ONE INDUSTRY, TWO CHINAS

One Industry, Two Chinas

Silk Filatures and Peasant-Family
Production in Wuxi County, 1865-1937

Lynda S. Bell

STANFORD UNIVERSITY PRESS
STANFORD, CALIFORNIA

Stanford University Press
Stanford, California
© 1999 by the Board of Trustees of the
Leland Stanford Junior University
Printed in the United States of America
CIP data appear at the end of the book

For Guangyuan and Margaret

Preface

This book has been a long time in the making. To begin, I traveled to China in February 1979, one of the first seven American exchange students in thirty years, generously supported with fellowship funding from the Committee on Scholarly Communication with the People's Republic of China (CSCPRC). My mood as we reached Beijing was ebullient but also apprehensive. We were all graduate students in Chinese studies from American universities—I was a Ph.D. candidate in the Department of History at UCLA—and our "mission," as we understood it, was to see if we could really do serious research in China. Would libraries and archives open their doors to us? Would the foreign affairs office staffs at the various universities with which we hoped to affiliate help or hinder our efforts?

As it turned out, at Nanjing University, where I went to pursue my Ph.D. research on the Wuxi County silk industry, a warm and helpful group of scholars and staff did their utmost to assist me. It was difficult at times because I had many requests and a full research agenda. I spent two years in Nanjing, and much of what appears in this book is the result of archival, library, and interview work begun during that time. Subsequently, as an assistant professor with additional fellowship support from the CSCPRC and the National Endowment for the Humanities, I returned to China in 1986 and 1987 for two research trips to the Institute of Economics of the Chinese Academy of Social Sciences in Beijing. It was there that another group of generous scholars and staff facilitated my work with the remains of a rare 1929 rural survey conducted in Wuxi by a research team led by the famous social scientist Chen Hansheng. Without access to this material, this study would have been completed much more quickly but in a very different fashion. It was this second round of research in China that allowed me to develop a detailed analysis of what transpired in the Wuxi countryside as silk-industry development occurred, and gave this book its final form.

Without the CSCPRC and its generous support of my work in China over the years, it would have been impossible to write this book. In their varied roles within CSCPRC (later known as CSCC, or the Committee on Scholarly Communication with China), Mary Brown Bullock, Bob Geyer, John Jamieson, and Fred Wakeman provided invaluable assistance. Other institutions also contributed financial support. Among these was the National Endowment for the Humanities, which granted me a year-long Fellowship for Independent Study and Research and a Summer Stipend. UCLA supported me with several fellowships, including a Hortense Fishbaugh Graduate Fellowship and a Distinguished Scholar Award while I was in the writing stage of my dissertation. The University of Illinois at Chicago and the University of California, Riverside, the two institutions where I worked as an assistant professor, also provided ongoing research support. The Center for Ideas and Society at UC-Riverside gave me a quarter free from teaching in the spring of 1992, when I was a resident faculty fellow there, and provided an intellectual environment in which I was able to work out complex theoretical and organizational issues that plagued me in the middle stages of writing.

Beyond funding, the personal assistance and moral support that various research institutions, universities, and individuals gave me over the years was exceptionally generous. At Nanjing University, Professors Cai Shaoqing and Yan Xuexi were the first to introduce me to the world of doing research in China, and personally arranged many of the interviews I conducted with former silk-industry participants. The interviewees themselves were very forthcoming, and I devote Appendix A to introducing them. In the foreign affairs office at Nanjing University, Zhang Rongchun and Chen Guanghua spent many dozens of hours negotiating access to libraries and archives. In Beijing, the eminent economic historian Professor Peng Zeyi, and former director of the Institute of Economics Professor Dong Fureng, made it possible for me to use the Wuxi rural survey materials. Professor Peng's help and support in particular I shall never be able to acknowledge adequately. In the modern history section at the Institute of Economics, members of the research staff, especially Liu Kexiang, Chen Qiguang, Zhu Yingui, Shang Lie, and Jian Ping, answered my constant stream of questions with immense generosity and patience. In Wuxi, I was assisted by personnel from Nanjing University; by Wang Yuancai and Tang Keke; and by personnel from the agricultural section of the Wuxi City Office of the State Statistical Bureau.

I am grateful to my host institutions as well for access to collections of archival and previously published, but often rare, materials at the following archives, museums, and libraries in China: the Number Two National History Archive in Nanjing; the Nanjing University Library; the Nanjing Municipal Library; the Zhenjiang Municipal Library; the Wuxi Municipal Library; the Wuxi Municipal Museum; the Shanghai Municipal Library; the Fudan University Library; the Beijing University Library; the Beijing Municipal Library; the Library and Materials Collection of the Institute of Economics of the Chinese Academy of Social Sciences in Beijing; and Beijing Teachers' College Library. In the United States, I used the East Asian collections of the Hoover Institution at Stanford University; the Library of Congress; Harvard University Library; the Regenstein Library of the University of Chicago; UCLA; and the University of California, Berkeley. I owe a debt of gratitude to each of these institutions as well.

Teachers, friends, and colleagues also gave me generous assistance for which I am grateful. Philip Huang mentored this project in its early stages. Others at UCLA, especially Bob Brenner, Fred Notehelfer, and David Farquahar, provided critical intellectual insight and support. Kathy Walker and Yip Honming were dedicated fellow graduate students, sharing knowledge as they completed their own local studies of economic development in early-twentieth-century China. Fellow graduate students in Nanjing, especially Kathy Walker, Helen Chauncey, and Randy Stross, provided models of hard work and dedication from whom I tried always to learn. Liz Perry was also resident in Nanjing as a research scholar while I was there, and was another model for me to emulate. In the postgraduate world of professional academia, colleagues in the history departments at the University of Illinois at Chicago and the University of California, Riverside, have given me heavy doses of support. Especially noteworthy in this regard have been Herman Ooms, Bill Hoisington, Carolyn Edie, Dan Scott Smith, Judy Coffin, Brian Lloyd, Arch Getty, Randy Head, Rob Patch, Sharon Salinger, and Roger Ransom. Other colleagues and friends outside my home departments gave me a great deal of moral support and guidance over the years as well, especially Tom Buoye, John Rohsenow, Carol Ruth, Steve Allee, Erna Marcus, Karen Turner, Melanie Manion, Vivian Nyitray, Ginger Hsu, Lucille Chia, Gene Anderson, Bernd Magnus, Emory Elliott, Steve Cullenberg, Susan Carter, Victor Lippit, Keith Griffin, Aziz Khan, Richard von Glahn, Bill Skinner, James Lee, Ken Pomeranz, Andy Nathan, Mary Rankin, Joe Esherick, Lillian Li, and Tom Rawski. In the last stages of manuscript preparation, Richard Sutch and Peter Lindert also gave me much-appreciated assistance and suggestions. Generous and helpful readings of the manuscript in its final stages were provided by Philip Huang, Kathy Bernhardt, Susan Mann, Sherm Cochran, Bill Kirby, and especially Jerry Dennerline.

At Stanford University Press, Muriel Bell and John Feneron were enormously helpful in steering the manuscrpt through to completion. Barbara James, at the Press, offered assistance in the early stages of submission, and in the final stretch, Sherry Wert performed expert copyediting. Invaluable research assistance was provided by Tu Xuehua (in Nanjing); Mary Lynn Dietche (in Chicago); and Denise Pan, Michelle Takahashi, and Lore Kuehnert (in Riverside).

Finally, there is my family to thank. My parents, Charles and Jane Schaefer, my sister Cynthia Wendt, her husband Vic, and her children, Katie and Kelly, gave me much loving support over the years. Guangyuan and Margaret Zhou, my husband and daughter, kept me honest and cheerful (most of the time) as this project neared completion. Above all, Guangyuan and Margaret, each in their own ways, convinced me of the value of finally finishing what had come to seem like the work of a lifetime. This book is gratefully dedicated to them.

Contents

18 pages of photographs follow page 108

Maps and Figures

Tables

Note on Wuxi County's Administrative Boundaries, Commercial Districts, and Size

In 1724, Wuxi County was split in two, roughly along a diagonal axis extending from northwest to southeast. The portion incorporating the western and southern districts retained the old name, Wuxi *xian* (county), while the portion incorporating the northern and eastern districts was called Jinkui xian. At the onset of the Republic in 1912, the two portions were rejoined as Wuxi County. Map 2 in Chapter 6 displays the shape of the Republican-period boundaries; for detailed maps and discussions of Wuxi and Jinkui counties during Qing times, see Zhu 1895, vol. 3. This source estimates that in 1895, Wuxi had three market towns (*zhen*); eight townships (*xiang*) with thirty-three periodic markets (*shiji*); and four commercial districts just outside the city. Jinkui is estimated to have had ten market towns (*zhen*); six townships (*xiang*) with twenty periodic markets (*shiji*); and one commercial district just north of the city (ibid.: leaves 39–42). In the Republican period, other sources count either sixty-five (Yin 1936, 1: 29–31) or sixty-six zhen (Wuxi xianzhengfu, Wuxi shizheng choubeichu 1930: insert map). The discrepancy with the previous numbers can be accounted for if both zhen and shiji subsequently were considered market towns. It is also useful to note that during Republican times in Wuxi, the term *shi* was used not only to refer to the urban center of the county (as in Wuxi shi [Wuxi City]), but also as a designation for densely settled townships. Other townships were referred to using the more common term, *xiang*.

Republican-period sources on physical size, cultivated land, and population contain numbers that vary, but the county extended approximately forty miles (120 li) from east to west, and thirty-six miles (110 li) from north to south (Wuxi xianzhengfu 1935, geography section: 1). In 1929, one source states that there was approximately 1,255,700 mu of cultivated land and a population of 971,800 (Chen 1929: 46–47). Another source estimates that in 1936, Wuxi had a total area of

1,973,700 mu, cultivated land of 1,259,501 mu, and a total population of 1,167,926 (Yin 1936, 1: 27–31). It is not entirely clear, but it is possible that the first population figure cited here refers only to those living outside the boundaries of Wuxi shi, the urban core at the center of the county.

Weights, Measures, and Exchange Rates

dan   A measure of weight equal to between 100 and 150 *jin*, with local variation; or, a measure of volume for grain approximately equal to 2.75 bushels, also pronounced *shi*. In the Character List, only the first character for "dan" can also be pronounced "shi"; this character is always used for specifying grain by volume. The second character with the pronunciation "dan" is used for measuring the weight of other items, such as cocoons. In Wuxi, one dan of rice (before milling) weighed between 135 and 150 jin.

fen   One fen equals 1/10 *mao*.

jin   (or catty) A measure of weight equal to between 1.1 and 1.3 pounds, with local variation.

li   A measure of distance approximately equal to 0.33 mile or 0.20 kilometer.

mao   One mao equals 1/10 *yuan*.

mu   A measure of area approximately equal to 0.67 acre.

picul   A measure of weight equal to 1,000 dan, or between 100 and 150 pounds. The national standardized weight of 1 picul was 133.33 pounds in the early twentieth century.

tael   The Chinese ounce, a measure of weight equal to one-sixteenth of a jin; also a unit of account (with varying values) for uncoined silver money. In 1921, 1 tael equaled US$0.76.

yuan (¥)   The Chinese dollar, the most common unit of account during the early twentieth century. In 1921, one yuan equaled US$1.04.

SOURCES: Rawski and Li 1992: xiii; *Webster's Third New International Dictionary* 1961; *A Chinese-English Dictionary* (Beijing: Shangwu yinshuguan, 1978); *Chinese Economic Monthly* 5 (Feb. 1924): 11.

ONE INDUSTRY, TWO CHINAS

1

Introduction: A Tale of Two Chinas

There are myriad ways to describe modern economic development. The most dramatic image is of smokestacks rising in large urban areas, where factory production heralds the dawn of a new era in the organization of labor and rapid, sustained gains in economic growth. But how best to analyze development? Should we be content with the standard narrative in which economic progress is synonymous in all times and places with the accelerated commercialization of rural economies, the end of peasant-family production, and the rise of an urban-based industrial order? Or should we respond to the calls of a new generation of historians for a different kind of emphasis, in which the focal point of early industrialization becomes the countryside, where merchants and artisans, and men and women in production, struggle for control of new economic processes?

Neither of these alternatives is entirely suitable for a study of economic development in modern China. We need, first of all, to erase old ideas about Chinese development before we can begin afresh to reconceptualize the issues. We have considered China a slow "responder" to international proddings for economic change, unlike Japan, which seemed to understand exactly what modern Western economies were all about by the end of the nineteenth century. Some have seen China as more problematic than Japan because of its domination by a conservative Confucian-oriented elite and its control by a backward and corrupt government with little will to promote significant economic change. Others have focused on exploitation by a rapacious West, eager to strip China of its political dignity and economic resources. From such visions have come efforts to apply dependency theory or world systems analysis, with China placed at one of the "peripheries" of the larger context of global capitalism.[1] But in reality, by the turn of the twentieth century, some areas of China were building new industries and entering successfully into the world marketplace, becoming part of new trends in the internationalization of modern development.

This study, which focuses on one of China's earliest and most successful new industries, modern silk production in Wuxi County in the Yangzi delta, carves out new terrain for analyzing modern development in China on its own terms. This is not to deny that the external pressures of imperialism made some difference in how these processes evolved or that the processes were in some ways predictable, guided by the "invisible hand" of modern market forces. But what was most distinctively Chinese about modern silk production in Wuxi can be summed up in the aphorism, "One industry, two Chinas"—a shorthand method for getting at the structural backbone of modern development in the Chinese setting. "One industry" speaks of a single developmental continuum taking shape by the turn of the twentieth century in places at the forefront of modernity in China, a continuum in which many private investors and an increasing number of state bureaucrats gave priority to new forms of mechanized factory production. Representing factories in China's developmental continuum in this study are Wuxi County's modern silk filatures, where steam-powered equipment spun silk yarn, or "raw silk," for export. At the same time, however, "two Chinas" emerged as part of the continuum—one populated by sophisticated, urban-based merchants and industrialists, the other by peasant families who remained in the countryside, producing the raw materials upon which silk filatures depended. In short, what was most distinctive about Chinese development in the early twentieth century was the fusion of modern factory production with peasant-family production, and the interdependence of the two systems.

Part of this book is based on quantitative analysis of economic data, especially from the Wuxi countryside. Peasant women were the majority work force within the silk-industry continuum. It is well known that peasant women went to work in significant numbers in China's early silk filatures and cotton mills, as they did in early textile industries worldwide. But the fact that peasant women also produced the raw materials for silk filatures, raising silkworms and cocoons in the context of peasant-family farming, has thus far received little analytic scrutiny. Some of the major quantitative questions posed in this study concern not just how peasant families fared as a result of their involvement in modern silk production but, more specifically, how peasant women fared. As a result of this approach, gender-related issues in the context of modern development come into sharper focus. Such issues include how labor was gendered overall in the context of peasant-family farming in Wuxi, and the implications of gendered labor patterns for peasant family structures and incomes.

To analyze China's new developmental continuum at the turn of the twentieth century also requires a sensitivity to the politics of industrial development. As governments came and went in China over the period covered by this study, the political landscape at the local level changed dramatically. In a place like Wuxi, where some members of the local elite were becoming prosperous merchants and industrialists in an important new export trade, the political stakes were significant. Silk-industry elites needed to discover how best to ally with new governments in the central China region and how to use their favor to bring about desirable policies in taxation and industrial regulation. It was also necessary to manage the peasantry politically, since silk-industry elites depended upon local peasant women for a steady supply of cocoons to keep their filatures operating. Struggles among silk-industry elites, peasants, and government over taxation, regulation, and prices produced a new political subculture in Wuxi through which state-directed industry under the Nationalists emerged. This outcome was one of the most significant features of China's developmental continuum by the 1930's, with important reverberations in China's economy and polity down to the present day.

THE DEBATE ON CHINESE DEVELOPMENT

Most of the previous literature on Chinese development has been mired in contentious debate. This debate first emerged in the 1920's, as Chinese intellectuals wrote prolifically about the problems of Chinese peasants. Many authors were particularly concerned with the effects of both imperialism and landlord-tenant relations on peasant livelihoods. For such writers, the roots of peasant poverty lay in the oppressive nature of imperialist domination and class relations, and these writers viewed revolution against both as essential if development was to proceed.[2] At the same time, other Chinese intellectuals were conducting quantitative investigations of Chinese agriculture with the help of foreign agricultural experts such as American John Lossing Buck. Although the studies and thinking produced as a result of such investigations did not deny that Chinese peasants were poor, they tended to emphasize the need for institutional reform rather than revolution, so that peasants could have better access to credit and modern technology. Rural banks and cooperatives might thus pull peasants out of poverty, with the implication that violent revolution was unnecessary to move Chinese development forward.[3]

Revolutionary options eventually won the day in China with the victory of the Chinese Communist Party in 1949, but the ongoing debate on

Chinese development did not subside. A generation of Marxist historians in China argued, for example, that indigenous "sprouts of capitalism" had emerged in China during the Ming (1368–1644) and Qing (1644–1911) dynasties, but that the Western intrusion of the nineteenth century had nipped them in the bud, forestalling successful native industrialization.[4] In the United States, the devastating interventionist policies of the Vietnam War prompted a generation of young China scholars to take aspects of the revolutionary analysis of the Chinese economy more seriously as well. Western imperialism became an emphasis for many young writers in their wake-up calls to a senior generation of China scholars, in which they argued that China had not been shaken out of its conservative doldrums by the West, but had been forced onto a new developmental path that destroyed older patterns of production, to the detriment of an already poor and suffering peasantry.[5] To make such arguments more convincing, new scholarship was needed. No matter where one stood in the debate in an ideological sense, there was simply an insufficient empirical base for arguing that the West had done in the Chinese peasantry with its new style of economic imperialism.[6]

Thus, a new round of scholarship in the United States attempted to fill in some of the empirical gaps about Chinese development. Victor Lippit's important studies on the size of the economic surplus siphoned off by the Chinese landlord elite, or gentry, argued that even without the added stresses of Western pressures to restructure the economy, Chinese peasants were deprived of the ability to accumulate savings for new forms of investment by a corrupt class system.[7] Philip Huang's pivotal studies on the Chinese countryside also provided new empirical insights into the internal dynamics of Chinese small-peasant-family farming. Huang demonstrated how the system of production in the Chinese countryside was predicated on intensive use of family labor, resulting in steady gains in total output, but at declining returns to labor. Huang thus provided an entirely new way of viewing the structural dilemmas of the rural economy—as long as the system of small-peasant-family farming was in place, China would continue to experience "growth without development," Huang's shorthand for referring to rising levels of output at declining marginal returns to labor.[8]

Despite the important new empirical ground broken by such studies, the atmosphere of contentious debate about Chinese development still refused to subside. Studies by Loren Brandt and David Faure, for example, provided new empirical data on peasant wages and incomes in areas of accelerated commercialization in the early twentieth century, arguing for the positive benefits of increased incomes among the peasantry as a result of Western-oriented production and market growth.[9] A new all-encompassing argument about Chinese development was also provided by Thomas Rawski, who argued, through careful reassessment of nearly all the quantitative data for both industry and agriculture in the early twentieth century, that China had, in fact, reached a "take-off" stage of economic growth, characterized by rising per capita incomes in both rural and urban areas.[10] The juxtaposition of Huang's and Rawski's sharply different views sparked a round of detailed critiques and counterarguments by a wide range of China scholars, in which Huang's negative arguments and Rawski's positive ones became representative of two seemingly irreconcilable points of view on Chinese development.[11]

This study enters the debate on Chinese development, but with a different approach and a revised agenda. Its central premise is that quantification of Chinese development, in and of itself, will never provide sufficient information to characterize China's developmental path. In addition to ongoing efforts to quantify, we need a new window into Chinese development that includes consideration of complex political struggles among elites, peasants, and the state that conditioned economic performance in the late imperial and Republican periods. Once issues of class, culture, politics, and gender in the Chinese setting are factored into the debate, we can begin to generate a new, more fully nuanced picture of exactly who gained and who lost as new industries were built in the early twentieth century, and how the developmental continuum shaped both private economic decisions and state planning for the economy over the course of the twentieth century.

This book has taken shape in a period in which writing about development issues, especially early industrialization, has reached new levels of sophistication among European historians. Debates about protoindustrialization in the European context, about the ways in which peasant-family structures affected development, about the roles of guilds, and about female labor have all reshaped the contours of thinking about early modern development in various European locales.[12] At the same time, however, this study also constantly has had to return to the specific context of an underdeveloped China at the dawn of the twentieth century, and to aspects of the development experience that were different from Europe because of China's third-world status as a relative latecomer to modern development. Thus, though some of the ideas here take inspiration from the new gains in European scholarship, I have had to adapt and reformulate arguments to make sense of these issues in a specifically Chinese context. Elites in China were not the same as elites elsewhere; likewise, peasant-family farming in China had its own distinctive contours, with gender relations within families and assumptions about male and female roles in labor processes very different from those in various European settings. Perhaps most different of all was the Chinese state, if one can say it existed at all at the turn of the twentieth century. How did rising and falling governments support or hinder development in the Chinese case, and what did the rise of the Nationalists in the 1930's, a government nearly universally condemned by its former analysts, really have to do with supporting or harming Chinese agriculture and fledgling industry?[13]

ELITES, POWER, AND DEVELOPMENT

An important component of the analysis in this book is a new approach to the study of Chinese local elites and their roles in modern development. The central premise of this approach is that elites built on an evolving cultural repertoire in the local setting in Wuxi, enabling them to actively, and successfully, promote modern development. At the core of this cultural repertoire were power relationships embedded deeply in local society, and used very profitably by some local elites to maintain and elaborate ongoing patterns of local social dominance. Dissenting from much of the previous literature on Chinese local elites, this study argues that such individuals were not interested in local autonomy from the state, nor in the creation of a new public sphere of bourgeois activity; rather, they wanted to find new ways to collaborate with, and gain added legitimacy from, rising governments in the Yangzi delta region to promote industrialization.[14]

Most local elites in Wuxi were men who came from locally prominent families of the Confucian-dominated, bureaucratic-office-seeking past. But during the late nineteenth century, some such men became the primary investors in new forms of cocoon marketing and silk-filature development. As they proceeded along their new career paths, they at once became more political as well, entering into new forms of intraelite association designed to promote the cocoon trade and the local filature industry. These new silk-industry elites needed both the peasantry and the support of local governments in Wuxi to make their new investment paths work. They needed peasants to produce cocoons, and they needed local government to help them achieve favorable tax policies. Without satisfactory performance in these two critical areas, their fledgling silk filatures stood no chance of success in the long term. Moreover, these new elites also needed to generate ongoing methods of raising capital among themselves, to guarantee that investment in silk filatures would become a permanent part of the economic landscape. For all of these needs, guild-type organizations arose within the context of local elite participation in silk-industry development in Wuxi, and I devote considerable time to analysis of their goals and performance. In addition to such formal organizations, informal modes of association based on personal networks served these elites well. By the 1930's, there were fifty silk filatures in Wuxi, with a full complement of well-networked local elites operating at their core.

These are examples of the issues to which I shall often refer in the context of this study as part of the cultural repertoire of local elites. Prasenjit Duara's influential construction, positing a cultural nexus of power among local elites in the context of rural north China, is similar, but not identical, to the analysis I propose here. Duara relies upon the idea that the cultural nexus was composed of "hierarchical structures and overlapping nodes" that spanned a wide range of potential sources of power, from the accumulation of wealth through landholding, to lineage supervision, to the management of temple organizations for the worship of local rural deities. Political problems emerged in full force by the 1910's and 1920's, as one government after another subverted the cultural nexus in efforts to collect badly needed additional tax revenues. They did this in the form of assessing *tankuan* taxes on village communities, supplementary land-tax levies so onerous that traditional villages leaders were reluctant to fulfill their regular obligations to serve as tax guarantors because the danger of impending financial disaster was so great. Rather than attempt to collect tankuan, many simply left their communities altogether, creating the potential for unscrupulous profit-seekers to become tax agents, brokering tax agreements between state representatives and village communities.[15]

Duara's formulation is important because it allows us to view power as a locally generated phenomenon, moving away from overly universalistic notions of what power is or where it resides. But unlike Duara, who is concerned with the structures of power, I concentrate on the ongoing evolution of local practice within such structures. I use "practice" here in the sense suggested by Pierre Bourdieu—a set of culturally conditioned behaviors, changing and developing over time, used to express and execute dominance, or power, over others.[16] Because I am interested in how local elites built upon long-term patterns of commercialization in Wuxi not only to launch modern silk production but also to maintain the industry by continuing their dominance over the local peasantry, I look for continuity as well as sharp ruptures or breaks, even in the tumultuous decades of the early twentieth century. Like Duara, I recognize an intensification of conflict between local elites and government over matters related to taxation, but I also find elites at work in Wuxi who were much more tenacious than those he finds in the villages of the north China plain. Local elites involved in silk-industry development in Wuxi did not give up power within cultural hierarchies so easily, nor did they bend to the state's demands for an increasing share of local resources without forcing compromises. In the end, some silk-industry elites in Wuxi were successful in forging newly powerful alliances with state agencies to promote their local social dominance through silk-filature growth.

SOURCES AND APPROACH

My work on Wuxi silk production has benefited from several periods of research in China, where I supplemented printed sources such as commercial journals and newspapers with extensive interviews of former silk-industry participants.[17] After conducting a first round of interviews, I approached the printed literature armed with new insights. Of greatest value were reports contained in intragovernmental communiques concerning silk-industry growth and regulation. Important disputes over taxation and silk-industry reform surfaced, allowing me to consider various forms of elite-state interaction as the silk industry evolved. I also discovered archival materials on such issues at the Number Two History Archive in Nanjing, a repository of central government documents from the era of Chiang K'ai-shek's presidency. For the portion of my work that deals with filature development, I began to probe the motivations of investors and their interactions with government using such materials.

While in China, I also was given access to a large number of materials called *wenshi ziliao*, an enigmatic term used to describe compilations of recent historical events written by participants, or local historians, in the tradition of compilers of local gazetteers of the past. Although scholars in the West have used various translations to render this term into English, I prefer the translation "cultural history materials" because it captures the intent to record varied aspects of the local historical experience. Wuxi has had several groups compiling wenshi ziliao series under various titles since the early 1980's, and they were an important extension in written form of the personal interviews I had begun earlier. The voices heard in various essays appearing in Wuxi wenshi ziliao are very similar to those I heard in interviewing situations, but often provide more detail, and more historical context, for local events related to Wuxi silk production. Wenshi ziliao have filled in many important facts that otherwise would have remained unknown as I have tried to piece together biographical sketches dealing with identities and intentions of silk-industry participants.[18]

For the rural portion of my work, I have been very lucky with sources. Although I started out with an excellent survey of three Wuxi villages conducted in 1940 by Japanese researchers from the South Manchurian Railway Company (commonly referred to by its abbreviated Japanese title, Mantetsu),[19] in the midst of my work in China I began to read about another survey of rural conditions in Wuxi carried out by Chinese researchers in 1929. Although it took some time to track down,[20] the Chinese survey of rural conditions in Wuxi has turned out to be an invaluable source for studying the role of the Wuxi peasantry in modern silk production and the effects of new industrial development on peasant per capita incomes, one of the principal issues at stake in the debate on Chinese development. The survey was organized by the Social Science Research Institute (SSRI) of the then–newly established Academia Sinica, a unit headed up by the well-known social scientist Chen Hansheng.[21] Chen had been educated in the United States and Europe, where he was trained in methods of social-science survey technique, and was eager to employ these methods in rural surveys back home in China. Chen was a native of Wuxi, making it easier for him to establish the contacts needed there to execute the survey.[22]

The scope of the SSRI survey included twenty-two villages scattered widely throughout the county, villages chosen for their diversity in terms of proximity to the urban core of the county, land-tenure conditions, and relative levels of wealth and poverty. In all, 1,204 households were surveyed using a twenty-six-page printed questionnaire, one that had been improved after several trial runs. The final version of the questionnaire solicited information on amount of land held, cropping patterns, tools and animals owned or borrowed, labor days worked, yields, prices received for the main crops of rice and wheat, and so forth. There was an attempt to tally the number of people in the household and their participation in the overall work effort. Substantial amounts of data were also gathered on silkworm raising, including both the amounts and the prices of cocoons produced as well as the amount of labor time invested and by which family members. Land-tenure practices were also of great interest to the research group, and an array of land-tenure categories were catalogued and rent payments recorded. A multitude of data was collected on hired labor practices. There were also attempts to inventory household belongings, to determine alternative income-earning activities, to figure the degree of indebtedness, and to learn something about tax obligations.[23]

The SSRI survey is unique for the degree of detail it contains, both quantitative and qualitative, concerning conditions in the Chinese countryside in the late 1920's.[24] Approximately 800 of the original questionnaires survive, presenting a daunting task for analysis. The lack of experience among some of the interviewing staff affected the quality of the responses that were elicited in some cases.[25] I found that the only way to get a feel for which data were usable was to read through a sizable number of the questionnaires to see which categories were handled most successfully by different interviewers. After ten months of effort, I had coded a sample of well over 100 households concentrating on farm size, cropping patterns, output, and prices; labor expenditure in agriculture, sericulture, and other subsidiary occupations; and land-tenure relationships, rent, and debt.[26]

Although I do not focus exclusively on the quantitative outcomes of silk-industry development on the Wuxi peasantry, I have developed an analysis that combines new quantitative estimates of per capita incomes with a qualitative inquiry into how peasants developed different work strategies as their roles in modern silk production evolved. My findings concentrate on gender differences in terms of work and on peasant decision-making within changing family structures. This focus differs from all previous studies of the Chinese countryside to date, thanks to the richly textured and highly detailed findings of the SSRI survey. I owe a great debt to Chen Hansheng and his research team as a result, and I can only hope that my interpretation of their findings lives up to the high standards of inquiry that their work embodies.

LOOKING AHEAD

The chapters in this book are arranged both chronologically and topically. The temporal pivot point is the period 1865 to 1937, from the end of the Taiping period in the Yangzi delta, to its occupation by advancing Japanese troops in the early stages of World War II. It was during this period that modern silk production originated in Wuxi, due in large part to the initiatives of members of the Wuxi local elite in promoting new forms of commercial and industrial activity.

But commercialization had a longer history in Wuxi, and in Chapter 2, I present a brief overview of those events during Ming and Qing times. Prior studies of the delta economy have analyzed commercialization in relationship to demographic growth, the rise of small-peasant-family farming, and the problem of low per capita incomes. Though these are important issues, my principal concern is to move away from an analysis that concentrates on the failures of development in the delta to demonstrate how elites, peasants, and the state, each with their own activities and rationales, created a highly stable, long-lasting commercialized agrarian order. Changing class relations and state fiscal problems created the potential for ruptures in this order, but it was only with the onset of difficulties created by new state policies on commercial taxation in the wake of the Taiping Rebellion, and the encroachments of imperialism, that serious cracks in the system emerged.

Chapter 3 explores how traditional and modern silk production in the delta proceeded side by side from the 1860's onward. The global context plays a major role in this story because it was through increased world-market demand for Chinese raw silk that Wuxi developed as a new co-coon-producing and marketing center. I am concerned with elite activities in the course of silk-industry growth, especially with evolving elite competition for the development and control of marketing networks involving local peasantries. Wuxi became a new silk-producing center because neighboring districts to the south and east had such long and strong traditions of merchant organization and control of handicraft silk-producing and marketing processes. A major effect of the world market was to intensify efforts by local elites to retain and/or develop prerogatives over marketing relationships with discrete groups of peasant producers of raw materials. Highly specialized marketing networks between local merchants and peasants were the result.

Chapter 4 continues the story of escalating political activity on the part of local elites in Wuxi to defend local interests against outside merchant competitors and the state. I take up several examples of how intraelite organizations in Wuxi attempted to defend their self-defined rights to regulate and control markets and to influence rates of commercial taxes. There was potential for competition between local elites and the state over the profits of the cocoon trade, but a desire on the part of both sides to unite whenever possible to promote a new form of commercial development. These findings challenge prevailing notions that an independent public sphere of local elite activity was emerging in highly commercialized areas of China in late Qing times. I argue instead that local elites continued to ally with the state for assistance, protection, and legitimacy whenever possible.

Chapter 5 takes up problems of investment and management in early silk filatures in Wuxi. Because merchants in the Yangzi delta had long-standing traditions of "layering" their commercial activities, such techniques were adapted to deal with the high risks of building silk filatures and entering the expanding global market for raw silk. A system of "split ownership/management" appeared in the filature industry, with investors divided into two distinct groups—those who built filatures, and those who rented and operated them on a yearly, contractual basis. This split meant that early filature operation was sporadic, or "speculative," leading to problems in capital reinvestment. Contemporary observers believed that "split ownership/management" was a major obstacle to future silk-industry growth. But I argue that we should see these developments in silk-industry organization differently—as a way to spread risk by a few key owners to a less-powerful stratum of silk-filature managers. Silk-filature operation may have been sporadic, but the total number of filatures in Wuxi rose rapidly during the 1920's, suggesting that new methods were afoot to spread the risks of filature operation downward further still, to the ranks of the Wuxi peasantry.

Chapters 6 and 7 shift focus from elite-centered concerns in silk-industry development to those of the peasantry. Chapter 6 uses the rural survey materials introduced above to explore how patterns of peasant production in Wuxi changed as sericulture and cocoon marketing entered the local scene from the 1860's onward. A combination of low land-per-person ratios and substantial rent demands meant that the earnings of commercialized farming dissipated quickly, even with new employment opportunities for peasant women through sericulture. Other forms of nonfarm work were also important for sustaining peasant livelihoods in Wuxi, but such opportunities were limited. As a result, peasant women worked at the difficult and time-consuming task of silkworm raising for much lower returns to labor than those accruing to their fathers, husbands, and brothers in farming and other forms of male-dominated work. Out-migration was also a painful step taken by adult male members of some peasant families with farms too small to support them, and lower per capita incomes resulted for the women and children who remained behind. In Chapter 7, we witness the attempts of sericulture reformers from the ranks of the local elite to improve the quantity and quality of cocoons produced by Wuxi peasants, and consider the complex cultural expectations of individuals on each side of the reformer/peasant relationship. The fact that most people involved in these processes on both sides were women sheds new light on the ways in which both gender and class added to problems facing sericulture reform, one of the key issues affecting silk-industry growth.

By the early 1930's, under the added stresses generated by the Great Depression, ongoing problems for silk-industry development came to a head. Chapter 8 explores new solutions to these problems, generated by a growing collaborative relationship between the Guomindang government and a handful of powerful filature owners, including a new overarching plan for silk-industry control. Under this plan, Wuxi became a new Model Sericulture District, with elaborate plans for state officials to monitor all aspects of further silk-industry growth, from cocoon quality, to filature development, to levels of taxation on the cocoon trade. This new institutional arrangement favored a small group within the Wuxi silk-industry elite as suitable collaborators with state interests. One man in particular, Xue Shouxuan, became especially influential during this period. Under Xue's influence, cocoon prices were set by government decree through the Model District program, thus passing the costs of silk-industry reform downward to the peasantry.

In the concluding chapter, I summarize how the rural economy and modern industry merged in Wuxi over seven decades. Within "one industry," there were "two Chinas" firmly in place. This analysis differs from many previous studies that have posited uneven regional development or a growing urban/rural divide. Instead, my study shows, in areas like Wuxi, at the forefront of China's new efforts to industrialize, there was a single developmental continuum, in which the wealth and power of silk-industry elites depended on peasant-family production, especially the poorly paid, but much in demand, hand labor of peasant women. Since peasant families had ongoing needs for income from sericulture, they had little choice but to absorb the costs of new elite-orchestrated, state-legislated programs for cocoon quality and price control. The legacy of state policies favoring industry over the countryside would linger into future decades, as a returning Guomindang government in the 1940's, and a fledgling Communist government in the 1950's, found it difficult to move beyond the "one industry, two Chinas" continuum that dominated early efforts to industrialize.

2

Markets and Power in the Late Imperial Era

Wuxi County is located in the heart of the Yangzi delta, an area that experienced extensive commercial development beginning in the Song dynasty (960–1279). To set the stage for activities related to silk production in Wuxi, we should have some understanding of prior patterns of commercialization in the delta. During Song times, cities such as Hangzhou, Ningbo, and Suzhou became entrepôts for trade in grain, cloth, and luxury goods. Such cities also became centers of intellectual and cultural pursuits, as wealthy landowners and merchants resided increasingly in urban locales and developed strong traditions in pursuing education, civil-service degrees, and positions in officialdom. During the Ming (1368–1644) and Qing (1644–1911) dynasties, commercialization reached a new high, as market-town development throughout the countryside soared and rural society became highly market-oriented.

Previous studies have concentrated on the parallel paths of commercialization and demographic growth in the delta from the Song through the Qing. They have stressed that market development and commercialized rural production generated ongoing growth in total economic output. But because of steady population growth, these gains were achieved only at the expense of stagnating per capita incomes among the peasantry. Though there have been different ways of characterizing these trends, from placing them at the heart of why China did not produce its own industrial revolution (Elvin 1973), to using them to explain why peasants remained poor even in the face of dramatic market growth (Huang 1990), the overwhelming conclusion has been that Chinese development was on a negative path in the late imperial era.[1]

We should not downplay the significance of these developmental dilemmas, but my emphasis here is different, moving away from an analysis that concentrates on the failures of development in the delta toward one that explores the tenacity and strength of the rural economy over such a long period. At the core of the efforts to reshape the delta's economy in the late imperial era was a series of actions in the arenas of class and state power, contributing to the desire and urgency among local elites and the state to foster rural market growth. By the late nineteenth century, on the eve of the emergence of modern silk production in Wuxi, the combined effects of the Taiping Rebellion and Western imperialism had generated fissures of a new type in the edifice of the delta's highly commercialized but fragilely balanced agrarian order.

COMMERCIALIZATION AND DEMOGRAPHIC GROWTH

Trends in population growth and commercialization proceeded side by side in Wuxi during Ming and Qing times, as elsewhere throughout the Yangzi delta. Ping-ti Ho and Dwight Perkins have produced demographic growth estimates for eighteenth-century Jiangsu Province, where Wuxi is located, in the range of 0.8 to 0.9 percent growth per annum.[2] For Wuxi alone, population figures culled from local gazetteers yield an estimate of 1.2 percent growth per annum over the period 1726 to 1795.[3] In and of themselves, these rates of demographic growth are not particularly unusual or startling, falling in a range that was standard for premodern economies worldwide. What made the situation in the delta different was that at the start of the late imperial era, even as early as Ming times, population was very dense given the amount of arable land available for peasant farming. By the 1790's, Wuxi had only 1.3 mu of arable land per capita—just 0.09 hectare, or one-fifth of an acre.[4] This was an extremely low land-per-person ratio by world standards, and the Wuxi situation corresponds with conditions prevalent in other delta counties by the late eighteenth and early nineteenth centuries.[5]

The density of population in the delta led to grain-deficit conditions, as did the tax burden of the delta relative to other areas of the country. The delta was part of an eight-province region of south-central China from which the state demanded additional sums of "tribute grain" (cao-liang), based on the fact that these provinces had long been the richest and most productive in the country. By Qing times, however, areas of Anhui and Jiangxi provinces to the south and west of the delta had become the new grain-surplus regions, and imported rice into the delta.[6]

Given these conditions, Wuxi became an important locale for rice marketing. Its strategic location just south of the confluence of the Yangzi River and the Grand Canal and on the northeastern bank of Lake

Tai made Wuxi a good choice for such activity.[7] State policy contributed
to Wuxi's rise as a rice-marketing center, since the Qing government
designated Wuxi as a concentration point for the collection of tribute
grain before it was sent via the Grand Canal northward to Beijing. As
surcharges on tribute grain mounted and certain portions of the total tax
were converted to cash equivalents, officials increasingly collected them
in cash rather than in kind. They then purchased grain to meet the portion of the total tax still demanded in kind by the central government in
Beijing. In this way, officials helped to increase the volume of rice traded
in various central China locales, and Wuxi emerged as a leading center
for rice-marketing activity.[8]

Contributing further to Wuxi's new patterns of commercialization,
peasants began to produce handicraft cotton cloth, referred to in local
sources as *mianbu* or *huabu*. A 1752 gazetteer explains the intricacies of
Wuxi peasant participation in cotton production and marketing:

> Of five counties in Changzhou Prefecture, Wuxi is the only one that
> does not cultivate cotton of its own; yet cotton cloth is even more im-
> portant here than in the other counties. Wuxi peasants get only enough
> grain from their fields for three winter months' consumption. After
> they pay their rents, they hull the rice that is left, put some in bins, and
> take the rest to pawnshops to redeem their clothing. In the early spring,
> entire households spin and weave, making cloth to exchange for rice to
> eat because by then, not a single grain of their own is left. When spring
> planting is under way in the fifth month, they take their winter cloth-
> ing back to the pawnshops in order to get more rice to eat. . . . In the
> autumn, with the slightest rainfall the sound of looms echoes through
> the villages once again and peasants take their cloth [to market] to ex-
> change it for rice to eat. Although there are sometimes bad crop years
> in Wuxi, as long as other places have good cotton harvests, our peasants
> have no great difficulties.[9]

Thus, Wuxi peasants developed a complex pattern of spinning and weaving cotton, pawning clothing items made of cotton, and selling cotton
cloth to supplement their grain supplies. As they did so, entire peasant
households, including women and children, became involved in making
cotton products, while men remained the principal work force in grain
production.[10] Caught up in the demographic/production/marketing
surge of delta as a whole, Wuxi peasant households seemed to have little
choice but to respond in such a fashion.

Though these were significant developments, if we view Wuxi's
trends in commercialization and population growth against the backdrop of an evolving body of scholarship on such issues, they alone are insufficient evidence for a permanently negative trajectory of develop-

ment. For example, critics of protoindustrialization theory, in which scholars have linked rural production of goods for market with earlier marriage, higher fertility rates, and an almost "natural" progression to full-scale industrialization, have found that many areas of rural manufacture in Europe actually experienced "de-industrialization" instead. This finding forestalls any easy, determinative links between demographic growth, changes in peasant-family structure, and new forms of production.[11] Robert Brenner also has argued quite convincingly, through comparisons of demographic trends in western and eastern Europe, that the relative decline or persistence of the institutions of serfdom, rather than population growth, effected the emergence of rural capitalism.[12] And in a wide-ranging comparison of demographic trends in France's *ancien régime*, the Ottoman empire, and late Ming China, Jack Goldstone has argued that the potential for demographically induced state crises was so common in the premodern world that population growth alone cannot account for the varied patterns of economic development that emerged to stave off or quell such crises.[13]

In light of such evidence and arguments, I believe it is important to supplement study of peasant-family production, commercialization, and demographic growth with a more thorough look at issues of class and state power in relation to new market growth. Rural markets were places where peasants went to buy and sell, but they were also institutions built by local elites eager to develop new sources of wealth, power, and legitimacy in a time of steadily rising population and fundamental changes in the structure of property rights. Moreover, the Qing state was eager to assist local elites in their efforts, for a strong state depended on a thriving rural economy. The activities of local elites and the state in the commercial arena generated a new urgency about finding ways to legitimize their behavior, resulting in the formation of an "ideology of popular welfare" to support market growth.[14]

ELITES, MARKETS, AND THE IDEOLOGY OF POPULAR WELFARE

Proceeding apace with demographic growth and commercialization in the delta during Ming and Qing times were important new trends in intellectual life. Some of these trends took shape within a well-established discourse on Confucian statecraft, or *jingshi*, literally meaning "to order the world."[15] A fuller expression is also the four-character phrase *jingshi jimin*, "to order the world and provide for the people." The Chinese term that eventually came to mean "economics," *jingji*, is a compressed version of *jingshi jimin*, suggesting that some elites perceived "ordering the world and providing for the people" as an economic concern.[16]

Although there were many variants of statecraft argument, and although the degree to which it permeated elite discourse fluctuated, there was momentum for statecraft thought to become a strong counterpoint to the more orthodox set of Neo-Confucian theories and practice of the late imperial period.[17] During the eighteenth century, there was a lively and creative sense of urgency about statecraft goals. New academic schools flourished throughout the delta, based on strong lineages within certain prefectures of the region, with Wuxi being one of the important locales in which such schools thrived. Many men who participated in these schools were interested both in a return to the teachings of Han dynasty thinkers, who were concerned with the proper ordering of the world as opposed to philosophical pursuit for its own sake, and in rigorous philological study of rediscovered Han versions of Confucian texts. Many also turned to technical subjects such as astronomy, mathematics, hydraulics, and cartography as a way to better prepare themselves for roles as leaders of practical affairs in their home communities. It was in this dynamic intellectual milieu that renewed concern with statecraft emerged, as members of elite society focused increasingly on becoming better equipped to promote political reform on the one hand, and to provide for the people's welfare on the other.[18]

Some scholars have suggested that the evolving concerns of statecraft thinkers were related to escalating commercialization of the rural economy in the delta.[19] A review of the cultural repertoire of newly rising commercial elites will reveal, in fact, a strong desire to develop and promote what we might identify as an "ideology of popular welfare," emerging from prevailing trends in statecraft discourse. Identification of this activity as an "ideology" implies that it entailed more than intellectual discussions, including a growing body of cultural practices among some local elites in the delta, designed to impress their local communities with their interest in promoting new forms of commercial activity as Confucian-oriented moral men.[20]

One activity of newly rising commercial elites inspired by the ideology of popular welfare was the formation of *shantang*, or benevolent halls. As William Rowe has shown for Hankow, merchants organized shantang as neighborhood-based organizations, performing such functions as public burial, the operation of harbor lifeboats, and the distribution of winter clothing, tea, grain, and rice gruel. By the end of the nineteenth century, benevolent halls were expanding their activities to include dispensing free medicinal drugs, and were nurturing the moral well-being of their surrounding neighborhoods by handing out free stationery and providing rudimentary literary training for aspiring, but poor, local scholars.[21] Mary Rankin has chronicled similar activities on the part of merchants who organized shantang throughout Zhejiang Province in the post-Taiping period.[22]

Parallel activities by merchants in the name of popular welfare were also under way in Wuxi. A prime example is provided by the activities of the Hua family in the Wuxi market town of Dangkou, and its role in the formation of charitable estates, or *yizhuang*, during the eighteenth and nineteenth centuries. Yizhuang were designed to pool a portion of the material resources of the wealthiest members of an extended kinship group within a given locale in order to provide relief grain to poorer kin in times of trouble, and to perform other charitable functions such as the provision of support to widows and funds for education. The first charitable estate had been founded in the delta during the Song dynasty, but the eighteenth century marked a new stage in forming corporate lineage organizations of this type.[23] Local developments in statecraft thought were linked with such efforts. Locally prominent intellectuals spoke eloquently of the concerns of Hua estate founders in providing for the welfare of the "descent group" (*zong*) as one means to better organize and provide for societal well-being at large.[24] Yet the positions of Hua family members as prominent merchants in Wuxi were also clear, and their founding of charitable estates was one means to consolidate some of their hard-won commercial wealth while simultaneously promoting their reputations in the context of local society.

The story of the founding of the "New Hua Charitable Estate" underscores these connections. Plans to form this estate began to percolate among four Hua family brothers during the mid-nineteenth century. Significantly, none of the four brothers were degree-holders, placing them outside gentry circles of activity and behavior, at least in a formal sense. Rather, their impetus for pooling some of their wealth to provide for the welfare of their less fortunate kinsmen came from their success in Dangkou as local merchants. Jerry Dennerline describes them as "local merchants, manufacturers, and purveyors of the wine and soy sauce for which Dangkou was known."[25] By the time the son of one of the Hua brothers, Hua Hongmo, founded the estate in 1875, he had passed the prefectural and provincial examinations, upgrading his status to that of a member of the upper gentry as well as a locally prominent merchant. Under his directorship, the "New Hua Charitable Estate" amassed landholdings of nearly 4,000 mu. Hua Hongmo also made his private rice warehouses in Wuxi City property of the estate, thereby "channeling revenues earned from storing the grain of inland merchants en route to Shanghai into the Huas' Dangkou projects."[26] By founding the "New Hua Charitable Estate," Hua Hongmo not only fulfilled his Confucian responsibilities to provide for popular welfare, he also assured that his commercial fortune would not be divided among his heirs upon his death, as was customary. Instead, Hongmo's commercial wealth remained intact as a means to promote the economic well-being and local prestige of the Dangkou Huas at large.

What we have, then, in these portraits of benevolent halls and charitable estates is evidence for how commercial elites used welfare institutions to promote their status and leadership roles in local communities.[27] When elites expanded their cultural repertoires in this way, they adhered to the spirit of Confucian statecraft by demonstrating a strong impulse to provide for kin-based and community-oriented welfare. However, we should not ignore other motivations of local elites to build up private fortunes and bolster their dominance in local society through such activities. Commercial wealth was important in assuring that elite families could fulfill their community obligations, enhance their moral reputations, develop their capacities as local leaders, and retain their power and prestige across generations. Thus, the "gentry-merchants," or *shenshang*, who began to appear with great frequency in local histories during Qing times, were also working hard to achieve permanent, and legitimate, positions for themselves via their evolving ideology of popular welfare.

Sometimes the very act of forming a commercial network was portrayed by such men as a form of Confucian-inspired institution-building. We have an example of a market-town founding from Wuxi, where one of the best-loved folktales of the region enshrined the "origin myth" of Dangkou, originally founded during the Ming by yet another Hua family scion, former Hanlin Academy member Hua Cha. As the story goes, Hua Cha was suspected of trying to usurp the power of the emperor by naming his new market town "Longting," or "Dragon Pavilion." In order to dispel such fears, as imperial guards advanced on the town, overnight Hua Cha had the local bean-curd shop print "Dongting," or "Eastern Pavilion" on its wares instead, and had the product distributed throughout the area to the local people. The ruse worked, and Hua Cha is well remembered "as the man who fooled the emperor and shared his bounty with the people."[28] This long-standing legend, surviving well into the twentieth century, suggests the degree to which the Hua family, important local gentry-merchants in Wuxi throughout Qing times, had succeeded in creating an image of their beneficence in their local market-town community.

Other evidence leads to similar conclusions about market foundings and the ideology of popular welfare. Throughout the delta during Ming times, elites consecrated their efforts to found new markets by constructing temples to local gods within market sites (Hua Cha himself was one such example), demonstrating that they were acting for the benefit of communities as a whole.[29] And as Susan Mann has recently pointed out, when local governments set commercial-tax rates and made decisions about the licensing of local merchants, they had to act cautiously so as not to violate persistent imperial edicts that proclaimed the importance of *anmin tongshang*, "making the people content and facilitating the activities of merchants."[30] The fact that Qing emperors proclaimed the links between market development and the people's welfare suggests the high degree of success for merchants in promoting new markets and the ideology supporting them.

Thus, the commercialized agrarian economy of the delta gained some of its momentum and staying power through elite efforts not only to promote and build local markets, but also to make them legitimate in a Confucian sense. Though this seems to fly in the face of conventional Confucian thinking about merchants and their "parasitic" nature (more on this problem below), the evidence is overwhelming that it had become more than acceptable for important local families in the delta to strive for the status of "gentry-merchant," in which they combined pursuits in Confucian education, degree-seeking, and commerce. It might be tempting to conclude that such activities also signaled the emerging potential for such men to promote still more developmental breakthroughs. Such speculation is appealing because of the corporate nature of both the shantang and the yizhuang, and parallels with merchant corporate wealth in the West.[31] However, to evaluate the potential for delta elites to become leaders in new forms of innovative investment, we cannot view their activities in isolation from other events in the arenas of power during the Qing, where the actions of peasants and the state with respect to the rural economy were also significant.

STRATEGIC SHIFTS IN PATTERNS OF CLASS DOMINANCE

While local elites became increasingly involved in managing new markets and founding corporate welfare organizations, the delta peasantry engaged in new forms of commercialized cropping and handicraft activity in the context of an evolving system of small-peasant-family farming. The ideal of the independent smallholder as the mainstay of the rural order had existed in China since at least the Han dynasty (202 B.C.–220 A.D.), but over the centuries there had also been a tendency for officials and other wealthy members of elite society to amass large estates. With the onset of Qing rule, however, this tendency was undercut throughout the empire by vigorous state policies eradicating large, estate-type holdings. These state policies were accompanied at the time of the Ming-Qing transition by protracted struggles of the rural population against various forms of servile status, with the resulting elimination of most forms of bond servantry and slavery by the early decades of Qing rule.[32] By the eighteenth century, rural cultivators fell into one of three main types: the owner-cultivator, who owned the land that he worked; the tenant, who rented one or more parcels from landlords, who were increasingly absentee; or the part owner-cultivator, part tenant, who owned some land of his own and rented the rest from landlords. Landholdings for most were small and fragmented, with cultivators often working several tiny parcels, scattered throughout the countryside surrounding their home villages.

As commercially oriented small-peasant-family farming developed, so, too, did landlord-tenant struggles. New aspects of land tenure in the delta were products of peasant efforts to retain their hard-won freedom from more oppressive forms of landlord control, and concomitantly, of peasant attempts to find new forms of economic security in the face of commercialization.[33] A new system of dual-ownership rights to the land that came to exist throughout the delta by the high Qing period had the potential to contribute to the preservation of peasant rights in an atmosphere in which the risks of commercial cropping increased anxiety about economic security, and in which new forms of landlord engrossment were always possible.

Although the origins of the system are obscure, dual-ownership rights to the land were prevalent throughout the Yangzi delta by the eighteenth century. The system went by various names in different locales, but such arrangements had one essential characteristic in common: the land was divided into "topsoil" (tianmian) and "subsoil" (tiandi), with each of the two strata having ownership associated with it. The subsoil right could be owned by someone who did not cultivate the land himself, but collected a rental payment from someone who worked it. In turn, the cultivator owned the topsoil right, which gave him the right to work the land in perpetuity, pass it on to his heirs, and even sell or let the privilege of cultivation to another. In general, rents were lower when tenant-cultivators possessed topsoil rights.[34] Rental rates on land with top-soil/subsoil divisions were also very stable, with the amount of rent fixed in kind at the start of the arrangement generally remaining the maximum rent for the land, even when the topsoil rights changed hands. Although tenants often had to pay a substantial rent deposit in order to acquire topsoil rights, once this had been done, those defaulting on rental payments usually could not be evicted from the land until the sum for which they were liable equaled either the amount of the original deposit or the outright "purchase price" they had paid to acquire the rights.[35]

Data on the topsoil/subsoil system at work in Wuxi during the early twentieth century allow us to view the degree to which the system pre-vailed and to observe its complex workings. Although we cannot pre-sume that all aspects of the situation in Wuxi in the 1920's were identi-cal with mid-Qing practices, the more general accounts of the system throughout the delta during the mid-Qing, as summarized above, sug-gest that the basic contours of the system were similar.

Among a sample of 196 households from villages throughout Wuxi in 1929, data on topsoil and subsoil rights associated with 477 parcels of land distributed among these families indicate that only 82 of the par-cels, or roughly 17 percent, had no topsoil privileges associated with them; conversely, 83 percent had topsoil privileges.[36] Seen from another perspective, looking only at data for twenty-four households that could be called "pure tenants," meaning that all of the land that they worked had some form of rental payment associated with it, 27 parcels from among their total of 88, roughly 31 percent, had no topsoil rights. Al-though this is a higher percentage of land parcels with no topsoil rights than among those held by the population as a whole, only seven house-holds among the "pure tenants" were completely devoid of topsoil privi-leges. The remaining twenty "pure tenant" households rented at least one parcel, and sometimes two or three, on which they held topsoil rights.

Terminology associated with land-rental arrangements reveals the complexities of topsoil/subsoil arrangements in Wuxi. One SSRI inter-viewer attempted to clarify a confusing array of local terminology with the following explanatory note:

[Land with the designation] subsoil-land/living-land (*tianditian/huotian*) is commonly called rented land (*zutian*). The seller (*maizhe*) sells the land to a [new] owner (*zhuren*) for about 75 yuan, called one mu's rental amount (*zu'e*). Responsibility for paying the land tax is discussed at the time that the price for the land is set. If the price is low, then the buyer will be responsible for the tax, and if the price is high, then the seller will be responsible; [in any case] the land deed will pass to the buyer's hands. This method [of selling cultivation rights] is the same as borrowing [against land as collateral]. The seller henceforth pays one dan of rental rice (*zumi*) [yearly], considered to be interest (*lixi*) on the [purchase price of] 75 yuan.[37]

This passage describes one way in which subsoil rights to land could be sold in Wuxi, and simultaneously, the way in which the original peasant cultivator, the "seller," managed to retain topsoil privileges for the indefinite future. In the situation described here, a peasant-cultivator in need of cash puts his land forward as collateral, and in effect "sells" the subsoil rights to a buyer for about 75 yuan; the transfer of subsoil rights is implied by the fact that the land deed passes into the buyer's hands. Every year thereafter, the cultivator, in return for retention of the right to work the land and to redeem the land deed in the future, pays approximately one dan of rice to the buyer, which in local terminology is referred to as "interest" against the original "purchase price," a loan of 75 yuan.

The mixing of market terminology (buying, selling) with terms associated with land rental and borrowing (rental amount, rented land, interest) provides important insight into the degree to which commercialization of the rural economy had its impact on land-tenure possibilities. Rights to cultivating the land were bought and sold, thus creating a situation in which peasants and landlords alike each attempted to use the marketplace to their own advantage. Potential advantages for peasants were embedded in this system—they could raise cash through a land "sale" while retaining the rights to cultivate the land and redeem it in the future. Moreover, the responsibility of paying taxes on the land might be bargained away as well; by accepting a lower sum of cash at the outset of the transaction, the cultivator could negotiate for the buyer of the subsoil rights to become liable for yearly tax payments.

As the Qing wore on, peasants increasingly improved their control over proceeds from the land not only by striving to hold topsoil rights, but also through rent and tax resistance. The government declared failure to pay rent a crime in the early eighteenth century, and began to assist landlords in the dunning and incarceration of defaulting tenants, recognizing that without the regular payment of rents, landlords would be less likely to meet their yearly tax obligations. Kathryn Bernhardt argues that it was the rise of commercialization, the subsequent removal of many landlords to newly emerging urban areas and market towns, and the general climate of economic insecurity generated by market relationships that generated these trends in peasant resistance.[38] She also argues that landlords were the ultimate losers in these struggles, as their economic position eroded to a precarious point by the early twentieth century in the face of ongoing peasant action.

What can these findings on peasant struggles over land rights and rent and tax resistance during the Qing tell us about economic development? One rather obvious point is that changes in land tenure and agrarian class relations contributed to land parcelization. Demographic growth also played a role, as did the cultural preference in Chinese society for partible inheritance, or *fenjia*, which helped to reduce farmsteads to minuscule size.[39] Parcelization meant that the most important component of rural capital, the land itself, was widely dispersed among the farming population, making it very difficult for those who remained in farming to accumulate wealth and invest innovatively. In addition, because landlords were increasingly unable to secure stable incomes from their landholdings, they were less likely to commit to improvements in the land, or to other innovative agrarian techniques.

But if peasants had little capacity to invest, and landlords little incentive, we are still left with an unsolved problem—why did gentry-merchants like the Huas of Wuxi, men who had amalgamated economic pursuits including both land ownership and commercial activity, not become innovators in this evolving economic milieu? If land had become such a tenuous investment, would making the most of one's commercial ventures not have taken on greater urgency, at least for some? Mark Elvin has suggested that the availability of cheap peasant labor and the scarcity of resources relative to population worked against innovations in technology and production.[40] But in other economic environments, most notably in England and later Japan, when commercial elites were faced with an abundance of labor, they turned around to employ it in new manufacturing enterprises very cheaply; and when faced with scarce resources, they helped launch new efforts to capture or produce them. Were there, then, other factors that inhibited investment? To explore this question, we should consider more fully the gentry-merchants' relationships both with the peasantry—not just as tenants, but also as producers of raw materials and handicraft goods—and with the Qing government, on which they depended for favorable tax policies.

MERCHANTS, PEASANTS, AND THE FISCAL CRISIS
OF THE QING STATE

Scholars have long argued one of two variants of why Chinese merchants did not become sources of economic innovation and investment. Both variants are related to the hypothetical position of merchants based on the traditional Confucian order, where they occupied
the lowest position in the social hierarchy because they were not "productive" but rather were "parasitic" members of society, who made
their profits from the hard work of others. According to the first variant, deprived of the capacity to obtain high social status as merchants,
men who made their fortunes through commerce sought status-laden
degrees and official positions, and merged with the bureaucratic-
landlord elite. Much of their money, therefore, went to the pursuit of
education and the purchase of land as solid, acceptable social and economic investments. The other variant argues that merchants' profits,
by their very nature "parasitic," were always the universal target of
high tax rates. Thus, merchants were unable to accumulate large sums,
and failed to generate significant investment potential.[41]

These observations about merchants, Confucian cultural values, and
the state contain an important insight into the problems that commercial elites faced over the centuries in China in establishing a fully
autonomous position in society. The system of bureaucratic officialdom
promoted by the state made merchants relatively conservative regarding
at least some of their investments. However, to rely on the idea that lack
of merchant autonomy was a permanent, insurmountable problem for
Chinese development ignores the important changes in merchant behavior, and state support for that behavior, as commercialization swept into
rural areas throughout the Yangzi delta during the Qing.

One way to alter this picture is to consider how commercial elites and
the state related to the small-peasant-farm economy in highly commercialized areas such as the Yangzi delta by Qing times. Since raw materials and finished handicraft products were both produced by small-peasant-farming households, merchants worked hard to build up ongoing exchange relationships with such households within local areas. The result
was that merchant/small-peasant nexuses came to dominate production
and marketing relationships. As we shall see in Chapter 3, in the context
of handicraft silk production in the delta, such nexuses were very powerful mechanisms for the further extension of commercial capital into the
countryside—so powerful, in fact, that they tended to spawn ever more
elaborate subnetworks of commercial exchange rather than stimulate

interest or incentive among their merchant organizers in managing production.[42] Moreover, once such nexuses were in place, elites and the
state both had something to gain, with commercial wealth augmenting
elite incomes from landholdings, and potential tax revenues collected
from peasant smallholders providing a stable source of income for the
state. The problem with this scenario by late Qing times was that in an
era of rising population and relatively scarce land resources, it became
increasingly difficult to maintain the delicate balance of interests that
gave such nexuses their legitimacy and staying power.

A key question, therefore, is not whether merchants were in a position to establish their autonomy from the state, but rather why they
found it increasingly difficult to maintain the peaceful coexistence with
the state that had marked the early Qing. When we review the record of
evolving taxation, we shall see that early Qing policies toward commercial profits were quite lenient, with low tax rates and other special efforts directed toward protecting the profit-making capacities of merchants. The Qing state often premised these policies on ideas similar to
those expressed through the ideology of popular welfare and touted so
widely by delta elites. However, by late Qing times, escalating state demands for commercial taxes emerged as a problem for Chinese merchants. It is important to understand the reason for this shift in state policy in light of the structural evolution of the agrarian economy as a
whole, and its relationship to the growing fiscal instability of the Qing
state.

Eighteenth-century tax reform. During the eighteenth century,
the Qing government faced several problems in balancing its budget. The
first was that the Kangxi emperor had frozen land-tax rates in 1712, de-
claring that the *ding*, or head tax on all adult males of working age, would
be permanently merged with the land tax. To make the arrangement pal-
atable to all, he also declared that the rate at which the land was taxed
would be fixed in perpetuity. As the population continued to increase,
the merger of the head tax with the land tax meant that the state permanently eliminated its capacity to capitalize on this situation by taxing
more people. At the same time, because the land-tax rate was fixed, the
state could not secure claims to a share of increased levels of agricultural
productivity. On top of these structural difficulties with the land-tax
system, the rate of taxation was fixed at a relatively low level, even by
premodern standards. In the Yangzi delta, it averaged 4.5 to 6.8 percent of
an average to excellent rice harvest during the mid-eighteenth century.[43]

By the early 1720's, the Qing central government was on the verge of bankruptcy. Thus Kangxi's son, the Yongzheng emperor, set out to accomplish another round of tax reform. The key reform, enacted in 1723, was designed to create a legitimate new surcharge to be retained in the province of origin, providing local officials with substantially increased salaries as well as more funds to run their governments. It was called *huohao guigong*, "returning the meltage fee to the public coffers." As Madeleine Zelin has shown, this was technically "a charge added to regular tax remittances to compensate for the inevitable loss of silver that resulted when taxes were melted down into large ingots for transporting to the central government."[44] However, in reality, it became an important method for adding a range of new surcharges on taxpayers to generate revenues for local governments.

Almost as soon as the reform was instituted, it became clear to the central government that new legal surcharges on the land tax alone would be insufficient to deal with the problem of revenue flow. There were key regions—including the Yangzi delta—that were so chronically in arrears in paying their taxes that huge deficits had accumulated and continued to grow. Thus the emperor declared a massive investigation of tax arrears, concentrating on the Jiangsu portion of the delta. The investigation revealed a number of ongoing difficulties in tax administration. Prevailing tax-collection procedures, most notably "proxy remittance," or the payment of taxes to a third party, who then forwarded them to the local government, had become a widespread vehicle in the delta promoting embezzlement and engrossment by sub-bureaucratic clerks and runners. Importantly, many of these sub-bureaucrats had close ties with local gentry members, or were themselves members of locally important families, allowing gentry-landowners to falsify their tax obligations, or to avoid tax payment altogether.[45]

At the root of all these problems was the fact that tax records were extraordinarily complex in the delta, making it difficult to know who was responsible for paying the tax on any given piece of land to begin with. In fact, in a passage bearing an uncanny resemblance to the interviewer's note on the sale of topsoil rights in Wuxi quoted above, Madeleine Zelin describes how the nature of land transactions in the delta led to problems in tax accountability:

> One common practice used by wealthy households to evade taxes involved their role as moneylenders to the poor. Rather than sell land outright, a poor household would often mortgage it to a wealthy household. The original owner would receive perhaps half the value of his land, but had the right to buy it back within a fixed time period. Use of the land generally passed into the hands of the holder of the

mortgage, but title was not necessarily transferred to the wealthier party. Consequently, the property was lost to the original owner, but his tax liability remained. . . . The party mortgaging his land did not have the ability to pay his taxes because he could no longer farm it, or was able to do so only by paying the mortgage holder rent. The person who had lent him the money for which his land was collateral was equally unwilling to pay the tax, because technically the land was not his own. As a result, the tax went unpaid and the government could not determine responsibility for the plot.[46]

Thus, the dual-ownership system of topsoil/subsoil rights to the land was a key factor contributing to the ambiguity of land sales and resulting tax liabilities. Although buyers and sellers of topsoil privileges were supposed to make clear who would be responsible for tax payments in the future, actually implementing such a procedure was difficult indeed, as it was in the interests of both parties to keep the agreement as ambiguous as possible. If tax liability remained ambiguous, then perhaps tax payment could be avoided altogether.

In some areas, difficulties with the reform also included mass resistance against it. As local magistrates attempted to implement the reform, or officials from higher levels traveled from locale to locale to explain the new tax surcharges and how the problem of arrearage would be dealt with, they often met with spontaneous outbursts of anger, and sometimes even full-scale tax rebellions. One such incident occurred in Wuxi, when the local magistrate escalated his campaign to collect past taxes by making the heads of all households with arrears wear the cangue. A group of local people rioted in the local yamen and released prisoners held in the county jail. As a final defiant act, they burned government boats to prevent county police from pursuing them.[47]

Although the Qianlong emperor tried to make the reform work in the decades after Yongzheng's rule, in the end it died a relatively quiet death, and a new spate of illegal surcharges and payments of all types surfaced as the principal means used by local governments to finance their activities. The failure of the reform can be attributed not only to the complexities of landholding, but also to a vast empire's problems in dealing with premodern methods of communication, limited administrative capacities, and complications for relatively impoverished peasants in meeting any new demands for additional taxes. Although local governments needed greater revenues to govern and serve expanding populations under their jurisdiction, an increasingly strapped peasantry, suffering from the effects of demographic growth and land parcelization, was also more frequently unable to pay.[48] Thus, efforts to collect additional surcharges through legal channels subsided, and irregular methods of tax embezzlement, engrossment, and evasion all resumed as an accepted part of land-tax administration at the local level.

   The growing importance of commercial taxes. Against the backdrop of mounting chaos in land-tax administration, the Qing state constantly voiced concern over issues related to popular welfare. Such concern was at least in part responsible for the cessation of efforts to make land-tax reform work, as government officials worried about the inability of small-peasant-farming households to absorb still more tax requests. Concern for the people's welfare also affected the way the state responded to the escalating commercialization of the rural economy. As Susan Mann has so aptly shown, the Qing state was well aware that for the agrarian economy to flourish, and the people's welfare to be assured, appropriately lenient policies on commercial taxation were also of the highest priority. Thus, Qing emperors and high-ranking officials issued repeated proclamations and memorials urging the promotion of local markets, ideally to be organized and taxed by local merchants, who had some concern for the well-being and prosperity of their local communities.[49] Some markets had the title *yiji*, or "benevolent market," associated with them. In such markets, state-licensed brokers were prohibited from collecting taxes, in favor of a system where local merchant families organized the marketplace and collected a modest tax quota on the government's behalf. The results were favorable for both sides in the arrangement: local governments were able to secure badly needed revenues to sustain their governing efforts, and prominent local families were allowed to generate and retain a large proportion of commercial profits. At the same time, such families could, and did, enhance their reputations in local society as morally upright corporate groups and individuals interested in promoting popular welfare.[50]

   Meanwhile, as the state found it increasingly difficult to generate adequate revenues through the land-tax system, its demand for more commercial taxes mounted. Even as early as the 1720's, in the context of the attempts at land-tax reform under the Yongzheng emperor, informal customs duties and other local commercial duties were being converted into formally legalized sources of local revenue in many areas, including Jiangsu Province.[51] By the 1850's, delicately balanced state policy regulating and promoting market development was experiencing further shifts in favor of policies that would generate more commercial-tax revenues. New demands on the state's already strapped resources in the form of massive military expenses to quell the Taiping Rebellion, and war indemnities imposed by imperialist powers, combined to make the generation of additional revenues through commercial taxation urgent. The focal point of new state demands for commercial-tax revenue was a controversial new tax called the *lijin*—literally, "one-thousandth unit of currency," but in practice, a tariff, or surcharge, of 1 percent or more on the value of commercial goods. Devised by a county magistrate in Jiangsu as a way to pay for military expenses in the campaign against the Taipings, by century's end, the lijin and the new network of local tax bureaus it generated had become an important source of revenue for the central government.[52]

Local variations in the implementation of the lijin program were dramatic, based on the degree of commercialization of local areas as well as on the need and demand for revenue. Areas in which military demands were high and in which marketing networks were well developed tended to be the most affected. The Yangzi delta met both these criteria. Devastation of the region during the Taiping period had increased military expenses sharply, and restoration efforts were also costly. Meanwhile, not only were well-established trading networks being revived in the region following the defeat of the Taipings, but many new forms of trade also were evolving as foreigners congregated increasingly in Shanghai in the wake of the Opium War. Thus, the density of new lijin bureaus, most of them transit points at which the new levies were collected from Chinese merchants conducting domestic trade, was very high in the delta. Zhejiang Province, in the heart of the delta, reported 316 such bureaus in 1908, and Shandong Province, well to the north of the delta, only 14.[53] By 1908, after a half-century or so of lijin and other commercial-tax proliferation, total revenues derived from commercial taxes amounted to 65 percent of central-government income, with the land tax, which had once provided 74 percent of the total, amounting to only 35 percent.[54] The new lijin tax system, launched as a measure of expediency to pay for extraordinary military expenditures during the midnineteenth century, was but the tip of an iceberg of new commercial-tax policies and practices awaiting the commercialized rural economy.

Often, it was local merchants with whom the state entered into negotiation, conflict, and compromise over new commercial taxes.[55] We shall see in subsequent chapters that such activities in Wuxi generated new forms of merchant/state tension, contributing to the risks faced by silk-industry investors. To be sure, there were other risks involved in silk-industry investment, related to the ongoing dilemmas of peasant-family production and the ways in which Chinese silk entered the world market. We shall return to these problems below as well. Yet it would be unwise to view any of these issues in isolation. Evolving struggles in the arenas of class and state power had contributed to a distinctive, and tenacious, commercialized agrarian order during the late imperial era. In an environment of ongoing commercial development, Wuxi silk production emerged. Local elites and peasants who formed the new merchant/peasant nexus in Wuxi silk production would draw upon a legacy of strengths from older patterns of commercial production and marketing. But they also would face an uphill battle in terms of sustaining new patterns of investment, as it became increasingly difficult in the post-Taiping years to balance the interests of peasants, elites, and the state in politically infused commercial arenas throughout the Yangzi delta.

3

Why Wuxi? Merchant Competition and the Changing Contours of Yangzi Delta Silk Production

The 1850's and early 1860's were watershed years in the history of the Yangzi delta. The massive Taiping Rebellion, begun in southeast China, came to the region in 1853, with Taiping leaders making their capital at Nanjing, on the delta's western border. During the next eleven years, chronic warfare engulfed the delta, with many areas affected so severely that expanses of agricultural land were left uncultivated as peasants and landlords alike fled in large numbers, joined in the fighting, or faced death at the hands of competing troops. This situation disrupted marketing networks along with agricultural production, and both needed revival following the final Taiping defeat. Despite the devastation of war, repopulation of the delta was rapid, with returning peasants and migrants from other areas attracted by the opportunity to set up farming operations anew. Disruption of prior patterns of production and marketing, along with changing world-market demand for Chinese silk, laid the groundwork for new contours in Yangzi delta silk production.

Wuxi became a key area as these new patterns of sericulture and cocoon marketing emerged in the Yangzi delta in the post-Taiping period. But as events unfolded in Wuxi, older patterns of silk production and marketing in the delta did not dissipate entirely. Instead, parallel, competing commercial networks proliferated, with activities in the political realm supporting their growth. Antagonism between cocoon merchants in Wuxi and silk merchants in other delta locales arose, stimulated by competition to gain access to sericulture peasants and their products. The marketplace thus became an arena in which struggles for control over scarce resources were played out, and in which merchants defended their prerogatives over the peasantry. How Wuxi emerged as a new, permanent location on the silk-production landscape is best understood within this larger story of merchant competition and the changing contours of silk production throughout the delta as a whole.

SERICULTURE AND ECOLOGY IN THE
YANGZI DELTA

The Yangzi delta had a long history as one of China's premier centers for the production of handicraft silk. This history began with the arrival of sericulture from north China during the Northern and Southern dynasties (420–589 A.D.).[1] The ecology of the Yangzi delta played a role in how sericulture developed there, with certain areas better suited than others to mulberry cultivation and silkworm raising. In the atmosphere of increasing commercial competition that marked the late nineteenth century, ecological factors also played a role in Wuxi's development as a new sericulture area.

The boundaries of the Yangzi delta include territory within southern Jiangsu and northern Zhejiang Provinces. Since most of the delta lies south of the Yangzi River (with the exception of the two modern-day counties in Jiangsu Province, Nantong and Yangzhou, lying to the north), in Chinese the delta is usually referred to as "Jiangnan," literally, "south of the river." The East China Sea and Hangzhou Bay are the delta's eastern boundaries, and counties surrounding Tai Hu, a large lake straddling the borders of Jiangsu and Zhejiang approximately fifty miles inland from the sea, form its western edge. Moving southward, the delta's boundaries stretch to a point slightly south of Shaoxing and Ningbo, two of northern Zhejiang's largest commercial centers (see Map 1).[2]

Netlike waterways, both natural and man-made, stretch throughout the delta.[3] In the portion that lies within Jiangsu Province, the ratio of water surface to total land area is a relatively high 16 percent, and the land is low and flat.[4] To the south and east of Tai Hu, the land lies only 1.7 to 3.5 meters above sea level.[5] As a result of the sheer quantity of water and the low-lying nature of the land, inundation is frequent, especially during rainy seasons in spring and summer, and extensive pumping efforts are required.[6] Moreover, since the delta borders the sea, tides created by the ebb and flow of the Yangzi into small connecting rivers cause sluggish, swashing water, and contribute to inundation.[7]

The relationship of water to land in the portion of the delta that lies to the south and east of Tai Hu proved important in how peasants integrated mulberry cultivation into overall farming efforts. From the Song to the Ming, the first locales in the delta to introduce sericulture lay in areas most prone to inundation—Hangzhou, Huzhou, and Jiaxing prefec-

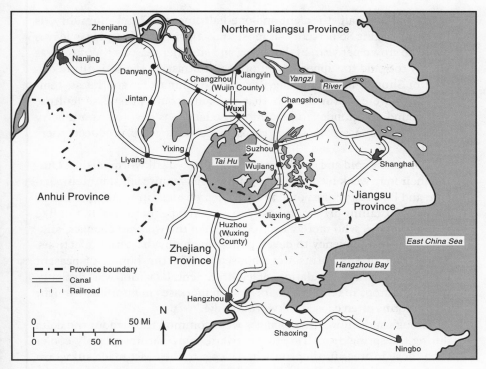

Map 1. The Yangzi Delta silk region

tures in Zhejiang Province, and Suzhou Prefecture in Jiangsu Province—
all south and east of Tai Hu.[8] Yet mulberries require adequate drainage
and grow best at elevations unlikely to experience flooding.[9] The strategy adopted for mulberry cultivation was thus to use the land on top of
embankments built for flood control and irrigation. From the Song dynasty onward, the building of embankment systems to surround low-
lying land had become an important part of land-management strategy.[10]
Low-lying land was made into rice paddies, with water pumped at appropriate points in the cultivation cycle from canals and rivers behind
embankments.[11] In winter, rice paddies were pumped dry and winter
wheat was grown.[12] Since embankments remained constantly above water, they became an ideal source of land on which to plant mulberries.[13]

   Although peasants could grow mulberry trees on embankment land,
other factors related to climate in the delta put limitations on the degree
to which sericulture could expand. Mulberries thrive in warm and hu-
mid conditions. Though the delta's nonfrost season is relatively long—

seven-and-one-half to eight-and-one-half months—and humidity is
high—averaging 80 percent—at most, only two crops of mulberry leaves
could be grown per year, in the spring and summer seasons.[14] Winter was
simply too cold to support the effort. By contrast, in the sericulture district of Shunde in Guangdong Province in China's far southeast, temperatures were warm enough that peasants could pursue sericulture
year-round. In Shunde, 70 percent of the land was devoted to mulberry
cultivation, and six to seven crops of cocoons were produced there
yearly.[15]

The delta's cold and damp springs also affected silkworm raising. During their four-week feeding period, silkworms require constant temperature and humidity,[16] responding to sudden changes in weather much as
humans do, falling prey more easily to certain types of illness. But unlike
many humans, who merely catch cold when the weather changes, silkworms have a tendency to develop life-threatening bacterial infections.
Since trays of silkworms were housed within the homes of peasant
households where regulation of environmental factors was difficult,
overnight drops in temperature or sudden increases in humidity brought
on by storms often caused silkworms to die.[17]

Though sudden weather changes were common throughout the delta
during the spring, from Tai Hu westward, temperatures slightly cooler
than those in areas further south and closer to the coast made silkworm
raising even more difficult. Thus, when new sericulture areas to the
north and west of Tai Hu developed from the late nineteenth century
onward, reports of cocoon-crop failure began to appear regularly in
newspaper and periodical reports. For example, in May 1916, Wuxi reported severe difficulties with its cocoon crop because of cold and rain.[18]
In May 1921, heavy rains had an adverse effect on cocoon crops throughout the delta region,[19] with the situation in Wuxi so bad that year that
the total cocoon crop was estimated at only 30 percent of its potential.[20]
In the 1920's, the first in-depth agricultural survey undertaken in Jiangsu
also reported that weather limited the expansion of sericulture into new
areas.[21]

Despite more severe problems with weather, many peasants in new
sericulture districts to the north and west of Tai Hu began to cultivate
mulberries more extensively. The combination of increased market demand for cocoons with the promise of new scientific techniques for sericulture improvement, including the application of bacterial disinfectants to quell the growth of silkworm disease, encouraged peasants to
devote larger portions of their land to cultivating mulberries and to start
larger silkworm broods. Instead of raising mulberries on embankments,

peasants used a new style of cultivation involving the conversion of former rice/wheat land to mulberries. The new mulberry fields that resulted have been referred to as *chengpian sangyuan*, or "tract mulberries"; these flourished from the 1870's onward in Wuxi, Jiangyin, Wujin, Yixing, Liyang, and Changshou, all to the north or west of Tai Hu.[22] Although they grew more mulberries than did most peasants in older sericulture districts, peasants in the newer areas still rarely converted all of their land, opting for a combined farming effort of summer rice and winter wheat in some of their fields, and mulberries in others. A less-than-ideal climate for sericulture remained an important factor in their decisions.

In Wuxi, certain ecological factors had more favorable effects, leading to the county's impending success among the new sericulture districts. Relatively high, dry land was one such factor. We have seen that the older sericulture districts lay in parts of Jiangsu and Zhejiang that were only 1.7 to 3.5 meters above sea level, with virtually no slope to allow for natural drainage. By contrast, the portion of the Yangzi delta in which Wuxi lay was 6 to 7 meters above sea level, and the majority of the arable land there was much less susceptible to inundation. The displacement of river water from the Yangzi by ocean tides formed a natural dike to the north of Wuxi and further protected the county from flooding.[23]

A second ecological factor that aided tract-style mulberry cultivation in Wuxi was the superabundance of canals, both natural and man-made, and their interrelationship with the surrounding environment. Rich mud deposits found on the floors of the canals were a unique product of the waterway system of the Yangzi delta, brought about by the combination of an extremely gentle land gradient and the presence of the Grand Canal. Because the delta is nearly flat between Wuxi and Shanghai, the flow of the canal was exceptionally gentle as it passed through Wuxi. Water also passed through the myriad smaller canals linked to the Grand Canal in Wuxi slowly and gently, to the point of being nearly stagnant.[24] Because the water was so still, plants and organisms thrived in Wuxi's canals, making the mud at their bottom an especially rich fertilizer for mulberries. Peasants of the area dredged it up themselves, or paid a small fee to people from northern Jiangsu who operated special boats for the purpose.[25]

Ecological factors, then, combined in the delta to support different styles of sericulture from one subregion to the next. Although the combination of these factors was not always ideal, the delta had nevertheless become China's premier center for handicraft silk production during Ming and Qing times, setting the stage for Wuxi's rise to preeminence using new-style "tract mulberry" cultivation. But before leaving the earlier history, we should also review other factors that supported the growth of sericulture and handicraft silk production in the delta during Ming and Qing times. These included government assistance, merchant activity, and commercialized household-based production in both urban and rural areas, factors that also affected the way in which Wuxi silk production would unfold.

THE IMPERIAL SILKWORKS, MERCHANTS, AND HOUSEHOLD-BASED PRODUCTION

Government support for silk production in the Yangzi delta began when the Song capital moved to Hangzhou in the heart of the delta in 1127, and demand for silk by the Imperial household and members of its bureaucratic staff stimulated more extensive sericulture development in the surrounding countryside. Not until the Ming (1368–1644) and Qing (1644–1911) dynasties, however, did the Imperial Silkworks system truly flourish, making the delta the most important silk region in all of China.[26]

As silk production developed its distinctive characteristics during Ming times, the first five stages of production—mulberry cultivation, incubation of silkworm eggs, silkworm feeding, cocoon collection, and reeling of silk fibers from cocoon casings—all took place within peasant households. Only the last stage—weaving—was performed elsewhere. This was because of the location of the Imperial Silkworks in three urban areas—Suzhou, Hangzhou, and Nanjing—and the relatively high degree of control exercised by the Silkworks over weaving procedures. In the early Ming, officials running the Silkworks chose silk weavers as their regular workers and then classified them as permanent and hereditary artisans. Some weavers worked full-time within workshops at the Silkworks; others worked only on a rotational basis.[27] By the fifteenth and sixteenth centuries, this artisan arrangement for silk weaving gave way to a putting-out system using merchants as middlemen. Under the new system, the Silkworks recruited private weavers who worked outside the factories under the supervision of a merchant guarantor (baolan ren). The guarantor bought raw silk from sericulture peasants and then distributed it to the weavers. In the early Qing, the merchant middlemen were no longer known as baolan ren, but rather as jihu, or weaving households. But the functions of jihu remained the same as that of their baolan ren predecessors—to serve as middlemen among sericulture peasants, weavers, and the Silkworks.[28]

By the high Qing, the middleman system sponsored by the Imperial Silkworks had grown larger and more complex. Large merchant enterprises known as account houses, or *zhangfang*, purchased raw silk, processed it, and distributed it to weavers, who themselves were now called jihu, or weaving households. Merchant account houses typically controlled 100 to 300 jihu. In Hangzhou in 1904, there were 3,000 looms, but each jihu had only two to three looms on average. Though jihu sometimes operated small workshops, they often subcontracted their looms and work assignments to yet another layer of subordinate weavers who worked in their own homes. Thus, though there was large-scale financing involved in this kind of silk weaving, the scale of production was usually quite small.[29]

Characteristic of the production and marketing of handicraft silk by Qing times, then, was the preponderance of exchange relationships among merchant middlemen and relatively autonomous sericulture peasants and weaving households. Organizational tendencies in this system over time were away from large-scale artisan-based production managed by the Imperial Silkworks, toward fragmentation and smaller-scale production. The zhangfang merchants who dominated the system by the high Qing had ties to small-scale, household-based production in two directions—toward peasant households who produced cocoons and silk yarn on the one hand, and toward weaving households (jihu) on the other. This was a more widely dispersed system based on small-scale production than had once existed during the Ming, when officials, and then merchant-guarantors recruited directly by the Silkworks, oversaw artisan recruitment and production.

The evolution of merchant activity in the context of delta silk production thus did not lead to larger-scale management of production, as occurred in some protoindustrial areas in the West. The commercial network of merchant account houses described here is an important example of how merchant/small-peasant nexuses became predominant in the delta during Qing times. From the account presented here, peasant-family production and the merchant/peasant nexuses associated with it appear to have altered the scale and organization of urban production as well. Although we have no direct evidence on costs of different methods of production, it was probably easier and cheaper for zhangfang merchants to purchase raw materials from one set of household-based workers, and then to put them out or sell them to another set of workers for weaving purposes, rather than to manage the larger, more complex oversight system that had existed during Ming times.

Beneath the merchant account houses, an array of other merchant activities also proliferated. These included merchant purchase and sale of warp and weft yarns of various types, as well as merchant-run shops for bleaching, dyeing, spooling, and pounding raw silk. There were also merchant establishments that sold finished products to specific domestic markets, and another separate stratum of merchant firms that acted as agents for export to various foreign markets. Few of these firms had true putting-out relationships with peasant producers, relying on the purchase and sale of items through the market rather than on fixed, contractual arrangements with peasants.[30] In short, the tendency in Yangzi delta silk production during Qing times was toward progressive elaboration and fragmentation of production and marketing among many layers of merchants and small-scale producers. This happened even as large merchant account houses bought up a substantial proportion of finished silk textiles from peasant weavers at the end of this string of relationships, to become the critical middlemen between the weavers and other merchants who sold the silk in disparate domestic and foreign markets.[31]

THE TAIPING WATERSHED AND THE
EXPANSION OF SERICULTURE

In this evolving milieu of handicraft silk manufacture, characterized by links between merchants and small-scale producers, Wuxi silk production emerged. But at the crucial moment of its origin, silk production in Wuxi was also a new phenomenon, made possible by the combined efforts of "restoration" of the delta following the Taiping Rebellion and world-market demand for new kinds of Chinese silk. There are several aspects to this side of the story: the effects of Taiping-period devastation on population, land-tenure relationships, and cropping patterns; efforts of the local elite to promote sericulture as part of the general plan of postwar rehabilitation of the delta; and increased demand for cocoons generated by new mechanized silk filatures in Shanghai. Behind all of these, competition with zhangfang-dominated networks for handicraft silk led to Wuxi's rise as a new sericulture district.

Warfare during the Taiping period affected areas throughout the Yangzi delta differently. Counties closest to the Taiping capital at Nanjing experienced the heaviest fighting; as a result, their population loss was exceptionally heavy. The area of the most severe devastation included Wuxi as its easternmost boundary.[32] Surviving cadastral records for the years 1830 and 1865 allow for an estimate of loss of life in Wuxi during the Taiping years. In 1830, the number of recorded male taxpayers stood at 598,483. In 1865, this number had dropped to 210,061.[33] Undoubtedly, the second figure reflects a certain degree of difficulty for government officials in reestablishing the former tax rolls in the first year following the Taiping defeat. Keeping in mind that the cadastral figures were an accounting of less than half the real population even in the best of times (see the discussion in Chapter 2, note 3), we can estimate that the population stood at approximately half a million in 1865, reduced by about one-half through death and flight.

In recounting the story of population depletion in the delta during the Taiping era, Li Wenzhi has shown that in the three prefectures to the east of Wuxi—Suzhou, Songjiang, and Taicang—population losses during the Taiping period were far lower than in prefectures between Wuxi and Nanjing. Many landlords in the less-severely affected prefectures had fled during the period of Taiping control, yet a significant number of cultivators remained on the land. Thus, Li argues that when landlords returned, they were able to reestablish their rights to land ownership and rent fairly easily. By contrast, in Jiangning, Zhenjiang, and Changzhou, the three prefectures straddling the area from Nanjing to Wuxi, more than 50 percent of the land remained vacant in 1870. Li reasons that with agricultural production so severely curtailed, landlordism itself was seriously challenged. Peasants who resettled dormant land either claimed the status of independent owner-cultivator or were in a strong position to resist rent collection. If rents were high, the cultivator could threaten to move to a new location, since vacant land was abundant; the landlord would then lose his tenant altogether. Because it was difficult to collect rents and keep tenants, many landholders preferred to sell their land, and large concentrated landholdings under single ownership were rare. Thus, owner-cultivator farms were able to gain a strong foothold in the post-Taiping period throughout the Jiangning-Changzhou corridor, the area stretching from Nanjing to Wuxi.[34]

Such changes in land tenure and population density in the delta may have been only momentary, as longer-term patterns seemed to reassert themselves in Wuxi by the 1920's (see Chapter 6 below). Nevertheless, a new window of opportunity for Wuxi silk production appeared in the wake of population depletion and unsettled land-tenure relationships.[35] One of the most significant results was the rapid expansion of sericulture into areas where peasants previously had not grown mulberries or cultivated silkworms. As we have seen, such areas were primarily to the north and west of Tai Hu, and Wuxi stands out as a prime example of how sericulture spread to this subregion of the delta in the post-Taiping years. In an 1813 local gazetteer from Wuxi, no mention was made of silk in the list of important native products.[36] However, in the 1881 revised version of the same gazetteer, the following section on silk had been added:

> In the past silk was produced only in Kaihua Township. From the early years of the Tongzhi reign [1862–74], conditions have been in flux with much vacant land and many people [coming to resettle it]. This has created an ideal situation in which to begin the planting of mulberries and the raising of silkworms. Sericulture has begun to flourish, and has spread to every township.[37]

This passage suggests that Taiping devastation in Wuxi created opportunities to transform patterns of cropping, sideline production, and local commercial activity. We should recall that in the eighteenth century, the principal sideline activities in which peasant households participated were cotton spinning and weaving. But Wuxi peasants had not grown their own cotton, relying instead on the importation of raw cotton from neighboring districts (see Chapter 2). Now, with a large proportion of arable land standing idle, a chance existed for peasants returning to the area, or for newcomers from other areas, to begin mulberry cultivation. As they did so, the disruption of land-tenure relationships in areas between Nanjing and Wuxi played a role in the degree to which mulberries gained ground. Because mulberry trees are a relatively long-term and substantial investment, requiring not only six to seven years of propagation before they produce a large quantity of leaves to feed silkworms, but also expenditure of large amounts of time in pruning and applying fertilizer,[38] peasants preferred growing them on land to which they held complete title (that is, both subsoil and topsoil rights), rather than on rented land.[39] During the 1920's, most mulberry land in Wuxi was still peasant-owned.[40]

As we shall see in greater detail in Chapter 4, local elites also played a role in the beginnings of sericulture in Wuxi, through various government-supported programs and private efforts to import mulberries, silkworms, and sericulture technique from northern Zhejiang. Undoubtedly, these elites saw new commercial opportunities for themselves, as well as benefits for local peasants, if Wuxi could become a new sericulture district. In Qing times, markets for rice, raw cotton, and cotton handicraft cloth had all flourished in Wuxi. But because Wuxi peasants who produced cotton handicraft products depended on raw cotton grown elsewhere, competition developed between Wuxi cotton merchants and sojourning merchants from cotton-growing districts. Competition with merchants from neighboring Jiangyin County, who organized cotton firms of various types in the marketing districts outside Wuxi City's gates, had been especially vigorous.[41] When sericulture began to spread to Wuxi, local elites established new marketing relationships with local peasants who produced cocoons. Although there was always the potential for competition with merchants from outside the county, it rarely materialized, with new cocoon firms organized almost exclusively by local merchants at the market-town level. The cocoon trade thus became an important source of commercial revenue for local merchants, a form of local marketing that they struggled to preserve as their sole prerogative.

WORLD-MARKET EFFECTS

If the end of war and devastation provided an opportunity for peasants to begin sericulture and for local elites to promote it, another major factor supporting Wuxi silk production in the 1860's was increasing demand for cocoons generated by Shanghai's new status as a treaty port and the building of silk filatures there. We have seen that handicraft silk production and marketing had long been organized under the auspices of the Imperial Silkworks. But the Taiping occupation not only devastated sericulture in the region, it also curtailed the activities of the Silkworks. Due to depressed domestic economic conditions that lingered even after warfare was over, the export market, with Shanghai as its new locus of entry into the potentially lucrative Yangzi delta trading networks, took on new importance as a stimulus for rehabilitation and expansion of sericulture and silk production.[42]

Even before the nineteenth century, export demand for Chinese silk had helped stimulate handicraft silk production in the delta. From the sixteenth through the eighteenth centuries, foreign merchants traded Chinese silk in Japan, southeast Asia, Europe, and the New World. The trade was in silk fabric as well as in silk warp and weft yarns, or "raw silk" (shengsi), as such yarns were called. Raw silk went to such countries as Japan and Mexico, where it was woven and sold domestically or re-exported.[43] However, nineteenth-century trends in silk export signaled important departures from the past. Western demand expanded dramatically, due in large part to increased need for filature silk, spun by steam-powered plants located in Shanghai, Guangdong, and, beginning in 1904, Wuxi.

Demand for filature silk was closely linked to the development of the power loom in England in the 1780's, and the spread of its use throughout Europe and the United States.[44] With the power loom, more silk could be woven in a shorter period of time, and finding an adequate supply of cocoons and raw silk became a major priority for the international silk industry. For different reasons, however, neither Europe nor the United States produced its own cocoons to meet the increasing demands of modern textile mills. In the European case, a massive outbreak of pebrine disease, a bacterial infection fatal to silkworms, began in 1854, and destroyed small pockets of sericulture activity in southern France and Italy. Louis Pasteur identified the organism responsible for pebrine, isolated it, and developed methods of treatment, but his efforts came too late to quell the most serious effects of the epidemic.[45] In the United States, on the other hand, potential labor costs made sericulture prohibitively expensive. Mechanization of the procedures of sericulture was not an option because the incubation and feeding of silkworms require meticulous monitoring. Therefore, the most reasonable option available to silk industrialists in Europe and the United States was to try to exploit and expand the existing areas of labor-intensive cocoon production in the peasant economies of both China and Japan.[46]

The power loom stimulated demand not only for increased quantities of raw silk, but also for improvements in quality. Raw silk spun by machine in steam-powered filatures was of more even twist and strength than its handicraft counterpart and broke far less often during machine weaving.[47] Thus, in the overall production of a finished silk textile product, filature silk could increase labor productivity as well as the fabric's quality. One estimate of the degree to which productivity could be enhanced noted that while preparing silk for weaving, workers using low-quality raw silk could spool only six to eight pounds per day; those using high-quality yarn could spool thirty-five to forty pounds per day.[48]

Because machine weaving stimulated demand for increases in both quality and quantity of raw silk, in the last decades of the nineteenth century, export demand from Western markets shifted to include the new filature variety. Although the technology for steam-powered silk reeling was developed in Europe, in order to be close to raw-material supply and to take advantage of lower labor costs, Europeans began to establish silk filatures in Shanghai in the 1860's, while Chinese investors began to build filatures in Guangdong in China's far southeast. Other scholars have explored the development of filatures in Guangdong, and I shall not repeat their efforts here.[49] Because my concern is with the Yangzi delta, I shall concentrate on Shanghai's earliest filatures and the reasons for their difficulties in the years immediately following their foundings.

Silk filatures in Shanghai used relatively simple machinery and, for the most part, employed unskilled female and child labor. The first process pursued in steam filatures is most properly called silk "reeling." Although this process fulfills the same function as spinning for other staple fibers such as cotton and hemp, reeling and spinning are actually two different techniques. Because cotton is only a few inches long, it must be tightly twisted together to produce sufficient length. Silk fibers, on the other hand, are much longer, and are simply "reeled" from the cocoon casing; four to nine of them are loosely twisted together as part of the reeling operation to produce silk thread. A second process, called "throwing" or "doubling," is then employed, in which varying numbers of silk threads are grouped together and twisted in different ways to produce silk yarn of various textures, weights, and strengths. Both reeling and throwing were performed in Shanghai filatures, and the finished product, called "raw silk," was then exported to fulfill new world-market demand.[50]

In the 1920's, the average Shanghai filature contained around 300 basins.[51] Each basin consisted of a vat for boiling water, where cocoons were placed to loosen their fibers, and a reeling wheel, located above the vat and powered by steam. At each basin there were two workers, one who replenished the cocoon supply and tended the water, and a second who sat in front of the vat pulling up the cocoon fibers and leading them to the revolving wheel on which the silk thread accumulated. Both workers were female, the vat tenders usually among the youngest girls to work in early Chinese factories.[52] There were also workers who sorted and peeled cocoons, ran the boiler room, and packed the raw silk. The latter two categories of workers were usually men.[53] But the majority of workers in the filatures—reelers, vat tenders, sorters, and peelers—were women and young girls, whose skill and wages were relatively low.[54]

Despite the rapid escalation of world-market demand for filature-produced raw silk, the European investors who owned and operated filatures had difficulty keeping them in operation. Although they built their filatures in Shanghai, a rapidly developing city that neighbored traditional sericulture districts in the delta, they could not secure adequate cocoon supplies. Jardine, Matheson, and Company, a British exporting firm with multiple business ventures along the China coast, built Shanghai's first filature in 1862. But it closed within four years, due primarily to inadequate cocoon supply.[55] Several other filatures built by Europeans in the 1860's failed due to lack of cocoons.[56] Only in the 1880's would this situation begin to change for the better, with sustained filature development in Shanghai under a new Chinese-owned and -operated system.

HANDICRAFT VERSUS FILATURE SILK

During the early 1880's, there were still only three silk filatures operating in Shanghai: one established by the American firm of Russell and Company; the second, a renewed effort by Jardine, Matheson, and Company, financed with 40 percent foreign capital and 60 percent Chinese; and the third, a new venture undertaken strictly with Chinese capital, established by Huzhou silk merchant Huang Zuoqing. But by 1900, there were twenty-odd filatures in Shanghai, and by 1930, at the pinnacle of their development, there were 107 filatures in operation.[57] Most of the earliest investors in new Shanghai filatures were Chinese compradors or men who otherwise had strong connections with foreign companies, a logical development given that such men had the greatest opportunity to learn about new business ventures geared to servicing foreign markets.[58] Later on, most filatures would revert entirely to Chinese ownership, with many of their owners having no direct links with foreign firms.[59]

Critical to the new success of the Shanghai filature industry was the way in which new investors overcame previous problems with raw-material supply. One might assume that filatures finally were more successful in tapping into existing supplies of cocoons in traditional handicraft silk districts. However, a very different pattern of raw-material procurement emerged, with areas entirely new to sericulture, especially Wuxi, playing a major role in new-filature success. Ironically, perhaps, an important stimulus to these developments was the persistence and adaptability of the old merchant account houses, or zhangfang, which had long supervised silk production and organized silk purchase in traditional handicraft districts. For the most part, zhangfang merchants did not switch to operation within new filature networks, but rather retained and adapted their existing marketing networks with peasant-family producers of silk handicrafts in the lower half of the delta. The preferred method for adapting to changing world-market conditions among zhangfang merchants was to urge peasants to modify production techniques to satisfy changing demand for different types of handicraft silk, while they marketed the products in more locations abroad.

Data in Table 1 demonstrate both the strength and the flexibility of the handicraft sector despite growing competition with filature silk within the changing international silk trade in the period from 1870 to 1930. Although the raw silk portion of the handicraft trade fell off after 1895 due to competition with filature silk, the silk fabric portion picked up dramatically beginning in 1910. This reflects the development of new

TABLE I

Silk Exports from China, 1870–1930

(in thousands of dan [piculs])

| Year | Handicraft silk | | Filature silk: |
	Fabric	Raw silk	Raw silk
1870	3.8	49.2	a
1875	6.5	79.9	a
1880	8.4	82.2	a
1885	10.3	58.0	a
1890	14.7	80.4	a
1895	23.1	83.6	27.0
1900	18.3	61.9	35.3
1905	15.7	60.6	45.3
1910	29.7	75.2	64.0
1915	41.1	79.9	63.2
1920	37.4	48.2	56.1
1925	31.3	64.7	103.3
1930	29.9	51.1	100.3

SOURCE: Adapted from Lieu 1940: appendix, 265.

aNo figures reported.

weaving efforts so that handicraft yarn could be woven by peasant or artisan households and then exported. Many new weaving centers developed at such places as Shengze and Huzhou in Zhejiang, and Danyang in
southern Jiangsu, to produce handicraft silk fabric for export.[60] Well-to-
do Chinese women living in treaty port cities also bought such silks to
keep pace with the fashions of their European and American counterparts.[61] Thus, under zhangfang supervision, delta weavers adapted their
skills to produce fabrics other than the high-quality brocades and satins
formerly demanded by the Imperial Silkworks. In this way, the handicraft sector persisted and grew according to the tried and true methods of
merchant links with household-based production, competing well with
filature silk on the international market.

Another reason why the handicraft sector continued to be successful
was that prices for handicraft silk remained far lower than those for filature silk (see Table 2). Lower-priced handicraft silk was especially attractive in Hong Kong, Singapore, India, and the Mideast, where substantial
exports of raw silk and silk fabric continued well into the twentieth century.[62] Among the most popular types of handicraft raw silk exported
were warp and weft yarns produced in the northern Zhejiang prefectures
of Huzhou, Jiaxing, Hangzhou, and Shaoxing.[63] Even as late as 1926, only
21 percent of Zhejiang's cocoon crop went to filatures. Peasants in Zhejiang continued to reel the majority of their cocoons by hand and to sell
their raw silk to well-established zhangfang.[64]

TABLE 2

Value of Raw Silk Exported from
China, 1895–1930

(in yuan per dan)

Year	Handicraft	Filature
1895	435	647
1900	516	707
1905	669	942
1910	598	1,040
1915	527	1,036
1920	653	1,331
1925	788	1,623
1930	673	1,353

SOURCE: Adapted from Lieu 1940: appendix, 265.

Lower brokerage fees, as well as lower tax rates and transportation costs, contributed to the lower price of handicraft silk. Though the evidence on such matters is scattered, it is suggestive of the ways in which more well-established zhangfang merchants were able to use to their advantage the evolving system of domestic trade linked to the world market. For example, silk that was destined for export had to pass through a group of fifty middlemen merchants who had dual identities—on the one hand, they worked as compradors for foreign firms exporting Chinese silk, but on the other, they themselves were often merchants within the zhangfang system or had very close relations with zhangfang merchants.[65] Under such conditions, advantageous terms of taxation and the levying of fees associated with various stages of preparing silk for export accrued to zhangfang merchants. Also, reports from various points in the delta region indicate that the cost of shipping raw silk to Shanghai was lower than the cost of shipping cocoons. These advantages included better rates on internal transit fees (more on this below) and lower transportation costs.[66]

By the turn of the twentieth century, as compradors became less important in the Shanghai silk industry and better transportation networks emerged for cocoons and filature silk, the advantages for merchants from the handicraft sector should have started to dissipate. Nonetheless, prices for handicraft silk remained lower well into the twentieth century (see Table 2). Undoubtedly, it was a third factor—the continued ability of zhangfang merchants to exploit low-cost household-based labor in *all* phases of the production cycle—that enabled handicraft silk to remain competitive.

Ironically for Shanghai filatures, the labor they hired, even that of women and children, turned out to be considerably more expensive than labor expended within household-based production. Although I shall return to this point in a more extended analysis of peasant-family production in Chapter 6, it is worth noting here that when women went to work in silk filatures in Wuxi in the 1920's, wages for the most skilled work as silk reelers ranged from forty to fifty cents a day. When women remained to work at sericulture within their households, their work was worth only about twenty cents a day. The higher cost of factory-based female labor resulted from various aspects of the physical removal of women from their households. In order to make women available for factory work, peasant households had to be compensated for the loss of the women's time in other household-based work, such as growing vegetables, cooking, cleaning, and caring for animals and children. Daily travel to and from the filature also had to be compensated. When women lived at or near the filature during its months of operation, the costs of daily subsistence also needed to be factored into the wage. Although women earned less than men when they went to work in early Chinese factories, even female work became more expensive when it was divorced from household-based production.[67]

Thus, filatures simply could not beat out their zhangfang competitors when it came to the price of labor. It was not the ability to produce raw silk more cheaply that fueled Chinese filature development, but rather the demands of the international weaving industry for more and better raw silk. As long as zhangfang merchants continued to adapt and to carve out part of the new export market for themselves with lower-priced handicraft silk, competition for access to sericulture peasants and their products would continue.

THE ORIGINS OF WUXI COCOON MARKETING

When silk filatures began to develop in earnest in Shanghai in the 1880's, they succeeded because they had come upon an entirely new strategy for cocoon purchase. Prompted by commercial opportunity, yet thwarted by zhangfang persistence, filature organizers began to send compradors to Wuxi and other districts new to sericulture to encourage local elites to develop methods for cocoon processing and purchase. The organizations that resulted were called cocoon *hang*, or firms, a term that referred to relatively small-scale, local commercial ventures. Cocoon firms began to organize cocoon processing and marketing, establishing links with peasant producers of cocoons. In Wuxi, the effect on production was monumental. By the early twentieth century, nearly every peasant family in Wuxi had switched from cotton weaving as a form of sideline activity and was growing mulberries and raising silkworms instead. From 1910 to the early 1930's, the number of cocoon firms registered for operation in Wuxi grew from 140 to 373, and the county became the premier cocoon-marketing center within the delta region.[68]

Because Wuxi lay at the hub of an extensive network of waterways, it was a good location for cocoon-marketing activity. Small canals served as the major route for peasant marketing of cocoons at the site of annual, and later biannual, cocoon-marketing operations. Cocoon firms were scattered widely, located in or near market towns throughout the countryside, and peasants made use of small canals to bring their cocoons to market.[69] Larger canals converging in Wuxi were also important for intercounty cocoon marketing. Seven major routes for steam-powered boats linked Wuxi with Liyang and Yixing Counties to the southwest and Jiangyin County to the north, as well as to the city of Huzhou on the southern shore of Tai Hu. Cocoon firms used these routes to ship their goods to Wuxi City for preparation and reshipment to silk filatures.[70]

The early cocoon-firm network in Wuxi is an important example of how world-market demand for a new product, in this case filature silk, penetrated and interacted with merchant/peasant networks of production and exchange. The pivotal role of Wuxi local elites as organizers of cocoon marketing, and their combination of traditional styles of merchant activity with new demand for raw materials to service modern industry, would become hallmarks of silk-industry development in Wuxi. Thus, interaction between the comprador system and Wuxi elites explains not only how the cocoon-marketing system was first organized, but also how new links formed between local merchants working on behalf of modern industry and peasant-family production.

Compradors and early cocoon marketing in Wuxi. The early cocoon trade in Wuxi was a product both of evolving comprador networks and of local marketing arrangements. Compradors were men hired in various capacities by foreign firms based in Shanghai and other treaty ports to facilitate new forms of trade and investment among foreigners and Chinese merchants in the post–Opium War period. Evolving commercial taxation in the delta demonstrates the advantages Chinese merchants enjoyed when they became linked to the comprador system. Though Chinese merchants were increasingly subject to accumulating transit taxes on trade—the infamous lijin taxes as described above in Chapter 2—foreigners, via their comprador agents, could apply for a permit that allowed their shipments of goods to bypass lijin assessment altogether, paying instead a single amount called the *zikou banshui*, literally "the export half-tax." Under this system, products shipped to Shanghai by foreigners were treated as goods for export and given an export-tax assessment; the taxation rate for internal transport was then set at half the export tax and paid in Shanghai. Customs authorities issued a document called *sanliandan*, "the triple-transport permit," to foreign shippers or their comprador agents for presentation at each lijin station, exempting the goods from additional taxation. The Shanghai customs bureau then forwarded a share of the "export half-tax" proceeds to the appropriate lijin authorities.[71]

Because "export half-tax" fees were lower than lijin fees, foreigners and their comprador agents had a distinct advantage in the early decades of the cocoon trade. A skillful comprador could arrange to have the cocoons he purchased on behalf of Shanghai filatures classified as foreigners' goods for export (since they would eventually be reeled and spun in filatures for export as raw silk), and thus exempt from normal lijin fees. In general, lijin were approximately 3 percent *ad valorem* at place of origin and an additional 2 percent at each lijin station en route.[72] Lijin fees for cocoons transported between Wuxi and Shanghai around 1910 were about 9 yuan per dan of dried cocoons, or 6 percent of value. The equivalent "export half-tax" was only 1.5 taels, approximately 2 yuan, or just over 1 percent of total value. Thus, compradors paying the "export half-tax" rather than the normal lijin fees on cocoons could provide a substantial savings for filatures, giving them an advantage over domestic merchants operating independently.[73]

We have seen that the predominant trend in early filature development in Shanghai was for Chinese to become joint investors with foreign firms or to manage filatures belonging to foreigners. Often the Chinese managers of filatures had foreign connections, working as compradors in the silk-export trade or in other areas.[74] In part, this was because of cheaper tax rates on cocoon transport for foreigners. Gradually, Chinese became full owners of most Shanghai filatures, but filature registration often remained in foreigners' names in order to take advantage of savings in transit taxes as well as in fees paid to Chinese supervisory officials.[75]

Though Wuxi's strategic positioning within the delta's canal and river system made it an excellent location for cocoon marketing from the beginning, the completion in 1904 of the Wuxi-Shanghai stretch of the

Shanghai-Nanjing railway worked as an additional impetus to cocoon-firm development. Compradors interested in securing contracts for cocoon purchase began to travel to Wuxi by train; they also made rail transport an important method for return shipment of cocoons to Shanghai. As a result, cocoon marketing grew even more rapidly, so that by 1909, Wuxi had seventy to eighty cocoon firms. While filature management was shifting over to Chinese entrepreneurs, foreign exporting firms remained active in this period in promoting cocoon-firm development. British, American, Italian, and Japanese firms all sent comprador agents to Wuxi, with the Japanese firm of Mitsui, as well as the British giant Jardine, Matheson, and Company, among the promoters of Wuxi's earliest cocoon firms.[76] A brief look at the careers of early cocoon-firm organizers in Wuxi will help demonstrate more concretely how the cocoon-firm system worked. All of the men involved were Wuxi natives, yet they also had important ties to urban-based commercial networks and some form of government or business experience outside the county, working with and for foreigners.

Zhou Shunqing made his initial fortune as a comprador in the Chinese iron industry. Working first as manager of the British-backed Shengchang iron brokerage firm, he later became sole owner of the firm and opened branch operations in several cities. Zhou then began to follow more traditional routes to elite status. First, he purchased official rank through a personal contact he had cultivated with an uncle of the Guangzu emperor. Through this connection, Zhou solicited deposits from members of the imperial court to found one of China's first modern banks, the Xincheng, with branches in Beijing, Tianjin, Nanjing, and Wuxi. When the dynasty fell, the bank closed, and depositors lost 4 million yuan; yet Zhou survived the crisis, salvaging private reserves of 1.2 million yuan. With his profits in his comprador and banking activities, Zhou became a large-scale landowner in his home county. In the name of his lineage organization, he bought more than 3,000 mu of land at very low prices from peasants forced to sell in the drought-plagued northeastern section of Wuxi. He also purchased land for himself in the vicinity of his native village of Dongze in the southern part of the county, an important new sericulture district. He then single-handedly turned Dongze into a bustling market town by building facilities for shops, various local marketing firms, and pawnshops. He called his new creation Zhouxinzhen—Zhou's new market town—and built Wuxi's first silk filature there in 1904. Among his many early business ventures in Wuxi, Zhou operated seventeen cocoon firms.[77]

Whereas Zhou's career began with comprador activity and led into more traditional local elite roles, Xue Nanming's career took the reverse route. Born into a bureaucratic, landholding family, only later in life did Xue invest in new commercial and industrial ventures. Xue's father was Xue Fucheng, a holder of the highest-level *jinshi* degree, who had achieved national prestige and position in late Qing times, serving first as advisor to Zeng Guofan and later as ambassador to England, France, Italy, and Belgium. Xue Fucheng, a substantial landholder, also owned a large private granary in Wuxi. Xue Nanming began his own prestigious career in 1888, when Li Hongzhang appointed him to serve in Tianjin as a judge in court cases between foreigners and Chinese citizens. However, upon the death of his father in 1894, he returned to Wuxi and declined to resume office in Tianjin. Beginning in the late 1890's, Xue Nanming concentrated his efforts on the family's landholdings and new investments in silk production. In 1896, he collaborated with Zhou Shunqing in a brief filature venture in Shanghai. During this period, he also established ten-odd cocoon firms on behalf of Italian filatures.[78]

Rong Zongjing and Rong Desheng, brothers who became two of China's most important industrialists by the 1930's, had more modest claims to traditional forms of elite prestige than either Zhou or Xue. However, after sojourning careers in commerce, they, too, eventually settled down to make Wuxi their primary base for new-style investment activity. Their father, who owned only about ten mu of land, furthered family fortunes by traveling to Guangdong in 1883, where a relative working in Zhang Zhidong's administration helped him become a collector in two different locations for the new lijin taxes. He sent his elder son, Zongjing, to Shanghai at age seven to study in a firm manufacturing iron anchors. Soon after he arrived, Zongjing fell ill and returned home, but at age fifteen he went again to Shanghai to study old-style banking. He subsequently was a collection agent in Shanghai until the company for which he worked suffered financial difficulties at the time of the Sino-Japanese war. The younger son, Desheng, was apprenticed to a Shanghai old-style bank, and later worked under his father in the Guangdong Sanshui lijin bureau. Father and son returned to Wuxi in 1895, but in 1899, Rong Desheng briefly returned to Guangdong as an accountant in the provincial tax bureau. In 1900, he returned once again to Shanghai. At that point, he worked in an old-style bank that he and Zongjing had founded in 1896. Rong Desheng also set up a branch of this bank in Wuxi. Together, the brothers established several cocoon firms with funds borrowed from the Wuxi branch bank, on which they paid no interest as owners. They favored their native market town of Rongxiang as the location for their first cocoon-firm ventures.[79]

The details of the public lives of men who became some of Wuxi's first and most prominent cocoon-firm organizers make clear that there were two prerequisites for the successful organization of a cocoon firm—outside contacts and strong local roots. Zhou, Xue, and the Rong brothers were Wuxi natives, yet they all had supracounty economic and/or political activity in their pasts as well, including contacts with foreigners. They had studied modern business practice as it was evolving in Shanghai and elsewhere, and in the process learned that cocoons were in demand by Shanghai filatures. On the other hand, they were also returning members of the Wuxi local elite who chose their native place as the primary location of new investment activity. It was this combination in a few key individuals that gave Wuxi such a powerful start as a new center of cocoon-marketing activity.

Cocoon-firm facilities and the Wuxi local elite. Although initiators of the cocoon-firm system in Wuxi were local men with urban experience beyond the county, in the day-to-day operations at the local level another group within the Wuxi elite dominated the industry. These men were the owners and operators of cocoon-firm facilities. Unlike their urban counterparts working the Shanghai-Wuxi comprador circuit, local owners had more limited, immediate ties to rural areas in which cocoon firms were located, operating the facilities at cocoon-buying seasons through contractual arrangements with compradors. During the early stages of development, the relationship between compradors and cocoon-firm owners formed the essential operational link of the cocoon-marketing system. As the years passed and filatures were built in Wuxi as well as in Shanghai, compradors became less important, and local owners came to play the predominant role in the Wuxi. cocoon-firm system.

Cocoon firms were designed to operate seasonally, purchasing cocoons from peasants at the end of silkworm-raising seasons, heating the cocoons to a temperature high enough to kill the developing chrysalises inside, and arranging for shipment of the "dried" cocoons (*ganjian*) to filature warehouses. In the early stages of their development in Wuxi, cocoon firms set up operation only once a year, toward the end of the last week of May or early in June, conducting business for approximately ten days to two weeks. In the 1910's, a summer or fall buying season was added as sericulture experiment stations began to develop new varieties of silkworm egg that could be preserved by refrigeration and then induced to incubate later when peasants were ready to harvest a second crop of mulberry leaves. In most Wuxi locales, summer crops were rare, but fall crops were common by the 1920's.[80] In terms of their spatial distribution in the countryside, most cocoon firms operated at or near market towns, within easy walking or boating distance for peasant sellers.[81]

A cocoon-firm facility included areas for inspection and purchase of cocoons, rooms for drying cocoons with hot air, and space for storing cocoons for a short period before shipping.[82] The facility had spacious vacant areas for indoor cocoon collection, providing protection from the ever-present danger of rain. Peasant sellers came directly to the cocoon firm either by foot or by small boat, bringing relatively small quantities of cocoons, around fifty or sixty jin.[83] Employees of the firm inspected, weighed, and quoted a price for the cocoons, and gave the seller a receipt for which he could obtain payment from another employee responsible for cash disbursement.[84]

After the fresh cocoons had been purchased, cocoon-firm employees gathered them into large baskets and placed them on shelves in "ovens" the size of rooms, holding either 120 or 240 jin at a time and known respectively as single or double ovens.[85] For a period of five to six hours, heat from wood- and coal-burning furnaces dried the cocoons, with the temperature inside the drying rooms reaching 160 to 200 degrees Fahrenheit.[86] The drying rooms were constructed of concrete and raised a foot or two off the ground, providing space for a fire to be built beneath them.[87] Wooden racks were built along two walls for stacking the baskets of cocoons for drying. In the most advanced designs of the 1930's, the racks were metal, wheeled, and movable, and large metal fans were also installed in the center of each drying room to aid in hot-air circulation.[88] Drying was an essential step in cocoon marketing. Without it, the chrysalis within the cocoon would mature and emerge as a moth, destroying the delicate silk filament with its departure. The timing of purchase and drying was crucial because silkworm cocoons reached maturity within a week to ten days of formation. Cocoon marketing was a very urgent business as a result, with neither peasants nor employees of the cocoon firm getting much rest during the concentrated marketing period.[89]

Organizers of cocoon firms were men of some substance at the local level. In 1916, Japanese investigators who visited sites of cocoon marketing in Jiangsu described the owners of cocoon firms they observed as "local winemakers or wealthy men."[90] While such identification is only suggestive, it gives the impression that cocoon-firm owners were local elites able to tap readily into commercial networks at the market-town level, with sufficient funds to construct the rather elaborate cocoon facilities that were needed. The Japanese researchers further observed that

building the largest and most up-to-date cocoon firm facilities in the late
1910's took an investment of "several tens of thousands of yuan."[91] Because "tens of thousands" is a stock phrase for "a great deal" or "a lot,"
we cannot say exactly how much capital it took to start a cocoon-firm
facility. But the impression conveyed is that only men of some substance
at the local level either could have invested money for a cocoon-firm facility or could have been in a position to borrow funds to do so.[92]

Links between potential cocoon-firm investors at the local level and
compradors dispatched to Wuxi by Shanghai filatures were initiated via
written contracts that served as legal documents specifying the detailed
terms of the business agreement. An early cocoon-firm contract from
1887 demonstrates how a comprador and one local cocoon-firm owner
established their relationship. This contract—between two individuals,
Gu Mianfu, a comprador agent dispatched from Shanghai, and Sun Boyu,
a local landlord—served as the legal basis of operation of the Renchang
cocoon firm with three sites in Luoshe zhen, a major market town in the
northwestern part of Wuxi. The signing of the contract was witnessed by
a county official so that it could also serve as the official license (tie), establishing local government recognition of the business and sanctioning
its operation.[93]

Ideally, we would like to know how much land Sun owned and what
role cocoon marketing played in his overall economic situation to place
him more precisely in the local social hierarchy. But it is more difficult
to develop profiles for market-town notables like Sun than for men of
higher social standing. The identification of Sun as a landlord at the
market-town level came via independent discussions with two informants who had collected information in the early 1960's on the
Renchang cocoon firm from Sun Bingru, a former secretary of the Wuxi
Silk-Filature Association.[94] The informants, men with extensive experience of their own in delta silk-production networks, insisted that men
like Sun Boyu, a landholder who also had commercial interests centered
in his market-town environment, were the main builders of cocoon-
marketing facilities.[95] An article published later by one of these informants stated that cocoon-firm owners were men of local gentry or merchant standing.[96]

Cocoon-firm contracts: split responsibilities and shared risk. Thus
far we have established that the cocoon-firm system evolved via a two-
tiered system of comprador agents and local cocoon-firm owners. A more
detailed look at cocoon-firm contracts will demonstrate how responsibilities and costs were spread between the two layers of cocoon-trade

merchants. There were several styles of contract possible, sometimes with different names or slightly different terms, but for purposes of our discussion here, I find it most useful to group them into three broadly conceived categories.[97]

1. Contracts in which the cocoon-firm owner assumed all costs of operation, including transportation of the cocoons to Shanghai, for which he was paid a flat fee per unit of cocoons ordered. Some of the local names used to describe this form of contract were *chaojiao*, "to take up delivery," *baojiao*, "to contract for delivery," and *baoshou*, "to contract for receipt."[98]

2. Contracts in which the comprador merchant rented out the cocoon-firm facility for a flat fee per drying room and then undertook all costs of operation himself. This type of operation was generally called *zuzao*, "renting the oven." A variation of this form occurred when the comprador sublet the facility to a third party for operation so that neither he nor the owner directly undertook the work. This was sometimes called *yujian*, "surplus cocoons."[99]

3. Contracts in which the costs and responsibility of purchasing, drying, and shipping the cocoons were shared between the comprador agent and the local cocoon-firm owner. This system was usually called *baohong*, "to contract for drying," but was sometimes known as *baozhuang*, "to contract business." In this system, an estimate of cocoon quantity desired and cost of its purchase for the owner was made before the season began. The comprador agent paid 70 to 80 percent of this cost before marketing and the rest after the cocoons had been delivered. For any unexpected discrepancies in cocoon quality or quantity, payment adjustments were made upon final receipt of the cocoons. The established rate of payment in Wuxi by the comprador to the owner per dan of dried cocoons under these arrangements was 11.5 to 12 yuan.[100]

Among these three types of cocoon-firm contracts, the third, or baohong, in which the costs of cocoon marketing were shared by cocoon-firm owner and comprador, was the most popular in Wuxi. Although it was more risky for owners to assume part of the cost of operation of the cocoon-firm facility than to simply rent the facility outright, they stood to gain larger profits if they did so. Tables 3 and 4 break down survey data collected on Wuxi cocoon-firm operation in 1916 to reveal exactly how the costs were shared between comprador and owner under typical baohong contract arrangements. Figures in these two tables indicate that

TABLE 3

Cost of Cocoon-Firm Operation for Comprador, 1916

(in yuan per 200 dan of dried cocoons)

Baohong fee (11.50 per dan)	2,300
Cost of sending 40,000 yuan in cash to Wuxi for cocoon purchase	80
Transportation of 600 sacks of dried cocoons from the cocoon firm site to Wuxi city	60
Storage charges in Wuxi for one month, 25 fen per bale	24
Zikou banshui (transit tax) charges in Shanghai, assessed in customs taels, 1.5 tael/dan	450
Weighing charges in Shanghai	6
Shipping cost by train from Wuxi to Shanghai, 25 fen per bale	150
Customs clearance handling charge	12
Coolie cart charge from Shanghai train station to warehouse, 600 bales, 9 fen per bale	54
Packing charge cost	18
Cocoon production tax for 200 dan, 8.85 yuan/dan	1,770
Water, fire, and theft insurance for 40,000 yuan at 1.25% of value	500
Cost for hiring small steam boats, 5 boats for 15 days	75
Small [hand-powered] boat hiring cost for 15 days	24
Miscellaneous costs	100
Wuxi headquarters expenses	200
Salary for 21 clerks-in-charge	505
Interest on 40,000 yuan (borrowed from Shanghai banks prior to the marketing period), at an interest rate of 0.8% per month	267
TOTAL	6,595

SOURCE: Tōa dobunkai 1920: 559–61.

under baohong agreements, such things as transit taxes, transport costs, and the majority of white-collar wages were the responsibility of the comprador, whereas local costs of drying the cocoons, miscellaneous service fees, and unskilled labor costs were borne by the cocoon-firm owners. For these arrangements, the comprador paid 11.50 yuan per dan, or 2,300 yuan per 200 dan, to the owner as a baohong fee. The owner, in turn, incurred expenses of 1,092 yuan, leaving 1,208 yuan in profit. In contrast, under the terms of pure rental contracts in Wuxi at the time, where cocoon-firm owners received a flat fee for renting their facilities and undertook none of the work and expense themselves, owners received only 1,000 yuan in rental fees per 200 dan.[101] Thus, under baohong agreements, in return for absorbing some of the risks associated with cocoon-firm operation, owners increased their income by about 20 percent over what they would have derived from pure rental contracts.

TABLE 4

Cost of Cocoon-Firm Operation for Owner, 1916

(in yuan per 200 dan of dried cocoons)

Cocoon firm rental middleman's commission	70
Local "gifts" (supplementary fees paid to local officials)	50
Reed mats for dirt floor	70
Expenses incurred during trip (of Shanghai merchant representative) to prepare for cocoon purchase—i.e., to secure the cocoon firm facility	100
Wages for 25 coolies to dry cocoons for 14 days, 30 fen per day per worker	105
Food for 23 clerks—four tables, 2 yuan per day per table (10 meal periods)	80
Go-between fee for coolies and other hired labor	50
Police protection	30
Miscellaneous coolie labor, 8 workers, hired at the rate of 1 person per time period, costing 5 yuan each	40
Food for coolie labor, 33 workers, 22 fen per day per worker, for 14 days	102
Wood for fuel, 600 dan, at the rate of 50 fen per dan	300
Wages for two clerks to supervise cash disbursements (to peasants) and drying operations	95
TOTAL	1,092

SOURCE: Tōa dobunkai 1920: 559–61.

One way to evaluate the significance of these cost-splitting arrangements is to consider potential rates of return on investment for each party. Since the comprador agent had no fixed capital investment himself, but worked on behalf of silk filatures for a wage or commission, there is little insight to be gleaned simply from the statement of his costs as reported above. These costs are more properly considered as part of the cost of filature operation, a topic to which I return in Chapter 5. As for the cocoon-firm owner, we have no precise figures on initial capital outlay used to construct a cocoon-firm facility. As noted above, the survey from which we have gleaned the above cost figures simply reports that it took "tens of thousands of yuan" to build a cocoon-drying facility. We do know, however, that a typical cocoon-drying facility in Wuxi in the 1910's had twenty-four drying rooms, and was capable of producing 720 dan of dried cocoons during a good spring season.[102] If the facility operated during a second season in late summer or fall, as many were starting to do in the 1910's and 1920's, it could expect to turn out approximately one-third the number of dried cocoons produced in the spring season, or about 240 dan.[103] Thus, at the rate of 1,200 yuan per 200 dan, income from baohong fees for the cocoon-firm owner for the year (after expenses)

would have amounted to about 5,760 yuan. For a twenty-four-room facility, cocoon-firm owners also had to pay some additional local taxes and
miscellaneous fees of about 450 yuan. These taxes and fees were all
strictly local in nature, including such things as licensing fees and building taxes paid to the county magistrate's office, and fees paid to village
and district heads.[104] Deducting this amount from the estimated yearly
income from baohong fees for the owner of a twenty-four-room cocoon-
firm facility, we have a new net yearly income figure of 5,310 yuan.

Since we have no way of calculating more precisely what this sum
represents relative to initial capital outlay, we might usefully consider
its meaning by comparing it to sums that could be earned from other investment options open to cocoon-firm owners. If one invested in land in
Wuxi, as most members of the local elite were prone to do, figures from
1929 indicate that a yearly rental rate on one mu of land stood at about 8
yuan (or the equivalent in rice and wheat), a 7 percent return on one's
initial investment (the same survey indicates that the average cost of one
mu of land, including both topsoil and subsoil privileges, was about 115
yuan in 1929). Thus, to bring in a sum comparable to that earned by operating a cocoon-firm facility, one would have had to have collected
rents on about 660 mu—a rather sizable amount of land to acquire in
tight land markets—and to have been content with a relatively low
yearly rate of return. Loaning money to peasants, another standard investment option in rural settings, could bring higher rates of return, with
yearly interest rates on loans in Wuxi averaging about 20 percent. But
making loans to relatively poor peasants was risky, as many could not afford to pay toward their debts at all in some years.[105]

Another way of evaluating the system of cocoon-firm contracting in
Wuxi is to consider its merits as a risk-sharing mechanism, designed to
delegate the responsibilities and liabilities of cocoon marketing to individuals best positioned to handle them within evolving commercial
networks between Shanghai and Wuxi. One of the most important tasks
that fell to the comprador agent was the arrangement of short-term loans
of large sums of silver to pay to peasants at the physical sites of cocoon
marketing. An extensive network of traditional-style banks, or *qianzhuang*, developed in Wuxi in response to this need, but the point of
origination of the loans was usually the much larger, newly developing
modern banks in Shanghai. Compradors, and former compradors, were
most active in managing the newly flourishing qianzhuang system
throughout the delta, and also seem to have had the most success in maneuvering on an equal footing with foreigners in the emerging world of
Shanghai banking. For this most critical aspect of cocoon marketing, it

appears that the "comprador connection" was vital, at least at the out-set.[106]

Other costs that fell to the comprador agent in the baohong system were those associated with the hiring of white-collar staff, the transport and storage of cocoons, and various transit fees and taxes on the trans-port of cocoons from Wuxi to Shanghai. Arrangements of this type also were best left to men with comprador backgrounds, who had sufficient experience and information about commercial networks between Wuxi and Shanghai. We have already seen how such advantages included fa-miliarity with the intricacies of the internal transit-tax system, and knowing how to avoid it by retaining foreign names for filature registra-tion.

The costs and responsibilities that fell to local cocoon-firm owners in the baohong system included hiring an unskilled, short-term work force, preparing the physical site for marketing activity, and paying govern-ment fees that were purely local in nature. Although comprador agents paid slightly higher fees to local cocoon-firm owners for handling such arrangements, it was probably well worth their while to do so, to insure that men who were familiar with the local commercial and political en-vironment made these processes and procedures flow as smoothly as possible. In addition, if sudden crises should arise, such as widespread failure in peasant cocoon crops in a given season, or an abrupt fall in raw-silk prices in Shanghai, the split responsibilities of the baohong system mitigated the effects by reducing the volume of losses that had to be ab-sorbed by each side.[107]

The picture we have, then, of the social dimensions of the cocoon-firm system shows that Wuxi elites of regional economic stature acted as comprador agents for Shanghai filatures, while members of the Wuxi lo-cal elite who lived and functioned primarily at the market-town level became cocoon-firm owners. This system bound two layers of mer-chants together in new ways in Wuxi, to enable filature operators in Shanghai to remain in operation and to respond more successfully to new world-market demand for Chinese raw silk.

MERCHANTS AND PEASANTS IN DELTA
MARKETING NETWORKS

By the early decades of the twentieth century, Wuxi had established a flourishing cocoon-marketing network, linking local merchants and peasants in a new world-market-oriented commercial enterprise. Other surrounding counties also had successful cocoon-marketing networks, although developments elsewhere were not as dramatic as those in Wuxi. Not surprisingly, the success of new cocoon merchants prompted a reaction from the older, more well-established merchant networks for handicraft silk. In 1915, the Jiangsu-Zhejiang United Silk Weavers' Association (Jiang-Zhe sichou jizhi lianhehui), an organization representing zhangfang merchant interests, lobbied the provincial governments of Jiangsu and Zhejiang for legislation prohibiting the further establishment of cocoon firms. This zhangfang-dominated organization argued that thousands of weavers would be deprived of work by continued expansion of cocoon firms; moreover, when peasants refrained from spinning silk and sold their cocoons instead, quantities of handicraft silk declined, and prices rose. Under pressure from the Silk Weavers' Association, the Jiangsu Provincial Assembly enacted the first measure controlling cocoon-firm expansion, limiting the number of new cocoon firms per county to five. Similar legislation was also enacted in Zhejiang. Perhaps most indicative of the depth of the Silk Weavers' Association's concern was the fact that six municipalities and counties in Jiangsu where handicraft silk was produced—Jiangning, Wuxian, Wujiang, Changzhou, Zhenjiang, and Songjiang—were prohibited entirely from licensing any additional cocoon firms.[108]

By 1917, organizations representing cocoon-firm merchants had launched successful counterlobbying efforts, urging the provincial assemblies in both Jiangsu and Zhejiang to raise the number of new cocoon firms allowed per county to twenty. In addition, in counties where the cocoon trade was especially active, such as Wuxi, merchants gained the right to petition the county magistrate for additional licenses for cocoon-firm operation. In 1920, when a five-year limit on the original 1915 legislation was due to expire, the Silk Weavers' Association once again stepped up its efforts, trying to secure a permanent ban on cocoon-firm expansion everywhere. But it failed to gain further limits on cocoon firms, and the revised 1917 legislation remained in place.[109]

At stake in these evolving disputes over cocoon-firm expansion were hard-won merchant links to peasant-family producers of cocoons and raw silk throughout the delta region. Though merchant/peasant marketing relationships were a long-standing tradition in the delta, an important effect of increased world-market demand for filature silk had been to create tensions among merchant groups striving for access to sericulture peasants and their products throughout the region.

Of great importance in the ensuing merchant-to-merchant struggle (on which I shall say more in Chapter 4) was that since Qing times, merchants had become relatively independent actors in evolving silk production and marketing networks in the delta. They no longer oversaw production directly, as in the old Imperial Silkworks system of Ming times, nor did they have any formal rights over the peasantry, or legal guarantees to peasant products. Instead, merchants depended on the needs and desires of peasant-family producers of silk products and cocoons to augment their incomes through commerce, and relied on peasants to respond voluntarily to market demand, producing the goods that merchants wanted to purchase. Although local elites were involved in promoting sericulture in the post-Taiping era in the delta, there is no indication that peasants were contracted by local merchants to cultivate mulberries or to raise silkworms, even in those merchants' alternate roles as landlords who made rental land and credit available to peasant-tenants. As world-market demand for filature silk escalated, it brought pressure for merchants to find new ways to create and control local markets, where they hoped that peasants would supply the goods they wished to purchase. But establishing new forms of control over peasants would prove difficult. We have seen that delta peasants had developed strong traditions of resistance to landlord dominance during Qing times (see Chapter 2). When confronted with merchant behavior that appeared unjust, delta peasants again found new ways to resist.

A description of merchant/peasant interaction in cocoon marketing in Wuxi comes from journal literature of the 1930's on peasant problems. Because this literature was written by leftist intellectuals, many of whom wanted to inspire their readers to develop revolutionary sentiments, it was notoriously pro-peasant and prone to hyperbole about the evils of local elites. The following passage is revealing nonetheless of the strains that developed at the marketplace between local cocoon merchants and peasants:

> At the time when cocoon collecting was at its height, the cocoon collectors deliberately spread rumors of political unrest, impending civil war, slump in cocoon prices, and even suspension of cocoon collection. These rumors were quite sufficient to trap the peasants, but there were also many other ways by which the collectors could get the better of the peasants. The peasants often had to bring their cocoons a long distance to the door of the collectors and, in spite of the crowd, the collectors would delay weighing for many hours. During the weighing the collectors would sham depression and poor business, thus deliberately lowering collection prices. Finally the peasants, exhausted by fatigue and hunger from early dawn, were forced to beg in pitiful tones for a little better price, which when granted only meant about ten or twenty cents extra. In addition, the Chinese system of "big" and "small" money [that is, silver and copper cash] gave the collectors a further op-

portunity to cheat the peasantry [through manipulation of the exchange rate]. At the end of the day there would still be peasants who had not sold their cocoons. They often made a great noise cursing the collectors, calling for fire from heaven, without realizing that the collectors' property was insured and that such a burning would be of actual benefit to the collectors.[110]

One way to read this passage is to try to see beyond its most obvious intent to expose peasant oppression, to consider the rather tortuous history of merchant competition for access to sericulture peasants that was its backdrop. Merchants were under pressure to secure adequate cocoon supplies at reasonable prices for filatures, and the temptation must have been great to manipulate local peasants to get the best price possible. Timing also added pressure to the situation, because the developing chrysalises inside the cocoons would burst out within ten days if not killed through the drying process. We shall see later that even with the cocoon-marketing system firmly in place in Wuxi during the 1920's, filatures continued to close sporadically due to problems with both quantity and quality of the cocoon supply. My goal, therefore, is not to condone or condemn unfair marketing practices, nor to try to determine whether they were the norm or the exception in local merchant/peasant relationships. Rather, I suggest that local merchants were more prone to unscrupulous behavior vis-à-vis relatively vulnerable peasants because they needed to use such cutthroat measures in order to succeed in a highly competitive, pressurized environment.

The perception that cocoon merchants were manipulative must have been strong among delta peasants, because they developed a range of resistant behavior. On several occasions, peasants formed villagewide groups to protest what they believed to be the arbitrary lowering of cocoon prices.[111] A dramatic display of peasant resistance came in 1929 in Wuxi, when peasants became so angered over prices that they began smashing equipment in the offices of a local sericulture cooperative.[112] Facing intense competition with other merchants, as well as unruly peasants, the merchants' next recourse would be to seek government assistance in protecting and preserving favorable market conditions. The case of the Jiangsu-Zhejiang United Silk Weavers' Association cited here is but one example of such efforts. As we examine cocoon-merchant organizations and their activities in Wuxi, we shall see that growing merchant/government interaction would become critical in future decades, shaping not only merchant/state relationships, but also the potential for future silk-industry growth.

4

Public Sphere or Private Interest? Defending the Wuxi Cocoon Trade

As sericulture spread to new areas in the Yangzi delta in the 1870's, local elites and government officials encouraged its growth. These developments were part of a larger effort to promote economic and political rehabilitation of the delta in the post-Taiping era. Some scholars have emphasized that initiatives undertaken by local elites during this period marked a new form of "local autonomy," contributing to the decline and eventual collapse of the Qing and the political "disintegration" of the Republican period. Others have seen such activities as a creative form of self-initiated political activity akin to the rise of an independent "public sphere" among emerging bourgeois groups in early modern Europe.[1]

In Wuxi, members of the local elite strongly promoted both sericulture and cocoon marketing in the post-Taiping period. Contrary to "local autonomy" arguments that posit a growing confrontational stance of local elites toward the state, the Qing impetus toward elite/state collaboration to promote commerce remained strong in Wuxi. The potential was strong for county government agencies and local gentry members to jointly encourage peasants to undertake sericulture, and for local government to guarantee the rights of local merchants to regulate and protect cocoon-marketing arrangements. If the "local autonomy" construct does not reflect the Wuxi situation very accurately, neither does the idea of an emerging public sphere among local cocoon-trade merchants in Wuxi mirror the reality of ongoing elite efforts to rely on state support in promoting new market-related activities. Only over time, as collecting taxes on the new cocoon trade became an increasingly urgent goal of the provincial government, did conflict between local cocoon merchants in Wuxi and state agencies flare.

In this chapter, therefore, I shall try to articulate more clearly local elite efforts to promote sericulture and cocoon-marketing activities.

How might we better understand the activities of a Chinese merchant guild in the context of late Qing/Republican local society and politics? How did local elites conceptualize, and act upon, their positions with respect to governments that came and went with increasing frequency as the twentieth century advanced? And finally, what did the boundaries of elite/state authority have to do with development?

THE BUREAUCRATIC PROMOTION
OF SERICULTURE

The first efforts at collaboration between elites and the state in Wuxi in the post-Taiping period have been referred to in past literature as the "bureaucratic promotion of sericulture." Such efforts had a long history, but also received substantial reinforcement in the proclamations and actions of government leaders throughout the delta in the post-Taiping period. National leaders serving in Nanjing and provincial governors in the region, including Zeng Guofan, Shen Baozhen, Zhang Zhidong, Zuo Zongtang, and Li Hongzhang, all stressed the importance of sericulture to restoring the people's livelihood. In response to bureaucratic urgings at higher levels, local magistrates in delta counties organized special government bureaus to promote sericulture technique, hiring experts from Zhejiang to teach local people how to plant mulberries and raise silkworms. As a result of these efforts, the famous *hu* variety mulberries from Zhejiang and various varieties of Zhejiang silkworms were imported into locales new to sericulture.[2]

The idea that bureaucrats and local elites should work together to promote sericulture fit well into the more general world of statecraft thought that had come to prevail in the delta during Qing times. As we have seen in Chapter 2, elites and government became firmly committed to the development of marketing relationships and commercial institutions to promote and preserve the people's welfare. Perhaps what was different at this point was only the urgency of the situation, as rapid reconstruction in the delta was of the utmost importance to elite and state efforts to remain solvent in an era of economic crisis. In Lillian Li's detailed account of the bureaucratic promotion of sericulture, we see how one of its primary proponents among officialdom was a magistrate serving in Dantu County, Shen Bingcheng. Shen was a native of Huzhou, where sericulture had a long history, and, according to the local gazetteer of Dantu, was also a statecraft proponent. Shen went on to write, or at least to sponsor, an influential sericulture manual, and to become governor of Anhui Province as well.[3]

Another example demonstrates exactly how bureaucratic promotion by men like Shen, serving as local magistrates and provincial governors, interacted with the local elite initiative. In the early 1870's, a local gentry member from Jiangyin County, bordering Wuxi to the north, purchased several hundred hu-variety mulberry trees and planted them experimentally. The county magistrate subsequently ordered the purchase of more mulberries and their free distribution.[4] The lessons learned through such examples were stressed in another sericulture manual written by Zhang Xingfu, a *juren* degree-holder from Huzhou in Zhejiang. Zhang emphasized that experiments in sericulture should be carried out primarily by local gentry rather than by local government officials because peasants tended to mistrust government.[5]

In an example of elite involvement in sericulture promotion from Wuxi, Yan Ziqing, a Wuxi native who had served as a county magistrate in Shaanxi Province, returned to his native town of Zhaimen in the northeastern Wuxi township of Huaishang in 1871. A posthumous collection of his writings records that one of his first projects upon returning home was to import 3,000 mulberry saplings from Jiaxing County in Zhejiang, an area long famous for sericulture and the production of handicraft silk. Yan had the saplings planted on a thirty-mu plot and erected a large residence next to it. Yan claimed that this was the first instance of planting mulberries in relatively large tracts in Wuxi. To demonstrate the importance of his effort, he placed a stone engraving above the door of his new residence, naming it the "Cottage for the Study of Mulberry Cultivation" (Kesang lu).[6]

Yan's naming of his residence in the fashion he did may seem at first a relatively trivial matter. However, the three-character name Kesang lu—literally the "study-mulberry-cottage"—apparently was chosen with some care, an adaptation of a well-known phrase, *quanke nongsang*, "to encourage and study agriculture and sericulture." This longer phrase was a traditional exhortation to all scholar-officials, urging them to fulfill their responsibilities as upright leaders to promote the people's livelihood.[7] Seen in this context, the term "kesang" took on a special function as Yan adapted it, announcing to the local community that he was a leader committed to promoting the people's welfare.[8] In more pragmatic terms, of course, it was to the advantage of both government functionaries and local elites to see sericulture succeed as a means to revive the region's economy, because tax, rent, and successful commercial management all depended upon a flourishing rural sector.

A second case suggests that local elites in Wuxi were not completely loathe to discuss their commercial motivations in more forthright ways. A letter written by a large landowner named Hua Guanyi to his daughter-in-law in 1873 recounts his planting of 3,000 mulberry saplings on fifteen mu of land. In the letter, Hua discussed in detail the potential profits from sericulture, explaining that only if the ideal ratio of trees to land was achieved would the maximum profit per tree be possible. Hua reported that he had planted 230 to 240 trees to the mu, that he anticipated his trees would be producing twenty jin of leaves per tree, and that each jin would be sold for ¥1.30 or ¥1.40.[9] Thus, through Hua's account, we see that from the point of view of the more obviously calculating world of production and exchange, fulfillment of Confucian duty could also be profitable.

A final example from Wuxi demonstrates the evolving complexity of local elite initiative as elites' desires to seek commercial profit and to promote improved welfare through sericulture became more firmly established in local communities. In this example, a Wuxi degree-holder who held public office in the final decades of Qing rule, a man named Yang Renshan, recalled that during his youth he worried about the problem of insufficient mulberry leaves at the peak of silkworm-raising season and the rapid escalation of leaf prices that sometimes occurred as peasant households turned to the marketplace to supplement their supplies of mulberry leaves. In his memoirs, Yang states that he had considered buying a ten-mu plot to create a situation of "ever-normal mulberries," using the term *changping sang* to describe his idea. Since the state had long had the ideal of promoting "ever-normal granaries," *changping cang*, to regulate grain prices, Yang's phrase was a well-crafted allusion to prevailing ideological trends on the importance of providing for the people's welfare. But he also candidly admitted that at just the moment when mulberry prices rose, if he were then to put his own mulberries on the market at a relatively low price, both he and local peasants would have had something to gain—himself, profits from the sale of leaves, and the peasantry, lower prices for the mulberry leaves they needed so urgently.

Among his official duties, Yang was assigned to investigate and report on the silk and tea industries. He returned to Wuxi to look into local silk production and realized that problems with low cocoon quality were directly related to mulberry supply. Facing the possibility of insufficient mulberry leaves, peasants often fed their silkworms less. This forced the silkworms to form cocoons too early, resulting in thin silk filaments that produced relatively low-quality raw silk. In search of a solution, Yang turned first to "big merchants" in the local cocoon trade, suggesting that cocoon firms purchase land to establish "ever-normal mulberry fields" (changping sangyuan). They might then flood the market with additional leaf supplies to force price stabilization, thus enabling needy peasants to purchase adequate quantities for their silkworm crops. One problem with his idea, however, was that since mulberries took at least three to four years to mature to a sufficient level to produce sizable leaf harvests, a waiting period was inevitable before this measure could work. So Yang also proposed an interim method—for merchants to contract for advance purchase of leaves during the winter months at fixed prices, a practice that was sometimes used among leaf growers and purchasers. In the spring, the leaves would simply be turned over to the merchants, and they could withhold them from the market until just the right moment, selling them at suitably low prices to needy peasants to achieve the desired price-stabilizing effect. Merchants could still expect to make some profit for themselves via this temporary method, and the urgent need for leaves among peasants would also be met. Yang hoped that through this method, merchants and peasants in Wuxi would both benefit, and ultimately the entire nation would also be enriched through improved raw-silk sales abroad.[10]

There is no indication from the subsequent record about mulberry cultivation and leaf sales in Wuxi that any of Yang's ideas were ever implemented. As we shall see later, the issue of cocoon quality was an important and complicated one, and the provisioning of additional mulberry leaves at cheaper prices would probably not have improved cocoon quality substantially. In any case, the major point to take away from this example is not the degree to which such ideas were implemented, but what their existence reveals about the evolving nature of elite/state interaction on the questions of sericulture promotion, commercial initiative, and the people's welfare by the final decades of Qing rule. Yang Renshan was a prime example of how local gentry members in Wuxi responded in the post-Taiping years to the challenge of rural reconstruction. The initiation of new commercial activities related to raw-silk production for the world market, activities from which elites and peasants alike could benefit, received a great deal of attention from government and members of the local gentry in Wuxi and elsewhere throughout the delta. It would not be long before their efforts resulted in the conversion of substantial portions of agricultural land to mulberry cultivation, the production of sizable quantities of cocoons, and the generation of new marketing networks managed, regulated, and controlled by an emerging stratum of local cocoon merchants.

THE COCOON TRADE AND GENTRY
ORGANIZATIONS

Although we do not have specific examples of how individuals made the transition from promoting sericulture to organizing cocoon firms, it seems obvious from the above accounts that knowledge about new commercial opportunities related to world-market demand for raw silk circulated rapidly among members of Wuxi's local elite in the post-Taiping years. As we have seen in Chapter 3, contractual arrangements between Shanghai-based filatures and local cocoon-firm organizers led to the emergence of cocoon firms in market towns throughout the county. In a completely new and rapidly expanding commercial enterprise such as cocoon marketing, local merchants and peasants were bound to experience problems as both sides struggled to establish their respective positions within the new framework. In such an environment, Qing traditions of market management by locally prominent individuals and families came to the fore in Wuxi, with new elite-run organizations serving as vehicles to regulate and protect the rapidly evolving cocoon trade.

Susan Mann's work on merchants during the Qing suggests that the Qing state found it advantageous to rely on the initiative of local elites to regulate, protect, and tax markets in their home communities. She uses several examples of how local markets were rid of problems of unscrupulous tax-brokering by outside, state-appointed agents through the less-intrusive method of self-regulation, or "liturgical governance" (Mann's term, borrowed from Max Weber) employed during the high Qing by welfare-oriented imperial administrations.[11] The evidence on the early cocoon trade and the organizations designed to regulate, protect, and tax it in Wuxi indicates that similar strategies were employed there.

The first organization created in Wuxi to regulate and protect the cocoon trade was the *wenshe*, or "culture association" of Kaihua township. Although the term *wenshe* is often translated as "literary society," I believe "culture association" comes closer to its organizers' original intent to promote and enhance the general culture in Kaihua, broadly defined. Clearly, the name also had symbolic value, with strong associations with elite promotion of popular welfare at the local level.[12] By using this term, local elites marked themselves as men of refined social status who also were interested in serving society at large via such organizations. The designation "culture association" was commonly chosen by local elites for locally run community-service organizations, but in the rapidly changing late-Qing environment, its symbolic significance could also be used to enhance the legitimacy of entirely new activities. For example, a core group of Republican army officers who began the 1911 revolution in Wuhan also called them-selves a "culture association." Likewise, the first seven members of the Kaihua wenshe were still firmly within the market-town world of local elite society—all held low-level examination degrees—but the as-sociation's main tasks revolved around newly developing cocoon-mar-keting activities within the township.

The activities of the Kaihua culture association began in the mid-1880's, with its seven lower-gentry organizers responding to local prob-lems generated by nonstandard cocoon scales and weighing procedures used by a new local cocoon firm. The cocoon firm in question was lo-cated in Xushe and, somewhat ironically, at least from the point of view of the local peasantry, was named the Qijun, or the "Even-hand-ed," cocoon firm. Because this cocoon firm was originally established by Xue Nanming, the upper-gentry member identified in Chapter 3 as one of the important early middleman contractors of cocoon facilities in Wuxi on behalf of Shanghai filatures and foreign export firms, the lo-cal peasants who lived in the vicinity of Xushe called all of the opera-tors of the Qijun cocoon firm *yangshang*, or "foreign merchants," an indication of their knowledge of and concern about the relationship of the operators to foreign economic interests and the special privileges they were prone to expect.[13] Local peasants had already experienced the tendency of the operators of this cocoon firm to petition the provincial government concerning local disputes, and to call upon local officials to suppress any potential disturbance. They had been amazed by such special privilege at first, but had come to expect that this particular co-coon firm might engage in dishonest, self-serving behavior.[14]

In 1886, cocoon-weighing procedures used by the Qijun cocoon firm caused local cocoon-sellers to congregate and complain, prompting concern among the cocoon-firm operators and a request to the local county magistrate for protection and suppression should the conflict escalate. A subsequent investigation revealed that peasants were com-plaining about the type of scale being used by the cocoon firm, one that required 18 ounces of cocoons to be filled to balance rather than the standard 16.4 ounces traditionally used in the local market by mer-chants who purchased hand-spun silk.[15]

At this point, seven members of the lower gentry, the core group of what would eventually be known as the Kaihua Culture Association, de-cided to intervene. They invited representatives of the Qijun cocoon firm to have tea with them and to discuss the local peasants' concerns about weighing procedures. Although the Qijun representatives showed up for the requested meeting, they took a confrontational stance immediately, asked the names of the local gentry members, and told them that they intended to inform Magistrate Pei of their activities. Once the magistrate was notified, he contacted the county education director for a report on the seven gentry members in question. Luckily for the seven, the education director happened to be their tutor and spoke immediately in their defense, insisting that they simply had the best interests of the local community at heart. Although the matter could have ended there, the seven proved indefatigable and persisted in finding out for themselves whether or not the scales used by the cocoon firm were different from local standards. When they went to the marketplace, they found that the peasants were correct in their assertions, and they went in person to Magistrate Pei to make their own report. Taking a precautionary stance, the magistrate told them that this was a serious matter, that it must be reported to provincial authorities, and that only when a response came down from above could action be taken. Temporarily satisfied, the seven men returned to the marketplace only to find that the cocoon firm had closed up its operations for the season, an indication that its operators had, indeed, been at fault, and had retreated as a result.[16]

The persistence of the seven gentrymen now began to pay off for them in bigger ways. From the perspectives of their tutor, the local magistrate, and the local community at large, they had now proved themselves to be virtuous defenders of local interests, earning the right to organize themselves into a more formal group dedicated to upholding and protecting local cocoon-marketing procedures in the future from unscrupulous manipulators of the system. The magistrate ordered that henceforth, anyone establishing a cocoon firm in Wuxi would have to register their scales officially with the local government, and paste the official seal of standardization on their scales for everyone to see. The news of the "victory" of the righteous local gentry spread far and wide, and the magistrate not only thanked them for their actions, but also encouraged them to establish a "culture association" for the purpose of promoting their own further study and continued advancement up the ranks of degree-holding. Magistrate Pei also sanctioned their right to collect a "culture association fee" from all cocoon firms established in the area, a means to build up their association coffers to promote their educational efforts. Their tutor also joined in encouraging them, and helped them to invite famous local scholars to their now-flourishing academy to promote intellectual activity in the surrounding community. They were so successful that more than 100 local scholars studied at their academy, with their education efforts continuing right down to abolition of the examination system in the first decade of the twentieth century.[17]

Membership in the Kaihua Culture Association flourished during the final decades of Qing rule to include over twenty members, including a clerical staff that featured an accountant, a manager, and a secretary. The core group of seven founders continued to make major decisions affecting cocoon marketing, and to collect licensing fees to support their activities. An indication of how widespread the respect was for their work came when Xue Nanming, the original contractor of the Qijun cocoon firm whose activities they had so roundly criticized, met with them and made a substantial monetary contribution to their activities. After Xue's contribution, the group built more extensive and lavish facilities from which to conduct their work, both educational and otherwise, and purchased land to further support the association's activities.[18]

The example of the Kaihua Culture Association is a rich one, filled with extraordinary detail about how local government interacted with local gentry members to promote the development of cocoon marketing in the final decades of the Qing. Obviously, cooperation could benefit both sides. In the matter of quelling a potentially inflammatory situation in which local peasants were threatening the disruption of business activity, Magistrate Pei received important assistance from the seven lower-gentry members. On the other hand, the gentrymen themselves enhanced their own reputations as a result of their activities, and benefited materially as well, receiving substantial monetary contributions from one of the wealthiest and most prominent upper-gentry members in their community. And finally, we should not ignore the precedent set by the county-government sanction of the "culture association fee" now collected by this lower-gentry association—in reality, a form of tax on the rapidly expanding cocoon trade for the purpose of promoting the organization and its educational activities. This was an important first step in enhancing the managerial functions of local elites associated with cocoon marketing in Wuxi, empowering them as the legitimate defenders and promoters of political activities associated with new silk-industry development.

THE ORIGINS AND FUNCTIONS OF THE WUXI COCOON-MERCHANT GUILD

Whereas local gentrymen in Kaihua were the first to organize an elite-based organization related to the cocoon trade, another form of organization at the county level soon formed for the purposes of regulating and protecting the trade. This organization was known as the Wuxi Cocoon-Merchant *gongsuo*, or Guild (Wuxi jianhangye gongsuo), and its membership included those involved in the organization and operation of cocoon firms at the local level in Wuxi. With its membership engaged in a common trade, the Wuxi Cocoon-Merchant Guild resembled one typical form of merchant organization that developed in large commercial centers during Qing times. We might well begin a discussion of its activities, therefore, with a brief overview of such organizations and their functions.

During the Qing it was common for merchant associations to perform the tasks of self-protection and self-regulation. In the post-Taiping years, traditional forms of merchant organization experienced a renaissance throughout the Yangzi delta, re-forming along traditional "single-trade" or "fellow-provincial" networks, or emerging anew along such lines to promote and protect new forms of trade. The names given to such organizations were varied, but two of the most common were *gongsuo*, literally meaning "public office," and *huiguan*, "meeting hall," terms that reflected both the influence of important individuals in organizing them, and the fact that they usually had specific physical sites—a building or group of buildings—where their multiple activities were carried on. Though it is usually thought that Chinese merchants sojourning in various urban locales favored the term "huiguan" to refer to their "fellow-provincial" organizations, and that merchants engaged in a common trade used the term "gongsuo," Bryna Goodman has found in her recent work on such organizations in Shanghai in the late Qing and the Republic that such distinctions were not rigidly applied. She finds that both terms were used to name organizations that bound together those from the same native place—merchants, artisans, and workers—to promote trade and to protect the economic interests of the group.[19]

Some studies of huiguan and gongsuo have focused on their roles as collectors of commercial taxes on behalf of state agencies. As demand for commercial taxes grew in the post-Taiping years, a range of new types of taxes were levied on merchants and collected by their organizations before being sent forward to government agencies. Such taxes included the infamous "transit taxes" on internal trade (*tongguo lijin*), taxes that many merchants came to resent because they either were not imposed at all on foreign merchants or were imposed only in lesser amounts (see discussion of this point in Chapter 3). Other new commercial taxes included various forms of tax on local products (*chandijuan*) and licensing fees (*luodishui*), also often collected by merchants' organizations and then sent onward to state agencies.[20] As Susan Mann has pointed out, by voluntarily collecting and handing over a portion of trade proceeds, not only did merchant organizations protect themselves from excessive taxation demands by unscrupulous officials, they also took on the quality of quasi-official government bodies, capable of working in concert with local government authority.[21]

Recent studies of commercial cities have tried to come to terms in more general ways with the character of urban organizations and their roles in city life. William Rowe has studied merchant guilds, among other forms of urban organizing, in Hankow during the late Qing, whereas Bryna Goodman has focused on organizations founded on the basis of native-place origins, or "fellow-provincial" ties, in Shanghai during the late Qing and the Republic. Rowe is firmly committed to demonstrating the high degree of similarity between merchant organizations in Hankow and the guilds of early modern European cities, especially in terms of their roles in sponsoring new political and welfare-oriented activities. Rowe views merchant organizing as part of a growing "public sphere" of elite activity, in which merchants increasingly committed themselves to a range of public-service-oriented programs distinct from state-sponsored projects. Goodman, on the other hand, is interested primarily in the ongoing commitment to native-place ties in Shanghai, a city made up largely of immigrants in the late nineteenth and early twentieth centuries. The "fellow-provincial" organizations she studies were not exclusively "merchant guilds" in the sense that Rowe uses the term, although many of their most prominent members were merchants and they were involved on one level in promoting local business interests. Goodman is much more interested in exploring the importance of a traditional native-place orientation among all strata of Shanghai residents, and fashions an argument about the adaptability of such sentiment for the promotion of nationalistic goals and the evolution of class consciousness.[22]

My analysis of the Wuxi Cocoon-Merchant Guild builds upon these insights from previous studies. Like Rowe, I believe it is possible to think of the gongsuo organization formed by Wuxi merchants as a "guild," promoting and protecting common business interests and sponsoring public-welfare-oriented activities. However, I am reluctant to accept the "public sphere" dimension of his argument because it seems to imply that once on their new organizational path, merchants were involved in promoting ineluctable, capitalist progress. In its Habermasian form, as the "bourgeois public sphere," there is also a further implication—that as an autonomous social force, merchants would pursue and discuss subjects of interest and concern to a newly expanding modern citizenry. As we shall soon see, neither of these assumed characteristics of the European "public sphere" help us understand or analyze very precisely the activities of the Wuxi Cocoon-Merchant Guild.[23]

Thus, I reject the parts of Rowe's analysis that focus on the "public sphere" qualities of merchant organizations. Instead, in analyzing merchants' political activities, I follow much more closely Goodman's views on Shanghai's "fellow-provincial" organizations. Paralleling Goodman's findings, Wuxi cocoon merchants used "fellow-provincial" (or in this case, "fellow-county") sentiments quite effectively to build their guild. They then used the guild to further their private goals through protective, exclusionary measures. There were sometimes occasions for guild members to protest provincial government policy, especially as it related to the pace of cocoon-firm growth and taxation. One particularly turbulent period of protest erupted in the 1910's and early 1920's. Despite such conflicts, a very different situation evolved locally, where ongoing collaboration with county government became the order of the day. It seems important, therefore, to underscore that there was little motivation among the emerging silk-industry elite in Wuxi to adopt a permanently independent, oppositional stance to the fiscally coercive aspects of modern statemaking in the name of a wider "public." Instead, Wuxi cocoon merchants' sights were set more squarely on the pursuit of private interest through ongoing organizational forms and strategies, including elite/state alliances, especially at the county level.

In this evolving institutional milieu, the Wuxi Cocoon-Merchant Guild began its pursuit of functions once performed by the Kaihua Culture Association and more. Instead of outside gentry observers of local marketing conditions, now it was the merchants themselves who undertook both self-regulation and self-protection in the interests of promoting a flourishing cocoon trade. Leading up to the formation of the guild were regular meetings throughout the 1890's during spring cocoon-marketing seasons, attended by Shanghai filature agents and local Wuxi cocoon merchants, at the Shijinshan temple located to the northwest of the city (in Huangbudun, near Huishan). The group underscored to the local community, as the Kaihua Culture Association had before it, the legitimacy of its new commercial role through appropriation of a well-established cultural form—in this case, the already existing temple buildings, and their aura of spiritual authority within the local cultural setting.[24]

In 1902, cocoon-trade merchants formally petitioned the Jiangsu provincial government to form a countywide guild organization. The request was granted, with a guild fee now incorporated into the local dried-cocoon tax assessed by the Wuxi County lijin bureau. Once again, much as the Kaihua Culture Association had done previously, the guild members used the revenue generated through new fees to build a new, permanent meeting hall and office facility of their own, located outside the western gates of the city at Huishan Creek. In 1909, the meeting-hall facilities were expanded to include "foreign-style" meeting rooms and a kitchen area, presumably for preparing banquets for the guild membership and guests.[25]

The early managers of guild activities were all local gentry members, firmly entrenched within local elite hierarchies and engaged in evolving styles of local gentry-management. These men were hired by the guild membership to carry out the day-to-day functions of guild work, a long list of duties that we shall review shortly. The first manager was Sun Xunchu, a degree-holder who left soon after the guild's organization to begin an official tour of duty as a government bureaucrat in Hubei Province. The guild then selected Zhang Ding'an as its new manager. Zhang was son-in-law of Zhou Shunqing, the upper-gentry figure from Kaihua Township whom we met in Chapter 3 as one of the early comprador agents for the cocoon-firm system. Zhou Shunqing not only contracted for early cocoon-firm development in Wuxi, he also established a new market town called Zhouxinzhen (Zhou's new market), where he built Wuxi's first silk filature in 1904, promoted several additional cocoon firms, and established local pawnshops. Zhang Ding'an had experience in managing affairs in these enterprises, and also in running a special school organized by Zhou Shunqing to teach business skills. When Zhang died, a *shengyuan* degree-holder (the lowest degree within the three-tiered system), Hua Yisan, became the new manager. Thus all of the first three managers of the Wuxi Cocoon-Merchant Guild fit the profile of local gentry-managers that had been evolving since Qing times, and one had close ties with one of the most powerful upper-gentry and newly emerging bourgeois figures in Wuxi.[26]

The functions of the Wuxi Cocoon-Merchant Guild reveal even more graphically than the identities of its managers how complex and tightly interwoven old styles and new forms of commercial activity were becoming as the cocoon trade evolved. Though self-protection and self-regulation were clearly within the purview of traditional merchant organizations, they were now performed to promote a new form of world-market-oriented trade. A list of these functions reveals how guild members merged old and new styles, forms, and strategies in a total program for the promotion of the cocoon trade, and, by extension, for the promotion of the modern filature industry to which the trade was so closely linked:

1. To petition the Bureau of Naval Police for protection for boats carrying cocoons after purchase by cocoon firms and the cash used for their purchase.
2. To petition the county magistrate to give notice prohibiting unauthorized peddlers from performing cocoon-marketing activities, including drying and buying cocoons, confusing the orderly arrangements of cocoon marketing.
3. For the lijin office, to issue licenses to cocoon firms after payment of taxes.
4. To jointly decide on prices for cocoons, starting dates of marketing, and methods for dealing with those who deviate from these decisions.
5. To examine and license scales.
6. To receive and return deposits from cocoon firms to guarantee their compliance with local regulations.
7. To dispatch agents to investigate cocoon firms for the number of drying rooms and to report on the buying of cocoons.
8. To distribute materials on silkworm cultivation and its scheduling in cocoon-marketing districts.
9. To dispatch personnel to rural areas to discuss methods for sericulture improvement and the timing of stages of sericultural production.[27]

Though some previous studies have emphasized the importance of traditional gentry-style organizations in taking up tax collection on behalf of the state, the total package of what the Wuxi Cocoon-Merchant Guild perceived as its legitimate scope of activity is equally important to consider. The above list allows us a rare opportunity to view the entire spectrum of what the guild thought it was entitled to manage and control. Their activities ranged from requests for government alliance and assistance in terms of facilitating the smooth functioning of the cocoon trade, to the protection of trade activities from manipulation by private parties, be they "outside" merchants or their agents, or unscrupulous "inside" merchants or peasant participants in the trade. Broadly construed, we might say that the interests of the local trading community at large were at stake, and anyone who tried to undermine those interests was likely to become the target of attack or protest. As we shall soon see, according to cocoon-trade merchants in Wuxi, potential opponents could include agents of the state if they posed barriers to the self-defined interests of local merchants engaged in cocoon-trade activity.

COCOON-TRADE MERCHANTS AND THE
DEFENSE OF LOCAL INTERESTS

In the 1910's, the Wuxi Cocoon-Merchant Guild increasingly worked to defend and develop local commercial interests. The first series of incidents we shall review involves requests and counterrequests made to provincial-level state agencies concerning the licensing of new cocoon firms in Wuxi and other locales throughout the delta region. I have already noted some of the issues raised by these requests in Chapter 3, to demonstrate how old and new networks of merchant/peasant interaction within delta silk production competed. I return to these events at this point to underscore how strong the local interests of cocoon merchants had become in Wuxi by the 1910's, and also how important it was for Wuxi merchants to make successful alliances with county-level government (as opposed to provincial-level agencies) as they staked out their prerogatives to control local cocoon marketing and the revenues that it generated.

First of all, we should recall the basic issues in the licensing of new cocoon firms around 1915. At their point of origin, the issues revolved around requests made by an organization representing silk merchants in the handicraft sector, the Jiangsu-Zhejiang United Silk Weavers' Association, to the provincial governments of Jiangsu and Zhejiang to limit the number of licenses issued to new cocoon firms. At stake was the ability of silk merchants to purchase adequate quantities of handicraft silk products spun and woven by peasant households. The logic of the case of the Silk Weavers' Association against licensing additional cocoon firms was that the escalating purchase of cocoons from delta peasants limited the quantity of cocoons available to other peasant households in the region who spun and wove handicraft silk. By extension, new marketing arrangements between peasant cocoon-producers and cocoon-firm merchants also undermined the marketing activities and profits of the silk merchants, who purchased handicraft silk products of various types from other peasant households.[28]

As we saw in Chapter 3, the Silk Weavers' Association initially appeared to be quite successful in its petitioning efforts to limit cocoon-firm expansion. In 1915, both Jiangsu and Zhejiang provinces passed legislation limiting the number of new cocoon firms per county to five.

Once these control measures were enacted, cocoon merchants countered quickly, petitioning the provinces via their local and regional guild organizations for revised legislation. They were successful by 1917 in raising the allowed number of new cocoon firms per county to twenty. In addition, in counties where the cocoon trade was especially active, such as Wuxi, merchants gained the right to petition the county magistrate for still more licenses for cocoon firm-operation. In such cases, the magistrate was to limit expansion to a 20 percent increase from the number of firms already in operation in 1917. Thus, within the provisions of the revised legislation, cocoon merchants created a clever loophole, allowing further expansion of cocoon firms under the supervision of county authorities.

When Jiangsu Province first enacted control legislation against cocoon firms, a five-year limit was prescribed on the measure. In 1920, when the five-year limit was due to expire, the Silk Weavers' Association petitioned provincial authorities once again, calling for the continuation of cocoon-firm control. At this point, the Silk Weavers' Association requested a new system of "absolute control," forbidding any further cocoon-firm expansion within the province. Six municipalities and counties in Jiangsu with large numbers of handicraft silk weavers— Jiangning, Wuxian, Wujiang, Changzhou, Zhenjiang, and Songjiang—had been prohibited from further cocoon-firm expansion beginning in 1915, and the Silk Weavers' Association now sought to have this measure adopted for all counties. However, the Jiangsu Provincial Assembly was persuaded to continue the terms of the revised 1917 legislation, including the loophole that allowed virtually unlimited expansion in certain counties via petition to the county magistrate.

In Wuxi, where the majority of cocoon firms operated, cocoon merchants appeared to be quite adept at using the loophole in the provincial legislation, with their guild organization acting as a powerful lobbying force for continued expansion of the local cocoon-marketing network. As a result, the number of cocoon firms in Wuxi grew at a much more rapid pace than one might expect from the formal terms of the legislation. In 1920, there were 223 registered cocoon firms in Wuxi;[29] by 1933, at the height of their development, there were 373 registered cocoon firms, roughly a 67 percent increase over a thirteen-year period.[30]

Another series of incidents from the late 1910's illustrates the growing power of the Wuxi Cocoon-Merchant Guild to defend local commercial interests. Since cocoon marketing was not specific only to Wuxi, but had developed in other counties throughout Jiangsu, Zhejiang, and Anhui Provinces as well, Wuxi cocoon merchants began to fear that they might lose the capacity to arrange contracts to operate their facilities to their full capacity. At this point, we should recall that the mode of operation of cocoon firms was both seasonal and contractual. Each spring, filature agents negotiated contracts with local cocoon-firm owners for the purchase of dried cocoons. As new cocoon firms were increasingly established in areas of Zhejiang and Anhui, where in 1917 alone, eighty new cocoon firms were built, Wuxi cocoon-firm owners became nervous about their continued ability to compete. The crux of the problem was that some locales, especially in Zhejiang Province, were closer to the coast and further south than Wuxi, and thus had warmer temperatures slightly earlier during the spring cocoon season. This meant that peasants in such locales would be ready to harvest their cocoons earlier than Wuxi peasants would, and thus merchants there would get a jump on the marketing season.[31]

Facing the prospect of declining business, the Wuxi Cocoon-Merchant Guild decided to move forward the dates of their cocoon-buying activity, despite the fact that the entire cocoon crop in Wuxi might not be ready at the start of the marketing period. Shanghai filature agents who tried to work the entire marketing circuit, beginning in counties in Zhejiang that were near the coast and working inland over a period of two to three weeks, were upset by the Wuxi merchants' action. They sent to Wuxi a representative from their own business organization, the Silk Producers' Guild headquartered in Shanghai, to negotiate the situation. The man they sent, somewhat ironically perhaps, was Sun Xunchu, a Wuxi native and the first manager of the Wuxi Cocoon-Merchant Guild.[32]

There were no subsequent journal or newspaper reports about this dispute, and we cannot follow it to its conclusion. Nonetheless, the actions taken by the Wuxi Cocoon-Merchant Guild reveal the intentions of its membership by the late 1910's in an increasingly competitive and growing market environment. Through this particular set of incidents, it is clear that the interests of local cocoon merchants in Wuxi and those of Shanghai filature agents did not always perfectly mesh, and in such cases, the Wuxi Cocoon-Merchant Guild functioned first and foremost to assist local cocoon-firm owners. By this time, local filatures were operating in Wuxi as well, adding an important new dimension to local interest in raw-material procurement. As we shall see, local alliances within the silk industry in Wuxi continued to develop as the twentieth century wore on, and the Wuxi Cocoon-Merchant Guild evolved accordingly, as a merchants' organization dedicated to preserving the prerogatives of local men over production and marketing arrangements.

Another example demonstrates the local-interest aspect of the Wuxi

Cocoon-Merchant Guild. A foreign competitor attempted to introduce freely determined prices for cocoons to undercut local cocoon firms' buying activities. This individual, a Japanese businessman named Katakura, established two silk filatures, one in Suzhou to the east of Wuxi, named the Ruifeng filature, and one in Qingdao, a coastal city to the north. In 1929, Katakura ordered the manager of the Ruifeng filature to send agents to Wuxi to contract with local cocoon firms, but he also insisted that the firms offer prices for cocoons that were substantially higher than the fifty yuan per dan agreed upon by the Wuxi Cocoon-Merchant Guild. During the newly established fall marketing period, the agents sent by Ruifeng, a man named Chen Zhongxing and his son, arranged contracts with three cocoon firms in Wuxi's Kaiyuan and Tianxia townships in which cocoons were purchased at a price of over eighty yuan per dan. At that price, the Ruifeng agents were able to buy 70 to 80 percent of the cocoon crop in Kaiyuan and Tianxia. As a result, many other cocoon firms in Kaiyuan and Tianxia found it impossible to purchase cocoons. When many of its members protested, the Wuxi Cocoon-Merchant Guild discovered that the agents commissioned by the Ruifeng filature had caused this problem, and it called an emergency meeting to discuss ways to handle the matter. Among the suggestions was a proposal to draft a petition to government ministries at the national level to take punitive measures against the Ruifeng filature.[33]

Once again, we are unable to follow this story any further due to the absence of subsequent reports. Nevertheless, this example also demonstrates important aspects of the increasingly defensive posture of the Wuxi Cocoon-Merchant Guild. In this case, we see that infringement of price restrictions determined by local, collective interests was unacceptable behavior according to guild rules. Local merchants wished to insure their profits by a system of price regulation that allowed only a small amount of upward and downward fluctuation around a price established before marketing began.[34] When this system was challenged, the reaction in defense of local interests was both swift and fierce.

The overall picture we have of the Wuxi Cocoon-Merchant Guild by the 1920's shows an organization with growing influence at both the local and regional levels. The guild membership seems to have been motivated above all to develop and protect the interests of a local commercial community against any outside interference. As we shall see, it was not long before the guild would attempt to use its defensive capacities to protect its membership against agencies of the Jiangsu provincial government, as those agencies developed new plans to control commercial-tax revenues from the cocoon trade.

ELITE/STATE CONFLICT: TAXES AND
COCOON-FIRM CONTROL

To understand the growing potential for conflict between cocoon merchants in Wuxi and state agencies at different levels, it is necessary
first of all to review the importance of commercial taxation in an era of
escalating political crisis. We have seen earlier that during Qing times,
the state's efforts to reform a faltering land-tax system ended in failure.
To complicate the fiscal picture further, by the late nineteenth century, new fiscal pressures were also present in the form of demands for
war indemnities by foreign powers and the need to quell peasant rebellion on a massive scale. In this context, new commercial taxes called
lijin were first created, in a system that was designed to be adminis-
tered at the prefectural level, but whose revenues were earmarked primarily for national government needs. Wang Yeh-chien has estimated
that by 1908, the lijin accounted for roughly 14 percent of the central
government's revenue, and that commercial taxes overall accounted
for nearly 65 percent of state income. Accordingly, revenue from the
land tax had declined from 74 percent of state income during the eighteenth century to approximately 35 percent.[35]

From its inception, the lijin system encountered merchant resistance.
As Susan Mann has demonstrated, that resistance took different forms
in different places, with some merchant communities attempting to protest and resist payment of ever-escalating lijin fees, while others simply
left certain trading networks altogether to avoid escalating tax burdens.
By the beginning of the twentieth century, the cumulative effects of
merchant action against lijin collection had led the Qing government to
return to well-established traditions of "liturgical governance," in
Mann's terms, allowing merchant guilds to act as agents of lijin collection. When merchant organizations assumed lijin-collecting responsibilities, they saved the government the cost of maintaining separate lijin
bureaus, and they were more apt to make sure that the taxes actually
were collected, since they then were able to procure a proportion of the
slated tax revenues for their own organizations' use.[36]

Another set of problems raised by the creation of the lijin system had
to do with spatial boundaries of authority over commercial-tax revenues. In the earliest phases of the lijin system, most of the revenues were
spent by provinces for military needs. But the allocation of such funds
was tightly controlled by the central government, who saw it to be in its
own best interest for provincial administrations to fund newly expanded
armies and militia to quell real and potential domestic upheaval. By the

1910's, as governments at all levels of the political hierarchy were trying to reestablish themselves in a new Republican format, increased commercial revenues were sought by all to assist in the escalating processes of modern state-building. While many called for the abolition of the unwieldy and complex lijin system, in reality, commercial-tax levies proliferated at all levels of the political hierarchy. At the local level especially, new commercial levies of various types were needed urgently to fund new schools, local police forces, and local projects for the promotion of economic development.[37]

The fiscal situation in Wuxi by the late 1910's demonstrates just how important new commercial-tax levies on the cocoon trade had become to the support of local government projects. In Wuxi, a new local tax had come into existence called the "tax levied for public benefit on dried cocoons" (ganjian gongyi juan). The revenues generated by this tax accounted for 36 percent of the county's total income in 1915, bringing in 20,700 yuan. Only one other tax, a levy on buildings used for commercial purposes, brought in more revenue—27,000 yuan, or 48 percent of the total. The Jiangsu provincial government formally approved the dried-cocoon tax in 1914, but in practice, it had been collected since the latter years of the Guangxu reign (1875–1908). Levied by the county tax office (shuiwu gongsuo), the amount of tax assessment was twenty-two fen on each dan of dried cocoons. Within each township, members of the Wuxi Cocoon-Merchant Guild served as collection agents on behalf of the tax office. The revenue generated by the dried-cocoon tax in Wuxi was used exclusively for the development of new schools within the county.[38]

The degree to which the county government in Wuxi depended on cocoon-trade taxes and the uses to which they were put suggest the potential for a relatively high degree of cooperation between the magistrate's office and the Wuxi Cocoon-Merchant Guild. Certainly, it was in the interest of each of them to see adequate funding generated for new schools dedicated to the promotion of modern education for native sons. With respect to the province, however, a very different picture emerged. At least as early as 1918, Wuxi cocoon merchants began to resist increased provincial demands for cocoon-trade levies. In that year, foreign silk producers in Shanghai, in cooperation with the Jiangsu-Zhejiang-Anhui Silk Producers' Guild (Jiang-Zhe-Wan sichang jianye zonggongsuo), a regional organization based in Shanghai to coordinate all aspects of the modern filature industry, organized the United Association for Sericulture Reform (Hezhong cansang gailiang hui). This new organization subsequently petitioned and received permission from the national-level Ministry of Agriculture and Commerce to use the proceeds from a new surtax to support research on new methods of sericulture improvement. Provincial departments of finance were to receive the proceeds from this surtax and forward them to the association. When the Wuxi Cocoon-Merchant Guild announced the enactment of this new tax and the procedures for collection, its members immediately raised objections and decided to resist payment. Because Wuxi cocoon merchants were in the majority among cocoon merchants throughout the three-province region, the new regional association had no choice but to acquiesce when Wuxi merchants failed to pay the new charges. The provincial Jiangsu Department of Finance, at a loss as to how to implement the new tax in the face of Wuxi merchant resistance, recommended abolition of the levy altogether. While waiting for further notification from the national Ministry of Agriculture and Commerce, the Jiangsu Department of Finance simply ignored the order to implement the new levy.[39]

These actions show how Wuxi cocoon merchants had the capacity to turn the corporate strength of their guild organization squarely against provincial government. In this case, their maneuvering was done openly, with their decision a matter of public record made at an officially convened meeting of the guild. In a second example, more covert methods were used.

In 1923, Wuxi cocoon merchants took an even more aggressive stance against the province on the issue of cocoon-trade taxes. In that year, the Wuxi County lijin bureau forwarded 60,000 yuan in cocoon-trade taxes to the provincial Department of Finance. In previous years, the cocoon-trade revenues collected by the lijin bureau in Wuxi and forwarded to the province had reached as high as 401,000 yuan. Thus, it seemed that many funds earmarked for provincial-tax payment remained that year somewhere within the county. The Wuxi case was not an isolated occurrence. The neighboring lijin bureau, which combined the two counties of Wujin and Danyang under its jurisdiction, was also in default. For the three years 1918 through 1920, this second bureau paid only 150,000 yuan to the province, whereas previously it had paid 98,000 yuan for just one year. The provincial governor's office expressed concern over this rather substantial loss of revenue between the two lijin bureaus of approximately 500,000 yuan, and dispatched special agents to look into the situation.

Preliminary investigations revealed that new agencies calling themselves lijin stations had sprung up in the rich cocoon-producing region between Wuxi and Changzhou, the county seat of Wujin, which bordered Wuxi to the northwest. Apparently, these were merchant tax stations operating with the sanction of county governments to collect new cocoon-trade surtaxes designed to remain within the county. The governor's special agents concluded that these new stations were directly responsible for the failure to transfer lijin funds to the province. The agents' mission was thus to determine exactly how much tax each of the new stations was collecting, and how much of it should be forwarded to the province.[40]

To what extent the missing taxes diverted by the new merchant-controlled tax stations were used for legitimate public interests is difficult to determine. By the 1910's and 1920's, local governments commonly had returned to well-established traditions of merchant tax-farming as a way to quell merchant tax protest over escalating commercial taxes. The result was a tendency for larger amounts of taxes to end up in government coffers, since merchants welcomed the return to more traditional modes of self-governance.[41] However, in this particular example from Wuxi, we also see the potential liabilities of sanctioning merchant management of county-based lijin collection; in the mounting competition between province and county for income from commercial taxes, provincial government was clearly at a disadvantage if merchants decided that the more appropriate venue for the expenditure of commercial-tax revenue was their home turf.

In this increasingly contentious environment, new provincial departments established in Jiangsu when the Guomindang came to power there in 1927 made a general call for a total reform of cocoon-trade taxation.[42] This call was part of a larger effort on the part of Chiang K'ai-shek's new government to reform tax programs of all types. Given the history of mounting competition for tax revenues among the center, provinces, and counties, the Guomindang's new programs called for a total reevaluation of how such revenues should be split. Proceeds from the land tax and a new business tax, meant to replace the lijin system once and for all, were to have gone to the provinces. Customs- and salt-tax revenues were slated for the central government. And local commercial and miscellaneous taxes, along with a portion of the new business tax passed down from the provinces, were to supply county governments with their revenue. This basic formula went through several phases of revision and refinement over the years from 1928 through 1934, with the important addition of a proposed new income tax. In practice, however, it would prove very difficult to put sufficient bureaucratic personnel in place to implement such a precise new plan, and also to completely eliminate prior patterns of behavior and expectations of local merchants responsible for lijin collection.[43]

Under the Guomindang's new system of cocoon-firm "control," as it was called, the central concern was no longer to limit the number of co-coon firms that could be licensed, as previous provincial governments had attempted to do in the 1910's, but rather to implement strict regis-tration and licensing procedures to guarantee the upward transmission of tax revenues. In this system, the Jiangsu provincial Department of Re-construction, through its agencies at the county level, called bureaus of reconstruction (*jiansheju*), was to receive fees paid by cocoon firms for registration and licensing.[44] Thus, through the bureaus of reconstruc-tion, the province would try to make a more direct claim on a portion of cocoon-trade taxes, hoping to override well-entrenched tax-farming networks.[45]

By this time, however, the tradition of the cocoon trade as an object of local purview was well established, and merchants continued to resist provincial efforts to tax them more directly. In order to insure proper payment of the new fees, the provincial Department of Agriculture and Mines instructed the bureau of reconstruction in Wuxi to begin a fining procedure in 1929 against merchants who did not comply with the new registration measures. The Wuxi bureau was to fine cocoon firms that had not yet applied for new licenses, as well as cocoon firms that misre-ported the number of drying rooms in operation, at the rate of 5 to 10 yuan per room, with no fine to be less than 100 yuan. In addition, the bu-reau was to fine silk filatures that had set up their own drying facilities and failed to register them as cocoon firms, thus avoiding cocoon-firm taxes that should have been passed on to the province.[46]

These orders for fining Wuxi cocoon firms that did not comply with new registration and taxation procedures marked a new degree of pro-vincial persistence in pursuing cocoon-trade tax revenues. As we shall see later, when we take up continuing Guomindang policies toward the Wuxi silk industry in more detail, this was only the start of a concerted effort by an increasingly coercive and intrusive state to bring the proc-esses of economic development and commercial taxation under its con-trol.

GENTRY, MERCHANTS, AND THE STATE

To a greater degree than we might have expected from previous re-search on elite/state relations during the turbulent years of Qing col-lapse and state reconstitution under the Republic, gentrymen, mer-chants, and state agencies in Wuxi attempted to collaborate to promote sericulture and build a flourishing cocoon trade. The pattern in the Wuxi cocoon trade differs from the vision that commercial elites functioned increasingly in a new public sphere by late Qing times. In the 1870's, gentrymen and local bureaucrats worked in concert to bring sericulture to Wuxi for the first time in the Qing spirit of promoting popular welfare. By the 1880's, gentry members and new merchants involved in a rapidly evolving cocoon trade in Wuxi founded organizations to promote the best interests of the trade, but often relied upon local government assistance and sanction in promoting their activities of self-regulation and self-protection. In this context, the well-established Qing tradition of merchant tax-farming was employed in the Wuxi cocoon trade, and county-level government and the Wuxi Cocoon-Merchant Guild established a close working relationship that seems to have been to their mutual benefit. It was only in the 1910's, when pressures to fund newly developing provincial and county governments became more severe, that the goals of Wuxi cocoon merchants—to defend their local commercial interests—and those of provincial government—to collect larger sums of commercial-tax revenue—came into serious conflict.

We have also seen that the cocoon-merchant community in Wuxi was complex. As men who operated comfortably within gentry traditions of local commercial management, yet who were also interested in promoting a form of commercial activity tied to the newly mechanizing silk industry based in Shanghai, cocoon-trade merchants in Wuxi defy easy classification. Such men relied on forms and traditions of gentry management developed throughout the Yangzi delta during the Qing, yet actively promoted a form of commercialization that would pave the way for modern silk-filature investment. In the next chapter, I examine the early silk-filature industry in Wuxi, and the careers, management strategies, and investment patterns of its organizers. Not surprisingly, there was overlap between some segments of the cocoon-merchant community in Wuxi and early filature founders. This overlap would influence the internal organization of early silk filatures and their potential for success in an increasingly competitive world-market environment for raw silk. Emerging struggles over commercial taxation in Wuxi also would have their impact on how far and how fast filature development proceeded.

5

Investors at Risk in the Wuxi Filature Industry

By the beginning of the twentieth century, three decades of cocoon marketing had laid the groundwork for investment in silk filatures by Wuxi local elites. Filatures were not the only form of industry in which elites invested, but they were by far the most influential in reshaping the rural economy in Wuxi, guaranteeing that nearly every peasant household in the county would venture into sericulture in the years ahead. Local silk filatures thus became the anchor in Wuxi for the "one industry, two Chinas" continuum taking shape.[1]

We have seen that as local elites in Wuxi delved into cocoon marketing on behalf of Shanghai filatures, they relied on a commercial layering strategy that paralleled other networks for handicraft silk production and marketing in the Yangzi delta region. Building on such precedents, another layered investment pattern emerged in the early stages of filature foundings in Wuxi. Two distinct strata of filature owners and managers appeared, producing a system of filature operation described in contemporary sources as "split ownership/management." In many ways, this was an ideal strategy for early silk-filatures founders, men who could raise capital through preexisting elite networks in local society but who faced a range of unfamiliar risks in filature operation and marketing conditions. By passing risk onto a lower stratum of managers, silk-filature founders produced the initial momentum they needed to get the industry started. However, over the longer term, investment and management patterns in filatures also exacerbated problems of capital reinvestment and low-quality raw silk. We shall see in later chapters that by the mid-1920's, as some filature owners began efforts to end "split ownership/management," the severity of accumulated silk-industry problems prompted them to shift risk in new ways, seeking government controls on all aspects of future silk-industry growth.

FILATURE FOUNDERS AND ELITE NETWORKS

Beginning in 1904, Wuxi became the third major site of filature development in China, following the Canton delta and Shanghai, the two sites where filatures had begun in the 1860's.[2] Although Chinese investors were most active in building filatures in the Canton area, most early Shanghai filatures were founded either by foreigners or jointly by foreigners and Chinese compradors. Once compradors gained sufficient knowledge of filature operation, they began to rent filatures from foreigners, to buy out their foreign partners, or to strike out on their own to found new filatures. By the beginning of the twentieth century, most Shanghai filatures were Chinese-owned.[3]

From the outset in Wuxi, all filature investors were Chinese. However, one important aspect of the Shanghai experience was replicated, with many early Wuxi filature founders being men of comprador background. The knowledge and contacts acquired through comprador experience seem to have given such men an edge in starting filatures. Foreign exporting firms based in Shanghai monopolized silk export, even going so far as to boycott the one Chinese investor who tried to build his own silk-exporting firm, forcing him into bankruptcy.[4] Under such circumstances, compradors were at an advantage, since they had the knowledge and experience necessary to negotiate successfully with foreign exporting firms for the sale of raw silk. Many filature founders in Wuxi were comprador agents for the early cocoon trade. Such men also hoped that through their contacts within local cocoon-trade networks in Wuxi, they would be able to solve the problem of inadequate, costly cocoon supplies, an issue that had plagued the Shanghai filature industry from its inception.[5]

It is not surprising, then, that Zhou Shunqing and Xue Nanming, two of the Wuxi men we have met before as comprador agents for the early cocoon trade, became Wuxi's earliest filature founders. We should recall that Zhou and Xue both had prior experience working as comprador agents for foreign-owned Shanghai filatures. Zhou became a banker in Wuxi and purchased a sizable amount of agricultural land within the county. By the start of the twentieth century, although Zhou had never held high official position, he had become a respected and powerful individual within the upper stratum of Wuxi's local elite. Xue's early background was more traditional than Zhou's. He was the son of a very high-ranking Qing official, Xue Fucheng, and also held important bureaucratic posts himself. He abandoned his official career in favor of business, but he and his family retained large landholdings in Wuxi and a large private granary.

Zhou and Xue's first effort at filature investment was made in 1896 in Shanghai, where they jointly organized the Yongtai filature. However, neither man had full knowledge of the internal workings of filatures, and their efforts to produce and market raw silk met with only mediocre success. Soon thereafter, Zhou withdrew his capital from Yongtai and returned to Wuxi. In 1904, he founded the Yuchang filature in his birthplace, the market town of Dongze, located about six kilometers south of the city. For the time being, Xue Nanming kept his capital investment in Yongtai and remained in Shanghai for several years, where he immersed himself in the study of new filature equipment and techniques for using it. In 1909, he, too, returned to Wuxi and opened the Jinji silk filature in a commercial district outside the west gate of the city.[6]

These ventures marked the start of the filature industry in Wuxi, with the construction of fifty filatures there by 1930.[7] In the early stages, comprador background remained important as Zhou and Xue were the most active in new filature foundings, building three and five filatures respectively. Another comprador, Zhu Lanfang, founded two more of Wuxi's earliest filatures, the Yuankang filature in 1909 and the Ganyuan filature in 1913. Over time, however, as knowledge of filature operation spread, not all filature organizers were compradors. Men with backgrounds as landlords, cocoon merchants, handicraft silk and cotton merchants, founders of native banks, and managers of an assortment of new Shanghai industries also started filatures in Wuxi.[8] Though not all of these men had experience as compradors, filature founders seemed to have had an aptitude for taking advantage of the distinctive and rapidly evolving commercial/industrial milieu in Wuxi. The chief attribute of men who succeeded in this milieu was an ability to combine new knowledge and skills with a capacity for maneuvering within long-standing local elite networks within the county.

The founding of Ganshen filature in 1909 by Sun Heqing further demonstrates how these combined abilities influenced early filature foundings.[9] Sun was a large landowner who lived in the market town of Shitangwan. In the first decade of the twentieth century, he began keeping accounts for Wuxi's first modern bank, the Xincheng yinhang, and forged a close friendship with the bank's manager, Gu Dasan. With Gu's help, Sun acquired seven mu of vacant land on Liangxi Road, a newly forming industrial district, and used the land as collateral to obtain a

loan from Xincheng to build a filature facility on the land. He then hired
several individuals from among the local elite in Wuxi to staff various di-
rectorships and managerial posts within the factory, and started operations in 1910.

The first five years of operation of the Ganshen filature, as the new
factory was called, brought only mediocre results, largely because Sun
understood little about the filature business. When his chief director retired in 1914, Sun invited his nephew Cheng Bingruo to enter the factory
as his "representative" to assume a wide variety of managerial roles.
Cheng was very young at the time, still in his twenties, but he seemed to
be just the sort of man needed to perform the range of tasks associated
with filature management. He had graduated from a modern school for
the study of "public affairs" (gongshi) and was pursuing a career as an
English instructor in a women's college.

From the time that he entered the Ganshen filature, Cheng set about
studying every aspect of filature operations, from cocoon marketing and
warehousing, to negotiating with foreign exporting firms in Shanghai.
His skill in English seemed to serve him well, as he studied reports on
raw-silk prices on the international market himself, not needing to rely
on secondhand information provided by compradors working for foreign
exporting firms in Shanghai. When more senior members of the local
elite who had founded filatures in Wuxi, men like Sun Heqing and Xue
Nanming, met together and discussed local affairs of a wider, more traditional variety, it was men like Cheng who paid close attention to important communiques from Shanghai about international business conditions. Under Cheng's growing influence within the day-to-day operations of the filature, Ganshen began to flourish.

In 1917, critical steps were taken to give Cheng Bingruo more authority within the management ranks of the Ganshen filature. He was given
the formal title of manager (jingli), and Sun Heqing became the equivalent of a general overseer of operations (zongli). At the same time, Sun
began to seek out other friends and relatives to become shareholders in
the filature, while he himself retained the position of chief shareholder.
Sun sold shares to six individuals, including Cheng Bingruo, for 900 taels
each, and began to pay out dividends to himself and other shareholders of
20,000 taels yearly.

As World War I came to a close and the international market for raw
silk flourished anew, Cheng Bingruo, while remaining manager of Ganshen, began a new filature venture of his own in which he and another
group of four additional investors from among the Wuxi local elite
rented an already existing filature facility, renamed it the Ganfeng fila-

ture, and began to run it in a fashion modeled after the Ganshen experience. In this second filature, Cheng Bingruo acted as general overseer, and his cousin, Wang Yisun, became manager. Meanwhile, under Cheng Bingruo's management, investors in Ganshen began to explore additional opportunities, renting out other filature facilities, often jointly with other investors for short periods, to enhance Ganshen's output potential, profits, and reputation. Cheng Bingruo began to purchase raw-silk trademarks with established reputations on the world market, and also to develop new ones for use in all of his filatures.

In 1925, Cheng Bingruo and his evolving cohort of fellow filature investors built a new filature facility by selling shares in the amount of 70,000 taels. In 1926, they rented this third filature to investors in the Ganfeng filature, where Cheng Bingruo was still manager, and Shan Youxian, son of one of the principal investors, became its manager. Finally, in 1927, the original founder of the Ganshen filature, Sun Heqing, retired from his position as general overseer. Although he retained some shares in the filature, he sold the bulk of his shares to Cheng Bingruo, who was still manager and now was principal owner as well.

The founding of the Ganshen filature and the expanding, interconnected networks of local elite investors it spawned provide an excellent starting point for exploring investment and management patterns that emerged in the Wuxi filature industry. For our ensuing discussion of these patterns, it will be useful to divide the phases of filature development in Wuxi according to three chronological periods: from 1904 to 1919, from 1920 to 1930, and from 1931 to 1937. In each of these phases, new developments in investment and management appeared. The first two phases are closely connected, however, and we can use the above story of Ganshen as a take-off point for examining investment and management trends during those two phases.

The most obvious points to make about the founding of the Ganshen filature concern the ways in which elite networks were used to form groups of investors as filatures were founded. In the earliest stage of filature foundings, from 1904 to 1919, investors built a total of eleven filatures in Wuxi.[10] The number of men involved in these foundings was relatively small, and as in the Ganshen example, many were close acquaintances or relatives. Also, like Ganshen, most early filatures were founded by a single individual who had the capacity to raise capital on his own to build the filature plant and to purchase and install reeling machines.[11]

As their businesses grew, filatures owners expanded by adding more reeling machines. During these expansionary phases, the original filature founders solicited additional investors, a step that was called *hezi*, or "pooling capital." Profit-sharing contracts were drawn up stipulating that the bulk of yearly profits be dispersed in the forms of bonuses for management personnel and shareholders' dividends. It was rare, especially in the earliest phases of filature development, for specific plans to be made for reinvesting a portion of yearly profits. As in the Ganshen case, new groups of filature investors were composed of friends and relatives from within the Wuxi local elite.[12]

In the second phase of filature development in Wuxi, from 1920 to 1930, rapid expansion occurred, with thirty-nine new filatures built during this eleven-year period.[13] Because growth was so rapid, this phase of filature development in Wuxi has often been referred to as the "golden age."[14] During this period, the "golden-age" phenomenon was not unique to the Wuxi filature industry, but occurred in other Chinese industries as well. Rapid industrial expansion was fueled by two factors—relatively cheap prices for Chinese products on the world market resulting from China's decision to remain on the silver standard while most of the rest of the world switched to gold; and a general resurgence of world-market demand for luxury products such as silk in the aftermath of World War I.[15] As opportunities to sell more raw silk in the world market emerged, investing in filatures became an attractive option for more members of the Wuxi local elite.

In this phase of filature growth, more networks of local elite investors proliferated. By this time, there were more young men on the local scene who had spent time abroad studying business and economics, and new ideas about the importance of modern industry were beginning to have a more firm grounding among local elites in Wuxi. Many had been to Japan or the United States, where they had opportunities to observe modern factory organization and operation firsthand.[16] Despite their new knowledge, tendencies already present in filature investment circles solidified, resulting in a permanent cleavage between initial investors and those responsible for the tasks of filature management.

As the divide between filature founders and managers developed into a routine and seemingly permanent feature of filature organization, a set term was used to refer to it—*shi/ying ye*, or "split ownership/management." One of Wuxi's earliest filature founders, Xue Nanming, was said to have designed the system as a way to accommodate his lack of expertise in filature operation. After Xue's cofounder of the Yongtai filature in Shanghai, Zhou Shunqing, withdrew from co-ownership, we have seen that Xue kept the filature operating. As he did so, he pioneered "split ownership/management" by renting the equipment to one Xu Jinrong, with an agreement that Xu could become a permanent investor in the filature provided that fixed capital and operating capital be kept separate. Over the next several years, he rented the facility to a series of managers at a rate of three to four taels per reeling machine. When the Yongtai filature moved to Wuxi, Xue retained the "split ownership/management" system.[17]

When new filatures were founded, other owners modeled their investment and management strategies on Xue's experience, also using "split ownership/management." According to this system, each filature was split into two separate entities, one called *shiyechang*, or the "industrial plant," and the other *yingyechang*, or the "managerial plant." In effect, what this meant was that one group of shiye investors pooled capital to build, expand, and maintain the physical aspects of the filature, including the buildings and reeling machines, and that a second group of yingye investors pooled a separate capital fund that paid for operating the filature, covering such things as cocoon purchase and workers' salaries. Yingye investors rented filatures from shiye investors, at monthly rental rates of two to four taels per reeling machine. In the process, they became very adept at gearing the scale of their operations to world-market demand for raw silk and cocoon availability.[18]

While in some instances shiye investors became investors in yingye operations, for the most part, owners of filature plants and equipment and those responsible for filature operations, or "managers" (*jingli*) as they came to be called, evolved into distinct groups.[19] Most early filature founders, as we have seen in the case of Sun Heqing above, became increasingly removed from day-to-day filature operations. Many of these men were high-ranking members of the local elite in Wuxi who had ongoing commercial investments and new industrial interests as part of their total portfolio, but who remained involved in a wide range of more traditional economic activities as well, including landowning and money-lending. The expanding coterie of filature managers, on the other hand, was less traditional in outlook and orientation, and many became more interested in investment and direct involvement in filature operations as a full-time career. However, cases like that of Cheng Bingruo, who rose from the position of manager to become principal owner of the Ganshen filature, were rare. Most filature managers circulated from plant to plant, seldom staying involved with a single filature throughout their careers.[20]

When observers of "split ownership/management" began to write about it in commercial journals during the 1920's, the system often came under harsh criticism. One of the key problems facing the Chinese filature industry was that the quality of raw silk produced in Chinese filatures did not come up to the same standards as Japanese silk, and thus did not command the same price levels or the same level of demand on the international market. It was relatively easy to accuse "split owner-ship/management" of being at the heart of these difficulties. Since fila-ture owners rented their equipment to others, they were blamed for hav-ing a "feudal" mentality, with relatively little interest in maintaining filature equipment and keeping it operating to its full potential. On the other hand, filature managers were criticized for being "speculators" who operated filatures only when the highest profits could be expected on the world market. The result of these attitudes and practices was that low rates of reinvestment in technical improvements doomed Chinese filature silk to remain of poor quality and in lower demand than Japanese silk.[21]

Contemporary criticism of "split ownership/management," then, ad-dressed low silk quality and intense competition with Japan, two key is-sues facing the filature industry in the 1920's. But given filature inves-tors' dependence upon an increasingly intricate web of commercial and production relationships—extending horizontally within local elite so-ciety but also upward into the international marketplace and downward to the Wuxi peasantry—we might do well to view this system differ-ently. "Split ownership/management" may indeed have contributed to low silk quality, but a litany of perceived and real risks emerging from within the silk-industry continuum was the ultimate source of filature investors' problems.

SILK-INDUSTRY RISKS: PERCEPTIONS AND REALITIES

When silk filatures were first built in Wuxi, the earliest founders, men like Zhou Shunqing and Xue Nanming, believed that there were clear advantages to moving their investments out of Shanghai to Wuxi.[22] Cocoon procurement was the first problem that they hoped to over-come. We have seen in Chapter 3 that early Shanghai filatures found it very difficult to secure an adequate supply of cocoons. Their response to this problem had been to encourage the development of new sericul-ture districts such as Wuxi, and to develop the cocoon-firm system, through which comprador agents for foreign filatures had come to Wuxi to contract with local merchants for the purchase of cocoons from local peasants. Although these developments had eased the diffi-

culties of Shanghai filatures in purchasing cocoons, enabling many filatures to remain in business over prolonged periods, the problem of cocoon supply never was eliminated completely. During the late 1920's,
many Shanghai filatures stood idle for months at a time due to inadequate cocoon supply.[23]

Early filature founders in Wuxi saw potential advantages in building
filatures closer to the site of raw-material procurement. They hoped that
filature agents responsible for cocoon purchase would have fewer costs
associated with their operations, saving on the transport of cocoons to
Shanghai and on warehousing there, as well as on the dreaded transit
taxes, most of which were levied on cocoons as they made their way
through transit-tax stations en route to Shanghai. Also, by locating filatures in Wuxi, early founders hoped for better access to cocoon-
marketing information, enabling them to contract for cocoon purchase
at locations within the county where cocoons were most plentiful and of
the highest quality.[24]

Another hoped-for advantage in moving early filatures to Wuxi was
potential savings on the cost of female workers. Filature founders were
seeking a young, female work force to fill most of the jobs in their new
plants, and they believed that hiring peasant women in Wuxi might be
even cheaper than employing young, unskilled women in Shanghai filatures. Although in Shanghai young filature workers were paid the lowest
wages of any factory workers in the city, the filatures often fed and
housed young women in dormitory-style living quarters. But in Wuxi,
since most female filature workers were daughters, daughters-in-law,
and young wives within peasant families who could live at home while
working seasonally in their filature jobs, the filatures would not have
had to absorb the costs of their food and lodging.[25]

Given such high hopes for more advantageous investment conditions
in Wuxi among early filature founders, it is somewhat ironic that when a
comprehensive article on the state of the Wuxi filature industry appeared in 1930 in the *Wuxi Yearbook*, a new publication of the county
government, filature investors in Wuxi still bemoaned the seemingly intractable problems of cocoon supply and workers' wages. The author of
the piece claimed that he could not know for certain whether these problems were genuine since the views he was reporting were taken from investigations among the community of filature investors in Wuxi. But for
our purposes, the article very usefully reveals what those involved in the
silk industry at the height of its "golden age" believed to be the most serious difficulties they faced.[26]

The portion of the *Wuxi Yearbook* article discussing silk-industry problems was divided into three categories: "raw materials," "products," and "marketing." The problem with raw materials was crystal clear, according to filature investors—peasants in Wuxi "rested according to custom" when it came to sericulture technique, refusing to change their conventional methods of mulberry cultivation and silkworm raising. Cocoon quality was low and quantity unpredictable as a result, affecting the production efforts of every filature.

As for "products," there were two difficulties. One was that taxes on raw silk had become onerous, now amounting to over 100 yuan per dan. The second was that filature workers were becoming contaminated by "Europeanization," demanding shorter working hours and higher wages despite the fact that their education and skill levels were very low. The combination of high taxes and troublesome, unskilled workers stymied innovation within filatures. The implication was that rising costs for filatures, in the form of higher tax rates and demands for increased wages by irresponsible workers, reduced the capacity to invest in innovative methods.

In "marketing," the problem was that foreign firms monopolized exporting procedures for raw silk, including quality inspection and the subsequent pricing of raw silk based on its grade. Fluctuations in silk-market prices were perceived by silk filaturists in Wuxi not as the result of ebbs and flows in supply and demand, or even as a result of competition with Japanese silk or new rayon products, but rather as Chinese producers' inability to attain a position of independence within the international network of raw-silk marketing. In Shanghai, filaturists urged the Chinese government to establish quality inspection stations of its own, and to make private investment in shipping and exporting more attractive by retrieving tariff autonomy, in an effort to resolve these "marketing" dilemmas.[27]

These, then, are the ways in which Wuxi filature investors viewed the problems facing further silk-industry expansion around 1930, just before the onset of the Great Depression. But what had become of the perceptions of an earlier generation of filature investors, who believed that filatures in Wuxi should have experienced clear advantages over their Shanghai counterparts in at least two of these areas? Digging a bit more deeply into the realities of risk associated with raw-silk production shows that Wuxi filature investors were not imagining their difficulties. As they faced serious risks in raw-silk production and export, even the advantages of their Wuxi location could not completely solve the dilemmas of filature operation. Filature founders in Wuxi thus would con-

tinue to employ the system of "split ownership/management" throughout the 1920's, to pass onward the real and substantial risks of raw-silk
production.

    Risk number one: cocoon supply. Despite the fact that Wuxi was
the cocoon-marketing capital of the delta region, the supply of cocoons
to Wuxi filatures never seemed to meet filature demand, with cocoon
purchase remaining the most vexatious of all problems facing filature
growth. A look at cocoon prices relative to the prices filatures obtained
for their raw silk in Shanghai prior to export, as shown in Table 5, provides insight into the cocoon-supply dilemma. Figures 1 and 2 present
these same data in graph form. In Figure 1, the two price series are
graphed literally. Figure 2 retains the same data points as in Figure 1,
but finds curves of best fit for the data (using polynomial equations) to
provide a picture of the central tendency of movement for each series
over the entire time period.

    Most apparent from these data is that while both sets of prices rose
over time, the prices of cocoons rose at a faster pace than those of raw
silk and tended to remain at a higher level (relative to the index year of
1896) over the entire period. Raw-silk prices also rose at first, but after
1907 they fell off at a sustained pace due to escalating competition with
Japanese silk. In the first decade of the twentieth century, Japanese silk
was entering the world market in large quantities, and it overtook Chinese silk very rapidly in terms of total quantity exported.[28] This shift
caused demand for Chinese silk to decline and prices to fall, especially
because Chinese silk was of lower quality than its Japanese counterpart.
This situation did not change substantially until World War I and after,
when the world silk market expanded anew with the growth of con-
sumer demand in the West for silk products.

    Cocoon prices also were more volatile than those of raw silk, with
much larger fluctuations both upward and downward from one year to
the next (see Fig. 1). The volatility of cocoon prices can be explained by at
least two factors. First was the tendency for inclement spring weather in
the Yangzi delta to adversely affect the quantity of cocoons. Since cocoon marketing lasted for only three weeks or so in the spring, and for
another similar period in fall, fluctuations in cocoon supply, or even expected fluctuations, could cause the price of cocoons to rise. Second, local political turmoil could also adversely affect cocoon marketing, as the
entire process depended upon large quantities of silver for cocoon purchase making their way to Wuxi from Shanghai via boat transport. Local
warfare, or the threat of it, could severely curtail these shipments, thus

TABLE 5

Cocoon and Filature Silk Prices and Their Indices, 1896–1929

(1896 = 100)

Year	Cocoon price (in yuan)	Cocoon price index	Silk price (in taels)	Silk price index
1896	30.00	100	580	100
1897	35.00	117	650	112
1898	38.50	128	650	112
1899	36.50	122	750	129
1900	45.00	150	695	120
1901	37.50	125	600	103
1902	65.00	217	820	141
1903	51.50	172	885	153
1904	39.00	130	750	129
1905	43.50	145	750	129
1906	45.00	150	770	133
1907	50.00	167	897	155
1908	53.00	177	823	142
1909	50.50	168	840	145
1910	57.00	190	795	137
1911	46.50	155	757	131
1912	31.00	103	673	116
1916	56.50	188	641	110
1928	47.40	158	808	139
1929	52.40	175	777	133

SOURCES: Data for 1896 through 1912 are reported in Suzuki Chifu 1981: 158.

The cocoon price as reported for 1916 is an average computed from cocoon prices for Wuxi reported in the newspaper *Minguo ribao* (Shanghai) from the spring of that year. The silk price is computed from data in L. M. Li 1981: 74–76.

Cocoon prices for 1928 and 1929 are computed averages from data appearing in *Guoli zhongyang yanjiuyuan shehui kexue yanjiusuo* 1929: tables on sericulture. Silk prices for those years are computed from data in L. M. Li 1981: 74–76.

NOTE: The prices of cocoons are average prices per dan of fresh cocoons observed at cocoon-marketing sites in Wuxi for the year. Silk prices are the average prices per dan of filature silk observed in Shanghai.

lowering the quantity of cash available for cocoon purchase. This is probably what caused the drop in cocoon prices in Wuxi in 1911 and 1912, when the collapse of the dynasty led to a period of instability.[29]

In more general terms, as we would expect, the price movements of cocoons and raw silk were closely related (see Fig. 2). Although cocoon prices remained at a more elevated level that those offered for raw silk at Shanghai after 1896, the price indices tended to move in tandem. It was undoubtedly the higher degree of volatility of cocoon prices that troubled silk-filature investors the most, since they found that the continued low quality of cocoons, regardless of the higher prices that fluctuations in supply forced them to pay, became more and more worrisome. As we have seen above, filature investors found low cocoon quality to be a par-

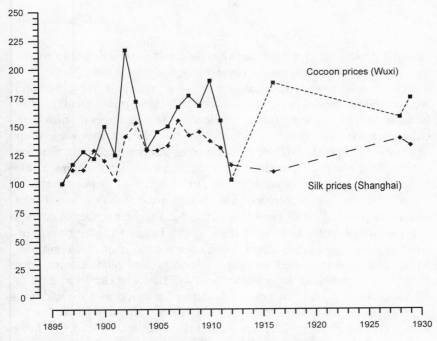

Fig. 1. Cocoon and filature silk-price indices, 1896–1929

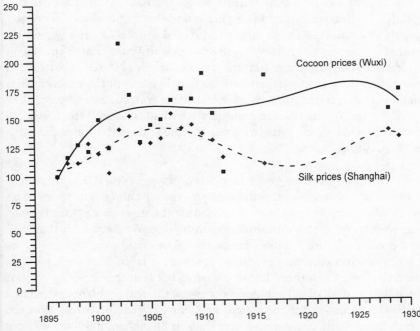

Fig. 2. Cocoon and filature silk-price indices, 1896–1929, smoothed curves

ticularly troubling problem, one they felt was intractable due to the backwardness of peasant production techniques.

Exactly who was responsible for the low quality of cocoons, and what could be done about it, are issues I take up in much greater detail later, as I explore peasant-family production and attempts by new sericulture experiment stations to intervene to help peasants raise their production standards. For the moment, it is important to note that the cocoon-firm system, through which the filature industry had been able to gain its capacity to develop in the first place, was at least partially responsible for the dilemmas of low cocoon quality. As the number of filatures expanded rapidly in Wuxi in the 1920's, the number of cocoon firms grew dramatically as well, from 223 in 1920 to 373 by 1933.[30] Instead of developing closer supervision over cocoon inspection and purchase, silk filatures relied as before on contractual relationships with cocoon-firm operators, men from the lower ranks of the local elite in Wuxi.[31] The processes of cocoon selection, sorting, and drying thus were entirely beyond the control of filatures. The rapid speed with which cocoon firms proliferated during the 1920's also seems to have caused a decline in their standards of operation, contributing to cocoon-quality problems.

In the end, like Shanghai filatures before them, Wuxi silk filatures had a difficult time remaining open year-round due to problems in cocoon supply. By the late 1920's, the commercial journals of the period reported numerous temporary filature closings in Wuxi related to cocoon shortages.[32] But because filature owners received fixed, prearranged rental fees from managers, and invested little if any of their own capital in filature operations, they stood to lose little from such short-term closings. Rather, it was filature managers who had to absorb the losses, as they struggled to keep their rented filatures adequately stocked with high-quality cocoons.

Risk number two: workers' skills and wage issues. Another problem facing filature investors in Wuxi was the cost and competency of its work force, a group that was composed for the most part of young peasant women from the surrounding countryside. We have seen that Wuxi's earliest filature founders hoped that they could save on labor costs by drawing on this pool of cheap, preexisting labor. But we have also seen that by 1930, other filature investors felt that this strategy had not brought the desired advantages. What were the real problems associated with the hiring and management of labor in Wuxi filatures? Was the work force really cheaper in Wuxi than in Shanghai, and did these potential savings bring any substantial advantages to Wuxi filature investors?

Data on the Wuxi filature work force indicate that the majority of workers fit the profile we would expect—young women from Wuxi who worked in filatures periodically, according to demand for them in any given season. A 1930 report on the filature work force showed that in 1928–29, of approximately 19,000 female workers in filatures, 79 percent were from Wuxi. In addition, the female work force in filatures was mostly young, with the largest number of workers in the age range from fourteen to thirty years.[33] Female workers were hired on a short-term basis, with the wages for the first part of their employment (two to ten weeks) held as a kind of "work deposit" to guard against losses by filature managers if the filature had to close. Thus, flexibility in work-force size and cost was maintained by filature managers to accommodate their own short-term arrangements for the renting of filature facilities.[34]

Despite their retention of a portion of workers' wages to guard against potential losses, Wuxi filature managers struggled constantly to keep workers' wages low. Data in Tables 6 and 7, comparing wage rates for female filature workers in Shanghai and Wuxi, present the best figures available on the comparative wage picture. In Table 6, we see that in 1916, daily wages for female filature workers in Wuxi were substantially lower than those paid in Shanghai. However, in 1926, the wage levels were much closer. This was the result of a major strike among filature workers in Wuxi in 1926, through which they managed to receive substantial wage concessions from filature managers.[35] By 1929, however, wages for at least some types of female filature worker had slipped back to levels below those of their Shanghai counterparts (see Table 7).

What may be even more important than relative wage levels when considering whether or not filature investors gained labor advantages in Wuxi is the question of skill levels of women workers. In Shanghai by the 1920's, there was a long tradition of filature operation, dating back to the 1860's. In addition, an urban-based work force had been forming there for three generations, and many women workers were passing on their jobs and skills to female family members.[36] However, in Wuxi, filature work was a newer option, and many women worked only seasonally, depending on the number of filatures operating and the demand for their services. Under these conditions, with a much larger pool of temporary female labor from the surrounding countryside in Wuxi, filature managers seemed to opt for the potential savings in wages that a work force of this type could bring them rather than tackle more directly the problem of low or nonexistent skill levels among young peasant women.

TABLE 6

Range in Daily Wages for Female Filature Workers
in Wuxi and Shanghai, 1916 and 1926

(in yuan)

Year	Wuxi	Shanghai
1916	0.12–0.25	0.25–0.55
1926	0.24–0.40	0.22–0.42

SOURCE: Gao and Yan 1987: 509.

TABLE 7

Comparative Daily Wages for Female Filature Workers
in Wuxi and Shanghai, 1929

(in yuan)

Type of work	Wuxi		Shanghai	
	Highest wage	Lowest wage	Highest wage	Lowest wage
Reeler	0.57	0.55	0.62	0.60
Threader	0.38	0.18	0.36	0.33
Joiner	0.55	0.45	0.68	0.63
Thrower	0.63	0.62	0.67	0.33
Cocoon sorter	0.55	0.30	0.60	0.36
Cocoon peeler	0.36	0.30	0.40	0.36

SOURCE: Gao and Yan 1987: 510.

Seen in this light, the filature investors' concerns about their work force become clearer. It is well within reason to assume that the skill levels of young peasant women who worked in filatures in Wuxi was very low, as the filaturists argued. But this problem was primarily a function of the desires of filature managers to save on wages by hiring an ever-rotating work force composed of young peasant women. Ironically, and very annoyingly from the filature managers' point of view, when labor organizers who had important information about wage levels in Shanghai encouraged women to strike for higher wages, as happened in 1926, the potentially advantageous trade-off—lower wages for less-skilled workers—evaporated. Based on their traditions of filature management, the continuing response of filature managers was to turn to the rotating labor pool of unskilled peasant women to keep wage levels from continuing to rise. But once again, because of the system of "split ownership/management," these problems with work-force reliability and cost were of little direct consequence to the senior stratum of filature owners. As with cocoon-supply problems, owners passed these dilemmas on to filature managers, who were left to deal with them accordingly.

Risk number three: commercial taxes and exporting. The final area of risk faced by filature investors in Wuxi was that of commercial taxes and the related problems resulting from exporting raw silk via foreign firms in Shanghai. As cocoons and raw silk (handicraft as well as filature varieties) made their way from delta locales toward Shanghai for export, they were subjected to an ever-changing and expanding array of local product and transit taxes.[37] Japanese observers of the delta silk industry estimated that cocoon-trade taxes, including local and provincial product and transit taxes of various types, amounted to about one-third of the price that filatures paid for cocoons, in the range of 12.80 yuan to 13.60 yuan per dan of dried cocoons, depending on the location in which they were purchased. After adding export taxes levied on raw silk in Shanghai, the total tax amount on one dan of raw silk leaving Shanghai was approximately 67 taels.[38] In the late 1920's, this amount was approximately 8 percent of the value of raw silk exported from Shanghai (see Table 5). By late-twentieth-century standards, this may appear to be a reasonable, moderate tax rate. For the times, however, and in comparison with prevailing tax rates for the Japanese filature industry, this level of taxation seemed shockingly high, leading Japanese observers to agree with Wuxi filature investors that taxes were undermining the ability of the Chinese filature industry to prosper.

The relationship between commercial taxes and the ability of the Wuxi silk industry to grow is thus a complex one. Though we cannot claim that in an absolute sense, "high" taxes were threatening the health and well-being of the industry, worries about continually rising and arbitrary taxes certainly had an effect. Perhaps the best way to explain the problem is to say that it was the combination of proliferating taxes and uncertain profit margins for raw silk that affected the attitudes of filature investors.[39] Foreign export firms and a secondary stratum of Chinese merchants resident in Shanghai, acting as intermediaries between exporters and filatures, controlled the external processes of raw-silk marketing.[40] By the 1920's, foreign buyers had set up their own silk-quality inspection stations in Shanghai, and only after evaluating raw-silk quality were price offers made. Chinese filaturists would have preferred a system over which they had more control, or, at the very least, to have dealt with independent Chinese shippers of raw silk. But the inability of Chinese governments to establish tariff autonomy had inhibited the development of the Chinese shipping industry.[41]

We have seen in Chapter 4 that trends in cocoon-trade taxation by the late 1910's prompted the Wuxi Cocoon-Merchant Guild to launch a va-

riety of efforts to resist or protest new taxes. In 1929, a new organization
called the Wuxi Silk-Filature Association (Wuxi sichangye xiehui) joined
the groundswell of tax protest. Lamenting the fact that cocoon quality
was low and supply insufficient, silk-filature investors in Wuxi petitioned the Jiangsu Department of Finance for elimination of all tax levies
that year on the fall cocoon crop. Because fall cocoon crops were relatively new, and their quantity smaller than spring crops, it was a logical
tactic for the filaturists to adopt. Hoping that the government would offer them tax relief to offset rising cocoon prices and labor costs, Wuxi
filaturists decided to focus attention on the fall cocoon crop before tax
policies were fixed.[42] At this point, an older, more well-established organization, the Jiangsu-Zhejiang-Anhui Silk Producers' Guild, based in
Shanghai and representing the interests of the filature industry throughout the region, stepped in to support the Wuxi filaturists' petition. Cit-
ing problems with cocoon quality and quantity and the rising costs of
raw-silk production that resulted, this larger association put its substantial influence behind the Wuxi filaturists' request.[43]

By November, the Jiangsu Department of Finance had finally acquiesced, at least partially, to the Wuxi Silk-Filature Association's request,
deciding not to impose taxes on fall cocoons that year. But overall tax
rates on raw silk remained unchanged, and as production costs for raw
silk had persistently exceeded the prices offered by agents for foreign export firms in Shanghai throughout the summer and fall months of that
year, the tax relief for fall cocoons came too late for many filature managers. Filatures began shutting down operations in large numbers until
their managers could be assured that total costs, including taxes, would
not exceed what they could earn by selling their raw silk for export.[44]
Thus, the final risk factor associated with filature operation—the threat
of escalating commercial taxes coupled with uncertain prices for raw
silk—sometimes became the death knell for individual filature operation, even at the high point of growth and expansion for the industry
overall.

RISK AND POWER IN THE WUXI
FILATURE INDUSTRY

Having reviewed the risks faced by Wuxi filature investors, we can
now return to the system of "split ownership/management" employed
in the filature industry to assess its meaning in the evolving context of
Chinese industrial development. Another observer of the Chinese silk
industry, writing in the Shanghai-based Banker's Weekly in 1929, gave

yet another rendering of the difficulties faced by the industry.[45] He argued that the most pressing problem of the filature industry was that multiple layers of production and marketing limited the flow of information among all parties involved, precluding the possibility of any substantial quality gains in either cocoons or raw silk. Potential lenders judged silk filatures to be a high-risk investment, especially modern bankers based in Shanghai. To purchase their yearly supplies of cocoons, filatures had to borrow large sums of silver from traditional native banks, whose interest rates were unregulated and thus were very high for the purchase of risky items such as cocoons. Native banks in Wuxi and Shanghai had gotten into the business of warehousing cocoon stocks purchased by filatures, and used these stocks as collateral for future loans. If raw silk could not be sold for high enough prices, filaturists simply refused to sell and were thus unable to pay off their loans in a timely fashion. Their cocoon stocks were then held hostage within the bank-controlled warehousing system. As a last point, this author also raised the old and lingering issue of the lack of an independent position for Chinese filaturists in the marketing of raw silk abroad. As we have seen, this issue could become the final straw on the backs of silk-filature managers in Wuxi, since a combination of uncertainty about tax rates and prices for raw silk could force them to shut down operations entirely.

Though the writer of this piece did not speak of the "split ownership/management" system directly, his observations about the problems imposed by the failure to develop a more unified system of production and marketing dovetail with our previous picture of Wuxi filature operation. Although one of the original goals of Wuxi filature owners was to move filatures closer to the site of the production of raw materials, they seem to have taken no steps toward integration of the industry, which would have enabled them to benefit from their move. Cocoon production, cocoon marketing, and raw-silk production remained separately managed activities, and even within filature operation, owners and managers remained separate, with neither group making long-term commitments to improve production technique and product quality. We have established that these were the preferred forms of operation of the Wuxi filature industry, but the question of why this was so deserves final scrutiny.

Some have argued that the filature industry throughout China suffered from a "rentier" mentality, with this metaphor conjuring up visions of filature founders who rented out their equipment as a natural tendency stemming from their alternative roles as landlords.[46] But as I have tried to demonstrate, the investment and management environment for filatures was much more complex than that. Well-established traditions of commercial layering existed among local elites in Wuxi before the earliest filatures were founded, and silk-filature founders adapted those traditions in their quest to deal with the panoply of risks associated with raw-silk production. Owners and managers of filatures were all "at risk," but through the system of "split ownership/management," the lion's share of that risk could be passed downward by senior owners to more vulnerable managers, who had to cope most directly with constantly changing conditions for cocoon supply, workers' low skill levels, potential labor unrest, and problems of taxation and export.

Another argument about why early silk filatures in China experienced difficulties has been that most Chinese industries, silk filatures among them, suffered from a critical shortage of capital. "Undercapitalization" thus limited production, and was the real reason, it has been argued, that reinvestment to improve product quality was so slow to occur.[47] But one Chinese scholar recently has shown that for Wuxi in particular, this viewpoint simply cannot stand up to the light of evidence. Large amounts of capital were invested in new industries in Wuxi, most of it generated from within elite networks of various types centered in the county.[48] This observation parallels what we have seen for the case of silk filatures in Wuxi, as substantial sums of capital were generated through elite networks to fund early filature construction and expansion.

What was really needed for long-term filature success was not only the ability to generate capital to build new filatures, but also a new outlook concerning internal industry organization and capital reinvestment to improve raw-silk quality, the only means through which Wuxi filatures could have recovered the market shares they were consistently losing to Japan. Despite the odds against their success, silk filatures proliferated in Wuxi until the eve of the Great Depression. We can only conclude that the system of "split ownership/management," while contributing to problems in raw-silk quality, was also carefully and purposively crafted, a method through which filature owners dealt with risk by passing it onto a rotating pool of ambitious but less-powerful silk-filature managers. Building on these risk-sharing precedents, a few of the most successful filature owners in Wuxi would soon find new ways to "reform" the industry, passing a greater share of the cost and risk downward further still, all the way to the Wuxi peasantry.

Chen Hansheng, director of the
SSRI rural survey in Wuxi, and the
author. At Chen's home in Beijing,
July 1981. Photograph from the
author's collection

Western-style building in Zhouxinzhen, site of early cocoon-firm activity and Wuxi's first
silk filature. Photograph by author

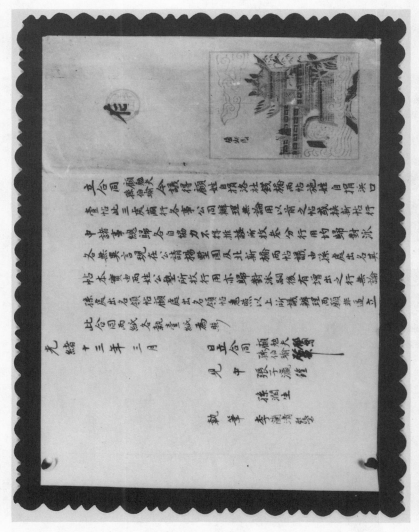

Cocoon-firm contract, between comprador Gu Mianfu and Wuxi landlord Sun Boyu, establishing the Renchang cocoon firm in 1887. Photograph from author's collection

Exterior of the Lüyuan People's Commune cocoon-purchasing facility in Xijiabian zhen; formerly the Huachang cocoon firm, built during the 1930's. Photograph by author

Interior view at the Lüyuan People's Commune cocoon-purchasing facility; entry to a cocoon-drying room, or "oven." Photograph by author

Rural homes and foot traffic in the vicinity of Zhaimen, site of Wuxi's first new experiments in sericulture during the 1870's. Photograph by author

Entryway to Yan Ziqing's former residence, the "Cottage for the Study of Mulberry Cultivation" (Kesanglu), in Zhaimen. One of the original stone tablets (engraved with the character *ke*) that once occupied now-empty space above the door rests on the ground to the left of the entryway. Photograph by author

Mulberry fields and rural housing in the vicinity of Rongxiang zhen, site of the Mantetsu rural survey. Photograph by author

A peasant home in the vicinity of Yangmuqiao, one of three villages of the Mantetsu survey. Photograph by author

A young peasant woman picking mulberry leaves. Photograph by author

A peasant woman feeding silkworms; in the background are traditional racks for stacking silkworm-feeding trays. Photograph by author

Silkworms on a feeding tray. Photograph by author

Cocoons on straw bundles (as prepared in the traditional fashion for silkworms to form their cocoons). Photograph by author

Buildings of the former Sanwuguan Silkworm-egg Breedery. Photograph by author

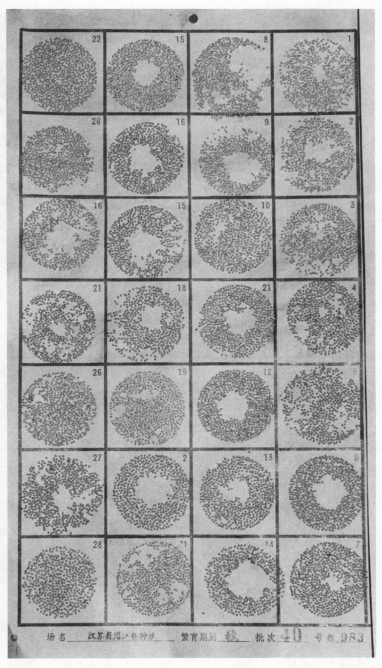

A silkworm-egg card, sold to Wuxi peasants by public and private silkworm-egg breederies. Photograph by author

民國八年男職員攝影

民國八年女職員攝影

Staff members of the Jiangsu Provincial Sericulture Experiment Bureau in Wuxi, 1919.
From Wuxi Ximenwai Jiangsu shengli yucan shiyansuo 1919–21

影 攝 理 調 所 分 一 第

影 攝 沙 除 所 分 一 第

Weighing mulberry leaves and feeding silkworms, at the Jiangsu Provincial Sericulture Experiment Bureau in Wuxi, 1919. From Wuxi Ximenwai Jiangsu shengli yucan shiyansuo 1919–1921

薛壽萱先生

A portrait of Xue Shouxuan, Wuxi's "silk-industry mag-nate" during the 1930's. From Wuxi Yongtai sichang disi-wu ceng lianxiban lianhe biye jinian tekan chuban weiyuan-hui 1936

"Revive the silk industry, develop the people's livelihood"—a modern sentiment in traditional guise, associated with efforts at silk-industry recovery orches-trated by Xue Shouxuan during the 1930's. From Wuxi Yongtai sichang disi-wu ceng lianxiban lianhe biye jinian tekan chuban weiyuanhui 1936

華新製絲養成所之前景

華新製絲養成所之後景

Exterior views of the Huaxin filature buildings. From Wuxi Yongtai sichang disi-wu ceng lianxiban lianhe biye jinian tekan chuban weiyuanhui 1936

永盛繅絲工場多緒繅車之又一景

永泰覆搖工場編絲部．

Interior views at the Yonsheng and Yongtai filatures—silk reeling and preparing silk thread for throwing. From Wuxi Yongtai sichang disi-wu ceng lianxiban lianhe biye jinian tekan chuban weiyuanhui 1936

華新覆搖工場之內形

丞泰生絲整理工場生絲纖度檢驗部

Interior views at the Huaxin and Yongtai filatures—silk throwing (top view) and grading raw silk (bottom view). From Wuxi Yongtai sichang disi-wu ceng lianxiban lianhe biye jinian tekan chuban weiyuanhui 1936

Urban canal in Wuxi City, in the vicinity of the Wuxi Number One Silk Factory (formerly the Dingchang filature).
Photograph by author

Exterior view, courtyard at the Wuxi Number One Silk Factory (formerly the Dingchang filature). Photograph by author

Sorting cocoons at the Wuxi Number One Silk Factory. Photograph by author

Cocoon-soaking trays at the base of reeling machines in the Wuxi Number One Silk Factory. Photograph by author

Mechanized silk-reeling in the Wuxi Number One Silk Factory. Photograph by author

6

Women in Sericulture, or How Gendered Labor (Re-)Shaped Peasant-Family Production

During the 1920's, a growing coterie of cocoon merchants and silk-filature investors stood at one end of the emerging silk-industry continuum in Wuxi, peasant families who worked at mulberry cultivation and silkworm raising at the other. Previous studies of the Chinese rural economy have argued that commercial activities like sericulture raised peasant-family incomes.[1] In Wuxi, though it was true that sericulture brought much-needed supplementary cash incomes to peasant families with small farms and substantial rent payments, this was only one of its multiple effects. Beginning with the questions of how and why peasant women worked at silkworm raising in Wuxi, we shall see that their returns to labor were lower than those for men in grain farming. But because female labor had a very low opportunity cost, this particular balance of male and female work within peasant families made perfect sense. By the 1920's, small farm size and large rent payments dictated that peasant families also find other forms of nonfarm employment. Precisely because filature demand for cocoons remained high and sericulture was women's work, it was usually men who left the farm in pursuit of other forms of urban-based work.

As some men succeeded in new strategies for earning larger incomes in commercial and professional pursuits in nearby cities and market towns, a few fortunate households enjoyed substantially higher income levels. But in the villages most remote from the urban core of the county, where men had to leave home permanently to seek nonfarm work, women and children who stayed behind fared less well. With no men to farm, and no guarantee that any substantial proportion of male migrants' earnings would flow homeward, households with small farms in distant villages had the lowest income levels in the Wuxi countryside. Thus, gendered labor, perpetuated by the ongoing demands of silk filatures for cocoons produced by peasant women, contributed to a pattern of gen-

dered wealth and poverty. Sericulture was a kind of crutch for densely
settled villages in Wuxi, but one that had little prospect of keeping its
female bearers walking steadily into a prosperous, more developed future.

PEASANT HOUSEHOLDS, FARM SIZE, AND
CROPPING PATTERNS

As discussed in Chapter 1 (and in Appendix B), the data on peasant-
family production considered here come from two surveys of rural
households in Wuxi, one conducted in the summer of 1929 by a Chinese research team of the Academia Sinica's Social Science Research
Institute (SSRI), and the second in 1940 by a Japanese research team of
the Shanghai Research Office of the South Manchurian Railway Company (SMR or, using the more common Japanese abbreviation, "Mantetsu"). The SSRI survey originally was conducted among 1,204 households in twenty-two villages scattered widely throughout the county.[2]
The Mantetsu survey, while more limited in scope, covering three villages in close proximity, with a total of just eighty households, is
nonetheless another valuable resource for studying the Wuxi farm
economy.[3] Map 2 displays the names and locations of villages studied
here, including thirteen of the SSRI-surveyed villages and all three of
the Mantetsu-surveyed villages.

Peasant families typically consisted of four or five people, conjugal
units that included a husband and wife, one or two children, and sometimes a grandparent or two. These families combined grain farming and
mulberry cultivation, with silkworm raising a nearly universal sideline
activity. Rice and wheat were the principal grain crops grown in Wuxi, as
in many other locations in the Yangzi delta, and accounted for the majority of arable land. Although this land was often called paddy land, or
shuitian in Chinese, rice/wheat land is a more precise designation since
it was devoted yearly to one crop of summer rice (harvested in the fall)
and one crop of winter wheat (harvested in the spring). Though nearly all
rice/wheat land in Wuxi was planted in rice every summer, in winter
some land was put to soil-enriching plants or vegetables, such as taro and
broad beans, that could be sold or consumed by family members.[4]

Mulberry fields, or *sangyuan* in Chinese, were almost always arranged in "tract" fashion in Wuxi (see Chapter 3), in contrast to other areas in the delta where mulberries were grown on embankments between
rice/wheat fields. Compared to other places in the delta, Wuxi had a substantial amount of land devoted to mulberry cultivation, because land

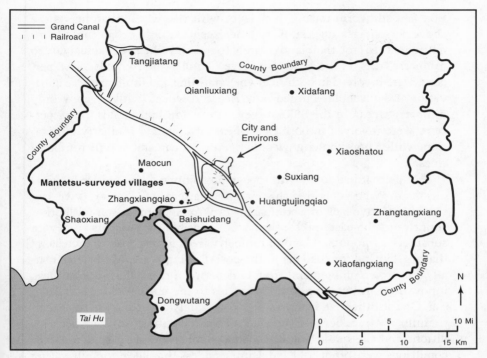

Map 2. Wuxi County and surveyed village sites

that had once been devoted to grain cultivation was given over to mulberries at the close of the Taiping period in 1865.[5] Most estimates of the
proportion of land devoted to mulberry cultivation in the 1920's and
1930's in Wuxi fell in the range of 20 to 30 percent.[6]

In the three villages of the Mantetsu survey, seventy-five households
worked approximately 190 mu of land; of this, about 146 mu, or 76 percent, was rice/wheat land; 43 mu, or 23 percent, was devoted to the mulberry; and 1 mu was used strictly for vegetable cultivation.[7] Vegetables
for home consumption were grown between mulberry trees. In thirteen
villages of the SSRI survey, 128 households held 976 mu of land, with
237 mu, or 25 percent, devoted to mulberry. Alfalfa, broad beans, and
other vegetables were grown in some villages on rice/wheat land during
the winter months (rather than devote all the land to a second crop of
winter wheat), and vegetables for home consumption were also grown
between mulberry trees.[8]

Although peasants gave over a substantial percentage of farm land in
Wuxi to mulberry fields, most households carried on mulberry cultiva-

tion and silkworm raising in tandem with rice/wheat farming, as the above percentages suggest. It was the exception rather than the rule for households to crop their land entirely to rice and wheat, or exclusively to mulberry trees. In the Mantetsu survey, 62 of 75 households, or 86 percent, were involved in both rice/wheat farming and mulberry tree cultivation; 8 households farmed only rice and wheat, while 5 grew only mulberry trees.[9] In the SSRI survey, 113 of 128 households, or 88 percent, were involved in both rice/wheat farming and mulberry cultivation, while 2 households grew only rice and wheat, and 13 only mulberry trees.

Factors that had to do with topography, climate, and marketing conditions in Wuxi supported this cropping pattern. In Chapter 3, we saw that the relative lack of waterlogging in Wuxi in comparison with other counties to the east and south made it possible for peasants to devote substantial amounts of land to mulberry trees in response to increasing filature demand for cocoons in the post-Taiping years. Mulberries usually had grown only on embankments between rice fields prior to these innovations in Wuxi and other counties to the north and west of Lake Tai. On the other hand, peasants in Wuxi rarely devoted all of their land to mulberry trees because the risks associated with spring weather conditions and the marketing of cocoons were too great. Spring weather conditions were often cold and damp, and less than ideal for cultivating silkworms. Sudden rains and the dampness that followed often led to bacterial infection among silkworms and the total destruction of some households' yearly crops.[10] In addition, prices for cocoons varied widely from one day to the next, and also varied among marketing locations during the cocoon-buying season.[11] Because climate and marketing conditions made income from cocoon sales difficult to predict, in some years many families spent more fertilizing their mulberry fields and buying silkworm eggs than they were able to earn by selling their cocoon crops.

Most important of all was the small size of farms in Wuxi. The Mantetsu research team was so stunned by the small size of farms they observed that they commented at great length on the situation in their survey report, referring constantly to landholdings in Wuxi as *reisai*—fragmented, small-scale, or petty—even in comparison with the farms they had observed in fieldwork in other delta locations. The average size of a farm among the seventy-five farming households in the Mantetsu survey was only 2.54 mu, or about one-third of an acre.[12] As Table 8, with data compiled by the Japanese research team, reveals, the median figure was lower than this, with nearly half the farms working 2 mu or less, and

TABLE 8

Farm Size in Three Mantetsu-Surveyed Villages, 1940

(N = 75)

Size of farm (in mu)	Households	
	N	%
≤1	13	17
1.1–2.0	23	31
2.1–3.0	18	24
3.1–4.0	13	17
4.1–5.0	4	5
5.1–7.0	4	5

SOURCE: Mantetsu 1941: 88.
NOTE: Land amounts include both owned and rented land.

TABLE 9

Farm Size and Cropping Patterns in SSRI-Surveyed Villages, 1929

(in mu; N = 128)

	Mean	Median	s	Min.	Max.
Farm size	7.62	5.50	6.27	.30	38.50
Rice/wheat land	5.77	4.00	5.20	.00	28.20
Mulberry land	1.85	1.50	1.51	.00	10.30

SOURCE: SSRI survey sample; see Appendix B.
NOTE: s signifies standard deviation.

the largest farm only a meager 7 mu. The Japanese researchers found these figures so astounding because of the average farm sizes they had observed elsewhere—in Jiading, close to Shanghai, the household average farm size in Mantetsu-surveyed villages was 6.36 mu; in Changshou, bordering Wuxi to the north, the average size was 5.28 mu; and in Songjiang, the average size was a relatively high 9.56 mu.[13]

In the villages surveyed by the SSRI research team, farms were larger on average than those observed in the Mantetsu survey, but there were still many farms that were very small by the prevailing standards of the delta region. Table 9 provides descriptive statistics on farm size, rice/wheat land, and mulberry land for households in the SSRI survey. The principal reason that farms were larger on average than those in the Mantetsu survey is that some farms were far larger than any observed by the Japanese. Average farm size was 7.62 mu, about the size of the largest farm size in the Mantetsu-surveyed villages, with the largest

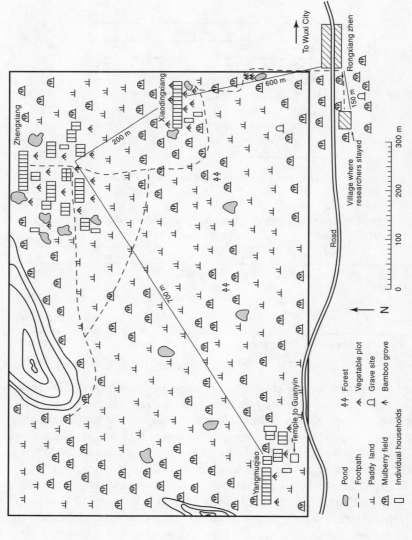

Map 3. The Mantetsu-surveyed villages and surroundings. Adapted from Mantetsu 1941

farm at 38.5 mu. Nevertheless, the median farm size in the SSRI-surveyed villages was still only 5.5 mu, with 50 percent of households working farms of this size or smaller.

LAND TENURE, OUTPUT, AND SUBSISTENCE

Further complicating farming patterns in Wuxi was the high degree of land parcelization there. For the Mantetsu-surveyed villages, the most common number of parcels per household was three to four, none of which exceeded 0.65 mu, for a total of 287 plots.[14] Map 3, based on a rendering of village locations and farmland surrounding them in the Mantetsu survey, gives some sense of what the fragmentation of land-holdings meant for cropping patterns. Rice/wheat land and mulberry fields were scattered throughout the entire area between village settlements, with little apparent pattern to their arrangement. An active land market for both topsoil and subsoil rights, in combination with land hunger among much of the rural population, contributed to this pattern of extreme parcelization.[15]

Much of this fragmented farm land in Wuxi was also rented at relatively high rates. For villages in the SSRI survey, 128 households held 338 separate parcels. Only 9 households had a single parcel, with the rest working from 2 to 5 parcels each. Of these parcels, 123 were rented, or 36 percent of the total. Likewise, only 24 households, or 19 percent, did not rent land; the rest worked from 1 to 4 rented parcels each. Yearly rental payments for tenants averaged 41 percent of total grain output.[16]

The combination of small farm size and substantial rent payments for many leads us to consider how Wuxi farming families met their consumption and reproduction needs. Although the concept of "subsistence" is variable in different spatial, temporal, and cultural settings, the definition I adopt here is that provided by the field survey work of John Lossing Buck in China during the 1920's and 1930's, and economist Dwight Perkins's later use and interpretation of Buck's data. Based on a thorough overview of Buck's findings, Perkins found that 400 jin, or cat-ties, of grain and grain substitutes (such as peas, beans, and so on) was the bottom level reported for yearly grain output per adult male in Chinese villages in the early 1930's. Perkins thus concluded that 400 jin (or 200 kilograms) per adult male constituted "something like a minimum level of subsistence."[17] One problem with using per capita grain output figures to estimate subsistence is that they tell us little about variation among farming households.[18] They also ignore the fact that many households had to use some of their grain to make rental payments on a portion

TABLE 10

Per Capita Grain Output in Wuxi Villages, 1929

(in jin; N = 128)

	Mean	Median	s	Min.	Max.	% house-holds be-low 400 jin per capita
Per capita rice/wheat out-put	533	438	431	0	2,202	45
Per capita rice/wheat out-put after rent pay-ments (in and out)	478	286	599	–92	3,110	66

SOURCE: SSRI survey sample; see Appendix B.
  NOTE: See note 18 for an explanation of the use of "per capita" here and in subsequent tables.

TABLE 11

Per Capita Grain Consumption Potential in Wuxi Villages, 1929

(in jin; N = 128)

	Mean	Median	s	Min.	Max.	% house-holds be-low400 jin per capita
Per capita grain consump-tion potential	946	652	1,160	25	8,700	27
Per capita grain consump-tion potential after rent payments (in and out)	896	509	1,393	–108	9,258	38

SOURCE: SSRI survey sample; see Appendix B.

of the land they worked. Thus, for a better sense of exactly how many peasant families in Wuxi met their subsistence requirements through farming, we also should look at more detailed household-level data on internal family composition in relationship to grain output, rent payments on land, and consumption.

Estimates for how well individual farming families in the SSRI survey were able to meet their subsistence requirements through rice/wheat farming are contained in Tables 10 and 11. Table 10 shows that average grain output per capita stood at 533 jin, but 45 percent of households fell below the minimum subsistence level of 400 jin. After rent payments, these figures fell to 478 jin for average per capita output, with 66 percent of households below the 400-jin floor. Table 11 uses available data slightly differently. Potential rice/wheat output for fields currently under mulberry cultivation is added to the total real output of rice and wheat, thus raising the potential levels of average per capita output below the 400-jin floor to 27 percent before rent and 38 percent after rent. The insight gleaned here is that even if all available land had been cropped to rice/wheat in Wuxi villages, a substantial proportion of peasant households would still have fallen short of owning and renting enough land to provide self-sufficiency in grain production at a minimum level of subsistence.[19]

Given small farm size and relatively substantial rent obligations, most peasant families in Wuxi had sideline employment to earn additional cash income. The major sideline in Wuxi was silkworm raising, with 92 percent of families in the SSRI survey engaged in it. But other sidelines were also important, with 62 percent of families having at least one family member, and sometimes more, working at other forms of cash-generating work. Though silkworm raising was women's work, we shall see that most other sideline activities were performed by men, creating a distinctively gendered pattern of work, wealth, and poverty in Wuxi villages.

SERICULTURE AND THE SEXUAL
DIVISION OF LABOR

There was a strong notion in Wuxi in the 1920's that sericulture was a more profitable activity than rice/wheat farming. This sentiment was expressed in a 1921 journal article as follows:

> Twenty years ago, peasants [in Wuxi] grew rice, wheat, and beans. In recent years, since the development of filatures, peasants have seen that sericulture is more profitable than rice/wheat farming and thus, in agricultural pursuits, have increased their involvement in sericulture.[20]

Not only did the idea that a commercially oriented activity such as sericulture have the capacity to enrich the peasantry prevail at the time, but a great deal of subsequent scholarship on the Chinese rural economy has also ascribed to it. Was this notion really true? In what sense can the profitability of one form of farming activity be assessed against that of another? And even more importantly, how might we better understand cropping choices made by peasants given the overall economic contexts in which they functioned?

To say that sericulture was more profitable than rice/wheat farming in Wuxi in the 1920's oversimplifies the effects of alternative gains and losses when members of the same farming household balanced the two activities. Table 12 summarizes data on returns to rice/wheat farming and sericulture (including both mulberry cultivation and silkworm raising) from households in the SSRI survey from two contrasting points of

TABLE 12

Comparative Returns to Land and Labor for Rice/Wheat
Farming and Sericulture, 1929

(in yuan; N = 98)

	Returns									
	Per mu					Per day[a]				
	Mean	Med.	s	Min.	Max.	Mean	Med.	s	Min.	Max.
Rice/Wheat farming	13.84	14.04	5.30	.00	26.92	.72	.75	.32	.00	1.36
Sericulture	14.31	10.72	18.63	−33.98[b]	73.75	.29	.26	.36	−.37[b]	2.13

SOURCE: SSRI survey sample; see Appendix B.

[a]"Per day" means "per labor day," or *gong* in Chinese. In rice/wheat farming, one labor day was six to eight hours while one labor day in sericulture was usually an entire twenty-four-hour period. Thus, "returns per day" for sericulture were in some sense even lower than the calculations appearing in this table.

[b]Negative "returns" are explained in the text.

view—returns to land and returns to labor time invested. Average returns to rice/wheat farming and sericulture per mu were roughly comparable, sericulture having the slight edge. On the other hand, for returns to labor, there was a dramatic difference, with rice/wheat worth 0.72 yuan per day versus only 0.29 yuan per day for sericulture. Thus, sericulture used much more labor time than rice/wheat farming to produce roughly the same average returns to the land. But maximum and minimum returns to both land and labor also reveal another dimension to the problem. The "shifts in the pendulum" for returns to sericulture were much greater than those for rice/wheat farming. The maximum earnings per mu for sericulture reached 73.75 yuan, a much larger figure than for rice/wheat farming, which brought in a maximum of 26.92 yuan. Negative "returns" were also possible for sericulture for both land and labor because many households began the process of silkworm raising, paying to purchase silkworm eggs and to fertilize their mulberry fields, but had no income from cocoon sales since their entire silkworm broods died.

Thus, one might say that the potential existed for sericulture to be more profitable than rice/wheat farming because of the possibility of greater returns per mu. But because of the risks associated with silkworm raising, including the possibility of silkworm disease and death during cold and damp springs, and unpredictable fluctuations in market conditions for cocoons, sericulture was also a greater liability. Having said this, we still must ask why most peasant households were willing to absorb the risks of sericulture and to accept returns to labor that were so much lower for sericulture than for rice/wheat farming. The simple answer to this is that sericulture used family labor of very low opportunity cost—female labor—and that peasant women would have been paid much less in other forms of readily available work. Behind this statement, however, is an array of expectations about what peasant women might and might not do, and also about women's responsibilities and liabilities in their family and work environments.

Data on the identities and sexes of those who participated in the work of silkworm raising in the SSRI survey make it clear that it was primarily a woman's domain. Among ninety-six households for which we have this form of data, ninety-three had one or more women engaged in sericulture for at least a month-long period each year. For all ninety-six households, the average number of days devoted to silkworm raising by women was fifty-two (this could include work by one or more women), while the average number of days devoted by men was only seventeen. Only two households had no women involved in silkworm raising at all, whereas forty-one households (among the ninety-six considered) reported that men did not contribute to silkworm raising.[21]

Women's work in silkworm raising corresponded to the well-known preference among Chinese peasants that women not work the fields in agriculture, but instead be occupied in work within the home. We have seen in Chapter 2 that in Qing times, the preferred form of work for women in Wuxi had been cotton spinning and weaving. But one reason women made the switch to silkworm raising was that it brought relatively higher returns to labor than work with cotton or, for that matter, any other forms of female home-work. At the time of the SSRI survey in 1929, cotton weaving brought in only 0.02 yuan per day in Wuxi; making hemp rope, 0.03 yuan per day; and lace making, 0.03 yuan per day.[22] These amounts should be compared to the average figure of 0.29 yuan earned per day through sericulture, and to the 0.72 yuan earned per day by men in grain farming, as seen in Table 12. Thus, in general, women's work was poorly paid. But under the pressure for additional cash income brought on by land scarcity and rent obligations, women needed the best-paying work available. Because silk filatures generated a steady demand for cocoons in Wuxi, women's work "of choice" had become silkworm raising.

Women began raising silkworms in Wuxi in mid-April each year, when delicate silkworm eggs were incubated, often strapped to a woman's body in the early stages to provide sufficient warmth. Once the eggs hatched, the pace of a woman's work was frantic because silkworms ate voraciously. For five feeding periods of four to six days each, large quantities of mulberry leaves had to be stripped from the trees and piled high every four hours or so on top of bamboo feeding trays. Five or six daily feedings thus went on round the clock, making it difficult for women to sleep at all during the month-long period of silkworm care and feeding. Trays had to be monitored carefully while the worms fed so that they remained evenly distributed, and droppings and moltings also had to be removed periodically.[23]

From the mid-1920's onward, some peasant women also tried to raise a second crop of fall silkworms by using scientifically cross-bred silkworm eggs and artificially induced incubation techniques. Promoted by sericulture experiment stations to meet escalating filature demand for cocoons, these techniques and those who promoted them in Wuxi brought additional complications for peasant women, which I shall review at greater length in the next chapter. Here, it is enough to note that the amount of time women spent in silkworm raising expanded with the addition of a fall silkworm crop, but because of their unfamiliarity with the more complicated techniques needed—from the use of refrigeration to delay incubation of eggs, to the application of new forms of chemical disinfectant to kill bacteria—it was difficult for the women to be successful with them. Thus, for peasant women, the hope that fall silkworms might bring some additional income rarely materialized. Even worse, women's return rate to labor time invested usually declined when they attempted fall silkworms, since the worms more often than not died off entirely.

Although peasant women worked long hours at silkworm raising, there is no evidence that they personally benefited much from their efforts. Their earnings were collected at the marketplace by their fathers, husbands, or brothers, and went into family coffers to help provide for household needs overall.[24] Moreover, as we have seen, silkworm raising was a tedious, risky business, and when silkworms died before reaching maturity, a reservoir of traditional beliefs about women's "polluting" powers during menstruation and pregnancy and following childbirth were often called upon to explain the tragedy. Such explanations for silkworm death could cast an unfavorable light on a woman's reputation, implicating her in an unfortunate series of events that were often beyond the range of her knowledge and control. Thus, peasant women worked hard for few personal gains through sericulture. Their primary goal was to bring supplemental incomes to their families, enabling consumption and reproduction needs to be met.[25]

GENDERED LABOR AND NONFARM WORK

The rationale for why women worked in sericulture leads us to consider the full range of options chosen by peasants as they looked for ways to support themselves. Decisions about what to do in an increasingly land-scarce environment in Wuxi during the 1920's included silkworm raising for women, but also other forms of nonfarm work for male and female peasants alike. To understand the fuller implications of the sexual division of labor supported by filature demand for cocoons in Wuxi, we can pursue the idea that all labor was increasingly gendered, with men seizing opportunities to leave farming altogether to seek other forms of nonfarm work.

Table 13 displays average per capita peasant incomes earned in 1929, dividing the SSRI-surveyed households into five wealth categories from "poorest" to "richest," then breaking down the average per capita incomes by source within each wealth category. Several aspects of income differentials among households are important. First, there is a clear contrast between per capita incomes among the poorest and richest households, a range that spans from 10.47 to 350.65 yuan. When incomes are broken down by source, significant patterns emerge. Households in the poorest category had the lowest average per capita incomes in all four major income-generating areas. Their low incomes in rice/wheat farming and sericulture may be attributed to having too little land to raise substantial grain and mulberry crops, and also to failing at their silkworm-raising efforts in the spring and summer of 1929. To reach the "middle" category, households did noticeably better in each income-earning endeavor than did their poorest neighbors. But to make it to the upper stratosphere of "richest," households had to move beyond both rice/wheat farming and sericulture into much more lucrative activities in the nonfarming arena.

If neither grain farming nor sericulture was making some peasants rich in Wuxi, what was it that allowed them to move in this direction? Tables 14 and 15 help to answer this question with additional data on household incomes for those in the "richest" category. Table 14 reveals that two of the richest households had no incomes at all from rice/wheat farming and that incomes from sericulture were very modest. On the other hand, nonfarm activities made per capita income figures for this group high relative to other households, with figures well over 200 yuan for five households. Per capita incomes from collecting rent were also high for three households.

TABLE 13

Average Per Capita Incomes by Source Among
Wuxi Rural Households, 1929

(in yuan)

Households[b]	Total income	Rice/wheat farming	Sericulture	Nonfarm activity	Rent
			Per capita income by source[a]		
All (N = 128)	57.57	21.67	6.84	24.42	4.64
Poorest (N = 20)	10.47	5.83	.06	4.32	.25
Poor (N= 64)	32.07	18.11	4.60	8.77	.58
Middle (N = 28)	64.88	34.29	12.01	17.34	1.25
Rich (N = 10)	118.63	43.96	14.80	42.02	17.85
Richest (N = 6)	350.65	16.36	15.88	262.11	56.31
eta^2	.87	.38	.31	.75	.48

SOURCE: SSRI survey sample; see Appendix B.

[a]The figures displayed here are stated in yuan, although not all income from rice/wheat farming and rent collection was actually a cash amount. For the sake of comparison with cash-income-earning activities, I have used data from the SSRI survey on grain prices and output, and on rental amounts paid in grain and their cash equivalents, to convert all income figures into cash equivalents.

[a]The household categories in this table were created through a quantitative measurement technique called clustering, in which individual cases in a given population are placed into groups, or "clusters," based on their relative degrees of closeness to a common mean. The households were thus not grouped arbitrarily, but rather, according to the significance of their income differences from other groups of SSRI-surveyed households. The specific technique used here is the standard SPSS quick cluster routine, which uses a squared-Euclidean-distance measure of variance between means. The eta^2 statistic reported in the last line of the table is similar to the r^2 statistic in regression analysis—the closer its value to 1.00, the more robust the findings. I chose cluster analysis over regression primarily because of non-normal distributions for most variables in the SSRI data. The distributions could be improved by removing outliers and converting the remaining data to logarithms. But in the end, this seemed fruitless since it was precisely the "abnormalities," or disparities in distribution, in which I was most interested.

TABLE 14

Per Capita Incomes by Source Among Wuxi's
Richest Rural Households, 1929

(in yuan)

Household	Total per capita income	Rice/wheat farming	Sericulture	Nonfarm activity	Rent
			Per capita income by source		
1	270.26	.00	8.89	256.67	4.70
2	207.64	42.92	19.40	58.96	86.35
3	517.92	27.45	8.29	450.98	31.20
4	265.75	.00	2.04	250.00	13.71
5	356.59	24.79	25.62	259.26	46.93
6	485.77	3.01	31.03	296.77	154.95

SOURCE: SSRI survey sample; see Appendix B.

TABLE 15

Nonfarm Incomes by Source Among Wuxi's
Richest Rural Households, 1929

(in yuan)

| | Nonfarm income by source | | | | | | | | | |
| | Cottage industry | | Commerce | | Teaching | | Doctoring | | Other | |
House-hold	Per capita	Total	Per capita	Total	Per capita	Total	Per capita	Total	Per capita	Total
1	0.00	0.00	0.00	0.00	173.33	312	0.00	0.00	83.33	150.00
2	0.14	1.20	58.82	500.00	0.00	0.00	0.00	0.00	0.00	0.00
3	0.00	0.00	450.98	2,300.00	0.00	0.00	0.00	0.00	0.00	0.00
4	0.00	0.00	250.00	700.00	0.00	0.00	0.00	0.00	0.00	0.00
5	0.00	0.00	0.00	0.00	37.04	200.00	222.22	1,200.00	0.00	0.00
6	0.00	0.00	135.48	840.00	0.00	0.00	161.29	1,000.00	0.00	0.00

SOURCE: SSRI survey sample; see Appendix B.

Table 15 probes further still into how some peasants were "getting rich" in the Wuxi countryside. One of the six richest households had total income from teaching and other unspecified nonfarm activities of 462 yuan, and households three and four made 2,300 yuan and 700 yuan respectively through commerce. The remaining households had large incomes generated through a combination of cottage industry, commerce, teaching, and doctoring. Thus, it appears that the richest households residing in Wuxi villages resembled their market-town and urban counterparts—engaging in a combination of mercantile and professional activity, coupled with some land rental—producing far more income with their nonfarm activities than with either grain farming or sericulture.

Given the scarcity of land in Wuxi, these developments in income-earning strategies made good sense. Both grain farming and silkworm raising were constrained by the amount of available farmland. Although some households bought mulberry leaves from their neighbors during silkworm-raising seasons, by far the more common pattern was for households to scale their silkworm-raising efforts to the amount of land they had for mulberry cultivation (more on this below). When farms dwindled in size, as they had for many households in Wuxi by the 1920's, the most logical strategy was for some household members to leave farming altogether to seek more profitable forms of work elsewhere. But it took a combination of luck, skill, and opportunity for peasants to make the leap out of farming into the kinds of quasi-professional activities described here. For most, alternative forms of work were much less lucrative, and not always available.

TABLE 16

Household Incomes from Nonfarm Work and Sericulture, 1929

(in yuan)

Form of work	Mean	Median	s	Min.	Max.
Artisanry (N = 33)	43.97	28.00	37.77	2.00	150.00
Cottage industry (N = 39)	5.35	4.00	4.65	1.00	20.00
Wage-work in agriculture (N = 9)	25.19	12.00	20.38	5.00	52.00
Other village-based wage work (N = 16)	40.99	19.50	45.12	2.00	144.00
Factory work (N = 8)	72.69	70.00	44.59	17.50	150.00
Urban-based wage work (N = 2)	55.00	55.00	35.36	30.00	80.00
Sericulture (N = 109)	31.28	18.00	38.83	.39	200.00

SOURCE: SSRI survey sample; see Appendix B.

The SSRI survey provides a wealth of information on other types of nonfarm work pursued by Wuxi farming households. We have seen that some households had opportunities for professional and commercial activities that brought much higher than average per capita incomes. For most households, however, the major forms of nonfarm work were more mundane. Such work included various forms of artisanry for men—brick making, tile making, carpentry, and tailoring—and also agricultural wage work, boat tending, and miscellaneous urban-based wage-earning activity, such as working as clerks in small shops. For women, cotton spinning and weaving, lace making, the twisting of hemp fibers into rope, and the making of paper money for holidays and religious purposes were the major forms of nonfarm work.[26]

Table 16 provides summary descriptive statistics comparing household earnings from the principal male activities, categorized here as "artisanry," with those from the principal female activities, categorized as "cottage industry." Other data in the table include earnings for male work as hired agricultural laborers; for male work in other wage-earning activities in the village setting, with boat-tending an especially important activity included in this category; for factory work, which was neither primarily male nor female work among these households; and for sericulture, which, as we have seen, was primarily female work.

Not all households had incomes in each of the categories displayed in Table 16, as the numbers listed under each form of work indicate. For those that did have incomes earned from some form of nonfarm work, what was earned through male work was much greater than what was earned through female work. For example, comparing the earnings from male work in artisanry with those for female work in cottage industry, we see that the average (or mean) income for male work was 43.97 yuan, versus only 5.35 yuan for female work. Moreover, the maximum income figure for male work was much higher than for female work—150 yuan for artisanry versus 20 yuan for cottage industry. Factory work had the potential to bring returns comparable to those from artisanry, but only eight households reported having any members with factory jobs. At the same time, the bulk of nonfarm incomes came from sericulture, although as we have seen, this meant long hours for peasant women, with no guarantee of substantial returns for every household.

Thus, as filature demand for cocoons stimulated the shift for women into silkworm raising in Wuxi and a proportion of relatively scarce farmland was converted to mulberry cultivation, male work became concentrated not only in farming but also in certain forms of relatively well-paying artisan jobs and other wage-earning work. As peasants made decisions about how to allocate their labor time, total returns to the family work effort were of primary importance, especially for farms that were very small and needed to push their nonfarm income-earning activities to the maximum. As these processes unfolded, "gendered" labor was employed not just in farming and silkworm raising, but also in most other forms of work. At the same time, the best-paying nonfarm jobs were the domain of male peasants, while women were primarily engaged in silkworm raising and a variety of much lower-paying forms of homework. Of course, it is also true that some peasant women, especially those who were young and unmarried, went to work in silk filatures and cotton mills in Wuxi City and in Shanghai. But as our data demonstrate, such opportunities were still relatively rare for peasant households even in the late 1920's, and the range of wage-earning opportunities open to peasant women was, for the most part, quite narrow.[27]

MIGRATION AND ITS CONSEQUENCES

The location of the village in which they lived also made a difference in the options for nonfarm work open to Wuxi peasants. When peasants lived in villages that were relatively close to the urban core of the county, they found more nonfarm work. Table 17 demonstrates how this logic operated.

There are important insights to be gleaned here about the relationships among income-earning strategies, farm size, and relative distance of one's village from the urban core of the county. First of all, as we might expect, per capita rice/wheat incomes were more substantial for

TABLE 17

Average Per Capita Incomes for Households Grouped by Farm
Size and Distance from Urban Core, 1929

(in yuan)

Farm size and distance from urban core	Total	Rice/wheat farming	Seri-culture	Nonfarm work	Rent
Large (> 5.5 mu) (N = 38)					
Far (N = 27)	46.34	29.59	10.79[a]	5.22[a]	.74
Close (N = 11)	47.02	29.20[a]	8.03	9.32[b]	.46
Small (< 5.5 mu)(N = 38)					
Far (N = 13)	32.35	15.95[b]	3.94	8.53[c]	3.94
Close (N = 25)	37.82	8.52[a,b]	3.53[a]	23.50[a,b,c]	2.28

SOURCE: SSRI survey sample; see Appendix B.

NOTE: To test for variance among group means within each variable, Tukey-b tests were used. Pairs of means that tested positively at the .05 level are indicated by matching letters (a, b, c) in each column.

larger farms. This same pattern obtained for sericulture, with larger farms earning more per capita from sericulture than smaller farms did. Because there were markets for mulberry leaves, we might have assumed that smaller farms would try to capitalize on that situation and raise more silkworms than their own mulberry land was capable of supporting. But the fact that all small farms earned very similar per capita incomes from sericulture—in the range of only three to four yuan—while their larger neighbors earned in the range of eight to eleven yuan, indicates that decisions about the scale of silkworm raising were also dependent on farm size.[28]

Differences in nonfarm per capita incomes are even more revealing. Large, distant farms earned only about five yuan per capita from nonfarm activities, while small farms close to the urban core earned nearly five times that amount, approximately twenty-four yuan. On the other hand, small, distant farms earned only slightly more than their larger, distant counterparts, approximately nine yuan on average. Thus, while all peasants with small farms may have needed incomes from nonfarm activities, being close to Wuxi City meant that they had more opportunities to pursue this strategy effectively. In addition, small farms rented out more land than their larger neighbors, an indication that as men sought relatively well-paying nonfarm jobs, they gave up some of their farm work in order to do so.

In Table 18, the same size/distance groupings are used to explore the idea that there was a final alternative for peasant families who had small farms—male migration on a permanent or part-time basis to seek work

TABLE 18

*Average Number of Household Members Present and Working on
Farms Grouped by Size and Distance from Urban Core, 1929*

Farm size and distance	Present			Working		
from urban core	Men	Women	Children	Men	Women	Children
Large (> 5.5 mu) (N = 38)						
Far (N = 27)	1.63[a]	1.74	1.48[a]	1.59[a]	1.67	0.37
Close (N = 11)	1.55	1.82	3.18[a,b,c]	1.45[b]	1.55	0.91
Small (< 5.5 mu)(N = 38)						
Far (N = 13)	0.77[a,b]	1.31	0.92[b]	0.69[a,b,c]	1.15	0.31
Close (N = 25)	1.44[b]	1.48	1.52[c]	1.28[c]	1.36	0.56

SOURCE: SSRI survey sample; see Appendix B.

NOTE: To test for variance among group means within each variable, Tukey-b tests were used. Pairs of means that tested positively at the .05 level are indicated by matching letters (a, b, c) in each column.

in urban settings. The data in Table 18 are grouped into two sets: average figures for resident men, women, and children in each household, and average figures for resident men, women, and children who worked. The fact that large, close farms had significantly more children present is not surprising. Such households had the combination of more farmland and more opportunities for nonfarm work than any of their neighbors, resulting in the largest per capita incomes overall (see Table 17). Thus, they could afford more children. On the other hand, farms that were small and distant from the urban core had significantly fewer men than any of the others. We cannot prove conclusively that the relative absence of men in distant households with small farms was a result of migration, but the logic of the situation—too little nonfarm work close to home—is highly suggestive of this possibility.

The SSRI survey also provides substantial commentary on peasant migration. When questioned about the number of people present in one's family, if someone in the household had left to seek work elsewhere, peasants often said it was hard to know whether or not to count that person due to the uncertainty of his or her return. Moreover, some peasants who migrated on a semipermanent basis sent or brought money home, but others who left permanently sent only minuscule amounts, or nothing at all, needing all the income they earned to forge a new life in an uncertain urban setting. Of course, it is also possible that some men absent from rural households had joined the ranks of the ubiquitous "floating population," on the move constantly as migrant agricultural laborers, beggars, bandits, or potential recruits into one or another of the competing armies that dominated China's political landscape during the 1920's.

TABLE 19

*Positions Within the Family of Migrant Workers
from Thirty-Seven Mantetsu-Surveyed
Households, 1940*

Position of migrant family member	N	%
Male household head	19	47.5
Eldest son	12	30.0
Younger son	2	5.0
Eldest son's wife	3	7.5
Other	4	10.0
TOTAL	40	100.0

SOURCE: Mantetsu 1941: 102.

TABLE 20

*Locations of Migrant Workers from Thirty-Seven
Mantetsu-Surveyed Households, 1940*

Location of migrant worker	N	%
Shanghai	33	82.5
Wuxi (city)	4	10.0
Changshou	1	2.5
Shengze	1	2.5
Suzhou	1	2.5
TOTAL	40	100.0

SOURCE: Mantetsu 1941: 99–100.

Data from the Mantetsu survey contained in Tables 19, 20, and 21 provide further evidence on the growing importance of male migration in Wuxi. Of the eighty households in the three Mantetsu-surveyed villages, thirty-seven had one or more family members living and working away from home on a permanent basis. Most of the forty individuals involved in this activity were male heads of households or eldest sons, and the largest number were employed in Shanghai, as seen in Tables 19 and 20. In Table 21, we see that most were working as skilled factory workers or as shop clerks. These facts on male migration, coupled with the ongoing importance of female involvement in silkworm raising, led the Japanese interviewers to conclude that in the villages they were observing, female labor had become primary and male labor secondary. They considered this a distinguishing characteristic of the agricultural system

TABLE 21

Occupations of Migrant Workers from Thirty-
Seven Mantetsu-Surveyed Households, 1940

Occupation	N	%
Store clerk	7	17.5
Clerk for butcher shop	6	15.0
Clerical worker	2	5.0
Skilled factory worker	15	37.5
Coolie	3	7.5
Female silk-filature		
worker	2	5.0
Ahmah (wet nurse)	2	5.0
Cook	1	2.5
Undetermined	2	5.0
TOTAL	40	100.0

SOURCE: Mantetsu 1941: 100.

operating in these Wuxi villages, a system shaped primarily by petty, fragmented landholdings and sericulture.[29]

Clearly, men from the Mantetsu-surveyed villages who had left were a relatively privileged group as far as migrants went. With so many of them able to find desirable jobs in Shanghai, they also sent relatively large amounts of money home.[30] One can imagine that because these villages were in the most prosperous area of the county with many strong commercial connections to Shanghai, personal networks had worked to assist some of these men in finding jobs. Many women in the Mantetsu-surveyed villages had become more responsible for farm management as their men left. As they did so, they relied on a combination of their own work, rental of some family-owned farmland, and the hiring of some male labor at peak periods of planting and harvesting. Most of the hired male labor came from among other male residents in the same villages, hired only for very short periods. Undoubtedly, this strategy made better sense for families with very small holdings than keeping their own men on the farm for the entire year, where they would have been severely underemployed. The better alternative was to hire in short-term labor when needed and for able-bodied males to seek full-time urban employment.[31]

When substantial proportions of nonresident men's earnings made their way back to the village, migration became yet another way to supplement meager family earnings from farming. However, there was no guarantee that such revenue flows back toward the village would materialize. Returning to the dilemmas of households in the SSRI survey who had the smallest farms and lived furthest from the urban core of the county, we should emphasize that small, distant farms had both the fewest number of resident men and the lowest per capita incomes (as seen in Table 17). This suggests that women and children who remained behind as their husbands and fathers migrated on a permanent basis, especially those who lived in areas remote from the county's urban core, were the poorest people residing in Wuxi villages.

As a final commentary on peasant poverty in Wuxi, I return briefly to the question of per capita incomes throughout the county as a whole. We saw earlier that small farm size precluded self-sufficiency in grain consumption for a sizable proportion of Wuxi peasant households. We also now have seen that many supplemented their incomes with a wide variety of nonfarm work, including sericulture. But taking into account income from all sources, 27 percent of households in the SSRI survey still had per capita incomes below twenty-four yuan, a rough cash equivalent to the "400 jin-of-grain" subsistence floor discussed earlier.[32] In addition, these were income figures tallied before rent payments and other expenses for miscellaneous items such as clothing, weddings, and funerals. We can only conclude that in any given year, a substantial proportion of Wuxi households—perhaps as many as one-third throughout the county as a whole—relied either on savings or on loans to meet their basic consumption requirements.[33]

SILK FILATURES, GENDERED LABOR,
AND RURAL POVERTY

To evaluate the effects of silk-filature demand for cocoons on peasant-family production, I have provided as complete a picture as possible of peasant work in the Wuxi countryside at the height of filature development. Silkworm raising was not the only form of sideline activity in Wuxi, but it was the most widespread because it combined the long-standing peasant preference that women refrain from work outside the home with the ongoing demands of silk filatures for cocoons. Thus, gendered labor solidified in Wuxi. While peasant women performed the laborious, troublesome tasks of silkworm raising, men worked in rice/wheat farming and other subsidiary occupations. In the process, mothers, wives, daughters, and daughters-in-law earned cash incomes through cocoon sales, contributing to their families' abilities to meet their consumption and reproduction needs even as family landholdings, and rice/wheat crops, dwindled.

By the 1920's, this rather precariously balanced system was showing signs of strain. Migration was the next step for some male peasants in Wuxi, especially those who had very small amounts of land and could not find alternative forms of work close to home. Among "large farms" (a genuine oxymoron in the agrarian environment in Wuxi), sericulture combined with rice/wheat farming provided a suitable means of securing per capita incomes adequate to sustain peasant families. When the population in some villages became so dense that farms were especially small, or when landlord-tenant relations were such that rent obligations were substantial, migration for some male peasants and smaller per capita incomes for the women and children who stayed behind resulted.

As we shall see next, peasant poverty in Wuxi contributed to ongoing difficulties with cocoon supply to local filatures. Ironically, and tragically, those who tried to assist peasant women in raising production standards never made the connection between rural poverty and silk-industry performance, struggling instead with what they believed to be peasant ignorance and superstitious belief when it came to difficulties in improving methods of silkworm raising. It would never occur to most of them that poor peasant women were unlikely recipients of their messages of modernity, especially in the absence of sufficient resources to make possible even the most basic forms of investment in agricultural improvements.

Imparting Modernity: Women and the Politics of Silk-Industry Reform

During the first decade of the twentieth century, Chinese exports of raw silk began to lag behind Japanese exports on the world market, prompting new concerns for silk-industry reform. Although there was some discussion of inadequate management and investment within Chinese filatures, as we have seen in Chapter 5, the far more important issue for most silk-industry reformers in Wuxi was the quality and quantity of cocoon supply. This issue had plagued filatures from the start, and Wuxi developed as a new sericulture district to meet increased filature demand for more and better cocoons. But by the 1910's and 1920's, cocoon supply had resurfaced as a central issue for the filature industry, with public and private resources devoted to finding ways to solve the problem.

The principal public institution that emerged in the early stages of silk-industry reform in Wuxi was a more specialized version of the "agricultural experiment station" so prevalent worldwide in agricultural-reform circles during the early twentieth century. This was the "sericulture experiment station," which, as we shall see, went through several variations in organization in Jiangsu Province and in Wuxi. There were also many ventures in publicly funded education in sericulture technique and also in the private "for-profit" business of silkworm-egg production. All of these activities, public and private alike, targeted the peasant population of Jiangsu Province—and especially of Wuxi, where sericulture was ubiquitous—as intended recipients of new knowledge and skills associated with scientific methods of silkworm raising, and also as potential consumers of scientifically crossbred silkworm eggs.

The story of silk-industry reform told here thus takes up strands of analysis from previous chapters on filature development, peasant involvement in sericulture, and local elite politics, and attempts to weave them together into a thicker, more richly textured whole. Chronologically, the bulk of this story occurs in the late 1920's, at about the time of the SSRI survey of peasant households in Wuxi. We shall see how Wuxi peasant women whom we have met through the SSRI survey became the intended audience for new "messages of modernity" carried by silk-industry reformers. We shall also explore why the fit between filature demand for cocoons and peasant supply was so poor, and why, even with a concerted effort, it still proved so difficult to fix. Finally, local politics plays an important part in this story as well, for as local elites pursued new careers in silk-industry reform, they not only met peasants close up for the first time, but also looked for ways to maneuver around other elite competitors. Almost inevitably, some succumbed to the temptation to manipulate fragile institutions through illicit means, further compounding the difficulties for silk-industry reform.

MODERNITY IN A LOCAL CONTEXT:
EARLY INSTITUTIONS FOR SERICULTURE REFORM

The bulk of previous scholarship on China's economic modernization in the late nineteenth and early twentieth centuries has been devoted to the thought, writings, and activities of individuals who were prominent at the national level in the pursuit of new policies and practices devoted to promoting modern industry.[1] My approach is quite different in that I am interested almost exclusively in silk-industry reformers at the very bottom of local elite hierarchies—the counterparts of the lowest rung of the cocoon-merchant community in Wuxi whom we met earlier, in Chapters 3 and 4. I am concerned with the interplay between such local elite "messengers of modernity," as I believe we might view them, and the peasantry in Wuxi.[2] In exploring instances of interaction between them, I am especially interested in the female members of both groups, and their struggles to find ways to understand each other's approaches to the problems of silkworm raising.

In terms of what modern science could do to improve, or "reform," sericulture in Wuxi, the most critical advances were in new knowledge and methods in silkworm-egg selection and cultivation. An epidemic of silkworm disease had nearly wiped out sericulture in southern Europe during the 1850's, prompting experimentation with selection and cross-breeding techniques to generate disease-resistant egg varieties.[3] The development of chemical disinfectants and new methods of application also fought bacterial infections. In addition, modern refrigeration equipment could be used to artificially delay egg incubation—an especially attractive technique for sericulture in Wuxi because of the possibility of increasing the number of yearly silkworm-raising periods to two, or even three, in spring, summer, and fall. If more silkworms were raised each year, and a larger proportion could be made disease-resistant, then the central goals of silk-industry reform—to produce larger quantities of higher-quality cocoons—might be realized.

In the Yangzi delta, new silkworm-egg varieties were generically termed "improved silkworm eggs" (*gailiang canzhong*) and were dispensed, or sold, "by the card," referring to pieces of lightweight cardboard, about nine by twelve inches in size, on which eggs were hatched by female moths.[4] Peasants had traditionally preserved their own eggs each spring on pieces of mulberry bark and hung them up in a dry, cool location until the following spring season. But as some filatures began to offer higher prices for cocoons spun from improved egg varieties, pressure on peasants to purchase the new eggs increased. One reason for filature preference was that it took fewer cocoons produced from improved eggs, as opposed to native varieties, to spin the same quantity of raw silk.[5] Moreover, using improved eggs meant that raw silk was of greater strength and higher quality, meeting escalating international demand for such a product.[6]

In the late nineteenth century, Japan progressed more quickly than China did in terms of importing and adapting modern methods of sericulture. Japanese governments at the national and prefectural levels played a role in the development of a network of sericulture schools and egg-production stations starting in the 1890's. Private filatures had also played an early role in sponsoring research teams pursuing crossbreeding experimentation and delayed incubation of silkworm eggs, making summer and fall crops possible. In the period from 1887 to 1907, Japanese production of summer and fall cocoons increased from 11,000 to 45,000 tons, to make up 35 percent of Japan's total yearly cocoon production. The Japanese government also developed an impressive network of domestic inspection stations to check and regulate cocoon and raw-silk quality, another measure designed to stimulate improved methods of sericulture.[7] At least in part because of early successes in the implementation of improved sericulture technique,[8] Japanese exports of raw silk rose rapidly from the 1890's onward, surpassing Chinese exports in total volume around 1909. Although Chinese exports of filature silk continued to rise as well, they never achieved the same pace of expansion as their Japanese counterparts. From 1909 to 1930, Japanese exports rose from 135,000 to 470,000 dan, while Chinese exports over the same period only rose from 130,000 to 152,000 dan.[9]

In the Yangzi delta, educational institutions devoted to sericulture also began to appear in the late 1890's, but did not take hold quite so rapidly as in Japan. Amidst several false starts by local gentry and county magistrates in various locales, two local schools for sericulture eventually succeeded, based on a combination of foreign advice, official support, and local student commitment.[10] These were the Hangzhou School for Sericulture (Hangzhou canxueguan) and the Hushuguan Sericulture School for Girls (Hushuguan nüzi canye xuexiao), about ten li outside of Suzhou. The Hangzhou school was established in 1897 by the local prefect, Lin Dichen, at the urging of the German customs commissioner in Ningbo, F. Kleinwachter, a man who took an active interest in silkworm disease and new methods for controlling it.[11] Kleinwachter was responsible for a Chinese student from Ningbo, Jiang Shengjin, traveling to France to study sericulture technique. When Jiang returned, the Hangzhou school was established by Lin Dichen under Jiang's supervision.[12] Japanese experts were hired to teach at the school, and many of the school's students traveled to Japan as well. Upon their return, the school used the students' newly acquired skills and commitment to the program to begin extensive development of its programs.[13] The Hushuguan school was founded in 1904 in Shanghai by a graduate of the Hangzhou school, Shi Liangcai. In 1911, the school began to receive provincial funding, and in 1912, it moved to Hushuguan.[14]

By the 1910's and 1920's, graduates of the Hangzhou and Hushuguan schools had founded private silkworm-egg breederies of their own and formed the core staff for additional schools and publicly funded extension stations. Thus, new sericulture-improvement specialists moved rapidly into careers combining public service with a new form of commercial venture—the selling of silkworm eggs to local peasants throughout the delta region.

Although there are no extensive family histories of sericulture reformers, we can deduce certain things about their social standing from available educational data. Reports on the staff of sericulture schools and extension stations, as well as brief biographical accounts provided by prominent individuals who engaged in sericulture reform, indicate a consistent picture of their educational backgrounds. Like the earliest Hangzhou school students, all received advanced training in technical programs related to sericulture, and many also went to Japan to study the latest developments in modern sericulture technique. Information culled from personnel records of silkworm-egg breederies in Zhejiang Province around 1930 indicates that all heads of such breederies had education in sericulture schools in the delta region, and many also had further training in Japan.[15] Data on five prominent individuals in Jiangsu Province point to similar patterns. Zheng Qunqiang, head of the Hushuguan school from 1918 through 1949, graduated from the Hangzhou School for Sericulture in 1902, stayed on as a teacher, and then went to Japan for further training.[16] Fei Dasheng, the elder sister of well-known anthropologist Fei Xiaotong and the wife of Zheng Qunqiang, was head of the extension office of the Hushuguan school in the 1920's and 1930's. She had attended Hushuguan as a student and had gone to Japan to study before assuming her position as head of the extension office.[17] Hu Yuankai, a teacher at the Hushuguan school in the 1930's, studied agriculture at the Wuxi Institute of Education from 1931 to 1934, and then went to Japan to study.[18] Chen Zirong, founder of the Sanwuguan egg breedery in Wuxi, studied at the Hangzhou School for Sericulture and got further technical training working for the Yongtai silk filature in Wuxi.[19] His sister, who was in charge of silkworm breeding and technical training at the Sanwuguan breedery, was also a graduate of Hushuguan.[20]

From this kind of biographical data, it is clear that sericulture reformers were part of a young generation of new local elites. Confucian examinations had been abolished in 1905, and new avenues for modern, technically oriented education evolved accordingly throughout the Yangzi delta. Modern schools replaced Confucian academies and trained students in a myriad of new skills. Sericulture schools provided one kind of new technical training, becoming an option for children of local elites to prepare for new career paths.

Unlike Confucian education before it, the new world of technical training in sericulture reform was open to women as well as men. New administrators of sericulture schools and extension stations tended to be male, but young women distributed eggs and taught improved technique among the peasantry. Because peasant women were mainly responsible for the work of silkworm raising, in theory at least, it was easier for female extension workers to establish necessary working relationships with them.[21] In the early 1930's, when a survey was taken in Wuxi of the staff of the provincial sericulture-reform program, twelve of thirteen top administrators were male, but 181 of 199 extension workers were women.[22] Although they filled more menial positions than their male counterparts, these women also had several years of special training in sericulture schools or extension-station programs.

When interviewed during the 1980's about their experiences, two people who had once been prominent in delta circles of sericulture reformers independently described themselves as *zhishi fenzi*, or "intellectuals." One of these individuals was Fei Dasheng, a woman and former director of extension work for the Hushuguan School, and the other was Hu Yuankai, a man and former instructor at Hushuguan.[23] Self-perception of their work in sericulture reform thus involved affiliation with traditional local elite status, long associated with intellectual pursuit, albeit of a very different type. Fei Dasheng's family also was described by her more famous brother, the eminent anthropologist Fei Xiaotong, as being of gentry status. Commenting on the gentry's fate during the 1940's, Fei Xiaotong described the gentry as "a product of history, caught in an impasse in the great transformation of the epoch."[24] While his comments referred primarily to the way in which the Communist revolution was putting an end to the gentry's roles as landlords and local wielders of power, in retrospect, his commentary might also be applied to a more gradual process of local elite transformation under way since at least the late nineteenth century. This transformation included a self-conscious turn among many local elites toward modernity, and involvement in a host of new economic activities at the local level designed to promote modern development. Where they succeeded, and how and why they sometimes failed, are revealed in part by the ways in which they applied themselves to the work of silk-industry reform.

ESCALATION OF GOVERNMENT SUPPORT AND
THE FAILURE TO MEET FILATURE DEMAND

Beginning in the mid-1910's, increased pressure from Western countries was brought to bear on Chinese silk-producers' organizations to work harder to improve the quality of Chinese raw silk. The United States, which feared that the Japanese would develop a monopoly for raw silk in the American market, was especially active in this effort.[25] In 1915, the U.S. Raw Silk Inspection Bureau invited representatives of the American and Chinese silk industries to a meeting in New York to discuss what measures were needed to raise the quality of Chinese raw silk.[26] In follow-up gestures, the American head of the bureau wrote to Chinese businessmen about new methods and personally visited China twice. He brought a film with him on these trips featuring new methods in sericulture technique and silk spinning.[27]

Increased foreign concern over the quality of Chinese raw silk resulted in 1918 in the founding of a new organization called the United Association for Sericulture Reform (Hezhong cansang gailiang hui). Members of this organization were all foreigners residing in Shanghai— French, Italians, British, Japanese, and Americans. Some members were filature owners, but most simply wished to import higher-quality raw silk produced in Chinese filatures. To this end, they established four experiment stations for silkworm-egg breeding funded jointly by foreign chambers of commerce in Shanghai and by a portion of Chinese tax revenue on the cocoon and silk trades.[28]

Initially the foreign chambers of commerce put up 30,000 taels to fund sericulture experiment stations. However, the foreign founders of the association also approached the Shanghai-based Jiangsu-Zhejiang-Anhui Silk Producers' Guild, an organization representing Chinese silk filaturists and cocoon merchants throughout the delta region, and urged them to find ways to provide long-term funding for such stations. The guild responded to this urging with a two-part proposal. First, cocoon merchants in Jiangsu, Zhejiang, and Anhui provinces were to pay a new surtax to the guild of one mao per dan of fresh cocoons purchased from peasants and forward the funds on to the new association. Second, the Yangzi River customs office responsible for collecting lijin and other transit taxes on the cocoon and silk trades would turn over 4,000 taels monthly to the association for programs in sericulture reform. The guild's proposal met with the approval of the governors and financial departments of Jiangsu, Zhejiang, and Anhui, and also of the national government.[29]

Although there are indications that this plan for increased public funding for sericulture reform met with localized cocoon-merchant resistance, the proposal seems to have taken hold and persisted well into the next decade.[30] By 1928, "reform surtaxes" levied on cocoon merchants (fuzheng gailiang jianshui or jianjuan) in Jiangsu existed to fund not only programs organized by the United Association for Sericulture Reform, but a whole range of additional government-sponsored efforts as well.[31] In 1929–30, sericulture-reform surtaxes on the cocoon trade in Jiangsu brought in 105,060 yuan, an amount equivalent to roughly 1 percent of the annual provincial budget.[32] Still more revenue was slated to come from new cocoon-firm registration fees, 50 percent of which were to fund sericulture-reform programs.[33]

Wuxi's preeminent position as cocoon-marketing capital of the delta region guaranteed that it would receive a sizable portion of this new sericulture-reform money. In 1918, two of the first four breederies established by the United Association for Sericulture Reform were located in Wuxi.[34] Also in that year, the provincial government of Jiangsu founded another public institution in Wuxi called the Sericulture Experiment Bureau (Jiangsu shengli yucan shiyansuo). The bureau had male and female staff and students who carried out experimentation and extension work. By 1921, the bureau had produced sixty-five varieties of improved silkworm eggs.[35] In 1923, the Wuxi County government also established a silkworm-egg breedery within the compound of buildings used by the

Wuxi Cocoon-Merchant Guild located in Beimenwai.[36] Meanwhile, private ventures in producing and selling improved silkworm eggs in Wuxi were flourishing as well, with at least five private egg breederies established from 1918 to 1926.[37]

When the Guomingdang established their new capital in Nanjing in 1927—one of the most important urban locales in Jiangsu Province— national government planning for economic development began to coincide ever more closely with programs for sericulture reform already in place in Jiangsu. Certainly, Guomindang statemakers saw potential political benefits in promoting economic development. Lloyd Eastman has pointed out, for example, that tapping new industry and commerce in Jiangsu for tax and loan support was a principal goal of the post-1927 Guomindang government.[38] However, as we shall see, promoting industrial development was an increasingly important goal in its own right for the Guomindang, and the Yangzi delta silk industry, centered to a large degree in Wuxi, became a project of special interest. In this context, public support for sericulture reform expanded rapidly in the years after 1927.

The new Jiangsu Department of Agriculture and Mines established under Guomindang supervision was charged with implementing national plans for economic development in the rural sector. Sericulture reform thus fell within its jurisdiction. Much of the department's blueprint for rural development in Jiangsu was presented in its first year-end report written in the summer of 1928.[39] In the report, the department urged each county in Jiangsu to focus on improvement in one "most essential" area of agriculture. Sixteen counties were to fund experiment stations for cotton, thirteen for rice, ten for other "mixed grains," fourteen for forestry, and eight for sericulture.[40] Standards were established for the level of funding per month for each type of station, and if the counties had insufficient funds, the province was to subsidize the stations up to the designated amount. Agricultural experiment stations were to be funded at the level of 600 yuan per month, forestry stations at 500 yuan, and sericulture stations at 400 yuan. A total of 234,210 yuan, or roughly 2 percent of annual provincial revenues, were to be available from the province for bringing the funding up to the suggested levels in 1929–30.[41] Among all Jiangsu counties receiving funding for programs in sericulture reform under these new guidelines, Wuxi soon emerged as the leader.

There were also two new heavily funded provincial agencies designed to reform sericulture established in Wuxi in 1928. The first of these was the Provincial Sericulture Experiment Station in Wuxi (Jiangsu shengli

Wuxi cansi shiyanchang). One hundred thousand yuan was budgeted for the founding of this station, which became the main institution for all of Jiangsu in the areas of silkworm-egg breeding, mulberry-sapling cultivation, and experimental work to develop new silkworm-egg varieties. The station planned to run thirty-four extension bureaus (zhidaosuo) in eight counties in the spring of 1929. Peasants receiving advice in silkworm raising from these bureaus were required to purchase improved silkworm eggs. In keeping with this policy, a second provincial agency established in Wuxi was the Silkworm Egg Inspection Bureau (Jiangsu shengli canzhong jianyansuo), which regulated egg cards produced by private breederies.[42] Thirteen such breederies were established from 1926 to 1929.[43]

As these provincial programs in sericulture reform were proliferating, filature investors in Wuxi were launching a new drive for expansion referred to as the "golden age." We have examined the details of filature expansion in the years from 1920 to 1930 in Chapter 5. We should note here at least one important fact associated with the "golden-age" phenomenon: the number of Wuxi filatures doubled in the space of just three years, rising from twenty-five in 1927 to fifty by the end of 1929. I have questioned just how successful this expansion was in terms of filature investment and management patterns. Most filatures continued to use the system of "split ownership/management," thus perpetuating long-standing problems in capital reinvestment. What I have not yet examined, however, is how the promise of extensive government support for sericulture reform worked to fuel filature-industry expansion. Filature investors in the Yangzi delta region had long worried about the problems of inadequate cocoon supply; once the Guomindang government stepped in with new funding for sericulture reform, new filatures were built at a staggering pace.

Despite the promise of larger quantities of high-quality cocoons, the sheer number of new filatures guaranteed that demand would escalate much more rapidly than new supply. In the fall of 1929, reports appearing in the Shanghai-based Banker's Weekly noted that only Wuxi and its neighbors to the west, Wujin and Zhenjiang, were able to implement programs in promoting new crops of fall silkworms immediately, and the quantity of new cocoons on the market thus failed to keep up with filature demand.[44] Filature demand for cocoons had been so intense in the 1929 spring season in Wuxi that by early September, all Wuxi filatures were anxiously preparing to send out cocoon-firm contractors, hoping to purchase as many fall cocoons as possible to avoid plant closures.[45]

Data on silkworm raising from the SSRI survey of Wuxi peasant households for 1928 and 1929 also point to the rather tenuous progress made in using improved silkworm eggs, especially for the new summer and fall crops so eagerly anticipated by Wuxi filature investors. Among the 128 households in the SSRI-survey sample, roughly half used improved egg varieties in the spring seasons in 1928 and 1929. But for the all-important additional summer and fall crops, these numbers were much smaller. Only twenty-six households attempted summer crops in 1928, with nineteen of those households using improved silkworm eggs and only eight households successfully raising their silkworm broods to maturity. For 1929, only slightly better results obtained—forty households attempted summer crops, thirty used improved egg varieties, and sixteen raised their broods to maturity. In the fall of 1928, the numbers were even less encouraging—only thirteen households started fall crops, all using improved silkworm eggs, with ten raising their broods to maturity.[46]

From these data, it appears that realizing the goal of substantially improved cocoon crops in Wuxi was not going to be a particularly easy, or speedy, task. To understand the uphill battle facing even the best-intentioned sericulture reformers and their peasant clients in Wuxi, we need to take a more detailed look at struggles to comprehend the complex constellation of factors necessary to produce more and better cocoons.

EXTENSION WORK: PERCEPTIONS OF "THE OTHER" AND THE PRACTICE OF SERICULTURE REFORM

Anthropologists and cultural theorists have analyzed visions of "the other" as one, often negative, outcome of encounters with strangers, both within and outside one's own culture. After listening to an interviewee's descriptions of her experiences in the countryside in the course of sericulture extension work, I began to believe that such visions factored into problems facing sericulture reform. As elite reformers and Wuxi peasants each looked at "the other" close up for the first time in the course of sericulture extension work, the subject's "gaze" became more than a metaphorical one—both sides stared long and hard at each other in a real sense, and experienced difficulties in interpreting the meaning of what they saw.

To begin exploration of this encounter, let us first consider what extension work actually entailed. Most extension workers were young female graduates of sericulture schools and experiment-station training programs. Their tasks required going out to the countryside in sericulture areas, making contact with peasant households, and explaining better sericulture techniques, or, in their view, imparting the "scientific truths" of silkworm raising to the peasantry. Two basic ideas formed the core of their message to peasants: silkworms died because of the spread of bacterial infections; and to prevent the spread of such disease, silkworms in their earliest stages of development required constant temperature and the separation of diseased silkworms from healthy ones. But as far as extension workers were concerned, peasants were resistant to these messages for two reasons. The first was that they lived in very "backward" (luohou) conditions, and the second was that they had their own "traditions" (chuantong), or customary ways of interpreting silkworm death. For the peasants' part, they were, indeed, skeptical about the messages they received from extension workers about silkworm raising. The language of sericulture reform itself must have sounded very peculiar to peasant women. What was "scientific truth," after all, and what was a "bacterial" silkworm disease? These words were not in the daily vocabularies of peasant women who cared for silkworms; how were they to interpret them?

The following passage from my interview with Fei Dasheng, head of the Hushuguan extension bureau, reveals the depth of the dilemma in establishing two-way communication on these issues:

In 1923, the Hushuguan school set up an extension bureau, and in the spring of 1924, we sent four people out to the countryside in the vicinity of Zhenze zhen in Wujiang County to start propagating advanced scientific methods. We organized the peasants into a group to cooperatively raise silkworms [in their first stages of growth] and started to train them in scientific technique. At first, the peasants didn't quite trust us, these "foreign teachers" (yang xiansheng). After a while, as they saw the advantages of scientific sericulture (kexue yangcan), they finally began to warm up to us. We set up a study group (xuexi ban) and had each household send one young woman to study with us. The peasants didn't understand the truth (daoli) of silkworm disease transmission, but, acting according to tradition (chuantong), thought that simply not letting outsiders (shengren) observe [their silkworms] would prevent disease. But later, after we got through to them, they understood silkworm disease prevention. In 1925, we organized five such instruction groups (zhidao zu). . . .

People who propagated scientific methods in the countryside had a really difficult life. In rainy periods especially, when we had to go out to instruct [the peasants] in techniques for keeping silkworms warm, the muddy roads were impassable and getting good results was really difficult.[47]

As seen through this account, vocabulary on both sides of the peas-
ant/reformer relationship reveals something about the difficulties in understanding "the other." Take, for example, the use of the term "yang
xiansheng" by peasants to refer to extension workers. "Yang" literally
means "foreign," and one might interpret its meaning here as having
something to do with the production of a different kind of silkworm to
meet demand by the modern silk-filature industry, a foreign-oriented
export industry. But the use of the term "yang" in the early twentieth
century was also very loaded—to describe something, or someone, as
"yang" indicated a skepticism and wariness, since such things, or people, had the potential to change things in unpredictable, incomprehensi-
ble ways. The use of the term "xiansheng" here is perhaps even more
telling. Meaning "teacher," "sir," or "gentleman," it was a term used to
show deference to superiors. But superiors who were also yang were
most likely considered dangerous, or at least worthy of suspicion, on the
grounds that their intentions could not be easily ascertained. It is worth
noting as well that to address women with this term was unusual, indicating that when they viewed extension workers in their midst, peasant
women may even have lost the capacity to see them as members of the
same sex.

For the extension workers, as they observed peasant life, they seem to
have become ever more solidly convinced of their own validity as bearers
of the scientific "truth" of modern sericulture technique. In this short
passage, Fei used terms meaning "modern technique" or "scientific sericulture," or some combination of such terms, five times, underscoring
the importance and superiority of what extension workers had to offer
backward, tradition-bound peasant women. And Fei's final image of extension workers trudging through muddy, impassable roads seemed to
be a way to reemphasize that it was the backwardness of peasant attitudes and the resulting material conditions in which peasants lived that
made the realization of the benefits of modern sericulture so difficult.

Writings of Hushuguan extension workers dating from the 1920's
make similar points about peasant life and its impact on extension work.
In the early 1920's, the Hushuguan school began its own publication in
newspaper format called *Nücan* (Women's sericulture). In an article entitled "Opinions on Reforming Antiquated Methods of Silkworm Raising in Wuxi," one extension worker wrote that peasants simply could
not understand that bad weather affected silkworm raising, preferring to
attribute the problems to fate. In 1923, weather had been an important
factor in the spread of bacteria, causing silkworms to harden and die in
Wuxi, but peasants had difficulty accepting this explanation from out-

siders. Instead, they insisted on the roles of local gods and spirits in causing the problems.[48] In a second article written by an extension worker
about her experiences in Zhenze, the area discussed above by Fei Dasheng, problems with peasant belief in the intervention of evil spirits
were noted. The placing of red paper flowers for good luck in the center
of silkworm-raising trays was described as an example of how peasant
women clung to "superstition" in the area of sericulture technique.
They did so because their households' livelihoods depended so heavily
on silkworms. But it was extremely frustrating for extension workers
nonetheless, since such beliefs stood in the way of convincing peasant
women of the merits of scientific sericulture technique.[49]

If it was hard enough to convince peasant women of the benefits of
such relatively simple things as temperature and disease control, when it
came to more sophisticated, and more costly, efforts in sericulture reform, the difficulty of extension workers' tasks escalated accordingly.
Another critical component of their work was to promote and sell improved silkworm eggs to peasant households in sericulture areas, and to
introduce the benefits of refrigeration technique to produce second and
third crops of summer and fall silkworms. As early as 1899, the second
year of operation of the Hangzhou school, students there had produced
and marketed 1,000 cards of improved silkworm eggs. In the following
years, egg cards were purchased at the school by a Nanjing native named
Zhang, and distributed to peasants in Jiangning County surrounding
Nanjing.[50] By 1900, the school also had sold egg cards of crossbred varieties, and sent students into areas where peasants used them to check on
their progress.[51] By the 1920's, it was clear that the goal of many students
of the sericulture school in Hushuguan was to establish their own private silkworm-egg breederies, and to sell improved variety eggs to the
peasantry throughout the delta region.[52]

Many breederies established by Hushuguan graduates and others were
located in Wuxi. This move made a great deal of sense, since, as we have
seen, Wuxi was the most important locale in southern Jiangsu by the
1920's for sericulture and the cocoon trade. Peasants in Wuxi primarily
had cultivated their own eggs for the spring silkworm season each year
by allowing a portion of their cocoons to hatch and lay eggs, preserving
them in a cool, dry location until the following spring. The type of egg
used for this procedure went through only one development cycle per
year. However, there also had been an egg type available in Wuxi that
would incubate four times during the warm months from spring to fall.
Some Wuxi peasants had raised a second and third crop of summer and
fall silkworms with this egg type, but it had been time-consuming and

troublesome for peasants to constantly attend to the egg-incubation process. Most peasants thus had opted to use the first type of egg and to raise only one crop of spring silkworms.[53]

In 1925, the Hushuguan school first imported refrigeration devices that allowed for the artificial creation of a cold dormant period for silkworm eggs, and thus offered a new means to raise fall silkworms. Using refrigeration, a proportion of each spring's eggs were stored by breederies and experiment stations at a temperature of 2.5 degrees centigrade or below, for a period of forty to fifty days. This created an artificial winter, after which eggs could be brought out to hatch, sometime in late August. Although the Hushuguan school pioneered these techniques with the help of a visiting Japanese instructor, they spread quickly to Wuxi and further stimulated the development of private breederies there.[54] The Sanwuguan breedery in Wuxi purchased equipment for its own refrigeration room and allowed other breederies to use the room as well.[55] In the area of public facilities, the Jiangsu Department of Agriculture and Mines allocated 30,000 yuan for the installation of an Amana refrigeration room in the Provincial Sericulture Experiment Station in Wuxi, which all breederies throughout the province could use.[56]

Although the availability of improved silkworm eggs and refrigeration made possible the expansion of summer and fall cocoon crops, we already have seen from data on such crops from Wuxi in 1928 and 1929 that the hoped-for expansion did not materialize very rapidly. We have no firsthand accounts of the reactions to refrigeration in Wuxi, but we can only surmise that peasants would not have been inclined very favorably toward its use, at least at first. If "foreign" extension workers were a problem, how could the "foreign" equipment that they brought into rural areas have been any better from the peasants' point of view? But as the possibilities for using refrigeration and improved silkworm eggs expanded rapidly in Wuxi from the mid-1920's onward, other events coalesced in ways that only added to peasant skepticism.

EGG-SALE ABUSE: LOCAL ELITE COMPETITION
AND PEASANT RESISTANCE

In an absolute sense, improved silkworm eggs were not terribly expensive. In the spring of 1929, peasant households in the SSRI survey who used improved silkworm eggs spent an average of 1.82 yuan on their purchases.[57] Yet even in a prosperous place like Wuxi, we have seen that many peasant households were relatively poor. None of the twenty households in Mantetsu-surveyed villages in 1940 had much cash to spend on what the Japanese researchers referred to as "productive investment," spending less than 1 percent of their cash incomes in this way. The largest "productive investment" outlays were for mulberry-leaf purchase, with a total of about 13 yuan spent on mulberry leaves among all twenty households. Other "productive investments" included a total of 10 yuan for agricultural wage labor; 3 yuan for silkworm-egg card purchase; 2 yuan for farm-animal maintenance; and 2 yuan for fertilizer purchase.[58] Most of the cash income among all 80 households in the three Mantetsu-surveyed villages was used to purchase rice for consumption and for rent payments.[59] Among households in both the SSRI and the Mantetsu surveys, debt was also an important issue. Ninety-four of 128 households in the SSRI survey sample were in debt, at the average rate of 188 yuan per household.[60] Eleven of the 20 households in the Mantetsu survey for whom loan data were solicited were in debt, with 7 households owing 100 yuan or more.[61]

The point to be made here is not that purchase of improved silkworm eggs from private breederies or state-supported experiment stations was an onerous economic burden for Wuxi peasant households. Rather, in an economic environment in which choices had to be made about how to invest relatively scarce surplus cash, peasants first had to be convinced that silkworm-egg purchases would be beneficial. Concrete demonstration of improved volume and quality of cocoons was thus necessary in an immediate sense. Reliable results were critical since, as we have seen, peasant women were skeptical of what extension workers told them about improved methods of sericulture in the first place, and needed tangible reassurance that new methods, and products, would improve their cocoon output.

Unfortunately for sericulture workers intent on winning the confidence of the peasantry and furthering the progress of silk-industry reform, the atmosphere of rapid filature expansion and escalating competition for cocoon purchase that marked the late 1920's also created new opportunities for manipulation of silkworm-egg sales. The first hint of problems with selling silkworm eggs appeared in reports circulating in commercial journals in the fall of 1929. The words "profiteer" (jianshang) and "speculation" (touji) began to appear with increasing frequency in general assessments of silkworm-egg sales. Because of escalating demand by filatures for cocoons produced from improved egg varieties, prices for egg cards began to rise. One method designed to combat this problem was the organization of egg-selling cooperatives by several breederies in the Hushuguan area, to sell eggs directly to peasants at controlled prices. Silkworm-egg cards were also imported from Japan to help alleviate an anticipated 100,000-card shortage in the spring season of 1930. The Jiangsu Department of Agriculture and Mines planned to buy 10,000 such egg cards at two yuan per card, a price higher than that charged for Chinese improved varieties. The department hoped that a plan could be worked out by the Provincial Sericulture Experiment Station in Wuxi to sell them to peasants more cheaply.[62]

Despite these good intentions, reports began to circulate widely in the fall of 1929 that high-priced, bad eggs were sold to peasants since the supply of good eggs was insufficient to meet demand. In Wuxi, an incident occurred in which Japanese businessmen used Chinese agents to go to silkworm-egg breederies, buy eggs, and sell them at prices higher than those prevailing in the market. This happened in six townships in Wuxi in the fall of 1929. The agents were able to get the higher prices they asked by telling peasants they would get eighty yuan per dan for their cocoons. This created a mad rush to buy the eggs and a general state of confusion. Moreover, when peasants began to incubate the eggs, they discovered that they were inferior in quality, falling ill instead of developing into worms, and dying. In this case, not only did peasants pay higher prices for eggs, they also lost their entire year's silkworm crop.[63]

As reports on problems with egg sales began to accumulate, the Jiangsu Department of Agriculture and Mines decided that an investigation was called for, and it dispatched an agricultural affairs investigator, Qian Shilin, to the field. On October 27, 1929, Qian spent the day in four villages of Ward (qu) Two in Jiangyin County, where he witnessed several cases of peddlers selling eggs, falsely claiming they were from Hushuguan and other provincial institutions. They often charged an inflated price of 1.5 yuan per egg card, when the average price for egg cards was around 1 yuan. Qian suggested that the head of each ward, the quzhang, put a stop to these practices in all counties where this occurred, including Wuxi. He also suggested that identification badges be worn by official sales representatives of breederies and that the names of the varieties available for sale by breederies be posted publicly.[64] The quzhang was a likely choice by the provincial investigator to take responsibility in these matters since the qu, or ward, had been created in 1927 as a subcounty agency of Guomindang provincial authority.[65] We shall see shortly how the quzhang became an increasingly important figure in matters involving the silkworm-egg trade.

Additional cases of egg-sale profiteering reported in Wuxi, Wujin, and Jiangyin counties in the fall of 1929 finally led the Department of Agriculture and Mines to ask county governments to become more fully involved in investigating cases of egg-sale abuse.[66] Under pressure from the provincial government to get egg-sale problems under control, the Wuxi County government undertook investigations of two serious cases of egg-sale abuse during the fall months of 1929. Much to the dismay of provincial authorities, these two cases did not involve unscrupulous strangers roaming the countryside and randomly preying upon peasants. Rather, they concerned two trusted members of the local elite who were professionally involved in the business of producing and marketing improved silkworm eggs.

The first full-scale investigation of a serious case of egg-sale abuse in Wuxi centered on Sun Zhongjun, head of the Provincial Sericulture Experiment Station. Sun had been an active and aggressive leader of sericulture reform in Wuxi in 1928 and 1929. He attended provincial meetings called by the Department of Agriculture and Mines to discuss sericulture reform.[67] He also attended meetings of the Wuxi County government in April and May 1929, where he acted as an advocate to secure county-level funding for the Sericulture Experiment Station.[68] For these efforts, Sun was praised highly by the provincial Department of Finance and Department of Agriculture and Mines, and was held up as an example for other county officials to follow. Both departments urged all counties to use the same method of negotiation at county government meetings that Sun had employed to determine funding levels for agricultural reform.[69]

At precisely the same time Sun was performing his public duties so admirably, he also was lapsing into misuse of county experiment-station facilities for his own private gain. In the spring of 1929, Sun and his assistant manager at the station, Xu Yiru, agreed to let some of the experimental eggs hatch into cocoons and to sell them. They publicly reported only 413 yuan of revenue from these cocoon sales, but private account books later revealed that they had actually earned 1,652 yuan. Sun and Xu then proceeded to establish a private breedery named Dafeng, using the money they had made from these illegal cocoon sales as initial capital. But instead of setting up this new breedery in a separate location, they simply used the personnel, buildings, and eggs of the county station, producing and selling egg cards to peasants under the name of the Dafeng breedery. It was impossible to differentiate between the private breedery and the county station since they had now become one and the same operation.[70]

All of this might have passed unnoticed if Sun and Xu had not sold 10,000 cards of inferior-quality silkworm eggs to Wuxi peasants in the spring of 1929, eggs that were so bad they failed to form cocoons. Complaints brought this matter to the attention of the county government. An initial investigation was conducted in August, implicating Sun and Xu as the culprits behind this scheme. However, the county government did not report this incident to the provincial Department of Agriculture and Mines until November, and the department was incensed that neither Sun nor Xu had yet been fired or brought to justice by the county government. Although the department insisted that prompt action be taken, it still left the matter to the jurisdiction of the county, with a recommendation that a county court trial begin immediately. To insure that the two men would be brought to justice, however, the Department of Agriculture and Mines confiscated all the account books involved as well as reports of county investigations of the matter. The department seemed to be looking for ways to gain leverage to guarantee that the trial would begin immediately.[71]

A second serious case of egg-sale abuse in Wuxi investigated by the county government in 1929 involved Gong Canju, the local manager of the United Association for Sericulture Reform's Office Thirteen, located in Wuxi. This office was set up to sell silkworm eggs produced at the Zhenjiang breedery of the association to peasants in the area of Yuqi zhen in Wuxi.[72] In March 1929, a sericulture cooperative also was established in Yuqi zhen, called the Dongfang cooperative. One hundred and twenty households joined the co-op, paying membership fees of three yuan each. Gong Canju was also the principal organizer of this co-op.[73]

The organization of sericulture cooperatives of this type had become part of Jiangsu provincial policy on sericulture reform. Promoted by provincial and county extension bureaus, co-ops were collectively to buy and cultivate silkworm eggs.[74] Co-ops also assisted peasants with bringing their eggs through the difficult early phases of growth by housing them in a special building where disinfectant use and temperature control were monitored carefully. After this period had passed, the worms were distributed to individual member households.[75] An attractive feature of cooperative policy was that organizers were eligible for bank loans from the newly established Jiangsu Peasant Bank (Nongmin yinhang).[76] These loans were both long-term and low-interest, and thus were very desirable.[77] Because of these loan policies, co-op organizers had at their immediate disposal not only membership fees but also large sums of borrowed cash, often amounting to several thousand yuan, which they invested in silkworm-egg purchase.

As head of the Dongfang sericulture co-op in Wuxi, Gong Canju made arrangements for a first purchase of silkworm eggs in the spring season of 1929 that served his own interests as well—7,000–8,000 Zhenjiang egg cards from Office Thirteen of the United Association for Sericulture Reform, of which he was also manager. However, instead of providing the contracted number of egg cards to the co-op, Gong supplied only 3,000, and substituted cards made with another egg variety from the Anding breedery in Wuxi to make up the balance. The peasant members of the co-op had no trust in this second type of egg, and the Dongfang co-op, under Gong's direction, rapidly capitalized on this situation. A co-op outlet store (*menshibu*) was set up where the Zhenjiang-variety eggs were sold to co-op members at a price of 1.2 to 1.5 yuan instead of the normal price of 1 yuan on the grounds that the eggs were in such great demand. Meanwhile, co-op members who had contracted to buy eggs ahead of time and who had had them delivered by co-op personnel to their homes received the Anding-variety eggs instead of those of the Zhenjiang variety. This state of affairs so angered co-op members that three of them, Feng Yibao, Mei Guihe, and Gong A'liu, went to Office Thirteen to vent their frustration. There they smashed equipment and the sales counter, seized the person working as clerk at the time, and carried him off to the ward office, where they demanded an immediate judgment on the situation by the quzhang.[78]

The quzhang initially chose to confront only one of the issues at hand—inflated prices charged for Zhenjiang-variety eggs. He suggested a compromise solution, establishing a ratio of value whereby every ten Zhenjiang egg cards would be worth eleven Anding cards. This seemed to satisfy everyone for the moment, and the daily disputes that had been raging stopped. But the issue of Gong Canju's manipulation of his dual status as manager of Office Thirteen and of the Dongfang co-op remained unsettled. Indeed, the quzhang and Gong actually collaborated to conceal his involvement, leaving his name out of the report on the matter entirely. Only the three Dongfang co-op members who were involved in damaging Office Thirteen were named in the quzhang's report.[79]

In the aftermath of the violence at Office Thirteen, the Zhenjiang breedery of the United Association for Sericulture Reform asked the quzhang to investigate further and to find a way to pay for damages done. The Wuxi County government then also asked the quzhang to come up with a "peaceful settlement" of the matter. The new settlement suggested by the quzhang ordered the payment of damages by the three co-op members who had been involved in the incident, and financial restitution by Office Thirteen to peasants who had bought eggs at higher prices. However, the quzhang still did not name Gong Canju as a responsible party in this affair and recommended no action against him. As a result, the peasants continued to "buzz," and the Jiangsu Department of Agriculture and Mines decided to step in.[80]

A new investigation was conducted by the Wuxi County government under pressure from the Department of Agriculture and Mines during which Gong Canju's role in the whole affair was finally revealed. The Department of Agriculture and Mines was indignant because the county government and the quzhang had tried all along to conceal Gong's pivotal role. They therefore made a request to the highest authority possible, asking the national-level Ministry of Agriculture and Mines (Nong-kuang bu) to "allow" Wuxi County authorities now to accuse Gong as they saw fit.[81]

These two cases of abuse of government-sanctioned silkworm-egg sales in Wuxi provide important insights into the complicated dilemmas of sericulture reform. Sericulture reformers were dedicated increasingly to promoting a new form of modernity among the local peasantry in Wuxi. However, once they wielded a certain degree of political power derived from their new roles, acting simultaneously as representatives of government agencies and as managers of new private ventures in silkworm-egg production, the potential arose for abuse of these positions. When such abuses occurred and provincial-level officials attempted to curb them, the first inclination of those involved in the abuse was to turn to bureaucrats at the county and subcounty levels for protection and support. As we saw in Chapter 4, when local cocoon merchants in Wuxi experienced frustration with provincial government on the issue of escalating cocoon-trade taxes, they, too, turned to county-level officials for assistance in finding or creating loopholes in new laws. These actions on the part of cocoon merchants and sericulture-reform specialists were, in the end, a form of reliance on past traditions of local governance through which local elites and local government had often allied in the defense of common, local interests. Thus, even the apparently "criminal" behavior of a man like Gong Canju could be concealed by county-level officials, as he was a man upon whom the county government counted for the implementation of ambitious, and well-funded, provincial programs for sericulture reform.

On the other side of things, of course, stood frustrated peasants who tried to purchase reliable strains of improved silkworm eggs at agreed-upon prices. When emotions escalated, and disruption of the normal business of selling silkworm eggs occurred, it was the peasants involved in resistance who first were required by county government to make amends. Luddite behavior was not to be tolerated in the arena of silk-

152 Imparting Modernity

industry reform, and the protection of property associated with modernity had now become one of the new responsibilities of local government. In the face of such government action, we are left to wonder how peasant attitudes about sericulture reform were affected. Could peasants possibly have become any more sanguine about modernity in relationship to sericulture, as local officials stepped in to support even its most manipulative messengers?

TOO LITTLE, TOO LATE?

Previous studies of the Chinese silk industry in the early twentieth century have concluded that mediocre results in improving the quality of raw silk for export were a case of "too little, too late" in the area of sericulture reform. Behind such a conclusion is the assumption that because China's early effort to industrialize had no strong government support, as it did in Meiji Japan, for example, the modern silk industry in China was doomed to failure.[82] But we have seen in this chapter that efforts to improve raw materials to support modern silk production in the Yangzi delta had both private and public support from the 1890's onward. And in the 1920's, as the Guomindang government came to power in the region, large sums were poured into programs to support sericulture reform, especially in Wuxi. To suggest that public support was not forthcoming to assist modern silk-industry development in China is thus an insufficient explanation for the relatively slow pace at which sericulture reform proceeded.

Having viewed close-up some specific events and problems encountered in the process of sericulture reform in Jiangsu Province and in Wuxi, we have seen that a complex constellation of factors contributed to its slow momentum. Elite reformers and their peasant audience, especially female members on both sides, found communication difficult when it came to delivering and interpreting the messages of sericulture reform. Reformers insisted on the backwardness of the peasantry and their inability to understand their "messages of modernity" as the chief obstacle to successful implementation of new technique. Peasant women, on the other hand, were skeptical of outsiders who claimed to have miraculous cures for the ongoing problems of silkworm disease and death. Complicating the situation was the relative scarcity of ready cash among the peasantry to invest in new sericulture methods. Proof that new methods and improved silkworm eggs would produce substantial, immediate gains in cocoon output were essential if obstacles to communication and trust were to be overcome.

The uphill battle to make progress in sericulture reform became steeper still when a few among the reformer community at the local level in Wuxi misused their new positions of prominence as leaders in state-supported institutions. Ironically, it was the environment of rapid expansion of sericulture reform, marked by the input of substantial provincial funding after 1927, that created the potential for manipulation of silkworm-egg sales. Rapid filature growth in the same period created an upsurge in demand for more and better cocoons, further expanding the potential for manipulation. But when peasants resisted unscrupulous behavior among sericulture reformers, they faced local government officials who seemed more interested in concealing the activities of local elite wrongdoers than in fully rectifying the situation.

While provincial- and national-level agencies of the Guomindang government were concerned about the behavior of county-level officials in such matters, it would take several more years before new government-sponsored programs to control abuses in the area of sericulture reform would materialize. And as we shall see in Chapter 8, despite the Guomindang government's good intentions to more fully regulate both the cocoon trade and sericulture reform, these programs, once in place, also had the potential to produce serious negative outcomes for the peasantry. Guomindang regulation included not just the correction of abuses of the past, but also new plans to set cocoon prices by government decree, a critical issue on which peasant livelihood in Wuxi rested.

8

Success at Last? Bourgeois Practice and State Intervention Under the Nationalists

The early 1930's proved to be a critical period for revamping the Wuxi silk industry. While the temporary collapse of the world silk market during the Great Depression created a new sense of urgency for all filature-industry investors to achieve the goals of silk-industry reform, it was a new alliance between one powerful filature owner in Wuxi, Xue Shouxuan, and an increasingly interventionist Guomindang state that shaped new institutional structures to promote silk-industry growth.

This chapter proceeds on two fronts, beginning with elements of Xue Shouxuan's new "bourgeois practice" in relationship to Wuxi silk filatures. On one level, "vertical integration" of management and production might be seen as the heart of Xue's new plan, a style of bourgeois strategizing that economic historians since Alfred Chandler have considered an important model for achieving industrial success.[1] But on a second level, we shall also see that "merger" was another important tactic employed by Xue, as he forcefully took over failing filatures following the darkest years of the Great Depression.[2] The second major area of inquiry in this chapter thus focuses on the ways in which a more overtly activist approach by Xue—one might even be tempted to characterize his behavior as "coercive" with respect to other filaturists, cocoon merchants, silk-industry reformers, and the peasantry—came together with a new style of Guomindang state-making. The result was a powerful coalition between bourgeois practice and state policy to more thoroughly regulate, and ultimately to control, Wuxi silk-industry development.

NEW DIRECTIONS FOR WUXI FILATURES

We have seen in Chapter 5 that the predominant form of silk-filature organization in Wuxi was based on the principles of "split owner-ship/management." In this system, two independent groups—filature owners, and filature managers who rented the plants from owners on a yearly basis—kept their investment capital and operating capital separate, with neither side investing heavily in plant upgrades or routine repair, or in the internal reorganization of work within filatures that new equipment might require. Although the filature-investor community in Wuxi was reluctant to attribute poor silk quality to low rates of investment in capital improvements, other observers of the filature industry pointed increasingly by the 1920's to the system of "split ownership/management" as one of the critical weaknesses of China's modern silk industry.

By the mid-1920's, plans to change internal filature organization began to emerge in Wuxi, pioneered by Xue Shouxuan, a man with a long family history in Wuxi silk-industry development. Xue Shouxuan was the grandson of Xue Fucheng, a prominent late-Qing statesman who had served in diplomatic missions abroad in the 1880's, and who took an active interest in the modern economies he observed in his travels.[3] Xue Shouxuan's father, Xue Nanming, had been a comprador who had helped initiate the cocoon trade in Wuxi and also had founded some of Wuxi's earliest filatures, as we have seen in Chapter 3. Xue Shouxuan himself went abroad to pursue modern education, studying railway engineering and management at the University of Illinois.[4] Upon his return to China, he went back to Wuxi, his native place, and assumed control over the Xue family's silk-industry enterprise.

In 1926, Xue Shouxuan took over primary responsibility for five silk filatures in Wuxi organized over a fifteen-year period by his father.[5] Like other early filature organizers in Wuxi, Xue Nanming had used the system of "split ownership/management," renting filatures to managers in return for fixed rental fees per reeling machine.[6] Xue Shouxuan's sojourn abroad, however, seems to have set him apart from his fellow filaturists in terms of new ideas for industrial management.[7] When Xue Nanming died in 1926, his son ended old-style "split ownership/management" practices within the family enterprise. Although Xue Shouxuan assigned several men to manage the family filatures, they did not rent the filatures and pay the Xue family a fee in return; rather, they became Xue's hired employees and acted primarily as his personal assistants.[8] From this time onward, Xue set about to supervise filature development more directly.

Under his new personal management system, Xue's first effort was to improve the silk-reeling equipment in his filatures. He began with the Yongtai filature, the oldest of the family filatures, replacing old-style Italian reeling equipment, at which women worked in a seated position, with new equipment from Japan, at which women worked while standing.[9] The advantage of the Japanese machine was that two functions that were performed by two separate workers using the Italian machine—tending the cocoons as they bobbed in hot water to loosen their silk fibers, and reeling the silk from the cocoons—could be performed by the same worker using the Japanese machine.[10] Thus, with the new-style Japanese equipment, labor costs could be cut and output per worker increased.

Xue Shouxuan also organized a large new filature soon after he assumed directorship of the family business—the Huaxin filature, built in 1928—and equipped it completely with new-style Japanese machines.[11] In 1931, Xue started management- and worker-training programs, as well as a combined live-in boarding and training program (yangchengsuo) for female workers, at the Huaxin filature.[12] The goal of these programs was to improve managers' and workers' knowledge of silk-filature administration or reeling technique, thus further improving the filature's capacity to produce high-quality raw silk. Many male trainees were sent to Japan for further technical training under the auspices of the Huaxin program.[13] In its seven years of operation, Huaxin trained more than 3,000 filature workers and over 200 technical specialists.[14]

Other aspects of Xue's new plans for the silk industry extended beyond the reorganization of silk filatures. In 1930, he set up a sericulture affairs office (canshibu) under the direction of the Yongtai filature, and built two egg breederies in Wuxi and Zhenjiang. The Yongtai sericulture affairs office also began to organize sericulture cooperatives, promoting extension work and sale of egg cards produced by the Yongtai breederies.[15] Under this system, the breederies prearranged contracts with peasants to purchase the cocoons they raised from Yongtai's improved egg cards. Xue's goal for this operation was not only to improve the quality of peasant cocoons available to Yongtai, but also to guarantee their continuous supply. In an effort to increase his capacity for control at the opposite end of the marketing process, Xue also established an office in New York in 1930 to act as a direct exporting agency for raw silk produced in his filatures.[16] These projects were intended to increase the quality and quantity of silk exports and to enhance Xue's control capacities in all stages of silk production and marketing.

By the eve of the Great Depression, Xue Shouxuan had begun important innovations in reorganization of the Wuxi silk industry. With this start in a different style of silk-filature management, Xue seemed to be staking out new leadership territory for himself in the area of silk-industry development. As we shall see, the Depression soon had a devastating effect on the central China silk industry. But Xue Shouxuan would survive intact, and in the end would prove capable of using the negative effects of the Depression to further increase his own control of the silk industry.

The effects of the Depression on the central China silk industry were felt progressively over a period of three years. Volume of trade and value of silk sales began to decline in 1930, but it was not until 1932 that the market finally bottomed out. Table 22 reports volume and value of raw-silk sales from 1926 through 1932. As we see from data in this table, there was a period of substantial gain in the late 1920's, an era we earlier characterized as the "golden age" of Wuxi silk production. We saw in Chapter 7 how new Guomindang policies in the area of sericulture reform helped to spur this sudden growth spurt. Other factors in international currency markets also contributed to this upsurge. An international fall in silver prices after 1926 contributed to a period of overall prosperity for Chinese industry. Since silver prices were declining during these years, and China was the only major country still using a silver standard, the effect was a substantial devaluation of China's currency and an expanding market for Chinese exports. Foreign investment was also attracted to China by this situation, and wholesale prices in Shanghai increased by nearly 25 percent from 1926 to 1931.[17] Under these conditions, the Chinese silk market suffered only moderate declines in 1930 and 1931, but by 1932, the "golden age" was clearly over. Sales volume plummeted to 78,219 dan in that year, only 41 percent of the 1929 figure. The decline in raw silk value was even more drastic, with the 1932 figure of 32,932,250 taels only 22 percent of the 1929 high.

As demand for raw silk on the international market declined, filatures were unable to sell enough silk to repay the substantial loans they assumed each year for cocoon purchase. Banks then began to refuse further loans, making it virtually impossible for the silk industry to function. This created a crisis for the banks and filatures alike, since filatures had been among the banking industry's most important customers.[18] Given this state of affairs, filatures in both Shanghai and Wuxi began closing. Wuxi filature difficulties began as early as January 1930, with five filatures reporting closure.[19] In the course of the next three years, all of Wuxi's filatures closed for extended periods of time, except for three of the biggest—the Yongtai and Huaxin filatures, belonging to the Xue fam-

TABLE 22

Chinese Raw-Silk Sales, 1926–32

	Quantity (dan)	Value (customs taels)
1926	168,563	144,826,358
1927	160,002	128,705,732
1928	180,186	145,443,481
1929	189,980	147,681,338
1930	151,429	109,181,124
1931	136,160	84,680,482
1932	78,219	32,932,250

SOURCE: Kong 1935: 73.

ily, and the Gansheng.[20] Moreover, in 1931–32, it was reported that ap-proximately half of Wuxi's qianzhuang, or native banks, had closed due to the crisis in the silk industry.[21]

The first response to this situation came from the national Ministry of Finance, with arrangements made late in 1930 for a government bond program to subsidize the failing silk industry. A meeting was held on December 24, 1930, at the Central Bank offices in Shanghai, chaired by Zhang Shouyong, vice-head of the Ministry of Finance. Ten silk industry leaders from Shanghai, Jiangsu, and Zhejiang attended the meeting, where plans for the bond program were formulated. Among these ten were four men from Wuxi, including Xue Shouxuan.[22]

Initially the industry leaders attending the Shanghai meeting pro-posed that 10,000,000 yuan in bonds be issued for the program, but Zhang urged lowering the figure to 7,000,000 yuan. Of this amount, 6,000,000 yuan were to be dispersed immediately to filatures to make up for losses incurred due to declining silk sales, and 1,000,000 yuan were to be used for sericulture schools and extension work to attack the problem of poor silk quality. January 5, 1931, was set as the target date for issue of the bonds pending approval from the Executive Ministry and a rework-ing of the provisions by the Ministry of Law.[23]

By the time the provisions had been revised, the total amount of the bond program had been raised to 8,000,000 yuan, and the date of the bond issue delayed until April 15, 1931. Half the amount of the bonds was to be used for raw-silk export subsidies (at the rate of 100 yuan per dan),[24] one-quarter for improving filature equipment, and one-quarter for sericulture-reform programs. A committee was organized to administer the disbursement of funds, composed of two representatives from the Ministry of Industry, one from the Ministry of Finance, three from the filature industries of Jiangsu and Zhejiang, and three technical experts in sericulture. Initial interest payments on the silk bonds were to be funded by a special customs-tax levy on raw-silk export at the rate of 30 yuan per dan.[25] A second committee was organized to oversee accumulation of bond revenues and payment of interest to bondholders; this committee was composed of two representatives from the Ministry of Industry, one from the Ministry of Finance, one from the Ministry of Audit, two from the Jiangsu and Zhejiang filature industries, and one from Jiangsu or Zhejiang financial circles. Interest payments to bondholders were to be made every six months and were to be paid via one of four national banks—the Central Bank (Zhongyang yinhang), the Native Goods Bank (Guohuo yinhang), the Bank of China (Zhongguo yinhang), or the Bank of Communications (Jiaotong yinhang).[26]

The central problem addressed by this new program was low investment in Wuxi filatures. The problem was so key to filature recovery that when Japanese troops attacked Shanghai in January 1932, disrupting the initial bond program, a new program to raise 3,000,000 yuan was instituted soon thereafter.[27] The two government committees designed to supervise the silk-industry bond program then met monthly during the rest of 1932, and became involved in a wide range of supervisory and inspection functions. The subsidy dispersal committee reviewed inspection reports prepared by the Raw Silk Inspection Bureau (Shengsi jianyanju) to make sure that prescribed quality standards were met before subsidies were granted.[28] Committee members also personally visited individual filatures and inspected silk to see if each dan of raw silk prepared for shipment came up to the minimum weight of eighty jin.[29] The four banks managing disbursement of bond subsidies to the filatures also began to take an interest in supervisory functions, asking to review and appraise the quantity of cocoons needed per dan of raw silk.[30]

By the fall of 1932, the bond program had produced substantial positive results for the silk industry. In Wuxi, approximately twenty-five filatures were able to operate, at least part-time.[31] However, as silk exports began to pick up, and the two supervisory committees began to receive more requests for subsidies, insufficient funds were available to continue paying them out.[32] When the government could not keep pace with filature reopenings stimulated by the bond program, the Ministry of Finance ordered an end to the subsidy program by May 1933.[33]

Despite the fact that the bond program ended after only several months of operation, important precedents had been set for the future of the silk industry. National government committees composed jointly of representatives of government and industry had cooperated to raise capital. Moreover, there were signs that large national and provincial banks based in Shanghai would play a supervisory role in the silk industry. This new alliance between national government ministries and Shanghai banks on the one hand and silk industry leaders on the other was forged to cope with problems endemic in the filature industry and exacerbated by the Depression. In the post-Depression years, these new alliances would become the driving force of silk-industry development.

By 1934, the joint interactions of silk-industry leaders and the Nationalist government gave rise to new institutional structures designed to promote future silk-industry growth. While joint activities during the height of the Depression had been ad hoc and temporary, the new institutions put in place beginning in 1934 were meant to be regular and long-lasting, providing an ongoing means to regulate all aspects of silk production and marketing. On the surface, these new institutions and the policies they enacted had the potential to strengthen the competitive capacity of Chinese raw silk on the world market; when viewed more closely, however, we shall see that they also favored certain groups and individuals within the constellation of silk-industry participants, with Xue Shouxuan and his closest allies the prime beneficiaries.

The impetus for reorganization of the silk industry by the Guomindang government came via the Commission for the National Economy (Quanguo jingji weiyuanhui), a subunit of the Executive Ministry.[34] Under the leadership of the commission, new plans for silk-industry reorganization began to gel by early 1934, through a series of specialty commissions created first at the national, then at the provincial and local levels.[35] On February 19, the commission announced the formation of a subgroup called the Commission for Sericulture Reform (Cansi gailiang weiyuanhui). Immediately thereafter, the Reconstruction Departments of Jiangsu and Zhejiang provinces each organized their own specialty subcommissions as well. In Jiangsu, this was called the Commission for the Administration of Sericulture Improvement (Canye gaijin guanli weiyuanhui). Finally, selected counties throughout Jiangsu where sericulture was important were also given one of two new designations—Model Sericulture District (Cansang mofanqu) or Sericulture Reform District (Cansang gailiangqu)—and officers at this level were made directly responsible for the implementation of new national and provincial policies designed to tighten up regulation of the cocoon trade and the silkworm-egg breeding business. Altogether there were two Model Sericulture Districts—one in Jintan County and the other in Wuxi—and eleven Sericulture Reform Districts.[36]

The rapid and dramatic proliferation of new institutional structures devoted to silk-industry development in 1934 was accomplished by appointing people who were already in bureaucratic positions as the leading officers of these new structures and by drawing upon the experiences and talents of rising industrial leaders, who were invited to sit on policy-making boards. So we see, for example, that the Jiangsu provincial Commission for the Administration of Sericulture Improvement was headed up by Shen Baixian, who was already the head of the provincial Department of Reconstruction, and that the commission's remaining membership was composed of nineteen provincial silk-industry leaders.[37] At the county level in Wuxi, prominent silk-filature owners sat on the policy committee for the Model Sericulture District, with the county magistrate, Yan Shenyu, serving as its head.[38] Among the several silk-industry leaders who were tapped for service was Xue Shouxuan, who sat on the boards of both the provincial-level commission and the Model Sericulture District in Wuxi.

For Xue Shouxuan, participation in these institutional structures added to an already rich and growing repertoire of methods he used to build his reputation and power within central China silk-industry circles. We have already seen that Xue was part of a prominent former gentry family in Wuxi. As a member of an important local elite family, Xue Shouxuan proved very skillful at using a combination of old and new methods based on intraelite relationships at the local level to build up his position.

Marriage strategy was one such method, and Xue used it to its fullest potential. By marrying the daughter of Rong Zongjing, Xue solidified his ties to one of the most important industrialist families in all of China. Like Xue's father, Rong was one of the early local founders of the cocoon trade in Wuxi (see Chapter 3), and by the 1930's, he and his brother Rong Desheng were among China's most important industrialists. Rong Zongjing was known as China's "textile magnate" by the 1920's, owning some of China's largest and most successful cotton mills.[39] Not surprisingly, Xue's ties to the Rong family proved to be a valuable asset in generating much-needed capital for his filatures during the worst years of the Depression. With the personal introduction of his father-in-law to the general manager of the Bank of China, Zhang Gongquan, Xue was able to arrange loans to keep his filatures operating even before the bond issues discussed above began to assist the industry more widely.[40]

Thus, by the time of the establishment of the Model Sericulture District in Wuxi, Xue Shouxuan was in a strong position to continue to build his influence in the local silk industry in Wuxi and beyond. To understand exactly how he did this, we should first explore the programs of the model district. The major issues addressed by the model district were ongoing problems with levels of taxation on the cocoon trade and programs in sericulture reform. While the district's methods in dealing with these issues appeared even-handed and "rationalizing" on one level, they also had the effect of forcing out the smallest, least-heavily capitalized competitors, leaving only the biggest fish in the Wuxi silk-industry sea to maneuver in still more highly advantageous waters.

Regulation of the cocoon trade: taxes and quality control. We have seen in Chapter 4 that by the late 1920's, the Guomindang already had begun serious attempts to collect more cocoon-trade taxes. We saw there that this was a logical outcome of Guomindang state-making, since new agencies at all levels of the political hierarchy were competing for scarce funds. In Chapter 7, we saw that new programs in sericulture reform during the 1920's required state expenditures for sericulture experiment stations, education efforts, and equipment. What remains to be seen is how the Guomindang government and important silk-filature owners worked together in Wuxi through the Model Sericulture District to pass downward the burden of payment for these new programs. Their first targets were local cocoon merchants, who were asked to pay a new surtax on the cocoon trade earmarked specifically for sericulture reform.

New surtaxes on the cocoon trade were part of a larger program propagated by the model district aimed at cocoon-firm "control," as the program was routinely called. In the two model districts, in Wuxi and Jintan, new regulations stipulated that builders of new cocoon firms would be required to use the most up-to-date, Japanese-style hot-air blowing equipment to insure more uniform and complete drying of cocoons.[41] Small cocoon firms of four drying rooms or less, and those that had failed to be rented for two years or more, would no longer be allowed to operate.[42] And new surtaxes were to be levied on cocoon firms to support provincial efforts in the area of sericulture reform.[43]

Details of the new surtax program were first publicized in May 1934, and were designed for implementation no later than May 1935. One proposed levy was a three yuan per dan "security deposit" (baozhengjin) to be paid to the model district; the second was a twelve yuan per dan combined fee to pay for silkworm-egg purchase, sericulture reform, and filature development. This fee was really an augmented version of a former three yuan per dan sericulture reform fee (gailiangfei)—one of the basic taxes paid by cocoon firms to the province since the late 1910's—and was often referred to by this name. The local cocoon-industry association was to continue to collect this tax and forward it to the province.[44]

Although up to one year's grace period was allowed by the province before implementation of new cocoon-firm regulations, when the policy committee of the Wuxi Model Sericulture District met for the first time on May 16, 1934, it ordered immediate enactment of both the new security deposit and the augmented improvement fee for the spring cocoon season already at hand. The meeting had been called by the county magistrate and head of the Model District, Yan Shenyu, and its vice-head, another bureaucrat named Cai Jingde. The other fifteen members of the committee were Wuxi silk-industry leaders, headed by three of the most prominent Wuxi filaturists, Qian Fenggao, Cheng Bingruo, and Xue Shouxuan.[45]

Given that the Wuxi Cocoon-Merchant Guild, or gongsuo, had a well-established tradition of protesting government policy in defense of local interests (see Chapter 4), it is not surprising that the Wuxi Cocoon-Industry Association, a renamed version of the local gongsuo, produced a flurry of protest against the Model District's decisions.[46] They made three requests of the Model District: that cocoon firms of less than four drying rooms, as well as those which had not operated for two years, be allowed to open; that cocoon firms be allowed to follow their old registration procedures, with the association collecting all fees, rather than pay the new three yuan per dan security deposit directly to the Model District; and that the sericulture reform fee remain at three yuan per dan instead of being raised to twelve yuan.[47] Clearly, cocoon merchants were attempting to reassert what they believed were their legitimate rights in these matters: to retain the privilege of self-regulation of cocoon-firm marketing arrangements and facilities; to remain the sole collectors of all county and provincial levies on the cocoon trade; and to protest when the province decided unilaterally to raise the basic provincial-level tax on the trade to four times its previous level.

After the Cocoon-Industry Association made public its new demands, the first reaction of the Model District was to threaten cocoon merchants with harsh action if compliance was not forthcoming. The Model District's vice-head, Cai, ordered banks and qianzhuang to withhold loans to cocoon firms that refused to comply and threatened to fine them if they went ahead with loan arrangements. However, the banks made no response to this order, and the district leadership began to soften.[48] Abandoning their confrontational stance almost as quickly as they had adopted it, Yan and Cai resolved to take the requests of Wuxi cocoon merchants to the head of the Jiangsu Department of Reconstruction. They went to Zhenjiang, the provincial capital, on May 25, but Shen Baixian, head of the department, refused to negotiate with them. Instead, Shen adopted a hard-line stance, threatening to confiscate the cocoons of any cocoon firms refusing to comply, and to charge them a doubled improvement fee and fine. Yan and Cai returned on May 26 with no recourse but to attempt to implement the new policies.[49]

Despite the resolution of the province to enforce cocoon-firm regulation, Wuxi cocoon merchants stood firm in their refusal to pay new fees. Indeed, they threatened not to pay even the old rate for improvement fees of three yuan per dan if their requests were not met.[50] Under mounting pressure and with the opening of the cocoon-marketing season in Wuxi imminent, Yan and Cai made a second trip to Zhenjiang. This time Shen acquiesced, allowing for a one-year moratorium on the new regulation measures. Cocoon firms with less than four ovens were allowed to open. Registration of cocoon firms was to proceed as in previous years, with a three yuan improvement fee paid via the Cocoon-Industry Association. The only new point that remained in effect was the security-deposit system whereby each cocoon firm was to pay three yuan per dan to the Model District.[51] Through this compromise solution, the crisis was averted, and cocoon marketing was able to proceed.[52]

We see from these events that the antagonistic relationship first observed in the late 1910's, between provincial government on the one side and county government leaders and local cocoon merchants on the other, retained many of its essential characteristics nearly twenty years later. Cocoon merchants, as collectors and transmitters of taxes on their trade, continued to assert the kind of political leverage this unique position afforded them. When provincial-tax assessments climbed beyond amounts they were willing to pay, cocoon merchants threatened to resist payment of taxes altogether. For their part, county bureaucrats opted to lobby on behalf of cocoon merchants' interests in this matter, even though they had been ordered to implement the new policies. As we have seen earlier, county-government defense of cocoon merchants was grounded in mutual self-interest—keeping as much commercial-tax revenue as possible at the local level was something from which both groups could benefit as local statemaking proceeded. Finally, the role of the province in this three-sided scenario was to push constantly to force county bureaucrats and local merchants to relinquish their claims to control over taxes and other matters regarding regulation of the industry.

What is perhaps most striking about this new round of struggles over the issue of cocoon-trade taxes and other regulation procedures is the role played by some filature owners in Wuxi, a role that now set them apart from other local elites involved in ownership and management aspects of the local silk industry. The resolve on the part of this newly emerging stratum of filature owners to work with Guomindang statemakers at the provincial level is striking. Although two points that Wuxi cocoon merchants demanded were granted by the province—the opening of small cocoon firms and permitting the basic tax to remain at three yuan instead of raising it to twelve—these provisions were granted for one year only. By 1935, all the original terms of the new control policies for cocoon firms were to be implemented as planned.[53]

To this end, in January 1935, Guan Yida of the provincial Department of Reconstruction visited Wuxi to discuss the proper implementation of cocoon-firm control with the Cocoon-Industry Association.[54] However, Guan had also been commissioned by the provincial department to begin the process of removing Yan Shenyu, magistrate of the county and former head of the Wuxi Model Sericulture District, from his position of authority within the model district administration. Shen had already been demoted to vice-head, and Cai Jingde, former vice-head of the district, had been promoted to the position of head. Guan Yida traveled to neighboring Yixing County, where the vice-head of the Sericulture Reform District there, Zhou Yuanxun, was interviewed for possible transfer to Wuxi, where he would become vice-head of the model district.[55] Obviously, the province was determined to have no repeat performance of the previous spring, when county-level officials had acted as negotiators on behalf of Wuxi cocoon merchants. Apparently, Yan Shenyu had been the guilty party in assisting merchants in their petitions against new regulations. By February, in the aftermath of Guan's visit, an official order for cocoon-firm control was passed down from province to county to confirm the January discussions. The province wished to insure that by cocoon-marketing season, all opposition would be quelled, and control policies would proceed as planned.[56]

When the spring marketing season arrived in Wuxi in 1935, any potential that may have existed for a renewed confrontation between cocoon merchants and provincial authorities had been dissipated successfully. No protests were heard from the Cocoon-Industry Association, and new control policies were implemented as planned. In the end, this had serious consequences for the cocoon-merchant community, because their long-standing prerogative to collect all taxes on the cocoon trade was now substantially altered. Among the new control measures, the "security deposit" was a fee paid directly by each cocoon firm to the Model District administration. With this measure, the Cocoon-Industry Association was circumvented as a taxation agency for the first time. A new precedent was now established for the province to assert more direct control over taxes on the cocoon trade.

While the motivations of provincial statemakers to collect more taxes are clear enough, we might well ask exactly what the filaturists who sat on the Model District board had to gain from the implementation of new policies on cocoon-firm control. To begin with, we should recall the difficulties experienced in silk-industry reform during the late 1920's. By 1934, the most powerful among filature owners and managers in Wuxi were well aware of the need to improve raw materials in order to regain position for Chinese raw silk on the world market. Someone had to pay for these efforts, and although the province made policy and allocated funds for sericulture reform, the industry itself also had to help pay. As we have seen in Chapter 3, the men who operated cocoon firms in Wuxi did so on a year-to-year contractual basis for Wuxi and Shanghai filatures. Despite the collective strength of their industry association as a lobbying agent with government, these men were clearly less prominent in local elite circles than were those who had managed to make the leap into successful management and/or ownership of several silk filatures. From the point of view of the filature owners and managers, if someone had to pay for silk-industry reform, why not try to rest the burden on cocoon merchants? After all, cocoon merchants were in the best position to try to recoup any "losses" caused by higher taxes by trying to pass the burden one step further down to the peasantry in the form of lower prices paid for cocoons. And we shall see shortly that just such "next step" actions did, indeed, materialize by 1936, although in a rather unexpected fashion.

Many other activities associated with cocoon-firm reorganization were also under way by the 1930's, indicating that at least a few filaturists, and especially Xue Shouxuan, had plans to more directly supervise and manage cocoon production and marketing. It is probable that Xue saw certain future advantages to forcing out the smallest, least modernized cocoon firms through a combination of higher taxes and implementation of new model-district policies on other aspects of cocoon-firm "control." As noted above, another aspect of cocoon-trade regulation associated with the model-district program was a new series of rules concerning the construction and operation of cocoon-firm facilities. The new restrictions stipulated that all new cocoon firms had to install Japanese-style hot-air blowers in their drying rooms, the most modern equipment available.[57] In addition, small cocoon firms of four drying rooms or less, likely to be the least technically advanced in their equipment and methods, were no longer allowed to operate.[58] On the surface, both of these measures were designed to guarantee higher-quality cocoons by providing optimal conditions for cocoon drying. For Xue Shouxuan, however, who had already begun to install the most advanced Japanese-style drying machines in cocoon firms who contracted with his filatures, these measures also helped him force out competitors in a new bid to more closely control cocoon marketing in the central China region as a whole.[59]

Evidence supporting this view of cocoon-firm control comes from a situation that began to unfold in Jintan County, a locale near Wuxi, in which Xue Shouxuan rapidly expanded his cocoon-marketing influence under the model district program. It is somewhat surprising that Jintan was made a Model Sericulture District—only one of two throughout all of Jiangsu Province—since it was not a major producer of cocoons when the program was established.[60] Once we realize that Xue had important personal connections in Jintan, however, the rationale for granting the county model district status becomes clearer. Xue cultivated close friendships with the county magistrate of Jintan, who also served as vice-head of the model district, and with the head of the Jintan police bureau.[61] With the assistance of these two county-level officials, agents sent by Xue to Jintan were able to rent many cocoon-firm facilities. Once these facilities were rented, Xue set about renovating the existing drying rooms under model district guidelines, installing new-style drying equipment that he had imported from Japan. These new machines, installed in large chambers, were each capable of drying as many cocoons as twelve old-style drying rooms.[62] Although this must have required a substantial capital outlay for Xue, he was willing to do this because once such machines were in place and his agents were guaranteed the right to rent these renovated facilities, he quickly established the capacity to buy and process a large proportion of Jintan cocoons. At the time he began this system in Jintan, Xue also began to cultivate friendships with the magistrates of Yixing and Liyang counties, having similar plans to gain a foothold in their emerging cocoon trades.[63]

Silkworm-egg breeding and model-district policy. The second major area of model-district policy in Wuxi had to do with regulation of improved silkworm-egg breeding and sale of such eggs to the peasantry. We saw in Chapter 7 that some members of the local elite in Wuxi were prone to manipulation of the silkworm-egg breeding business, to the point that they even engaged in the sale of inferior-quality eggs to peasants. The method employed by the Model District in Wuxi to end egg-sale abuse was simple, straightforward, and harsh—no longer could improved silkworm eggs be sold directly to peasants by individual breederies, be they state-run or privately owned. Instead, all egg cards were now required to be sold first to the Model District, and then resold to peasants at a fixed price of five mao per card, only one-half the previous average price paid by peasants to the breederies.[64] In order to guarantee the production of high-quality egg cards, only five mao was paid by the model district per card to the breederies initially, with a balance of up to seven mao to be paid once the results of the egg cards were actually in. Since peasants were now to pay only five mao to purchase egg cards, the balance of the purchase price was to come from new surtaxes on the cocoon trade. Moreover, any breederies producing over 5,000 egg cards were required to sell one-third of their cards outside the province, a safety measure designed to undercut the dumping of bad eggs. An expert of the Commission for the National Economy, Ni Shaowen, was sent to the field throughout Jiangsu in the spring of 1934 to make sure all breederies complied with the new system. Wuxi was his first stop.[65]

During the fall season of 1934, like its cocoon-merchant counterpart, the industry association of silkworm-egg breeders in Wuxi complained about these new measures. However, this group seemed far less able than the Cocoon-Industry Association to generate any significant protest. Silkworm-egg breeders were a much newer group than cocoon merchants, and had no long history of organizing for protection of their corporate interests. Their efforts brought only a slight change in the terms of payment by the Model District for egg cards, raising the maximum price from seven mao to eight.[66] The basic contours of the system whereby the Model District purchased egg cards and then resold them to peasants remained in effect. In January 1935, the association tried once again to get the measures rescinded, appealing to principles of free enterprise. But the Model District continued to hold firm, and egg-card sales to peasants went ahead as planned.[67] In February, peasants were ordering eggs from new advisory bureaus of the Model District, and in March, a meeting was held for personnel of the bureaus to make preliminary plans for egg-card distribution.[68]

Like the new policies on cocoon-firm control, silkworm-egg control measures were designed to give the Model District and its administrative personnel in Wuxi greater input in regulating problematic aspects of the silk industry. And, as with cocoon-firm control measures, Wuxi filaturists had something to gain from new efforts at silkworm-egg control. Most obviously, they were more likely to improve cocoon quality, an issue with which filaturists had always had to contend. But we should not be surprised to learn that Xue Shouxuan once again had an unusual role to play, and a unique set of advantages to gain, in the reorganization of silkworm-egg breeding under the model-district guidelines.

Although model-district policy held that breederies could no longer sell improved silkworm eggs directly to peasants, there was one exception to this rule. If the breedery was willing to take the time and effort to establish egg-raising cooperatives with peasants, instructing them in new techniques to lower the risk of cocoon-crop failure, then they could retain the right to sell their own egg cards.[69] Under this provision, Xue Shouxuan's Yongtai and Huaxin filatures, which already had begun to develop such a system of cooperatives, continued to run breederies that sold egg cards directly to peasants. In 1934, the Huaxin filature prepared female extension workers to organize new-style contractual cooperatives, where filature staff sold egg cards to peasants and required that the cocoons raised from those cards be sold back to filature-controlled cocoon firms.[70] In 1935, the model-district extension program sent out 100 workers, but Yongtai and Huaxin sent out another 100 workers in Wuxi and surrounding counties to set up contractual co-ops.[71] Not only was Xue able to closely monitor cocoon production for his filatures via this program, he also retained the capacity to sell silkworm eggs to peasants just when other egg breeders were being forced out of their independent, privately run businesses by the model-district program.

The ultimate benefit reaped by Xue from this cooperative program was the ability to more closely influence cocoon pricing. Although cocoon-merchant organizations had long been responsible for setting a cocoon price at the beginning of the each marketing season, we have seen that prices ebbed and flowed daily, sometimes even hourly, at cocoon-marketing sites (see Chapter 3). But under Xue's cooperative program, peasants were required to sell their cocoons only to cocoon firms that contracted with his filatures. When selling their cocoons to these firms, peasants were given certificates of the weights received but without a stated price. About a month later, the filatures announced their cash payments for cocoons divided into three grades. The price paid for cocoons in the first grade were set slightly above the market price, but

Xue's filatures paid well below the market for the second and third grades. The key to price advantages in this system was cleverly designed. Since everyone wanted higher-quality cocoons, Xue could claim that by using this grading system he was introducing incentives for peasants to produce such cocoons. However, since his own organization controlled the grading procedures, and only a very small proportion of the total quantity of cocoons was given the highest grade, Xue's filatures paid substantially below market price for the majority of the cocoons they purchased through the cooperative program.[72]

Thus, model-district policy as it emerged in 1934–35 in Wuxi demonstrates the strength of the new alliance between the Guomindang government and prominent silk filaturists in Wuxi, especially Xue Shouxuan. The goal of their collaboration was to design and administer programs to assist in future silk-industry growth following the Great Depression. But it was not accidental that model-district policy was also in the best interests of the most powerful filaturists. Early in 1936, a final step was taken by Xue Shouxuan to solidify his growing prominence within central China silk-industry circles—the creation of a new joint-stock company designed to guarantee the capacity to generate capital on a large scale and bring the majority of Wuxi filatures under Xue's direct management.

FORMATION OF THE XINGYE SILK COMPANY

One way to describe Xue Shouxuan's activities during his rise to prominence is to point out his resemblance to those who had led the managerial revolution in American big business a generation earlier, a process made famous by the eminent business historian Alfred Chandler. Chandler argued that what made certain American industries more successful than others in the last decades of the nineteenth century was the growing ability of a new class of professional managers to build both forward and backward linkages for their production processes, more tightly controlling (or managing) pricing mechanisms and the production and selection of raw materials on either end. The term most often used to describe this overall effort is "vertical integration," and Chandler claimed that the "visible hand" of the manager is what made it happen, rather than "invisible" forces of the market. Another part of Chandler's story involves a revolution in accounting methods that made real costs clearer, and required managers to come up with better ways of meeting them to improve profit margins.[73]

Subsequently, Naomi Lamoreaux's work on what she called "the great American merger movement" improved on Chandler's original vision, making it clear that it was only under certain well-specified conditions that really powerful, long-term successes emerged in the ranks of American big business. Among these conditions was the fact that a depression occurred in the early 1890's, making it necessary for businesses who wanted to survive to design a new strategy for long-term success. The strategy they came up with included merging with competitors to eliminate price wars, one of the principal problems causing businesses to fail in the preceding period.[74]

Recalling that Xue Shouxuan had studied railroad management at the University of Illinois in the early 1920's, we might conclude that some of what he did with Chinese silk production in the early 1930's was modeled on his American predecessors' management activities. And, as we know from Chandler's work, it was precisely in the American railroad industry of the late nineteenth century that some of the most important managerial innovations had begun. On the other hand, Xue was also working under the pressures of a depression, and as in Lamoreaux's story, he began to use the "merger" strategy that such a critical moment for business survival was capable of prompting.

As early as 1932, prominent silk filaturists in Wuxi had begun to promote the idea that concentration of capital under unified management would be necessary for the revival of the Wuxi silk industry. At a meeting of the filature association of Wuxi held in May 1932, Qian Fenggao, association head and a close associate of Xue Shouxuan, argued that old, outdated reeling equipment was the primary cause for the failure of Chinese raw silk on the world market, and that up to 1,000,000 yuan would be needed to replace old machines in Wuxi filatures. Moreover, Qian suggested that several filatures combine assets in order to implement this change.[75]

In 1934, this suggestion was raised publicly once again by Zheng Bingquan, another filature owner who was part of an emerging silk-industry oligarchy. Zheng proposed the formation of a silk-filature cooperative group that would negotiate the marketing of Chinese raw silk abroad, the buying and warehousing of cocoons, and all other tasks associated with silk production so as to avoid excessive competition through self-regulation. Zheng further proposed that the Ministry of Industry and the Ministry of Foreign Affairs negotiate with relevant foreign embassies and consulates in China to establish direct marketing channels abroad. Resurrecting the nineteenth-century term "official supervision and merchant management" (*guandu shangban*) to describe his proposal, Zheng sent it off to the Jiangsu Sericulture Commission and the Wuxi Model Sericulture District for consideration.[76]

It came as no great surprise to anyone who followed developments in the silk industry when in January 1936, the formation of the Xingye Silk Company (Xingye zhisi gufen youxian gongsi) was announced in Wuxi. Heralded in news reports as a boon to the Chinese silk industry, the new company was authorized to sell stocks worth 1,000,000 yuan, to be deposited with the Shanghai and Wuxi branches of the Bank of China, the Bank of Communications, the Bank of Jiangsu, the Zhejiang Xingye Bank, and the Bank of Shanghai.[77] There were fifteen cofounders of the Xingye Company, all members of the powerful silk-filaturist group. Xue Shouxuan and his close associates, Qian Fenggao, Zheng Bingquan, and Xue Runpei, were among the organizers.[78] Hua Shaochun, head of the Cocoon-Industry Association, was commissioned by the cofounders to begin the work of setting up the new company offices.[79]

The significance of the Xingye Silk Company was twofold. It was a true joint-stock operation with the potential to raise capital far beyond the circles of friends and relatives that had always been the mainstay of filature investment in Wuxi, but that, as we have seen, also led to inefficient management practices and the yearly dissipation of filature earnings in the form of large profit-sharing dividends. The Xingye Silk Company was designed to end these chronic problems in filature investment and management once and for all. Further, the Xingye Silk Company was now to provide the framework within which competition for raw materials and external markets would be made more manageable.

To consider this second point, we should recall that the late 1920's had seen a rapid proliferation of new filatures in Wuxi, with the total number of filature plants doubling from twenty-five in 1926 to fifty by the end of 1929. This rapid expansion had occurred in a favorable political climate for the silk industry in central China, in which the Guomindang came to power with extensive new plans for silk-industry reform (see Chapter 7). However, after 1930, the Great Depression had created an economic atmosphere in which the sheer survival of most filatures was at stake. Although the bond program of 1932 helped ease that pressure somewhat, the danger that there would be drastic raw-silk price reductions as silk merchants struggled to regain lost market shares loomed large on the immediate business horizon of filature investors in Wuxi and Shanghai. In the face of these conditions, the Xingye Silk Company, under Xue Shouxuan's guidance, began filature consolidation, a process we might liken to the "great merger movement" in American business in the 1890's.[80]

Among the first tasks undertaken by the newly founded Xingye Silk Company was the rental and reopening of closed filatures in Wuxi. In 1934 and 1935, only fifteen filatures had been able to open. These included six filatures owned by Xue Shouxuan, two owned by his colleague Cheng Bingruo, and seven others that were run on the old "split ownership/management" system.[81] However, by February 5, 1936, the new Xingye Company had already made arrangements to rent and open eight more filatures.[82] Xue Shouxuan also made plans to rent twelve filatures on his own and to open them along with the six he already owned.[83] By June, reports held that more than forty silk filatures were under Xue's individual influence as owner or lessee, or under his corporate influence, through the Xingye Silk Company. Speculation was that Xue would soon begin to purchase the filatures he did not already own.[84]

Although details of the internal workings of the Xingye Silk Company are unknown, there was no doubt in any contemporary reports that Xue Shouxuan, as its director, was also its controlling force.[85] Indeed, it was very likely that through his own privately negotiated bank loan from the Zhejiang Xingye Bank, Xue was able to buy a majority of shares in the company from the outset.[86] Simultaneously, Xue continued to rent more cocoon-firm facilities, so that prevailing estimates held that he controlled over 400 cocoon firms throughout Wuxi and surrounding areas in 1936.[87] Filature managers who tried to remain independent during this process resented Xue's growing influence, and some vehemently resisted his efforts to consolidate their support behind him.[88]

Despite resistance by some filature managers, the Xingye Silk Company, as the Model Sericulture District before it, seemed to stimulate positive developments for the faltering silk industry. The first indication of this was the announcement in April 1936 of the formation of a Shanghai bankers' consortium to handle future silk-industry loans. Nineteen banks and qianzhuang formed the consortium at the behest of the silk-filature associations of Shanghai, Zhejiang Province, and Wuxi. Thirty million yuan divided into 600 portions of 50,000 yuan each would be available that season to filatures for cocoon purchase. The loans were for three months at the rate of 0.85 percent interest per month.[89] Once again, short-term, low-interest loans, which were of such vital importance to the filature industry for cocoon purchase, were available in ample supply.

At the same time that the Xingye Silk Company was generating positive developments for the silk industry as a whole, Xue Shouxuan was able to use his new position as director of the company to augment his growing personal control of all aspects of silk-industry functioning. The link between the Xingye Company formation and Xue's growing power can be seen in a final example—the process through which cocoon prices were decided in Wuxi in the spring season of 1936.

We have seen previously that cocoon-merchant organizations met each spring to deliberate on prices offered to peasants for their cocoons. However, in 1936, the Commission for the National Economy announced that it would decide each year on a uniform nationwide price for cocoons based on raw-silk prices on the international market and average production costs for Chinese filatures. For the spring season of 1936, the commission decided that the price offered to peasants would be thirty yuan per dan.[90] Although raw-silk prices had recovered to 74 percent of their 1929 level by that time, this suggested price for cocoons was only 42 percent of pre-Depression highs.[91] When the Wuxi Cocoon-Industry Association met on May 31, it merely reaffirmed the thirty yuan price. Hua Shaochun, one of Xue Shouxuan's personal associates, headed this association, accounting for the rapidity with which the organization agreed to the new system.[92] Whether Hua had been installed by Xue or was cultivated by him after assuming his position, the effect was the same—a decision that clearly favored Xue and the Xingye Silk Company by assuring that cocoons could be bought at lower prices.

When cocoon marketing began and thirty yuan per dan was offered to peasants for their cocoons, the Wuxi Agricultural Association, or *nonghui*, an organization representing local landlord interests, decided to protest the price. Members of this association met with the Cocoon-Industry Association and representatives of the Xingye Silk Company over this issue, and the three groups agreed jointly to petition the national-level Ministry of Industry and the Jiangsu Department of Reconstruction to raise the price to forty yuan. The reasoning offered for this request was that peasants could not meet their production costs if only thirty yuan were offered for their cocoons.[93] For landlord members of the Agricultural Association, lowered cocoon prices would have meant increasing peasant defaults on rents as well. In response to this joint petition, the head of the Jiangsu Sericulture Commission, Zeng Jikuan, traveled to Wuxi to discuss the matter. Although he met with representatives of the Agricultural Association, the county magistrate, and the head of the Model Sericulture District, Zeng made his final decision on cocoon prices only after he had met with Xue Shouxuan in his role as dir-rector of the Xingye Silk Company. After Xue visited Zeng at the county government offices, the cocoon price was raised to thirty-two yuan per dan, a compromise solution, but one that clearly continued to favor Xue. Cocoon merchants were notified immediately, since the cocoon-marketing season had already begun.[94]

This final incident reveals the degree to which the Guomindang government in tandem with Xue Shouxuan exercised a new measure of control over the Wuxi silk industry by the mid-1930's. Both sides of this alliance had common motivations—to improve the quality of filature silk so as to bolster China's silk exports on the international market. However, their political fusion to achieve these ends also spelled the beginning of the end for less powerful competitors. Cocoon merchants, silkworm-egg breeders, and silk-filature managers were all potential losers in this new organizational scheme for the central China silk industry. In addition, peasants found themselves with a diminishing capacity for price bargaining within the cocoon-marketing system in Wuxi, and thus became the last, but certainly the most significant, group to "share" the costs of silk-industry reform and control.

THE SHIFT TOWARD STATE CONTROL

By 1937, Xue Shouxuan's growing reputation earned him the title "silk-industry magnate" in contemporary reports on silk-industry developments. Depending on the context of the report, and the exact term used (siye jutou, siye juzi, or siye dawang), the title frequently had a pejorative ring to it. Clearly, there was good reason for peasants and their advocates among increasingly radical left-leaning intellectuals to be unhappy with the new price arrangements engineered by Xue and his Xingye Silk Company.[95] But surviving silk-industry reform specialists and silk-filature managers whom I interviewed who knew of Xue's activities also had nothing good to say about his efforts to consolidate the Wuxi filature industry under his own personal management system. Although they generally applauded Xue's efforts to improve equipment and introduce more efficient work and management practices in the Xue family filatures, they had little patience for his efforts to control virtually all filatures in Wuxi, usurping the autonomy of other members of local elite silk-industry circles.[96]

In the summer of 1937, with the threat of Japanese invasion of the central China region looming larger on the horizon, Xue Shouxuan left Wuxi for Shanghai, traveled to Hong Kong, and eventually fled to New

York. He took a large sum of cash with him, invested in war bonds, and worked for a time in New York in a managerial position for an auto company. But through a combination of bad investments and fines for income-tax evasion, Xue ended up financially destitute, supported by one of his sons who was an engineer. He died in New York in 1972, an apparent shadow of his former "silk-industry magnate" self of the mid-1930's, when his dual roles as director of the Xingye Silk Company and advisor to the Guomindang government had made him one of the most powerful industrialists in China.[97]

What is perhaps most important about Xue Shouxuan's story, at least from the point of view of the larger possibilities for development, is the degree to which Xue and the Guomindang collaborated in support of modern industry. A previous generation of scholarship on the Guomindang decade, spanning the years from 1927 to 1937, tended to be uniformly negative about the Guomindang's capacity to support economic development, focusing on government corruption and ineptness in management of government tax revenues.[98] Chinese scholarship on related issues, but with a later chronological focus on the postwar 1940's, developed a rubric of "bureaucratic capitalism" to describe such problems, and blamed corrupt and inept Guomindang government bureaucrats and big bankers in state-owned banks for the ruination of fledgling Chinese industries.[99] Books by Parks Coble and William Kirby have gone a long way toward revising these views, pointing to the formation of important government commissions during the Guomindang decade that established new programs for economic development and helped generate bank loans to assist new industries.[100]

One of Kirby's insights is worth highlighting here because of its bearing on how we might finally interpret Wuxi silk-industry reorganization during the early 1930's. Kirby's work concentrates on the role of German advisors to the Guomindang and their impact on economic planning. The Commission for National Resources was one of the most important government bureaus organized by those within the Guomindang leadership who were interested in the German development model, and through that commission, the Guomindang government was systematically preparing for direct government ownership of industries involved in strategic resource production by the mid-1930's. Kirby concludes that it was left to the Chinese Communist Party to take up where the Guomindang left off, but that the seeds had already been sown during the early 1930's for state direction of industry.[101]

One way to interpret the interactions we have observed here between Xue Shouxuan, the Guomindang's Commission for the National Economy, and silk-industry policy in Wuxi after 1927 is to see these events as a path parallel to that observed by Kirby for strategic resources. Silk was not a "national resource" in the same sense that energy sources and other potential war materiels were. Nonetheless, since the late nineteenth century, when raw silk had become *the* leader among Chinese exports in the newly dawning industrial era, progress in Chinese silk production had been of great interest to government. We have seen throughout this study how governments at all levels became involved with various aspects of promotion and regulation of the modern silk industry as Wuxi emerged as a strong leader in cocoon production and silk-filature development from the 1860's onward. When the Guomindang government stepped in with full support for Xue Shouxuan, a man who showed signs of being able to more fully "control" silk-industry problems of the past and provide a faster path toward continued silk-industry expansion, government officials undoubtedly hoped that decades of slower, more uneven growth in silk-industry output for the world market finally would be superseded.

Reflecting on the policies implemented under the Model Sericulture District in Wuxi, the start of what I believe we might, in this larger developmental context, think of as the beginning of state "directorship" of Wuxi silk production during the late 1920's, we can also see that the kinds of policy pursued by the district had a very sound logic. District policies focused on the two big issues that had always most plagued filature investors—state demands for more commercial-tax revenue via the cocoon trade, and the improvement of raw-material supply. By the late 1920's, the question being asked by government and silk-industry participants was not *whether* more cocoon-trade taxes were going to be paid, nor *whether* cocoon quality was going to improve, but rather, *who* was going to be responsible for the financial burdens of paying more taxes and improving cocoon quality?

Seen in this broader context of silk-industry history over several decades, Xue Shouxuan's final moves to set cocoon prices in 1936 take on the quality of a logical, methodical effort to bring industry and government into perfect concert on the critical issues facing silk-industry development. If peasants were forced to accept lower prices for cocoons, then middlemen cocoon merchants would have less reason to resist paying higher cocoon-trade taxes. And if more tax revenues materialized, not only would the government be satisfied, but more public funds might be slated (as promised) for the important work of silk-industry reform. Of course, we have seen that resistance and struggle were endemic in the arenas of cocoon-trade taxation and sericulture reform, and because Japan invaded central China in 1937, we shall never know the full range of potential economic outcomes of collaborative efforts between China's first truly "big business" in raw-silk production and the Guomindang. But we have already glimpsed the political outcomes—the emergence of an increasingly interventionist Guomindang state by the early 1930's, with government officials and their carefully cultivated silk-industrialist allies taking a controlling role in the area of state-directed development.

9

Conclusion: Peasants, Industry, and the State

From start to finish, building a modern silk industry in Wuxi meant bringing together peasant-family production and silk filatures. As this process unfolded, every economic step taken by silk-industry elites, from organizing the cocoon trade in the 1870's to Xue Shouxuan's creation of the Xingye Silk Company in 1936, was also politically infused. Political strategies designed to triumph over commercial competitors, to prompt peasant women to produce more and better cocoons, and to force fellow filature owners and managers out of business altogether, were on the agenda of the most powerful and prominent silk-industry investors. The ultimate successes came for those who discovered that government intervention in silk-industry development could be useful if it resulted in policies supporting their private goals and interests.

In the final analysis, the Wuxi silk-industry story forces us to come to terms in new ways with Chinese industrialists who were also powerful local elites, cultivating and reformulating strong traditions of local social dominance. By the 1930's, increasingly interventionist and controlling state institutions tried to direct industrial development, but they could not succeed without allies among local elites. At the same time, peasant families remained the source of raw materials and labor supply. The legacies of early industrialization did not pave the way for a better "fit" between modern industry and peasant-family production; rather, "one industry, two Chinas" remained a stubborn, troublesome feature of modern economic development into future decades.

THE SILK-INDUSTRY CONTINUUM: SILK FILATURES AND PEASANT-FAMILY PRODUCTION

Until now, we have understood very little about the fusion of peasant-family production with early Chinese industry, the phenomenon I have referred to as a silk-industry "continuum" in Wuxi. This book has asked new questions about Chinese development through a case study of the silk-industry continuum, exploring how silk filatures affected peasant-family production and how filatures fared as they relied on peasant women for labor and raw materials. We have seen that the relationship between silk filatures and the Wuxi peasantry first took shape in the post-Taiping years. Prior to that time, Wuxi was not involved in sericulture; rather, it was an area in which cotton grown in other delta counties was spun and woven by Wuxi peasants as their principal form of home-based production for the market. After 1865, as world-market demand for Chinese raw silk escalated in tandem with advances in mechanized spinning and weaving technologies, Shanghai and Wuxi became new sites for mechanized-filature spinning of raw silk for export. To circumvent competition with well-entrenched commercial networks for handicraft silk products controlled by merchants in locales to the south and east of Wuxi, Shanghai's filature investors and the merchants who purchased cocoons on their behalf developed new sericulture areas. Via this route, Wuxi became the principal site in the Yangzi delta for cocoon marketing for the Shanghai filature industry, and Wuxi peasants took up cocoon production to service world-market demand for machine-spun raw silk.

Through detailed household-level data on peasant work strategies and incomes, we have seen that nearly every peasant household in Wuxi engaged in cocoon production for the local silk industry; that peasant women raised silkworms for low returns to labor compared with men's earnings in other forms of work; and that sericulture incomes were one critical component of a total income-earning package necessary to meet basic subsistence requirements for the majority of Wuxi peasant households. Despite the fact that most peasant families engaged in sericulture and sold cocoons, we have also seen that this was not the way to "get rich" in the Wuxi countryside. The richest households were those whose men had found ways to make the leap out of farm work almost entirely, engaging in urban-based or urban-oriented activities such as commerce, teaching, and doctoring. Furthermore, gendered labor patterns in the Wuxi countryside, characterized by women's work in silkworm raising and men's work in grain farming, also carried over into other forms of higher-paying artisan or urban-based jobs for peasant men. This meant that when someone migrated from the countryside in search of a higher income, it was usually a male member of the family. Women and children who remained behind had the lowest incomes in Wuxi villages during the late 1920's.

One may draw many conclusions from these observations. On the one hand, silk-filature demand for female peasant labor did not enrich the Wuxi peasantry. A critical limiting factor for sericulture and its contribution to the economic well-being of Wuxi peasants was the land itself. When factoring in considerations of risk associated with climate and yearly uncertainty in world-market demand for Chinese raw silk, Wuxi peasants rarely committed all of their land to mulberry cultivation, but preferred to keep a portion for the more steady staple food crops of rice and wheat. In addition, the land was very densely settled in Wuxi, limiting the degree to which individual households could expand their farming efforts in any endeavor, be it grain farming or mulberry cultivation. Under these circumstances, incomes from cocoon sales were an important component of Wuxi peasants' livelihoods, but almost never their major source of income. By the 1920's, sericulture was less important than other forms of nonfarm work. Given the inability to expand sericulture much further in Wuxi, we can appreciate more fully why Xue Shouxuan, Wuxi's most powerful filaturist by the mid-1930's, was aiming to promote and control cocoon production in other counties.

Because the living conditions of many peasant households in Wuxi were close to subsistence level, a situation arising from a combination of small farm size and rental obligations associated with land-tenure arrangements, programs introduced to improve cocoon quality and output by using improved silkworm eggs met with only mediocre success. Although sericulture-reform experts were usually well intentioned, they had little capacity to convince peasant women that scarce household resources should be invested in a second crop of silkworms using improved eggs. Peasant women needed ample, concrete evidence in the form of thriving silkworm broods and higher cocoon prices to be persuaded that investing in raising more silkworms would be worthwhile. Complicating this situation was the fact that some important individuals within Wuxi sericulture-reform circles abused their positions for private gain, selling bad silkworm eggs to peasants, or manipulating their positions to charge higher prices for eggs. "Modern science" in the area of sericulture reform seemed not to possess the final answers to the complex issues of improving cocoon output and quality in Wuxi, battling as it did with complex sociocultural expectations on the part of both peasants and elites about their roles in sericulture processes.

It was against this evolving backdrop of relationships among peasant producers of cocoons and silk-industry elites that the Model Sericulture District in Wuxi finally took shape in the mid-1930's. Although cocoon production was not the only issue with which the Model District was concerned, it was one of the most significant. As we have seen, the Model District was a product of a new alliance between powerful filaturists in Wuxi, especially Xue Shouxuan, and the Guomindang's Commission for the National Economy, a bold institutional attempt to conquer the problems of cocoon supply for Wuxi filatures. Cocoon merchants were charged new surtaxes on the cocoon trade to pay for sericulture reform under model district guidelines, and private breederies were no longer allowed to sell silkworm eggs directly to the peasantry. Elaborate regulations for selling silkworm eggs to the district and reselling them to peasants were designed to curb the egg-sale abuses of the past while providing the peasants with high-quality eggs at controlled prices. But Xue Shouxuan also found ways to make the model district program work to his own best advantage, to the ultimate detriment of peasants involved in cocoon production. The costs of sericulture reform, although paid in theory by higher cocoon-trade taxes, were in fact skillfully pushed downward onto the peasantry in the form of legislated lower prices for cocoons. District bureaucrats set cocoon prices in 1936, in close consultation with Xue Shouxuan as director of the new Xingye Silk Company, at less than half the best market price for cocoons before the creation of the model district. With these actions, the Guomindang favored the interests of industrialists over those of peasants as one method to promote modern economic growth.

LOCAL ELITES, MODES OF POWER, AND THE STATE

Local elites in Wuxi were the intermediaries between modern industry and peasant-family production, acting first in new roles as orchestrators of the cocoon trade to service the Shanghai filature industry, and later as builders and managers of silk filatures in Wuxi and as sericulture-reform specialists. As local elites became involved in new forms of commercial and industrial development in Wuxi, they did not jettison their past traditions of cultivating social dominance in the local setting. Instead, they used organizational strategies and modes of behavior that skillfully combined aspects of their past cultural repertoires with new opportunities to build up wealth, reputation, and power. Through this process, collaboration with government agencies and structures occurred, modeled on past traditions of local elite cooperation with the magistrate's yamen to promote community well-being and the execution of state power.

The involvement of local elites in commerce was nothing new in the

Yangzi delta during the late nineteenth century. Throughout the delta during Qing times, as the economy underwent significant structural change in the direction of more cash cropping and home-based production of handicraft products for the market, Wuxi peasants became involved in cotton spinning and weaving. At the same time, land-tenure relationships were changing. From the Ming/Qing transition onward, peasants striving for more security as tenants increasingly challenged landlords, who granted permanent cultivation rights to many. Under these conditions, local elite families in Wuxi, as elsewhere throughout the delta, crafted new strategies to solidify their hold on local social dominance. These strategies included increasing involvement in managing commercial activities and an ideological rationale for doing so. The ideological dimensions of these activities were positioned soundly within a reformulated Confucian statecraft tradition, with frequent reference by local elites to a revived Confucian dictum on pursuing proper statecraft to promote the people's welfare (jingshi jimin). A strategic shift was to link elite intentions in this regard to the promotion of various forms of commercial activity at the local level. We have reviewed the case of the gentry-merchant Hua family from the Wuxi market town of Dangkou as an example of how this new form of elite strategizing worked.

Although the Qing state was supportive of these local elite activities during the eighteenth and early nineteenth centuries, by the 1860's the state had other structural difficulties with which to contend in the area of state finance. As population growth continued at a steady pace with little new land being brought under cultivation, especially in heartland areas like the Yangzi delta, the state found it increasingly difficult to collect land taxes. Despite efforts of the Yongzheng emperor in the mid-eighteenth century to introduce reforms that would generate more land-tax revenue, the Qing state, depending as it did on the cooperation of local elites to help execute policy, found it impossible to accomplish these goals. It was not just that local elites did not want to pay increased taxes themselves, although this was certainly one issue that stood in the way of tax reform; relatively poor peasants were simply unable to meet the state's tax demands, struggling as they were on farms of declining size as the Qing wore on. The double shock of the Opium War and the Taiping Rebellion brought home the need for new forms of state revenue in still more urgent ways, so that by the century's end, the Qing government placed increasing emphasis on the creation and collection of new forms of commercial-tax revenue.

In Wuxi, we have seen that elite/state interaction in commercial development and tax collection by the late nineteenth century focused on a few key issues: the joint "bureaucratic promotion" of sericulture following the Taiping Rebellion; the establishment of new intraelite associations to promote and protect local cocoon marketing; and the simultaneous development of such associations as government-sanctioned tax-collection agencies. The Kaihua Culture Association and the Wuxi Cocoon-Merchant Guild stand as important examples of how local elites adapted sociocultural practice of the past—the creation of intraelite associations to promote commerce—to launch a new form of cocoon marketing tied to changing world-market conditions and modern industry.

Until the 1910's, the interests of local elites involved in such associations and those of the state dovetailed rather well in Wuxi, with county magistrates especially helpful in implementing policies allowing for the expansion of the cocoon trade. Only from the late 1910's onward did a new level of concern among cocoon-trade merchants about escalating taxes begin to jeopardize the high degree of elite/state collaboration that had marked earlier decades. But as new tensions over taxes mounted, silk-industry elites never appeared to be in open revolt against the government, casting doubt on long-standing notions that "local autonomy" of elites from the state was endemic everywhere during the late Qing and the Republic. Even during the 1930's, when the Model Sericulture District took over cocoon-trade taxation, the desire to preserve elite/state collaboration remained strong. To illustrate this point, we have seen that as model-district bureaucrats raised cocoon-trade taxes to help pay for silk-industry reform, they also accommodated the interests of silk-industry elites by legislating low prices for peasant cocoons.

As local men in Wuxi became investors in silk filatures, they relied on still more aspects of past practice as local elites to deal with the risks of new economic activity and to solidify their evolving social positions. Commercial "layering," a technique used by merchants during Qing times in the delta to buy and sell silk products, was adapted by silk-filature founders as a way to cope with the high risks of modern silk production. "Split ownership/management" in filatures resulted, with the risks of inadequate cocoon supply, difficulties with labor, and commercial shipping and taxes passed on by filature founders to a substratum of filature managers. Filature founders also tapped networks of relatives and friends in elite society to pool capital for building and expanding their plants. Over time, the most successful new industrialists also used long-standing traditions of elite intermarriage to bolster their power and prestige in local society. Building upon such strategies, a few key silk-industry elites emerged in Wuxi by the 1930's, with Xue Shouxuan standing out above all the rest as the most successful at fusing old traditions of local social dominance with new bourgeois behavior. Seen in this light, the merger of Xue's "bourgeois practice" with Guomindang policy-making seems less a radical break with past traditions than a revised form of local elite/state collaboration. Far from going to war with a totally new brand of local industrialist, the Guomindang state committed itself to ongoing collaboration with men like Xue—painstakingly amalgamated, reconstituted local elites—to promote the goals of state-directed development.

THE STATE'S ROLE IN LOCAL DEVELOPMENT

The Wuxi silk-industry story is but one of many local scenarios of modern development unfolding in China during the early twentieth century. Since the magisterial work of G. William Skinner on China's regional systems during late Qing times, we have come to think about Chinese development in regional terms. Although the eight macroregions Skinner delineated were based on environmental factors such as river systems and watersheds and their accompanying agricultural/commercial potentials, his analysis also brought into play various forms of human intervention that helped shape patterns of regional development. Especially important for Skinner was the positioning of cities in commercial and administrative hierarchies. Skinner made two critical points in this regard. The first was that Chinese governments in late imperial times often looked to emerging cities that were high ranking in central-place (i.e., commercial) hierarchies for new administrative sites. The second and more subtle point was that some high-ranking central places never achieved concomitant administrative status because it was ultimately in the interests of Chinese rulers not to let commercial and administrative boundaries overlap too closely, especially in densely populated, highly commercialized regional cores. It was in such areas that powerful local elites with too much direct access to formal power might rise up to challenge state rule. Thus, it was also an important state strategy for dealing with central-place hierarchies and their relationships to state-constructed administrative networks to prevent administrative and economic boundaries from converging too perfectly, especially in regional cores.[1]

Important studies dealing with the Chinese economy and politics since Skinner have used or adapted his framework for regional systems.[2] But because new findings from recent studies of regional and local development are accumulating, the time is now ripe to begin to reformulate Skinner's original vision, especially for the critical decades of the early twentieth century. Kenneth Pomeranz's study of the inland North China plain, which looks at regional economic change over time and seeks in various ways to refine Skinner's notions of what contributed to the making of cores and peripheries within the north China macroregion from the 1850's onward, has begun this process. Pomeranz's major contribution has been to show how changing state goals and policy contributed to rapid economic degeneration in what was once the core of the region. Responding to the pressures of imperialism, the Chinese state adopted what Pomeranz calls a "quasi-mercantilist" stance, with state policy focusing on ways to promote coastal trading centers and railways as opposed to continuing state support for the natural inland core. Through policy maneuvers in the areas of credit markets, cropping patterns, and reforestation, Pomeranz argues that late Qing and Republican governments were major contributors to the "hinterland" nature of inland north China by the early twentieth century.[3]

One way to assess the very different story of modern development in Wuxi, and the state's role in that process, is to see them as the flip side of Pomeranz's scenario. Wuxi lay in the center of the Lower Yangzi macroregion's core, with the relatively high ranking of "regional city" in Skinner's central-place hierarchy. Yet during Qing times, Wuxi had never achieved a concomitantly high position in the urban administrative hierarchy, remaining only a "low-level" county capital. Based on what we have seen of the rising importance of Wuxi as a locale with many government programs to promote the modern silk industry there, we might argue that a new kind of state strategy was emerging by the early twentieth century, aimed at fusing rather than splitting economic and political hierarchies of urban places in the cores of certain prosperous macroregions.

But we must be cautious about viewing the Guomindang state as the sole mover in Wuxi's rise to prominence. As Kathy Walker demonstrates in her study of cotton production in Nantong, another Yangzi delta county, the state's targeting of particular industries and counties for government support also depended on local elite initiatives. The nationally prominent early industrialist Zhang Jian had founded one of China's first modern cotton mills, Da Sheng, in Nantong at the turn of the century, and it had flourished aided by government tax relief. However, by the 1920's, Da Sheng's operations began to fail as the plant was taken over by banks and other independent commercial creditors. In addition, as Da Sheng's status was fading, the famous Rong brothers' cotton mills in Wuxi and Shanghai were rising in stature. These newer mills were successful competitors with Da Sheng for raw cotton throughout the delta region, contributing to its demise. The Rong brothers, like their native-place compatriot, Xue Shouxuan, were favored participants in the constellation of Guomindang commissions, committees, and model districts that singled out certain key industrialists in the Yangzi delta region for more direct involvement in government policy-making with respect to industrial development.[4]

So the state clearly played an increasingly important role in development, or underdevelopment, throughout China during the early twentieth century. However, the key to whether or not a particular locale would succeed or fail in new efforts to modernize involved more than state initiatives. We have seen throughout this study that Wuxi's rise to prominence in silk-industry development lay not in increased state support alone, but rather in an evolving complex of state/elite/peasant relationships with deep roots in the agrarian/commercial past. Because of long-standing traditions of local elite involvement in the commercialized rural economy, when newly oriented governments signaled their readiness to promote modern development, local elites in Wuxi became their agents with relative ease. In the process, they built upon their past roles in shaping local political culture and learned to generate new commercial and industrial wealth by using female labor embedded in the economic substructure of peasant-family farming. These observations for Wuxi may be applicable to other areas of China as well; only future local studies will be able to determine whether Wuxi was a developmental "outlier" during the 1920's and 1930's or, as I suspect may be a more accurate assessment, a place at the cutting edge of a much wider sociocultural tendency for local elites to adapt their private interests to new state plans for promoting and controlling modern industrial growth.

FROM THE GUOMINDANG TO THE CHINESE
COMMUNIST PARTY: LEGACIES OF STATE CONTROL

In the course of conducting the research for this book, I visited Wuxi several times and also traveled to other locales in the Yangzi delta, to meet with people who had participated in silk-industry development. At the time, I was struck by the apparent aplomb with which many such individuals seemed to have weathered decades of antibourgeois political campaigns. Those who were the most dynamic and eager to discuss their experiences were former silk-filature managers and sericulture-reform specialists. I had expected at least some degree of reluctance on the part of such people to speak out about their pasts, but in retrospect I believe I can now explain why the opposite was true. The key to understanding the high degree of pride and self-assurance on the part of the lower stratum of Wuxi's former silk-industry elite is that their expertise about technical aspects of silk-industry development allowed them to step into the vacuum created by Xue Shouxuan's sudden departure from China in 1937. Such people became the local life-blood of evolving government policy for state-directed development.

The story of Gao Jingyue, a highly successful Wuxi silk-filature manager, provides a vivid illustration of how a few key individuals from among the lower stratum of the silk-industry elite developed their careers through ongoing cooperation with government. Gao's father had been a local cocoon merchant in Wuxi, contracting with Shanghai filatures for cocoon purchases among the local peasantry, and going on to become one of several cofounders of Wuxi's Shengyu silk filature. In 1927, upon Gao's graduation from a Zhejiang technical college, his father enlisted him to work in the Shengyu filature. In 1928, he went to Japan for two years to study modern methods of silk-filature operation. When he returned to China, the Wuxi silk industry had begun to decline because of the onset of the Great Depression. Gao wanted to assist in the industry's recovery, but had little capital to invest. During this period, he published at least one article about reforming organization and management practices in filatures. Prior to 1937, Gao also had gone to work for the Ganshen and Gantai filatures to help restructure their financial and labor practices, becoming an advocate of "scientific management."[5]

After Japanese occupation of the delta began in 1937, Gao Jingyue went to Shanghai to avoid cooperating with the Japanese Central China Silk Company, an occupation-government joint-stock venture organized for raw-silk purchase at controlled prices throughout the delta. Gao returned to Wuxi in 1945, and immediately became chairman of the Wuxi Silk-Industry Association (Wuxi sijianye tongye gonghui) and a member of the Jiangsu-Zhejiang-Anhui Silk Producers' Guild (Jiang-Zhe-Wan sichang jianye zong gongsuo).[6] Clearly, Gao was an emerging figure with increasing visibility and prestige in these government-sponsored industry associations, organizations that were thoroughly engulfed by Guomindang policy for silk-industry development during the late 1940's.

Gao Jingyue continued his rise to prominence after the coming of the Communist government in 1949, remaining chair of the Wuxi Silk-Industry Association.[7] In 1955, on the eve of implementation of new Communist government policy to convert all industries to "joint state-private management," Gao was manager of the Zengxing filature, one of Wuxi's largest surviving filatures. That year, as part of the new policy regarding filature organization, twenty-seven filatures were collapsed into seven larger plants. Government bureaucrats became the chief managing officers of these new factories, and several former silk-filature managers emerged in the new configuration of management personnel as factory vice-heads. Gao Jingyue made this next transition successfully as well, appointed as first vice-head of the "Number One Joint Public-Private Silk Factory." Finally, in 1956, Gao made the full-fledged leap to government bureaucrat-expert, appointed in that year to be vice-head of the Jiangsu Provincial Silk-Industry Bureau (Jiangsusheng sichou gongyeju).[8]

Although Gao Jingyue's rise to prominence is impressive, he was not the only member of the lower stratum of the Wuxi silk-industry elite to make a successful career transition into the 1950's. Lü Huantai, whom I also interviewed in Wuxi, had worked for Xue Shouxuan, employed during the early 1930's in the Yongtai filature's New York office, established for the purpose of directly exporting raw silk to the United States.[9] In the mid-1950's, Lü Huantai emerged with Gao Jingyue in the new leadership configuration of the Communist government's plan for silk-industry reorganization, becoming a vice-head of the reorganized Yongtai filature.[10] In another case, Zhang Enshen, a man who had been a local cocoon merchant in Wuxi during the 1930's, reported that during the Japanese occupation period, he became an organizer of a new form of smaller-scale filature that operated in rural areas in Wuxi, avoiding Japanese price controls on raw silk by smuggling some of his product around Japanese agents and exporting it directly from Shanghai. Before the Japanese occupation ended, Zhang reopened larger filatures; after 1945, he entered into a range of filature-management and silk-industry association activities under the returning Guomindang government.[11] He also emerged as a top filature manager in the early 1950's, and became one of several vice-heads of the "Number One Joint Public-Private Silk Factory" with Gao Jingyue.[12] A final example is that of Gu Suruo, who also made the successful transition from private filature manager to bureaucrat-manager in the restructured silk industry after 1955. Gu began his transition by keeping cocoon prices low, establishing a new state-managed company for cocoon purchase in the Wuxi countryside in the spring of 1949, and also by developing filature worker-training programs and new methods of financial management.[13]

From these brief case histories, it appears as though a steady progression in silk-industry policy continued from the Guomindang years into the Communist period, through which both governments relied on the same technical, managerial, and financial experts from the Wuxi silk-industry elite to promote state-directed development. It would take another study to lay bare all the details of how this process unfolded after 1937, even for a single industry like modern silk production in Wuxi.[14] Nonetheless, ongoing trends in elite/state collaboration to promote Wuxi's modern silk industry are striking, and stand in distinct contrast to the prevailing images we have of a sharp rupture between the economic policies of the Guomindang and those of the early Communist period.

Finally, we might begin to better understand shifting Chinese agricultural policy after 1949 when we view it from the vantage point of problems inherent in the silk-industry continuum in Wuxi. As previous scholarship has argued, Mao Zedong's growing concerns about the problems of modern development during the 1950's had deep roots in his ideological notions of a rural, communal, and utopian future.[15] But based on what we have seen in this study, there were undoubtedly other factors behind Mao's attempts to elevate the countryside to center stage in future development planning. By 1955, Mao began to argue that radically new methods of organizing production, especially the building of a diverse range of new industries in rural areas, would be necessary to break the privileges of an emerging bourgeoisie within the state apparatus.

We have seen that men who might fit such a description in Wuxi were not just economically competent, nor were they only concerned with politics; rather, they were increasingly skilled in both areas. Local elites such as these emerged from the rich commercial traditions of the Yangzi delta and began to come into their own during the Republican years. The Communist government that ruled after 1949, like the Guomindang before it, may have needed such men to assist in industrial development, but local elites' potential to manipulate the resources of the countryside to their own advantage also was clear. Seen in this light, the "anti-bourgeois" political campaigns of the mid-1950's onward may have been a product not only of Mao's "radical utopian vision," but also of a realist political strategy aimed at helping peasants resist the power of local elites in places like Wuxi, where some had grown accustomed during earlier decades to pursuing their private interests through state-directed development.

Appendixes

Appendix A

Interviews

NOTE: Chinese characters for personal names, place names, and other terms appear in the Character List. In the list below, interviewees are arranged alphabetically by surname.

INTERVIEWING SITUATIONS

During the 1980's, I met many people in China who had firsthand experience in one or more aspects of silk-industry development in Wuxi. The large majority of these meetings were not chance occurrences; most were prearranged by one of my hosting institutions—the Foreign Affairs Office of Nanjing University, the Economic History Section of the Institute of Economics of the Chinese Academy of Social Sciences in Beijing, and the Wuxi City Office of the State Statistical Bureau. I have not listed all of the interviews here, only those cited in the text.

Questions were put to interviewees in one of two ways. On some occasions, I was asked to prepare questions in writing well in advance of the interviews so that the interviewees could have a chance to prepare comments. In most instances, I also received a written version of the prepared notes from which the interviewees spoke. The written comments were invaluable because many older people did not speak readily intelligible standard Mandarin, but spoke instead in Wuxi's version of Wu dialect. At times, I also received simultaneous translation of the interviewee's comments into Mandarin, but this often proved so tedious and time-consuming that we would stop this exercise partway through the interview. This proved more efficient in the long run, since I also recorded the interviews for transcription later. At the end of the formal presentations, I then was invited to ask other questions. In many instances, I also met with interviewees on second and third occasions, which were always more informal than the first. The second major form of interview was a completely open-ended session in which I was introduced to the interviewees as an American student (and later, a professor) studying the Wuxi silk industry. I then was free to ask whatever I liked with no prearranged areas of inquiry.

One important interview I pursued on my own. This was a meeting with Professor Chen Hansheng, the organizer of the SSRI rural survey conducted in Wuxi in the summer of 1929, as described and analyzed in Chapters 1 and 6 and in Appendix B. I was given Professor Chen's telephone number by a

Chinese mentor, phoned him myself, explained who I was and what I was interested in knowing—at that time, I wanted to find out exactly what had become of the remains of the rural survey—and he invited me to his home. The groundwork for such a generous response had been well laid by Professor Stephen MacKinnon and his wife Jan MacKinnon, who first met with Professor Chen in 1976 to talk primarily about his interaction with the American radical Agnes Smedley, who spent considerable time in China during the 1920's and 1930's. During the 1980's, the MacKinnons and a few other Americans met with Professor Chen to learn more about his political experiences. But to my knowledge, I am the only non-Chinese scholar to have gone seeking the remains of the invaluable and unique Wuxi rural survey. Professor MacKinnon has written a paper about Professor Chen's life (MacKinnon 1990), and several pieces have been written about him in Chinese publications (see, for example, *Zhongguo jingji kexue nianjian 1984* [A yearbook of Chinese economics for 1984] [Shijiazhuang: Hebei renmin chubanshe, 1986]: 870-73). He has also published his own autobiography, which appeared in China in the late 1980's (Chen 1988).

Professor Chen was elderly when I met with him in 1981, well over eighty years of age. Although his eyesight was failing rapidly, he was not yet completely blind. Because he was still a very lively man, he much preferred to speak with me in English rather than labor along with me struggling to understand his Mandarin, heavily influenced as it was by his native Wu dialect (he himself was originally from Wuxi). Some of the details of Professor Chen's life recounted here come from MacKinnon's 1990 paper on Chen; others are details from my own discussions with him in July 1981.

I know less about the backgrounds of most of my remaining interviewees (with the exception of Gao Jingyue, as noted below), and the details I relate here come from the contact I had with them in the 1980's. This does not mean that the information they gave me was not important, as the frequent citation of their interviews in this book makes clear. For example, my interview with Fei Dasheng made the analysis in Chapter 7 crystallize, and Lü Huantai, a former participant in the Xue family enterprises, gave essential insights that helped pull together the disparate information in Chapter 8. Nonetheless, I am able to provide only fragmentary information on these two individuals, as for the remaining interviewees.

INTERVIEWEES AND THEIR BACKGROUNDS

Chen Hansheng

Date of interview: July 26, 1981.
Location: At Chen's home in Beijing.

Chen Hansheng was born in 1897 in Wuxi into a gentry family. He was educated at the missionary-run Qinghua University in Beijing and then went to Pomona College in southern California, where he told me he learned his nearly flawless colloquial English. He graduated from Pomona in 1920, then went on to study history at the graduate level at the University of Chicago, where he earned an M.A.; then at Harvard; and finally at the University of Berlin, where he earned a Ph.D. in 1924. He joined the history faculty at Beijing University in 1924, where he met Li Dazhao, also a history professor and cofounder of the Chinese Communist Party. Through his contact with Li, Chen secretly joined the Comintern and went to Moscow in 1927, returning to Nanjing and then Shanghai by late 1928. In 1929, Chen became director of the Social Science Research Institute of the newly founded Academia Sinica, and began his famous rural field investigations, of which the Wuxi survey used in this book was the first.

Through a series of interviews with Professor Chen, Stephen MacKinnon has learned a great deal about Chen's political activities during the 1930's. He worked as a Comintern informant concerning the internal affairs of the Guomindang for a number of years, and had an active political relationship with the Comintern "master spy" in China, Richard Sorge. Chen joined the Chinese Communist Party in 1935, and in 1936, at the request of the Comintern, returned to the United States to work with the Institute of Pacific Relations in New York. In 1939, he moved to Hong Kong; during the 1940's, he spent time in India and again in the United States. From 1945 to 1950, Chen taught in several U.S. universities while serving secretly as the Chinese Communist Party's leading representative in the United States. After the People's Republic was established in 1949, Professor Chen turned down ministerial positions, preferring instead to remain in the unique role of "the intellectual," serving as an advisor to many, including Mao Zedong.

Chen Yaorong

Date of interview: May 23, 1980.

Location: At the Xizhang Silkworm-Egg Breedery (Xizhang canzhong zhizao-chang) in Wuxi, formerly the Sanwuguan Silkworm-Egg Breedery (Sanwu-guan canzhong zhizaochang).

Chen Yaorong was seventy-eight years old in 1980. His elder brother, Chen Zirong, graduated from the Hangzhou School for Sericulture (Hangzhou canxueguan) in 1925, and went to work as a technical expert for Xue Nanming's Yongtai filature. Because Yongtai was interested in improving the quality of its raw materials, the filature advanced a loan to Chen Zirong to start a silkworm-egg breedery, the Sanwuguan, founded in 1926. Chen Yaorong was one of Sanwuguan's original personnel.

Fei Dasheng

Date of interview: May 18, 1981.

Location: At the Suzhou Silk-Industry Institute (Suzhou siye yanjiusuo) in Suzhou, an affiliate of the Suzhou School for Sericulture in Hushuguan (Suzhou Hushuguan canye xuexiao).

Fei Dasheng was seventy-eight years old in 1981. She was a student of Zheng Qunqiang, the head of the Hushuguan Sericulture School for Girls

(Hushuguan nüzi canye xuexiao), whom she later married. She served as director of extension work at the school from the 1920's through the 1940's. In 1981, she was advisor at the Suzhou Silk-Industry Institute. Fei is also the elder sister of the well-known anthropologist Fei Xiaotong.

Gao Jingyue

Dates of interviews: (1) May 24, 1980; (2) October 20, 1980; (3) May 28, 1981.

Locations: (1) At the headquarters of the Wuxi Municipal Committee of the Chinese People's Political Consultative Congress (Zhongguo renmin zhengzhi xieshang huiyi Wuxishi weiyuanhui) in Wuxi; (2) at Mochou Lake (Mochou hu) in Nanjing; (3) at Xihui Park (Xihui gongyuan) near Huishan in Wuxi.

Gao Jingyue was seventy-three years old when I first met him in Wuxi in May 1980. After Chen Hansheng, Gao was my most important interviewee. He was a lively, natural-born leader who was vice-chair of the revived political organization known as the Wuxi Municipal Committee of the Chinese People's Political Consultative Congress and a central committee member of the Democratic State Reconstruction Association (Zhongguo minzhu jianguo hui). Gao's father was a cocoon merchant and filature founder in Wuxi, and encouraged his son to study silk-filature organization and enter filature management. Since I have discussed Gao's extensive silk-industry activities in Chapter 9, I will not recapitulate those details here.

Gao's biggest contribution to this study was to provide invaluable information on the activities of silk-industry investors and managers, including a detailed history of early cocoon-merchant activities and organizations in Wuxi. As a former leader in silk-industry organizations in Wuxi, and a former silk-filature manager, Gao had access not only to the record of his own personal experiences in the Wuxi silk industry, but also to accumulated written materials of the associations. He painstakingly put together for me brief histories of various stages and episodes of silk-industry development. Without his generous help, my analysis of local elite involvement in the Wuxi silk industry would have been far more difficult to achieve.

Gu Suruo

Date of interview: May 28, 1981.

Location: At Xihui Park near Huishan in Wuxi.

Gu originally was a manager of the Guanchang silk filature. After Liberation, he became head of the Wuxi Number Two Joint Public-Private Silk Factory (Wuxi gongsi heying saosi erchang). Gu's silk-industry activities also are discussed in Chapter 9.

Hu Yuankai

Date of interview: May 23, 1980.

Location: At the Jiangsu Provincial Silkworm-Egg Company (Jiangsusheng canzhong gongsi) in Wuxi.

Hu Yuankai was seventy-one years old in 1980. In 1935, he went to Japan to study. He graduated from a sericulture school in Tokyo in 1938 and returned to China, where he became a staff member of the Jiangsu Provincial Sericulture School (Jiangsusheng canye xuexiao). In 1980, he was an expert at the Jiangsu Provincial Silkworm-Egg Company (Jiangsusheng canzhong gongsi) in Wuxi.

Lü Huantai

Dates of interviews: (1) May 24, 1980; (2) May 28, 1981.

Locations: (1) At the headquarters of the Wuxi Municipal Committee of the Chinese People's Political Consultative Congress in Wuxi; (2) at Xihui Park near Huishan in Wuxi.

Lü Huantai was seventy years old in 1980. He originally was a staff member in the New York office of the Xue family's Yongtai silk-filature organization during the 1930's. In 1980, he was a standing member of the Wuxi Municipal Committee of the Chinese People's Political Consultative Congress and was a member of the Sericulture-and-Silk-Research Section of the Wuxi Municipal Association for the Dissemination of Science (Wuxishi kexue puji xiehui cansi yanjiushi). Lü's silk-industry activities also are discussed in Chapter 9.

Shen Yaoming

Date of interview: May 24, 1980.

Location: At the headquarters of the Wuxi Municipal Committee of the Chinese People's Political Consultative Congress in Wuxi.

Shen Yaoming was seventy years old in 1980. Prior to the Cultural Revolution, he had been a silk-filature vice-head in Wuxi. In 1980, he was collecting materials on the history of the Wuxi filature industry and was a representative of the Wuxi Municipal People's Congress (Wuxishi renmin daibiao dahui).

Wu Yaming

Date of interview: November 7, 1980.

Location: At the Sericulture-Research Institute of the Jiangsu Provincial Academy of Agricultural Science in Zhenjiang (Jiangsusheng nongye kexueyuan Zhenjiang canye yanjiusuo).

Wu Yaming was sixty-eight years old in 1980. He originally was a technical staff member in the Yongtai filature organization. Around 1935 he went abroad to study in Japan.

Xu Ruliang

Dates of interviews: (1) May 24, 1980; (2) May 28, 1981.

Locations: (1) At the headquarters of the Wuxi Municipal Committee of the Chinese People's Political Consultative Congress in Wuxi; (2) at Xihui Park near Huishan in Wuxi.

Xu Ruliang was sixty-six years old in 1980. He originally was a manager of the Zhenyi filature. After Liberation, he became head of the Wuxi Number Three Joint Public-Private Silk Factory (Wuxi gongsi heying saosi san-chang). In 1980, Xu was an engineer at the Jiangsu Provincial Silk-Industry Bureau (Jiangsusheng sichou gongyeju).

Zhang Enshen

Dates of interviews: (1) May 24, 1980; (2) May 28, 1981.

Locations: (1) At the headquarters of the Wuxi Municipal Committee of the Chinese People's Political Consultative Congress in Wuxi; (2) at Xihui Park near Huishan in Wuxi.

Zhang Enshen was seventy-one years old in 1980. He originally was a man-ager of the Ruilin filature and vice-head of the Wuxi Silk-Industry Associa-tion (Wuxi sijianye tongye gonghui). After Liberation, he became head of the Wuxi Number One Joint Public-Private Silk Factory (Wuxi gongsi hey-ing saosi yichang). In 1980, he was a standing member of the Wuxi Munici-pal Committee of the Chinese People's Political Consultative Congress. Zhang's silk-industry activities are also discussed in Chapter 9.

Zhang Kai

Date of interview: October 11, 1980.

Location: At the Jiangsu Provincial Academy of Agricultural Science (Jiangsusheng nongye kexueyuan) in Nanjing.

Zhang Kai had no early experience in silk-industry work, but he was none-theless one of my most important interviewees. Since the 1960's, he had been collecting materials on the history of silk production throughout the Yangzi delta, and was affiliated in 1980 with the Jiangsu Provincial Acad-emy of Agricultural Science in Nanjing. He had many important papers in his possession, including a copy of what he believed was the first cocoon-firm contract written in Wuxi in 1887. He provided a photographed copy of the document, which I have included in the photo section following p. 108; it is also discussed in Chapter 3.

Zhou Kuangming

Dates of interviews: November 8 through 13, 1980.

Location: At the Sericulture-Research Institute of the Jiangsu Provincial Academy of Agricultural Science in Zhenjiang.

Zhou Kuangming was a graduate of the Suzhou School for Sericulture in Hushuguan who started work at the Sericulture-Research Institute of the

Jiangsu Provincial Academy of Agricultural Science in Zhenjiang in 1952. He worked in areas of silkworm-disease prevention and egg breeding. From the time he was a student, he had been collecting information on the history of silk production in the Yangzi delta. In 1980, he was still affiliated with the Sericulture-Research Institute.

Zhuang Yaohe

Date of interview: May 27, 1980.

Location: At the Wuxi Number One Silk Factory (Wuxi saosi yichang), formerly the Dingchang silk filature founded in 1929.

Zhuang Yaohe was head of the factory-affairs office of the Wuxi Number One Silk Factory in 1980. This factory had been one of Wuxi's early filatures, the Dingchang, part of the Zhou family enterprises (Zhou Shunqing had founded some of Wuxi's earliest filatures—see Chapter 5). Zhuang had in his possession a draft history of the Wuxi filature industry, prepared in mimeograph form by the Silk-Industry Editorial Group of the Wuxi Municipal Textile-Industry Bureau (Wuxishi fangzhi gongyeju, saosi gongyeshi bianji xiaozu 1959). He quoted from this work throughout our meeting, and I also was allowed to take notes from it during the afternoon of my visit to the factory.

Appendix B

The Wuxi Rural Surveys

The following discussion clarifies technical issues regarding the two rural surveys introduced in Chapter 1 and analyzed in Chapter 6. Both are peasant-household-level economic surveys, one conducted by the Shanghai Research Office of the South Manchurian Railway Company in 1940, referred to as the "Mantetsu survey" (Minami Manshū tetsudō kabushiki kaisha, Shanghai jimusho chōsashitsu 1941), and the second conducted by the Social Science Research Institute of the Chinese Academia Sinica in 1929, referred to as the "SSRI survey" (Guoli zhongyang yanjiuyuan shehui kexue yanjiusuo 1929).

ISSUES OF RELIABILITY AND METHODS OF DATA COLLECTION

The single most pressing question raised about early-twentieth-century Chinese rural surveys is whether or not they are reliable. Philip Huang has discussed this issue in relationship to Mantetsu materials (Huang 1985: ch. 2), and I will not recapitulate his entire commentary here. But it does seem important to reiterate a few key points. The Japanese government sponsored the research work of the South Manchurian Railway Company in China ("Mantetsu," for short), leading some to question whether the research was falsified or slanted in a direction that would help justify Japan's colonial aspirations. Founded originally as a management body for Russian railroads in Manchuria, the SMR was acquired by the Japanese government following the Russo-Japanese War of 1904–5, and became committed to conducting research on the Chinese economy. Most of its research personnel were independent scholars in various social-science disciplines before joining Mantetsu, individuals who found expression of their views in Japan during the 1930's increasingly difficult since many of them had Marxist inclinations. Working as part of Mantetsu research operations in China, however, seems to have afforded them a higher degree of intellectual freedom than they had found at home, and they wrote and published prodigiously. These scholars often expressed concern about levels of peasant poverty in China but did not seem interested in making the situation bleaker than it really was. They aimed instead to explain as accurately as possible why the Chinese peasantry might be likely to turn to rebellion or be prone to accept the leadership of the emerging Chinese Communist Party. (An engaging introduction to Mantetsu research activities is contained in Fogel 1988.)

A second concern about Mantetsu materials has been whether outsiders to the Chinese rural environment, especially those employed by a colonialist government, would have been able to elicit truthful information from peasant households. But Huang has observed that Chinese villagers who had contact with Mantetsu research teams remembered them fondly even decades later, pleased that there had been people so meticulously interested in every detail of their daily lives. In addition, as the Mantetsu research team who visited Wuxi noted in the preface to its published report (Mantetsu 1941), the fact that the local county government sanctioned their visit often made their work easier. Peasants responded readily to any questions for which they believed the government needed their answers in order to assist them in improving their farming efforts—questions about landholding, cropping patterns, and prices, for example. On the other hand, the interviewers also felt that issues outside the legitimate purview of local government, such as popular cultural practices and patterns of social organization, might have met with better responses if local authorities had not been involved so directly. With constant escorts from the county government office, the interviewers were not always free to establish direct rapport and carry on extended conversations with their interviewees, a problem that has lingered into the late twentieth century for aspiring foreign field workers in the Chinese rural environment.

Further insights into the potential difficulties in interviewing Chinese peasants come from an Academia Sinica work report on the 1929 SSRI survey in Wuxi. As noted in Chapter 1, the Wuxi team surveyed twenty-two villages with a total population of 1,204 rural households. But even for native interviewers, executing a twenty-six-page printed questionnaire was a daunting task. Forty-five people were involved in collecting the data and spent a total of three months in the field, first perfecting and then executing the questionnaire. Most of the interviewers were natives of Wuxi or neighboring counties, a plan designed to cope with the problems of interviewing in Wuxi's local version of Wu dialect. Approximately one-third of the interviewing group no longer resided locally, but were students or graduates of major universities in Beijing and Shanghai who had studied either agriculture or social sciences. Another one-third were upper-middle-school students in Wuxi, and the last third were Wuxi primary-school teachers. The members of the Social Science Research Institute staff who traveled to Wuxi to supervise the survey trained this rather motley assortment of individuals in interviewing technique, split them into four groups, and sent them out to preselected villages. There was resistance in some villages at first, with peasants proclaiming that if it was more taxes that the interviewers were interested in, they would not answer questions even if "a huge army" was sent in to coerce them. In one village, peasant women organized on-the-spot action with mops used to clean their households' nightsoil buckets, beating the would-be interviewers over the head with their self-styled weapons of resistance. Obviously, if interviewing was to proceed, more groundwork would have to be laid (Liao 1930: 11–13).

The next step was to make contact with village-level leaders, preferably with men filling the post of *dibao*, the lowest-level administrative post. The interviewers then promoted good relations with such individuals and relied on their assistance in setting up interviews. One suspects that this sort of effort—referred to as "tugging relationships" (*la guanxi*) in Chinese—was also useful to the Mantetsu researchers. In any case, establishing connections worked well for the SSRI interviewers when the dibao had considerable influence in the village. Otherwise, they relied on the ability of the primary-school teachers who were part of the interviewing teams to create goodwill with the villagers, a task at which they excelled in several instances. Only as a last resort, when the influence of the dibao was weak or the teachers could not win over particularly recalcitrant interviewees, was the authority of local government used more directly by producing official documents authorizing the researchers' visits. If it was necessary to resort to displaying documents, the visit usually became more perfunctory, and the results of the questioning were more likely to be inaccurate (ibid.: 13–14).

Given the amount of care taken in arranging for the best interviewing situation possible, the SSRI survey was not only one of the earliest but also one of the most important surveys of Chinese rural conditions during the 1920's, and is probably among the very best surviving data we have from that period. Although John Lossing Buck's famous surveys of the same era cover a much wider geographical scope, few of them were conducted by on-the-ground field workers (see Buck 1937). Most of Buck's data were collected instead through a mail-in survey method, and its questionable reliability has been a constant source of frustration for later researchers. As for the SSRI survey, its strongest point is the depth of concentrated quantitative data it contains, collected through lengthy face-to-face interviews. Many interviewers added their own narrative notes in the margins of the printed questionnaires (one even wrote occasionally in French and signed himself Gustave), making for a fascinating source of information on everything from basic cropping patterns to the complexities of local practices in land tenure. Approximately 800 of the original questionnaires survive, housed now at the Institute of Economics of the Chinese Academy of Social Sciences in Beijing. In 1986 and 1987, I spent about ten months there familiarizing myself with the materials and working out a system for coding them for later computer analysis.

After using the two Wuxi rural surveys, I have concluded that their most serious limitation is not their reliability but rather their lack of time-depth. These surveys do not contain data from which time series can be extracted, and therefore should be used with the greatest of caution when developing hypotheses about rural development over the long term. I avoid the issue of changing wage rates over time, for example, one of the preoccupations of economic historians who have studied Chinese rural development, because there is no way intrinsic to the data to study such a problem (for further discussion of the limitations of changing-wage-rate analysis, see Esherick's 1991 critique of Brandt 1989). Instead, I have attempted to use quantitative methods and economic reasoning in ways that make good sense given the cross-sectional nature of the data in the SSRI and Mantetsu surveys, and to draw conclusions about longer-term patterns of economic development only when I have been able to find ways to do so primarily with information available in the surveys themselves.

THE SSRI SURVEY SAMPLE

The questionnaires from the SSRI survey contain data on landholding, family composition, crop production, land and crop prices, sericulture, subsidiary occupations, hired agricultural labor, land tenure, rent, and debt. Each questionnaire represents one household; all of the households interviewed were engaged in farming activities and/or other village-based income-earning activities. The large majority of households worked at both rice/wheat farming and sericulture. To create the sample used in this book, I chose questionnaires from thirteen of the twenty-two villages surveyed based on extensive reading of questionnaires from all of the villages. (Map 2 in Chapter 6 displays the names and locations of the villages; their names also appear in the Character List.) The thirteen villages chosen had the best-quality questionnaires—that is to say, the interview teams going to those villages used the questionnaires most consistently among interviewees with most of the questions asked and answered. I then chose ten households at random from each of the selected villages to whom the interviewers gave the classifications "middle peasant," "poor peasant," or "agricultural laborer." There is no available explanation for how the interviewers derived these classifications, but my impression after reading over hundreds of questionnaires is that they conformed to those of land reform led by the Chinese Communist Party, a movement taking shape concurrently. For the remainder of the sample, I included all sixteen households from the thirteen selected villages classified "rich peasant," "landlord," or "merchant." Since these three categories were used for only about 10 percent of the 800 households overall, they are somewhat overrepresented in the current sample. However, my rationale for allowing this imbalance was that I was interested in including the largest possible number of rural rich to make comparisons with the majority of poorer households.

Once the sample households were selected, I began coding raw data from the questionnaires, creating 283 variables. Later, I grouped these variables into eight topically arranged data sets—Farm Operations (OPS), Crop Output and Prices (CROPS), Sericulture Operations (SER), Supplementary Income (SUPINC), Hired Labor (HIRLAB), Land Tenure (LANTEN), Land Rents (RENT), and Debt (DEBT). Inevitably, when reviewing the data for analysis, missing information made it impossible to use a portion of the sample households that were originally selected. In the end, 128 households from all thirteen villages remained in the analyzed sample, including at least six from each village. All of the richer households selected originally remained. For identification of each household record and ease of analysis across all eight data sets, the first four variables appear in each set (see Table B1). The remaining variables in each data set follow.

Farm Operations (OPS) includes size of farm; amount of land devoted to each crop; cost of irrigation, plowing, fertilizer, and animal usage; family composition; and categorization of the household by land-tenure arrangements, employment status, and farming type. Note that the terms *gengdao*, *xiandao*, and *nuodao* refer to three different types of rice grown in Wuxi and throughout the Yangzi delta generally; gengdao is short-grain rice grown for daily consumption, the most common variety in the Yangzi delta; xiandao is early-ripening long-grain rice, more delicate than gengdao but with more kernels per stalk; and nuodao is glutinous rice, grown sparsely and consumed by most peasants only on special occasions because of its lower yields and higher price. (See Table B2.)

Crop Output and Prices (CROPS) includes data on output and prices for the three types of rice (gengdao, xiandao, and nuodao), wheat, and mulberry leaves for 1927–28 and 1928–29. (See Table B3.)

Sericulture Operations (SER) includes output of cocoons for 1928 and 1929; income from cocoon sales; costs of egg cards and mulberry leaves; and family and hired labor usage. (See Table B4.)

Supplementary Income (SUPINC) includes all types of nonland-based work, either inside or outside the village, and the incomes earned from it. Another definition of "supplementary work" as it is used here is any income-earning activity other than rice/wheat farming, mulberry cultivation, or cocoon raising. (See Table B5.)

Hired Labor (HIRLAB) includes long-term and short-term labor hired by the household, including number of people hired; wages paid yearly or daily; place of origin of long-term workers; and tasks and seasons for short-term laborers. (See Table B6.)

Land Tenure (LANTEN) includes information on land by parcel, specifying whether it was rented or owned; its price; whether it was rice paddy or mulberry; the density of planting (how many plants or trees per mu); the size of the parcel; and ownership status (i.e., whether the person who worked the land held topsoil rights, subsoil rights, or no permanent rights to ownership). (See Table B7.)

Land Rents (RENT) includes the total number of mu rented in and out; the number of mu in each rented parcel; the rental value per mu in grain volume (dan); the rental value per mu in cash; and the total rental value in cash for each parcel. (See Table B8.)

Debt (DEBT) includes the number of loan associations; the number of pawning arrangements; the number of loans of other types, both as debtor and creditor; the total amount of money borrowed and/or loaned; and the interest paid and/or received. (See Table B9.)

TABLE B1

No.	Variable name	Description of variable
1	ID	Questionnaire I.D. number
2	VILL	Village I.D. number
3	CLASS	Class status given by interviewer: 1 = agricultural laborer 4 = rich peasant 2 = poor peasant 5 = landlord 3 = middle peasant 6 = other (merchant, artisan, shopkeeper, etc.)
4	SIZE	Total number of mu farmed (one mu ≅ 1/6 acre)

TABLE B2

No.	Variable name	Description of variable
5	RICE1	Number of mu gengdao (rice type #1)
6	RICE2	Number of mu xiandao (rice type #2)
7	RICE3	Number of mu nuodao (rice type #3)
8	WHEAT	Number of mu wheat
9	MULB	Number of mu mulberry
10	OTHERLAN	Number of mu other farm land
11	CROPS	Other types of crops grown: 1 = soil-enriching, flowering 6 = peas (wandou) grass (ziyunying) 7 = melons (gua) 2 = celery (qincai) 8 = garlic (dasuan) 3 = broad beans (candou) 9 = taro (yutou) 4 = alfalfa (musu) 5 = green (leafy) vegetables (shucai)
12	R1WORK	Labor days per mu, gengdao
13	R2WORK	Labor days per mu, xiandao
14	R3WORK	Labor days per mu, nuodao
15	WWORK	Labor days per mu, wheat
16	MWORK	Labor days per mu, mulberry
17	BEAST	Animal usage: 1 = no 4 = yes, hired from another 2 = yes, owned outright 5 = yes, borrowed from 3 = yes, owned partially another
18	OWNANCOS	Cost of feeding owned animal per year
19	HIRANIR	Mu worked by hired animal for irrigation on rice/wheat land
20	COSTIRR	Cost per mu of hired animal for irrigation on rice/wheat land
21	HIRANPL	Mu worked by hired animal for plowing on rice/wheat land
22	COSTPLOW	Cost per mu of hired animal for plowing on rice/wheat land
23	MECHPUMP	Mechanical pumping: 1 = yes, hired pump on all land 2 = no, did not hire pump 3 = yes, but hired only for some land
24	MUPUMP	Mu of rice paddy irrigated by pumping
25	COSTPUMP	Cost per mu of pumping rice paddy

No.	Variable name	Description of variable
26	PLOW	Plow usage: 1 = owned plow 3 = shared ownership 2 = did not own plow 4 = borrowed plow
27	WATWHEEL	Waterwheel usage: 1 = owned waterwheel 3 = shared ownership 2 = did not own waterwheel 4 = borrowed water-wheel
28	FERTR1	Cost of fertilizer per mu of gengdao
29	FERTR2	Cost of fertilizer per mu of xiandao
30	FERTR3	Cost of fertilizer per mu of nuodao
31	FERTW	Cost of fertilizer per mu of wheat
32	FERTM	Cost of fertilizer per mu of mulberry
33	MW	Number of household men who worked
34	WW	Number of household women who worked
35	CW	Number of household children who worked
36	MP	Number of household men present (this usually meant "in existence" rather than "residing at home")
37	WP	Number of women present (same explanation as for 36)
38	CP	Number of children present (same explanation as for 36)
39	TENURE	Status by land tenure category: 1 = owner-cultivator 2 = pure tenant 3 = part owner-cultivator, part tenant 4 = part owner-cultivator, part tenant, and rents land out 5 = owner-cultivator and rents land out 6 = tenant and rents land out 7 = rents land out 8 = landless peasant or worker 9 = landless "other," e.g., merchant, teacher, shopkeeper, musician
	EMP	Status by employment: 0 = farming only 1 = in addition to farming, family had other employment 2 = rather than farming, family had other employment 3 = other employment only 4 = unemployed
41	FTYPE	Status by type of farming: 1 = farming only rice/wheat 2 = farming only mulberry 3 = farming rice/wheat and mulberry 4 = no farming

TABLE B3

No.	Variable name	Description of variable
5	OUTR1	Output (dan/mu) for gengdao, 1928–29
6	PRIR1	Price received (dollar (yuan)/dan) for gengdao, 1928–29
7	JINR1	Jin/dan for gengdao
8	BESTR1	"Best-ever" gengdao output, dan/mu
9	OUT2R1	Output (dan/mu) for gengdao, 1927–28
10	PRI2R1	Price received (dollar/dan) for gengdao, 1927–28

No.	Variable name	Description of variable
11	OUTR2	Output (dan/mu) for xiandao, 1928–29
12	PRIR2	Price received (dollar/dan) for xiandao, 1928–29
13	JINR2	Jin/dan for xiandao
14	BESTR2	"Best-ever" xiandao output, dan/mu
15	OUT2R2	Output (dan/mu) for xiandao, 1927–28
16	PRI2R2	Price received (dollar/dan) for xiandao, 1927–28
17	OUTR3	Output (dan/mu) for nuodao, 1928–29
18	PRIR3	Price received (dollar/dan) for nuodao, 1928–29
19	JINR3	Jin/dan for nuodao
20	BESTR3	"Best-ever" nuodao output, dan/mu
21	OUT2R3	Output (dan/mu) for nuodao, 1927–28
22	PRI2R3	Price received (dollar/dan) for nuodao, 1927–28
23	OUTW	Output (dan/mu) for wheat, 1928–29
24	PRIW	Price received (dollar/dan) for wheat, 1928–29
25	JINW	Jin/dan for wheat
26	BESTW	"Best-ever" wheat output, dan/mu
27	OUT2W	Output (dan/mu) for wheat, 1927–28
28	PRI2W	Price received (dollar/dan) for wheat, 1927–28
29	OUTM	Output (dan/mu) for mulberry, 1928–29
30	PRIM	Price received (dollar/dan) for mulberry, 1928–29
31	JINM	Jin/dan for mulberry
32	BESTM	"Best-ever" mulberry output, dan/mu
33	OUT2M	Output (dan/mu) for mulberry, 1927–28
34	PRI2M	Price received (dollar/dan) for mulberry, 1927–28

TABLE B4

No.	Variable name	Description of variable
5	SERYN	Engaged in sericulture: 1 = yes 2 = no
6	SPJIN	Quantity of cocoons produced spring 1928, in jin
7	SPINC	Income (before costs) from cocoons, spring 1928
8	SPEC	Cost of egg cards, spring 1928
9	SPMC	Cost of purchased mulberry leaves, spring 1928
10	SP2JIN	Quantity of cocoons produced spring 1929, in jin
11	SP2INC	Income (before costs) from cocoons, spring 1929
12	SP2EC	Cost of egg cards, spring 1929
13	SP2MC	Cost of purchased mulberry leaves, spring 1929
14	SJIN	Quantity of cocoons produced summer 1928, in jin
15	SINC	Income (before costs) from cocoons, summer 1928
16	SEC	Cost of egg cards, summer 1928
17	SMC	Cost of purchased mulberry leaves, summer 1928
18	S2JIN	Quantity of cocoons produced summer 1929, in jin
19	S2INC	Income (before costs) from cocoons, summer 1929
20	S2EC	Cost of egg cards, summer 1929
21	S2MC	Cost of purchased mulberry leaves, summer 1929
22	FJIN	Quantity of cocoons produced fall 1928, in jin
23	FINC	Income (before costs) from cocoons, fall 1928
24	FEC	Cost of egg cards, fall 1928
25	FMC	Cost of purchased mulberry leaves, fall 1928
26	SPW	Female family members engaged in cocoon raising, spring
27	SPWDAYS	Labor days (gong) expended in cocoon raising by female family members, spring

No.	Variable name	Description of variable
28	SPM	Male family members engaged in cocoon raising, spring
29	SPMDAYS	Labor days (gong) expended in cocoon raising by male family members, spring
30	SPC	Child family members engaged in cocoon raising, spring
31	SPCDAYS	Labor days (gong) expended in cocoon raising by child family members, spring
32	SW	Female family members engaged in cocoon raising, summer
33	SWDAYS	Labor days (gong) expended in cocoon raising by female family members, summer
34	SM	Male family members engaged in cocoon raising, summer
35	SMDAYS	Labor days (gong) expended in cocoon raising by male family members, summer
36	SC	Child family members engaged in cocoon raising, summer
37	SCDAYS	Labor days (gong) expended in cocoon raising by child family members, summer
38	FW	Female family members engaged in cocoon raising, fall
39	FWDAYS	Labor days (gong) expended in cocoon raising by female family members, fall
40	FM	Male family members engaged in cocoon raising, fall
41	FMDAYS	Labor days (gong) expended in cocoon raising by male family members, fall
42	FC	Child family members engaged in cocoon raising, fall
43	FCDAYS	Labor days (gong) expended in cocoon raising by child family members, fall
44	SPHW	Female hired laborers engaged in cocoon raising, spring
45	SPHWDAYS	Labor days (gong) expended in cocoon raising by female hired laborers, spring
46	SPHM	Male hired laborers engaged in cocoon raising, spring
47	SPHMDAYS	Labor days (gong) expended in cocoon raising by male hired laborers, spring
48	SPHC	Child hired laborers engaged in cocoon raising, spring
49	SPHCDAYS	Labor days (gong) expended in cocoon raising by child hired laborers, spring
50	SHW	Female hired laborers engaged in cocoon raising, summer
51	SHWDAYS	Labor days (gong) expended in cocoon raising by female hired laborers, summer
52	SHM	Male hired laborers engaged in cocoon raising, summer
53	SHMDAYS	Labor days (gong) expended in cocoon raising by male hired laborers, summer
54	SHC	Child hired laborers engaged in cocoon raising, summer
55	SHCDAYS	Labor days (gong) expended in cocoon raising by child hired laborers, summer
	FHW	Female hired laborers engaged in cocoon raising, fall
57	FHWDAYS	Labor days (gong) expended in cocoon raising by female hired laborers, fall
58	FHM	Male hired laborers engaged in cocoon raising, fall
59	FHMDAYS	Labor days (gong) expended in cocoon raising by male hired laborers, fall
60	FHC	Child hired laborers engaged in cocoon raising, fall
61	FHCDAYS	Labor days (gong) expended in cocoon raising by child hired laborers, fall season
62	SP28	Cocoon raising attempted in spring 1928: 1 = yes 3 = yes, but failed 2 = no

No.	Variable name	Description of variable
63	SP29	Cocoon raising attempted in spring 1929: 1 = yes 3 = yes, but failed 2 = no
64	SUM28	Cocoon raising attempted in summer 1928: 1 = yes 3 = yes, but failed 2 = no
65	SUM29	Cocoon raising attempted in summer 1929: 1 = yes 3 = yes, but failed 2 = no
66	FALL28	Cocoon raising attempted in fall 1928: 1 = yes 3 = yes, but failed 2 = no
67	FALL29	Cocoon raising attempted in fall 1929: 1 = yes 4 = interview too early in 2 = no year to know 3 = yes, but failed

TABLE B5

No.	Variable name	Description of variable
5	COT	Family member engaged in cottage industry: 1 = yes 2 = no
6	COTINC	Income earned from cottage industry (in yuan)
7	ART	Family member engaged in artisan activity 1 = yes 2 = no
8	ARTINC	Income earned from artisan activity
9	AGLAB	Family member hired out for agricultural work: 1 = yes 2 = no
10	AGLABINC	Income earned from hired-out agricultural work
11	WAGELAB	Family member hired for wage work in village: 1 = yes 2 = no
12	WALABINC	Income earned from wage work in village
13	FACT	Family member worked in a factory: 1 = yes 2 = no
14	FACTINC	Income earned from factory work
15	URB	Family member engaged in wage work in an urban locale: 1 = yes 2 = no
16	URBINC	Income earned from urban-based wage work
17	COM	Family members engaged in commerce: 1 = yes 2 = no
18	COMINC	Income earned from commerce
19	TEACH	Family member was a teacher: 1 = yes 2 = no
20	TEACHINC	Income earned from teaching
21	DOCT	Family member was a doctor: 1 = yes 2 = no
22	DOCTINC	Income earned from doctoring
23	OTHER	Family members with other source(s) of supplementary income: 1 = yes 2 = no
24	OTHERINC	Income earned from other supplementary activity

TABLE B6

No.	Variable name	Description of variable
5	MLNGNO	Male long-term laborers, number of people
6	MLNGWAG1	Male long-term laborers, wages paid to first worker
7	MLNGWAG2	Male long-term laborers, wages paid to second worker
8	MLNGLOC1	Male long-term laborers, location of origin for first worker
9	MLNGLOC2	Male long-term laborers, location of origin for second worker
10	WLNGNO	Female long-term laborers, number of people
11	WLNGWAG1	Female long-term laborers, wages paid to first worker
12	WLNGWAG2	Female long-term laborers, wages paid to second worker
13	WLNGLOC1	Female long-term laborers, location of origin for first worker
14	WLNGLOC2	Female long-term laborers, location of origin for second worker
15	CLNGNO	Child long-term laborers, number of people
16	CLNGWAG1	Child long-term laborers, wages paid to first worker
17	CLNGWAG2	Child long-term laborers, wages paid to second worker
18	CLNGLOC1	Child long-term laborers, location of origin for first worker
19	CLNGLOC2	Child long-term laborers, location of origin for second worker
20	MSRTDAY1	Male short-term laborers, number of days, first worker
21	MSRTDAY2	Male short-term laborers, number of days, second worker
22	MSRTDAY3	Male short-term laborers, number of days, third worker
23	MSRTWAG1	Male short-term laborers, wages paid to first worker
24	MSRTWAG2	Male short-term laborers, wages paid to second worker
25	MSRTWAG3	Male short-term laborers, wages paid to third worker
26	MSRTLOC1	Male short-term laborers, location of origin of first worker: 1 = this village 2 = outside village
27	MSRTLOC2	Male short-term laborers, location of origin for second worker: 1 = this village 2 = outside village
28	MSRTLOC3	Male short-term laborers, location of origin for third worker: 1 = this village 2 = outside village
29	WSRTDAY1	Female short-term laborers, number of days, first worker
30	WSRTDAY2	Female short-term laborers, number of days, second worker
31	WSRTWAG1	Female short-term laborers, wages paid to first worker
32	WSRTWAG2	Female short-term laborers, wages paid to second worker
33	WSRTLOC1	Female short-term laborers, location of origin of first worker: 1 = this village 2 = outside village
34	WSRTLOC2	Female short-term laborers, location of origin of second worker: 1 = this village 2 = outside village
35	CSRTDAY1	Child short-term laborers, number of days, first worker
36	CSRTDAY2	Child short-term laborers, number of days, second worker
37	CSRTWAG1	Child short-term laborers, wages paid to first worker
38	CSRTWAG2	Child short-term laborers, wages paid to second worker
39	CSRTLOC1	Child short-term laborers, location of origin of first worker: 1 = this village 2 = outside village
40	CSRTLOC2	Child short-term laborers, location of origin of second worker: 1 = this village 2 = outside village

No.	Variable name	Description of variable
41	DLABDAY	Day labor, total number of days
42	DLABDAYF	Day labor, total number of days in farming
43	DLABDAYS	Day labor, total number of days in sericulture
44	DLABWAG	Day labor, total wages paid
45	DLABDW1	Day labor, daily wage paid for first type of work
46	DLABTAS1	Day labor, category of first type of work:
		1 = rice farming 4 = cocoon raising
		2 = wheat farming 5 = other
		3 = mulberry farming
47	DLABSEA1	Day labor, season employed for first type of work:
		1 = spring 4 = winter
		2 = summer 5 = when things are busy
		3 = fall
48	DLABDW2	Day labor, daily wage paid for second type of work
49	DLABTAS2	Day labor, category of second type of work:
		1 = rice farming 4 = cocoon raising
		2 = wheat farming 5 = other
		3 = mulberry farming
50	DLABSEA2	Day labor, season employed for second type of work:
		1 = spring 4 = winter
		2 = summer 5 = when things are busy
		3 = fall
51	DLABDW3	Day labor, daily wage paid for third type of work
52	DLABTAS3	Day labor, category of third type of work:
		1 = rice farming 4 = cocoon raising
		2 = wheat farming 5 = other
		3 = mulberry farming
53	DLABSEA3	Day labor, season employed for third type of work:
		1 = spring 4 = winter
		2 = summer 5 = when things are busy
		3 = fall
54	DLABDW4	Day labor, daily wage paid for fourth type of work
55	DLABTAS4	Day labor, category of fourth type of work:
		1 = rice farming 4 = cocoon raising
		2 = wheat farming 5 = other
		3 = mulberry farming
56	DLABSEA4	Day labor, season employed for fourth type of work:
		1 = spring 4 = winter
		2 = summer 5 = when things are busy
		3 = fall
57	DLABDW5	Day labor, daily wage paid for fifth type of work
58	DLABTAS5	Day labor, category of fifth type of work:
		1 = rice farming 4 = cocoon raising
		2 = wheat farming 5 = other
		3 = mulberry farming
59	DLABSEA5	Day labor, season employed for fifth type of work:
		1 = spring 4 = winter
		2 = summer 5 = when things are busy
		3 = fall
60	DLABINS	Day labor, from inside the village
		1 = yes 2 = no
61	DLABOUT	Day labor, from outside the village
		1 = yes 2 = no

TABLE B7

No.	Variable name	Description of variable
5	NO1OWN	First parcel, rented or owned: 1 = rented 2 = owned
6	NO1PRICE	First parcel, price per mu
7	NO1TYPE	First parcel, type of land: 1 = rice paddy 2 = mulberry
8	NO1DENS	First parcel, density of crop (number of plants per mu)
9	NO1SIZE	First parcel, number of mu
10	NO1STAT	First parcel, ownership status: 1 = no ownership rights 3 = topsoil & subsoil rights 2 = topsoil rights only 4 = subsoil rights only
11	NO2OWN	Second parcel, rented or owned: 1 = rented 2 = owned
12	NO2PRICE	Second parcel, price per mu
13	NO2TYPE	Second parcel, type of land: 1 = rice paddy 2 = mulberry
14	NO2DENS	Second parcel, density of crop (number of plants per mu)
15	NO2SIZE	Second parcel, number of mu
16	NO2STAT	Second parcel, ownership status: 1 = no ownership rights 3 = topsoil & subsoil rights 2 = topsoil rights only 4 = subsoil rights only
17	NO3OWN	Third parcel, rented or owned: 1 = rented 2 = owned
18	NO3PRICE	Third parcel, price per mu
19	NO3TYPE	Third parcel, type of land: 1 = rice paddy 2 = mulberry
20	NO3DENS	Third parcel, density of crop (number of plants per mu)
21	NO3SIZE	Third parcel, number of mu
22	NO3STAT	Third parcel, ownership status: 1 = no ownership rights 3 = topsoil & subsoil rights 2 = topsoil rights only 4 = subsoil rights only
23	NO4OWN	Fourth parcel, rented or owned: 1 = rented 2 = owned
24	NO4PRICE	Fourth parcel, price per mu
25	NO4TYPE	Fourth parcel, type of land: 1 = rice paddy 2 = mulberry
26	NO4DENS	Fourth parcel, density of crop (number of plants per mu)
27	NO4SIZE	Fourth parcel, number of mu
28	NO4STAT	Fourth parcel, ownership status: 1 = no ownership rights 3 = topsoil & subsoil rights 2 = topsoil rights only 4 = subsoil rights only
29	NO5OWN	Fifth parcel, rented or owned: 1 = rented 2 = owned
30	NO5PRICE	Fifth parcel, price per mu
31	NO5TYPE	Fifth parcel, type of land: 1 = rice paddy 2 = mulberry
32	NO5DENS	Fifth parcel, density of crop (number of plants per mu)
33	NO5SIZE	Fifth parcel, number of mu
34	NO5STAT	Fifth parcel, ownership status: 1 = no ownership rights 3 = topsoil & subsoil rights 2 = topsoil rights only 4 = subsoil rights only

TABLE B8

No.	Variable name	Description of variable
		LAND RENTED IN:
5	INMU	Number of mu rented in
6	INDAN1	Rental rate per mu in dan for first parcel
7	INCAS1	Rental rate per mu in yuan for first parcel
8	INTOT1	Total rent payment for first parcel in yuan
9	INMU1	Size of first rented parcel in mu
10	INDAN2	Rental rate per mu in dan for second parcel
11	INCAS2	Rental rate per mu in yuan for second parcel
12	INTOT2	Total rent payment for second parcel in yuan
13	INMU2	Size of second rented parcel in mu
14	INDAN3	Rental rate per mu in dan for third parcel
15	INCAS3	Rental rate per mu in yuan for third parcel
16	INTOT3	Total rent payment for third parcel in yuan
17	INMU3	Size of third rented parcel in mu
18	INDAN4	Rental rate per mu in dan for fourth parcel
19	INCAS4	Rental rate per mu in yuan for fourth parcel
20	INTOT4	Total rent payment for fourth parcel in yuan
21	INMU4	Size of fourth rented parcel in mu
		LAND RENTED OUT:
22	OUTMU	Total number of mu rented out
23	OUTDAN1	Rental rate per mu in dan for first parcel
24	OUTCAS1	Rental rate per mu in yuan for first parcel
25	OUTTOT1	Total rent received for first parcel in yuan
26	OUTMU1	Size of first rented-out parcel in mu
27	OUTDAN2	Rental rate per mu in dan for second parcel
28	OUTCAS2	Rental rate per mu in yuan for second parcel
29	OUTTOT2	Total rent received for second parcel in yuan
30	OUTMU2	Size of second rented-out parcel in mu
31	OUTDAN3	Rental rate per mu in dan for third parcel
32	OUTCAS3	Rental rate per mu in yuan for third parcel
24	OUTTOT3	Total rent received for third parcel in yuan
34	OUTMU3	Size of third rented-out parcel in mu
35	OUTDAN4	Rental rate per mu in dan for fourth parcel
36	OUTCAS4	Rental rate per mu in yuan for fourth parcel
37	OUTTOT4	Total rent received for fourth parcel in yuan
38	OUTMU4	Size of fourth rented-out parcel in mu

TABLE B9

No.	Variable name	Description of variable
5	LOANASS	No. of loan associations participated in
6	PAWN	No. of loans from pawn shops
7	LOANIN	Total no. of loans in
8	LOANINAM	Dollar amount of loans in
9	LOANININ	Yearly interest on loans in
10	LOANOUT	Total no. of loans out
11	LOANOUAM	Dollar amount of loans out
12	LOANOUIN	Yearly interest on loans out

Appendix C

Data on Investment Patterns in Wuxi Silk Filatures

Among the most difficult data to collect on early Chinese industry are reliable facts and figures about investment patterns. In the *Wuxi Yearbook* for 1930, we have one of the best accountings by the county government of investment in Wuxi industry. Comparing the figures for silk filatures and cotton mills, where preprocessed cotton yarn was woven into cotton textiles, far less capital was needed to operate a filature. In 1930, forty-eight filatures reported a total capital investment of 2,388,000 yuan, or about 49,750 yuan per filature on average. The amounts reported for the cotton industry were 6,160,000 yuan for only five mills, or 1,232,000 yuan per mill on average. In Wuxi's other major industry, flour processing, trends similar to those in cotton obtained. For four flour mills, 1,680,000 yuan were invested, or 420,000 yuan per plant on average (Wuxi xianzhengfu, Wuxi shizheng choubeichu 1930, industry section: tables 1 and 2 following p. 30).

The reasons for the smaller sums invested per filature are obscure. To begin with, the figures for filature investment cited in the *Wuxi Yearbook* refer only to "management" capital, or the sums invested by the individual, or group of individuals, renting and operating the filature. As discussed in Chapter 5, and as seen in the following table, there were both "management" and "ownership" groups associated with each filature, and their capital was kept separate for accounting purposes. In addition, since silk filatures produced only for an uncertain and volatile export market, and had constant problems with raw-material supply, neither their owners nor their operators probably had much incentive to expand their plants beyond the scale and scope they achieved during the 1920's. Finally, silk spinning used relatively simple equipment and employed primarily young unskilled women, additional factors that kept costs relatively low.

The following table displays the best available data on investment per filature. It includes the name of each filature and its founding date; the amount of capital amassed to start the filature; the amounts of "ownership" (shiye) capital and "management" (yingye) capital; and other background information about filature founders and management patterns. This chart is adapted from a similar one by Professor Yan Xuexi of Nanjing University published in Gao and Yan 1987: 51–52 and 55–59; it was compiled from several published and unpublished sources, unearthed by myself and Professor Yan while I was resident at Nanjing University in 1979–81. Because such sources often contain scattered information on filature investment with no precise dates attached, it is virtually impossible to know from which years the investment figures come, or the nature of ebbs and flows in investment (for the frequent turnover in filature management, and the periodic closing of filatures, see Chapter 5). Most of the data on ownership and management capital probably represent approximate investment sometime during the 1920's, since they were taken from the 1930 *Wuxi Yearbook* and other 1920's and early 1930's sources.

A Comprehensive List of Wuxi Silk-Filature Investment

Filature name[a]	Year of founding	Founding capital (000 taels)	Management capital (000 yuan)	Ownership capital (000 taels)	Reeling machines	Founder or his agent[b]	Notes on filature founders, owners, and managers
uchang	1904	80	56	70	96–330	Zhou Shunqing	Zhou was a native of Wuxi who worked as a comprador cocoon agent for a Shanghai firm and managed Wuxi's Xincheng bank. He served as head of Wuxi's Chamber of Commerce (for more on Zhou's background, see Chapter 3). Yuchang was the first silk filature in Wuxi; it had 96 reeling machines to begin, and grew to 330 machines.
ıji	1909	75	50	140	410	A certain Mr. Xu	Little is known about Mr. Xu. This filature was soon transferred to the ownership of Xue Nanming, one of Wuxi's first native sons to found a silk filature in 1896 in Shanghai (the Yongtai filature; for more on Xue Nanming's background, see Chapter 3).
ankang	1909	77	60	65	320	Zhu Lanfang	Zhu was a Shanghai comprador. He served as head of Wuxi's Chamber of Commerce.
nshen	1910	50	140	100	568	Sun Heqing	Sun was a landlord in the market town of Shitangwan and the general manager of Wuxi's Chamber of Commerce.

Filature name[a]	Year of founding	Found-ing capital (000 taels)	Manage-ment capital (000 yuan)	Owner-ship capital (000 taels)	Reeling ma-chines	Founder or his agent[b]	Notes on filature founders, owners, and managers
Zhenyi	1910	100	140	140	520	Xu Daosun	Xu was a private tutor in Henglin Township in Changzhou Prefecture and later became a clerk in the Gong-heyong silk filature in Shang-hai, where he made connec-tions with foreign firms.
Ganyuan	1913	50	60	97	256	Zhu Lanfang	On Zhu's background, see above. The first manager of this filature was Xu Daosun. It was later leased by the Ganshen fil-ature.
Longchang	1914	52	70	90	328	Zhou Yueshan	Zhou was a commercial capi-talist from Jiangyin County. Not long after its founding, this filature was sold to Xue Nan-ming and later was incorpo-rated into the Yongtai filature organization.
Fuguan	1914	50	?	?	248	Shan Shaowen	Shan was manager of the Wuxi Chamber of Commerce and an investor in the native banking industry. Not long after its founding, this filature was leased to the management groups of the Xichang and Ruichang filatures.
Jiuyu	1916	40	?	?	232	Ding Xing-chu	Ding and eight fellow investors in this filature were handicraft silk-industry merchants. Not long after its founding, this fila-ture ceased operation and then was leased out.
Yongsheng	1918	50	40	90	298	Xue Nan-ming	On Xue's background, see Chapter 3. From 1925 to 1929 this filature was leased to the Zhenfeng filature and later was returned to its original man-agement.
Dexing	1919	100	70	100	480	Tang Baoqian	Tang was a handicraft cotton-cloth merchant who later be-came one of the founders of the Qingfeng filature. Not long af-ter its founding, this filature was leased to the Dedayu fila-ture management group.
Zhenguan	1920	100	70	100	304	Lu Peizhi	Lu was a Shanghai business-man.

Filature name[a]	Year of founding	Founding capital (000 taels)	Management capital (000 yuan)	Ownership capital (000 taels)	Reeling machines	Founder or his agent[b]	Notes on filature founders, owners, and managers
Shenchang	1920	42	42	80	272	Zhou Shunqing	On Zhou's background, see above and Chapter 3.
Yongji	1920	48	50	25	248	Xue Nanming	On Xue's background, see Chapter 3. This filature was leased to the Yifeng filature and later became part of the Yong-tai filature system.
Zhenyuan	1922	50	42	90	352	Huang Zhuoru	Huang was a manager of a local granary.
Taifu	1922	40	42	?	384	Wang Song-lu, Shen Zhonghua, and Ni Zicheng	All three founders originally were cocoon merchants.
Ganyuan	1922	50	60	97	264	Sun Xunchu	Sun originally was a cocoon merchant.
Hongxu	1922	50	?	?	272	Hua Yizhi	Hua was a big landlord in the Wuxi market town of Dangkou and also managed a cocoon warehouse. He founded this filature with the intention of leasing it out to collect rent. It was never managed by Hua.
Shenyi nchang	1922	50	70	70	308	Xu Daosun	On Xu's background, see above.
Jiguan (Hengyi)	1925	30	28	65	120	Cai Xiaofeng	Cai was a native of Zhenjiang who originally was a cocoon merchant. This filature installed special "double-reeling" machines. But because business was bad, this filature was sold to the Hengyi company, which ran it with regular reeling machines.
Wufeng	1926	50	?	?	272	Cheng Bingruo and four others	Cheng Bingruo followed Sun Heqing as the manager of the Ganshen filature. Cheng and four of his friends and relatives founded this filature together. Because five investors founded it, it was called Wufeng ("Five Prosperities"). From the outset, in management practices it looked like a second Ganshen filature, and eventually it was named Ganshen Filature Number Two (Ganshen erchang).

Filature name[a]	Year of founding	Founding capital (ooo taels)	Management capital (ooo yuan)	Ownership capital (ooo taels)	Reeling machines	Founder or his agent[b]	Notes on filature founders, owners, and managers
Hongyu	1926	40	50	27	276	Hua Yizhi	On Hua's background, see above. Hua founded this filature with the intention of leasing it out. For a relatively long time it was leased to the Ruichang filature under Zheng Ziqing's management.
Yongtai	1926	80	75	82	492	Xue Nan-ming	On Xue's background, see Chapter 3. This filature was jointly established in 1896 in Shanghai by Xue and Zhou Shunqing. In 1926, it moved to Wuxi.
Jingcheng	1927	50	42	80	262	Deng Peilin and Cao Yousheng	Both Deng and Cao were managers of silkworm-egg breeders and were cocoon merchants in Jintan County. Not long after its founding, this filature was leased out.
Minfeng	1927	80	100	170	520	Zhu Jing'an	Zhu was a comprador for a British firm in Shanghai. This filature was among the earliest in Wuxi to use Italian reeling machines and then changed to Japanese-style machines.
Yunda	1928	50	?	?	224	Shen Jusun	
Yusheng	1928	50	40	45	320	Ren Ruduo	
Nanchang	1928	70	40	45	320	Yu Yiting	Yu was a manager of a Shanghai iron factory. This filature began operations under a management group that renamed the Shengyu filature, with cocoon merchants Zhang Shupi and Gao Shufang, Gao Jingyue's father, as its managers.
Wanyuan	1928	50(a) 40(b)	30(a) 30(b)	12(a,b)	248(a) 256(b)	Shen Gengyang	In 1929, part (a) of this filature was leased by cocoon merchant Wu Shirong and became part of the Yongtai and Yongfeng filature management operation. Part (b) was leased by a high-ranking silk-filature clerk, Ji Yunchu, and became part of the Wanyi filature management operation.
Zikang	1928	30	?	?	144	Yang Zhongzi	

Filature name[a]	Year of founding	Founding capital (000 taels)	Management capital (000 yuan)	Ownership capital (000 taels)	Reeling machines	Founder or his agent[b]	Notes on filature founders, owners, and managers
Dingsheng	1928	60	70	120	348	Shi Liangcai	Not long after this filature was founded, it was leased to the Ruichang filature.
Yuguan	1928	50	42	60	208	Wang Yousun	
Xingsheng	1928	50	30	50	244	Yang Hanxi	Yang was a big landlord in Wuxi, the chair of the Wuxi Chamber of Commerce, and manager of a cotton mill. Later he became Minister of Health under Japanese occupation. This filature was built primarily for leasing out.
Gengyu	1928	100	63	100	240	Wang Juancang	Wang was manager of a flour mill. This filature was built to be leased out, and later it was converted into the Gengyu cotton-cloth factory.
Tongfeng	1928	30	28	30	160	Liu Yuqing	Liu was a merchant in the Wuxi market town of Luoshe.
Jinguan	1928	60	63	90	288	Wu Dengyun	Wu was an exporter of raw silk in Shanghai and a comprador for foreign firms.
Yongchang	1929	50	42	82	312	Tao Haiyong	Tao was a cocoon merchant.
Antai	1929	40(a) 30(b)	35(a) ?	90(a) ?	288(a) 144(b)	Huang Jinfan and He Xizhang	Huang was a Shanghai handicraft silk merchant (buying for export), and He was a manager of an oil-pressing factory. Part (a) of this filature was leased out to a management group who called their operation the Yichang filature; part (b) was leased out to a management group who called their operation the Rongji filature.
Rongyu	1929	70	56	85	480	Shen Yeyun	
Huifeng (Hefeng)	1929	60	42	100	346	Zhang Zizhen	Zhang was a cocoon merchant and a shareholder in silk-filature investment.
Rongfurun	1929	60	40	65	256	Qiang Zhuoren and Tao Haiyong	Qiang was a big cocoon merchant in Wuxi's market town of Meicun. Tao was also a cocoon merchant.
Ande	1929	40	42	60	240	Yang Ganqing	Yang was a manager of real-estate and cooking-oil firms.

Filature name[a]	Year of founding	Founding capital (000 taels)	Management capital (000 yuan)	Ownership capital (000 taels)	Reeling machines	Founder or his agent[b]	Notes on filature founders, owners, and managers
Fucheng	1929	50	42	85	264	Chen Zhuoyun and Ni Zicheng	Chen and Ni were investors in the Taifu filature.
Dingchang	1929	50	42	145	512	Zhou Zhaofu	Zhou was the son of Yuchang filature founder Zhou Shunqing. He never participated in filature management but recruited aides Zhang Zhanhua and Qian Fenggao to run it.
Runkang	1929	30	?	?	212	Shan Chongli	Shan was a cocoon merchant.
Huiyuan	1929	40	?	?	208	Wu Qifeng and Ma Hanqing	
Baotai (Baofeng)	1929	40	42	120	320	Chen Meifang	
Youcheng	1930	30	?	?	264	Lu Youfeng	
Jiatai	1930	58	?	?	304	Su Jiashan	Su was a native of Changshou County and a prominent person on the Shanghai bund. This filature was built to be leased out.
Huaxin zhisi yangcheng-suo (Huaxin silk manufacture training institute)	1931	50	?	?	292 standing machines	Xue Shouxuan	Xue was Xue Nanming's son. This filature was China's first to adopt the latest-style Japanese reeling machines (see Chapter 8 for more detail on this development). It also used "scientific management" techniques.

SOURCES: Gao and Yan 1987: 52–52 and 55–59.

NOTE: Chinese characters for personal names, place names, and other terms appear in the Character List.

[a]Filatures were constantly renamed; the names listed here, then, are not comprehensive. As discussed in Chapter 5, when groups of investors and managers in each filature shifted, they often used new names, or revived older ones, to accompany their new ownership and/or management regimes. At any given time, a filature might even have had two or three names associated with it, one used by the ownership group, the others by managerial groups. For the most part, the names appearing in this list were the names used at the time of filature founding.

[b]Most of the names here are those of the primary founder of the filature, although these individuals often enlisted investment capital and sold shares to other investors at the time of founding. In some instances, the names given are those of the "representative" or "agent" of the founder. This man could be a manager hired by the founding ownership group, or a manager who himself raised investment shares and rented the filature from the owners.

Reference Matter

Abbreviations

The following abbreviations are used in the Notes and Bibliography:

DELSDAG   *Dierlishi dang'anguan* (Number Two National History Archive, Nanjing)

GSBYK   *Gongshang banyuekan* (Bimonthly journal of industry and commerce)

JNSWB   *Jiangnan shangwu bao* (Jiangnan commercial news)

JSJSYK   *Jiangsu jianshe yuekan* (Jiangsu reconstruction monthly)

JSSGB   *Jiangsusheng gongbao* (Jiangsu provincial government gazette)

JSSYYZ   *Jiangsu shiye yuezhi* (Jiangsu industry monthly)

Mantetsu   Minami Manshū tetsudō kabushiki kaisha, Shanhai jimusho chōsashitsu (Shanghai Research Office of the South Manchurian Railway Company)

MGRB   *Minguo ribao* (Republican daily news, Shanghai)

NKGB   *Nongkuang gongbao* (Gazette of the Jiangsu Department of Agriculture and Mines)

NSGB   *Nongshang gongbao* (Gazette of the Ministry of Agriculture and Commerce)

NXB   *Nongxuebao* (Agricultural study news)

SB   *Shenbao* (Chinese daily news, Shanghai)

SSRI   Guoli zhongyang yanjiuyuan shehui kexue yanjiusuo (Social Science Research Institute of the Academia Sinica, Shanghai)

WXZZ   *Wuxi zazhi* (Wuxi magazine)

YHZB   *Yinhang zhoubao* (Banker's weekly)

Notes

CHAPTER I

1. See, for example, Moulder 1977 and So 1986.

2. Two important collections of such articles are Feng 1935a and 1935b. For a good introduction to this literature, see Faure 1989: ch. 1.

3. Stross 1986 provides an important study of the activities of outside reformers, including Buck, and their Chinese counterparts, as well as the general failure of their efforts.

4. For studies of the Ming/Qing economy discussing the "sprouts of capitalism" framework, see Xu 1981; Li et al. 1983; and Xu and Wu 1985.

5. In response to the Vietnam War, some scholars of Asia formed an organization called the Committee of Concerned Asian Scholars, and began a new publication called the *Bulletin of Concerned Asian Scholars*. The arguments on Western imperialism and China as outlined here appeared in the *Bulletin*. See especially Esherick 1972 and Nathan 1972.

6. One of the most eloquent calls for new scholarship was Lasek 1983.

7. Lippit 1974 and 1978.

8. Huang 1985 and 1990.

9. Brandt 1989; Faure 1989.

10. Rawski 1989.

11. Pertinent review articles include Martin 1991; Esherick 1991; Myers 1991; Wong 1990 and 1992; and Feuerwerker 1992.

12. Gutmann 1988 provides a good general introduction to new scholarship on European industrialization. Provocative recastings of the problem include Sable and Zeitlin 1985, and Liu 1994. My colleagues Judy Coffin and Randy Head have been supportive of my efforts to come to terms with the new literature on European industrialization.

13. Negative assessments of the Nationalists and the economy include Eastman's seminal works (1974, 1984); Fewsmith 1985; and Bergère 1983 and 1989. There are few studies other than those which analyze politics in relationship to modern industry in China. Two of the most important that deal specifically with silk-industry development, and to which I refer throughout, are L. M. Li 1981 and Eng 1986. So 1986 is also a useful work on silk-industry development, focusing on the Guangdong area. Cochran 1980 provides an invaluable study in the style of business history, evaluating the development of competition and entrepreneurship in the cigarette industry.

Though I have learned from all of these works, my approach is different because of the emphasis I place on the relationship between the industrial and agricultural sectors as silk filatures proliferated in Wuxi.

14. Philip Kuhn's classic study (1970) of the Taiping Rebellion, and the growing autonomy of local elites from the Qing state that followed in its wake, set the stage for an extended analysis by many scholars of elite alienation from government at the end of the nineteenth century. Other influential studies in this mode include Wakeman 1975; Kuhn 1975 and 1979; [Mann] Jones 1979b; Esherick 1976; Young 1977; and MacKinnon 1980. For the more recent emphasis on an independent "public sphere" of local elite activity, see studies by Rowe (1984, 1989, 1990, and 1993) and Rankin (1986).

15. Duara 1988.

16. Bourdieu (1977) defines practice as social strategies that move through time creating, recreating, or transforming hierarchical human relationships. Practice in this sense is more than material interactions, including symbolic behaviors used to help establish social dominance. Marshall Sahlins (1981, 1985) emphasizes that social practice in this sense does not always repeat, for as history moves, so, too, does practice change, with evolving social strategies transforming older patterns of dominance. In Chapter 8, I use these concepts of practice to analyze the behavior of Wuxi's silk-industry bourgeoisie of the 1920's and 1930's, building on my previous analysis in Bell 1990.

17. I conducted several interviews while in Wuxi, and in Nanjing, Zhenjiang, Suzhou, and Beijing. For a complete list of interviews and a discussion of interviewing situations and backgrounds of interviewees, see Appendix A.

18. Since wenshi ziliao are always classified as materials intended only for internal circulation among select scholars and party officials in China, I am grateful to Chinese friends and colleagues, especially in Wuxi, who provided me with copies. I should also note that Professor Yan Xuexi, with whom I worked at Nanjing University in the early 1980's, has published a book of documentary materials dealing with Wuxi silk production in collaboration with a former silk-filature manager from Wuxi, Gao Jingyue (Gao and Yan 1987). There are many additional materials of the wenshi ziliao type in this volume.

19. Minami Manshū tetsudō kabushiki kaisha, Shanhai jimusho chōsashitsu 1941. Several works have appeared in English using Mantetsu materials, including Huang 1985 and 1990; Myers 1970; Duara 1988; and Brandt 1989. For a discussion of the reliability of Mantetsu survey materials, see Appendix B. For more background on Mantetsu research operations, a standard reference work in English is Young 1966; another useful introduction to Mantetsu activities is contained in the memoirs of Itō Takeo, an important member of the Mantetsu research operation in the 1920's and 1930's, translated by Joshua Fogel (1988).

20. I had discovered the existence of the survey through my reading of the monthly bulletin of the Academia Sinica for the late 1920's, but I had not been able to locate any substantial publications based on it. I visited the director of the survey, Chen Hansheng, in July 1981, at his home in Beijing (for more on Chen Hansheng's background, see Appendix A), to ask what had become of the materials collected in the survey. Professor Chen told me that he suspected they were at the Institute of Economics in Beijing; later I learned that they had indeed ended up there, because the modern history section of the institute became the successor of the Social Science Research Institute of the Academia Sinica, the group responsible for the survey. In 1985, I visited with Professor Peng Zeyi of the Institute of Economics, and he was able to confirm for me that the materials were still at the institute. In 1986, with Professor Peng's help, and the kind assistance of the director of the institute, Professor Dong Fureng, I was able to start using the materials in Beijing. They had been crated up and placed in an underground vault during the Cultural Revolution, and thus were fairly well preserved.

21. Guoli zhongyang yanjiuyuan shehui kexue yanjiusuo 1929. I refer to the survey throughout simply as the SSRI survey.

22. Chen Hansheng interview, July 26, 1981.

23. This description comes primarily from my contact with the remaining questionnaires now housed at the Institute of Economics in Beijing. There are also brief discussions of the survey found in work reports of the Social Science Research Institute in the monthly bulletin of the Academia Sinica. See for example, *Guoli zhongyang yanjiuyuan yuanwu yuebao* (Monthly bulletin of the Academia Sinica) 1, no. 1 (July 1929): 103–4; 1, no. 3 (Sept. 1929): 7; 2, no. 4 (Oct. 1930): 90; 2, no. 5 (Nov. 1930): 38–41; 2, no. 7 (Jan. 1931): 29–33; 2, no. 9 (Mar. 1931): 29–36.

24. This statement is not meant to detract from the great value of the many Mantetsu studies that have been used by others studying the Chinese rural economy. But the Wuxi survey materials are different because of the rigorous way in which the same interviewing schedule was used in many villages for a relatively large number of cases. The possibility of creating a household-based random sample for statistical observation was present in the Wuxi survey materials, an opportunity that I have tried to exploit appropriately.

25. For a detailed account of how the interviewing team was selected and how the interviews were conducted, see Appendix B.

26. Appendix B provides a detailed explanation of the variables I developed and a discussion of how the sample was selected.

CHAPTER 2

1. One difference between the arguments of Elvin and Huang is that the causative effects of population growth are reversed. Elvin's analysis (1973) implies that population growth propelled commercialization, whereas Huang (1990) follows the "inverse Malthusian" logic of Ester Boserup

(1965), in which increased output via commercialization creates the pre-conditions for population growth. Huang also contributes a finely tuned mi-croanalysis of small-peasant-family farming as the context for population growth, whereas Elvin's analysis focuses on macro issues of diminishing re-turns to labor in the rural economy overall as a result of empirewide popula-tion trends.

2. Ho 1959: 64; Perkins 1969: 202–9.

3. To estimate Wuxi population growth, I have used population figures from 1726 and 1795 found in *Wuxi-Jinkui xianzhi* 1881, 8: 5–6. There are certain pitfalls in using such figures, but accommodations can be made to compensate for less-than-perfect data. The biggest problem in using Qing dynasty population figures is that instead of reporting the real population, gazetteer compilers reported the *ding*, a unit of taxation that was supposed to represent all adult males of working age. According to Ping-ti Ho (1959), over time the ding no longer bore any relation to the real number of adult males, evolving instead into a pure fiscal unit corresponding to a given lo-cale's total tax liability. Ho believes that during the early eighteenth cen-tury, the ding represented "substantially less than one-half" of the real population (p. 35). By the late eighteenth century, a series of tax reforms called *tanding rudi* or *tanding rumu* (literally, "spreading the ding into the land") began a new system of taxation based on land-ownership (rather than male head count) at a permanent fixed rate (p. 25). By the mid-1770's, as the reforms finally began to take hold throughout the empire, the Qianlong em-peror called for an annual accounting of true population figures and real grain output (pp. 47–48).

To derive population figures and calculate a rate of demographic growth for Wuxi, therefore, I have adjusted the 1726 ding figure of 142,509 to 475,030, assuming that the ding figure was about 30 percent of the entire population (using Ho's suggestion that the ding was "substantially less than one-half" of the population). Then, following Chinese population expert Liang Fangzhong (1980: 440–41), I assumed that by the last decade of the eighteenth century, ding figures reflected reality more closely, equaling about 53 percent of the total population. This made it possible for me to use the 1795 ding figure of 566,217 to calculate a total population in that year of 1,068,334. Finally, to estimate a rate of continuous population growth over the entire period 1726 to 1795, I follow the techniques suggested in Barclay 1958: 28–33.

4. Land per capita is calculated by using a population figure estimated from the ding statistics for 1795 in *Wuxi-Jinkui xianzhi* 1881, 8: 5–6 (ding statistics are described and explained in note 3); and land statistics for the mid-1770's in ibid., 9: 1 and 10: 1.

5. For estimates of land per capita for other delta locales, see Huang 1990: app. B.

6. The eight provinces responsible for tribute grain payments were Shandong, Hunan, Anhui, Jiangsu, Zhejiang, Jiangxi, Hubei, and Hunan. See Hinton 1956: 7. On shifting patterns of grain surplus and export of grain into

the delta, see Perkins 1969: 140–51. On Wuxi's role as a transshipment and marketing center, see Shehui jingji yanjiusuo 1935: preface and 1–2.

7. Sun 1959: 4 and 98; Wuxi difangzhi bianji weiyuanhui 1959: 36–40.

8. Hinton 1956: 1–15; Shehui jingji yanjiusuo 1935: preface and 1–2.

9. *Xi-Jin shi xiaolu* 1752, 1: 6–7.

10. On the specific nature of women's and men's work, see Bell 1994, and Chapter 6 below.

11. For classic studies in the protoindustrialization mode, see Mendels 1972 and Medick 1976. Gutmann 1988 provides a good summary of the critiques of protoindustrialization theory.

12. Brenner 1976 and 1977.

13. Goldstone 1991.

14. Douglass North (1981) has argued for the importance of new conceptions of property rights and welfare ideology in fostering the rise of capitalism in the West. My argument takes inspiration from North's approach but stresses the uniqueness, rather than the similarities, of the Chinese experience.

15. I-fan Ch'eng (1988) dates the origins of increased interest in statecraft among delta elites to the sixteenth century.

16. For one example of how *jingshi jimin* was employed by a Qing-period statecraft writer, see Priest 1982.

17. See Dennerline 1981a, esp. ch. 5.

18. This view of statecraft argument and how it fit into an increasingly proactive, reformist intellectual environment is based primarily on Benjamin Elman's account (1990) of developments in and around Wuxi and Wujin counties, and Changzhou Prefecture, of which they were a part, in the western part of southern Jiangsu Province.

19. See, for example, Elman 1984 and 1990, and Dennerline 1981a: 9–10 and ch. 3.

20. I use the concept of ideology here in a Gramscian sense, alluding to the centrality of ideas in shaping various forms of social and cultural practice to create legitimacy for those in powerful positions in society. See Gramsci [1929–35] 1971. For a helpful introduction to Gramsci's views on ideology, see Boggs 1976, esp. ch. 2.

21. Rowe 1989: 105–27.

22. See especially Rankin 1986: ch. 3.

23. Dennerline 1988: 100–101.

24. Dennerline 1981b: 45–47; and 1988: 99–100.

25. Dennerline 1988: 102.

26. Ibid.: 104–5.

27. Cf. the argument in Dennerline 1981b.

28. Dennerline 1988: 92–94.

29. Richard von Glahn (1993) makes these observations about temple-building in market sites during Ming times. On Hua Cha, see Dennerline 1988: 94.

30. Mann 1987: 27–28.

31. See, for example, Rowe 1990 and 1993.

32. For an excellent discussion of Japanese scholarship on these issues, see Walker 1999.

33. Research by several Japanese scholars argues that commercialization gave small peasants an opportunity to establish their independent reproduction capacities for the first time, and thus was at the heart of peasant struggles for improved status. See Walker 1999.

34. Rents were lower by several *dou*, with one dou equaling one-tenth of a shi, or approximately 0.275 bushels; rents averaged from 0.8 to 1.8 shi per mu, or roughly from 40 to 60 percent of an average to superlative yield of 2 to 3 shi per mu. See Bernhardt 1992: 21.

35. Ibid.: 25.

36. SSRI survey. Chapter 1 and Appendix B provide introductions to the survey. Chapter 6 provides detailed analysis of a great deal more of its quantitative data.

37. SSRI survey, interview no. 730.

38. Bernhardt 1992: ch. 1.

39. David Wakefield's work (1992) on fenjia has shown that the further fragmentation of already small landholdings during Qing times was one of its principal outcomes.

40. Elvin 1973: ch. 16.

41. A classic statement on the power of the Chinese bureaucratic system to absorb all elite contenders is found in Balazs 1964: pt. 1.

42. Although I do not have sufficient economic evidence to demonstrate exactly why such merchant/peasant nexuses became so dominant, I believe that economic historians who study the Qing would do well to investigate this issue further. Comparing rates of return on investments by local merchants who developed exchange relationships with peasant households with rates that obtained for leasing land or loaning money and grain, for example, would tell us a great deal about the economic incentives to establish such trade relationships. In addition, an effort to establish another level of comparison, between rates of return in relatively small-scale trading ventures and those for larger-scale merchant operations that resembled more closely the "protoindustrial" merchant-run manufacturing enterprises that emerged in some areas of early modern Europe, would provide clearer insight into why the tendency in China was to move away from larger-scale operations as the Qing period wore on. I shall have more to say on this issue in Chapter 3. Of course, as many scholars of early capitalism in the West have pointed out, merchants became innovators in some areas only because they operated in tandem with equally profound changes in the nature of rural production (enclosure in England, for example), and should not be viewed at all times and in all places as the inevitable forerunners of more advanced forms of development. In this regard, the provocative argument by Elizabeth Fox-Genovese and Eugene Genovese (1983) provides a good starting point for working through some very difficult issues on the "Janus face of merchant capital."

43. Ho 1959; Wang 1973; Bernhardt 1992: 44; Zelin 1984.

44. Zelin 1984: 88.   45. Ibid.: ch. 6.

46. Ibid.: 249–50.   47. Ibid.: 227.

48. Madeleine Zelin notes the relationship between failure of the reform and diminishing incomes among the peasantry as a result of demographic growth. She also notes that even the Qing government itself had begun to see the relationship between these issues. On these points, see Zelin 1984: 265.

49. Mann 1987, esp. ch. 2.

50. Susan Mann's study of one such market in Zhoucun, Shandong Province, in the eighteenth century, demonstrates how one local family used this strategy to build its own local power and prestige. The members of the Li family, who founded the benevolent market at Zhoucun, not only were important merchants in their community, they also sought degrees and official positions, and built up their own corporate property through a lineage organization, all in the name of promoting popular welfare. See Mann 1987: ch. 5.

51. Zelin 1984: ch. 5.   52. Mann 1987: 95.

53. Ibid.: 104.   54. Wang 1973: 80.

55. Susan Mann provides examples of such negotiations and their outcomes during the late Qing and into the Republic. See Mann 1987: chs. 7–9.

CHAPTER 3

1. L. M. Li 1981: 2–3.

2. For an authoritative discussion of the historical geography of the delta and its contours, see Huang 1990: ch. 2.

3. Ch'en et al. 1961: 5; Sun 1959: 271.

4. Ch'en et al. 1961: 5.   5. Ibid.: 3.

6. Ibid.; Sun 1959: 11 and 91.

7. Ch'en et al. 1961: 5–6; Sun 1959: 11.

8. Sun 1972: 79–85; L. M. Li 1981: 44; Shih 1976: 5.

9. Dongnan daxue nongke 1923–24, 2: 9; specifically, this source states that damp, low-lying land in the southeastern part of Changshou County was unsuitable for mulberry cultivation. Lillian Li also discusses the necessity of relatively high ground and adequate drainage for mulberry trees (1981: 11–12). Li bases her remarks on nineteenth-century sericulture manuals.

10. Ch'en et al. 1961: 2–3.

11. Sun 1959: 91.

12. See ibid.: 59–60, for a description of double-cropping rice/wheat, and pp. 65–66 for mulberry cultivation. For an extensive discussion of the Wuxi agricultural system combining all three crops, see Chapter 6 below.

13. See Zhang 1979, pt. 2: 53. Zhang points out that in 1855, a resident of Jiangyin traveling by boat to Zhejiang recorded that in the vicinity of Huzhou, mulberry trees had been planted on the banks of the Grand Canal. This method was in sharp contrast to the extensive cultivation of entire

fields of mulberries begun two decades later in Wuxi. Lillian Li also reports on the observations of Robert Fortune, an English botanist, traveling near Hangzhou in the 1850's, who pointed out that "the mulberry was seen extensively cultivated on all the higher patches of ground, and rice occupied the low, wet land" (L. M. Li 1981: 12). My own observations in the delta in 1980–81 indicate that the pattern of using higher ground between rice paddies and on the banks of canals persists as one important method of mulberry cultivation.

14. Ch'en et al. 1961: 4. On the length of the growing season and its range from north to south in Jiangnan, see also Sun 1959: 59 and 200.

15. Topley 1975: 70.

16. Food and Agriculture Organization of the United Nations 1980: 38–42.

17. For problems related to humidity control, drafts, and sudden temperature drops, see *JNSWB* (Apr. 21, 1900), commercial raw-materials section: 2; DELSDAG, file no. 3504, "Liangnianlai bensheng [Zhejiang] canzhong zhizao ji qudi jingguo gaikuang": 4; Sun 1931: 985.

18. *MGRB* (May 21, 1916), sec. 3: 10.

19. *MGRB* (May 11, 1921), sec. 3: 11.

20. *MGRB* (June 5, 1921), sec. 2: 8.

21. Dongnan daxue nongke 1923–24, 1: 6; 2: 49.

22. Zhang 1979, pt. 2: 53–54; Mantetsu 1940: 71–73; Kōain kachū renrakubu 1941: 795–96; Gao and Yan 1980: 4.

23. Ch'en et al. 1961: 2–3.

24. Sun 1959: 11.

25. Mantetsu 1940: 70; Kōain kachū renrakubu 1941: 793–95.

26. L. M. Li 1981: 2–3.

27. Peng 1963a: 39; L. M. Li 1981: 46–47.

28. Peng 1963a: 43–46; 1963b: 92–96; L. M. Li 1981: 47–50.

29. Peng 1963b: 112–15; 1963c: 64–66; L. M. Li 1981: 50–57.

30. Shih 1976: 18, 24–25.

31. Silk-production and silk-marketing networks spawned by the Imperial Silkworks have been the subject of a large body of literature in Chinese and Japanese, with many scholars arguing that because of the use of wage-based artisan labor, these networks were a form of incipient capitalism in the late imperial economy. In Chinese, the term used to describe these relationships is *ziben zhuyi mengya*, or "sprouts of capitalism." Lillian Li has discussed these arguments at length, and it seems unnecessary to recapitulate their details here (L. M. Li 1981: 57–61). Having reviewed the production and marketing systems that emerged under zhangfang auspices during the Qing, Li and I tend to agree on one fundamental point—the movement was not toward more elaborate forms of labor organization or concentrated supervision and management within the Chinese silk industry, but rather away from such developments. Thus the term "capitalism," at least as it is understood in the literature of classical political economy, seems ill suited for use in referring to the zhangfang system.

32. Li Wenzhi 1981: 84.

33. *Wuxi-Jinkui xianzhi* 1881, 8: 6–7; these figures are also cited in Li Wenzhi 1957, 1: 151.

34. Li Wenzhi 1981: 82–86.

35. Kathryn Bernhardt's study of the delta during Qing and the Republic (1992) reinforces and augments Li Wenzhi's picture of evolving land-tenure relationships in the post-Taiping years. What Bernhardt's study adds is a significantly greater emphasis on peasant resistance to land rents and taxes to explain the growing strength of tenants in the region, patterns that began even before the Taipings arrived in the region.

36. *Wuxi-Jinkui xianzhi* 1813, 31: 8.

37. *Wuxi-Jinkui xianzhi* 1881, 31: 1.

38. Lillian Li (1981: 142) cites several late-Qing sericulture manuals and a Huzhou gazetteer on the length of time needed for mulberry trees to mature and on the heavy labor requirements for cultivating them.

39. Sunan renmin xingzheng gongzhu 1950: 377.

40. Mantetsu 1941, table 5 following the text shows that only 14 percent of mulberry fields in three Wuxi villages were on rented land, versus 36 percent of rice paddies on rented land. See also Chapter 6 for more detail on mulberry cultivation in Wuxi.

41. Zhang and Zhang 1988: 249–53. Also, see Walker 1999 for a discussion of long-distance cotton marketing throughout the delta during the Qing.

42. L. M. Li 1981: 72, 118–29.

43. Ibid.: 62–72.

44. For development of the power loom by Dr. Edmund Cartwright, see Barlow 1884: 229–41.

45. Eng 1986: 26–27.

46. Ibid.: 27–28. Eng points out that incubating and feeding silkworms are tasks that defy mechanization. They require meticulous attention and, hence, a large amount of labor power. Thus, attempts at silkworm raising failed in the United States "not because of the unsuitability of the soil and climate to the cultivation of mulberries and silkworms, but because of the prohibitively high labor costs in a labor-scarce economy" (p. 28).

47. Watson 1930: 35–36.

48. *JSSGB* 1030 (Oct. 19, 1916): 8. In Chinese sources, the low quality of raw silk was a topic widely discussed beginning in the late 1910's. The American market and the declining position of Chinese silk relative to Japanese silk prompted this concern.

49. L. M. Li (1981), Eng (1986), and So (1986) all discuss the development of silk filatures in Guangdong.

50. Sheffield 1911: 27; another very useful discussion of these processes is found in the Encyclopaedia Britannica, 15th ed. (1982), vol. 7: 288, and vol. 18: 173.

51. L. M. Li 1981: 165–66.

52. Shih 1976: 14; Lieu 1933: 75–76.

53. Lieu 1933: 74.
54. Ibid.: 73–76.
55. L. M. Li 1981: 164; Sun 1972: 103–4.
56. Yin 1931: 12; Wuxi difangzhi bianji weiyuanhui 1959: 41.
57. Sun 1972: 105; L. M. Li 1981: 164–66; Lieu 1933: 1–2.
58. Wang 1979: 1272–76; Chen 1957–61: 112–13.
59. Eng 1986: 56–57.   60. L. M. Li 1981: 124–25.
61. Hauser 1962: 89–90.   62. Lieu 1940: app. table 3, 266.
63. Some of the better-known names for these silks were Tsatlees, or "fine silks," Taysaams, or "coarse silks," Kashings, and Haineen and Wuchun re-reels. L. M. Li 1981: 77–78, 27, 106–7.
64. Ibid.: 106–7.
65. Ibid.: 91.
66. Ibid.: 167.
67. SSRI tables on subsidiary work.
68. It is difficult to determine the exact number of cocoon firms in operation at any given time because filatures, and the cocoon-marketing system that serviced them, operated sporadically depending on market conditions for raw silk. I return to this problem in Chapter 5. Sources for the number of cocoon firms established in Wuxi and other delta locales include Gao Jingyue interview, May 24, 1980; Tōa dobunkai 1920: 528, 538–57; JSSYYZ 15 (June 1920): 74–75; NKGB 3 (Oct. 1, 1928): cocoon-firm tables following p. 48; Wuxi xianzhengfu, Wuxi shizheng choubeichu 1930, commerce section: 28–37; and DELSDAG file 3242, subfile 32472.
69. Sun 1959: 98.
70. Mantetsu 1940: 69–73; Kōain kachū renrakubu 1941: 795–96.
71. NXB 294 (May 1905): 3–4; NSGB 2, no. 1 (Aug. 1915), selections section: 14–15; Nie 1979: 44–49.
72. Wang 1936: 204–5.
73. NXB 294 (May 1905): 4; Gao Jingyue interview, May 24, 1980.
74. Wang 1979: 1272–76; Chen 1957–61, 4: 111–13.
75. Eng 1986: 56–57.
76. Xi-Jin xiangtu dili 1909, 1: sec. 34; JSSGB (May 16, 1923): 2–3; Gao Jingyue interview, May 24, 1980; Kaihua xiangzhi 1916, 1: 52–53.
77. Wuxi difangzhi bianji weiyuanhui 1959: 56–58; Qian 1961: 123–25; Xi-Jin xiangtu dili 1909, 2: sec. 3. Qian Zhonghan has also provided more specific details on Zhou Shunqing's cocoon firms and his role in new local political organizations such as the Wuxi Chamber of Commerce and Agricultural Association during the New Policies period. See Qian 1983.
78. Qian 1961: 126; Wuxi difangzhi bianji weiyuanhui 1959: 42. A recent translation into English of Xue Fucheng's European diaries by his great-granddaughter, Helen Hsieh Chien, helps to shed light on how the Xue family became so interested in, and involved with, things that centered on "the West." See Chien 1993.
79. Shanghai shehui kexueyuan jingji yanjiusuo 1962: 3–8.
80. A general idea of periods in which cocoon marketing took place in

the delta is derived from news reports in commercial journals and newspapers. The exact length of the marketing period in Wuxi was discussed when I visited Wuxi and had the opportunity to ask experts on past and present sericulture and cocoon-marketing how long the marketing period lasted. The fact that Wuxi peasants rarely produced summer cocoons is confirmed in tables on cocoon and silk output in Jiangsu for 1933 in DELSDAG file no. 3242. That year, Wuxi produced 56,100 dan of cocoons in the spring season, 18,785 dan in the fall season, and none at all in the summer season.

81. The dispersion of cocoon-firm facilities in many market-town locations is documented in *Xi-Jin xiangtu dili* 1909, and also in DELSDAG file 3242, subfile 32472.

82. This descriptive account of cocoon-firm facilities is based primarily on Tōa dobunkai 1920: 535–36 and 557–59, and on information gained from a personal visit in May 1981 to the former Huachang cocoon firm located at Xiajiabian zhen, then part of the Lüyuan People's Commune in Wuxi. The Huachang cocoon-firm facility was built around 1930 and was still in use in 1981, although under collective rather than private ownership.

83. Tōa dobunkai 1920: 558.

84. Ibid.: 557–59.

85. Ibid.: 535; see also cocoon-firm tables in DELSDAG file 3242 for the denomination "single" or "double" oven and the capacity of each for drying cocoons.

86. Tōa dobunkai 1920: 535–36.

87. Ibid.: 535; this is also the way the Huachang cocoon-firm facilities were constructed.

88. Observations on the two types of drying rooms were made during my visit to the Huachang cocoon firm, where both types were still in use.

89. Tōa dobunkai 1920: 559.

90. Ibid.: 535; it seems especially appropriate for Japanese investigators to use "winemaker" as a form of identification for local elites since in rural Japan, local landowners frequently engaged in sake brewing as a sideline occupation. It was also true in China that local elites made brews of various types, but we are much less apt to think of wine making as a major occupation of local elites in China than we are for Meiji- and Taisho-period commercial elites in Japan.

91. Ibid.

92. Gao Jingyue, a former filature manager in Wuxi, makes the related point that when borrowing funds for silk-filature operation, the "social standing" (*shehui diwei*) of the borrower was crucial. See Gao 1983: 106.

93. I received a photographed copy of the Renchang contract at an interview on October 11, 1980, with Zhang Kai, a Chinese scholar who has studied China's silk industry.

94. Sun Bingru had talked to Sun Boyu about the founding of the Renchang cocoon firm, and apparently was responsible for preserving the original contract signed with Gu Mianfu, presenting it as probable evidence that the Renchang was Wuxi's first cocoon-firm facility.

95. Gao Jingyue interview, May 24, 1980; Zhang Kai interview, Oct. 11, 1980. Gao Jingyue also provided an interesting array of further anecdotal evidence on early cocoon-firm organizing in Wuxi, collected from other Wuxi silk-industry participants in the early 1960's, in which they argued and speculated among themselves as to which cocoon firms were actually the first established. The comprador Gu Mianfu's name came up repeatedly as being an important figure in early cocoon-firm contracting arrangements, not only for the Renchang cocoon firm, but also for other competitors for the status of "Wuxi's first cocoon firm." One participant in these discussions suggested that Gu Mianfu and Xue Nanming collaborated to establish local contracts for several cocoon firms in various market towns throughout the county in the early 1890's. An interview with Xu Ruliang (May 24, 1980), a member of the Wuxi People's Political Consultative Congress formerly involved in the Wuxi silk industry, confirmed this interpretation of the structure of the early cocoon-firm system, claiming that "landlords" were the key link at the local level. One Japanese source states that "wealthy rural folk" fulfilled the role of cocoon-firm builder. See Mantetsu 1940: 794–95.

96. Gao 1983: 105.

97. Lillian Li has grouped cocoon-firm contracts used throughout the Yangzi delta into four categories (L. M. Li 1981: 177–78). I have consulted three sources other than those used by Li and have found it most useful to think of cocoon-firm contracts as falling into the three categories I describe here. What is most important, however, is not the number of categories, but whether or not the cocoon-firm owner maintained a degree of responsibility for operating the facility himself.

98. Tōa dobunkai 1920: 537; L. M. Li 1981: 178.

99. Tōa dobunkai 1920: 537–38; Gao 1983: 105; L. M. Li 1981: 177.

100. Tōa dobunkai 1920: 537, 561; Gao 1983: 105; Zhang Kai interview, Oct. 11, 1980; L. M. Li 1981: 177–78.

101. Tōa dobunkai 1920: 559–61.

102. Ibid.: 534–35. This source states that cocoon firms with fewer than twenty-four drying rooms were considered small and those with more were considered large. Moreover, in Wuxi in the late 1910's, there were some cocoon firms that had over eighty drying rooms; these were considered exceptionally large. Cocoon-firm output capacity was determined by using the average output of 30 dan per double drying room per marketing period reported in the cocoon-firm tables for Wuxi in DELSDAG file no. 3242.

103. The estimate of the size of the fall cocoon crop in Wuxi is based on cocoon-output figures reported in DELSDAG file no. 3242.

104. Tōa dobunkai 1920: 534.

105. All of the quantitative data reported here come from my computerized data sets drawn from Guoli zhongyang yanjiuyuan shehui kexue yanjiusuo 1929. For discussion of this source, see Chapter 1 and Appendix B. The observation that peasants were often unable to pay interest on their loans comes from this same source. From a sample of 135 outstanding loans

in 1929, no payments were made on 33 of them, roughly 24 percent of the total.

106. Although Wuxi had a long history of relatively well-developed financial institutions because of its status as an important regional center for rice marketing, the qianzhuang system there, as elsewhere throughout the Yangzi delta, saw rapid development in the post-Taiping period. In Wuxi, both the grain trade and the new cocoon trade contributed to the rapid proliferation of small-scale banks within this network. By 1920, Wuxi had twenty-three qianzhuang in operation. An extensive warehousing system for cocoons developed in conjunction with the banking network, as the banks required filatures to use stocks of cocoons on hand as collateral for loans for future cocoon purchase. Some scholars have argued that silk filatures eventually suffered from this system, becoming dependent upon it for the large sums of cash that they needed to purchase cocoons each spring. However, I believe that this line of argument leads to a far too simplistic understanding of the problems of the filature industry, a topic to which I return in Chapter 5. For the moment, it is important to note that at least two scholars, Nie (1979: 42–43) and McElderry (1976: 72–74), have interpreted the emergence of the qianzhuang system as an important component of the new comprador-dominated commercial networks spawned throughout the delta in the post-Taiping period. Other sources on the development of the qianzhuang system and cocoon warehousing in Wuxi include Qian 1961: 98–99; Mantetsu 1942: pt. 2; Mantetsu 1940: 73; Lieu 1933: 45–49; Zhang Enshen interview, May 24, 1980; Tōa dobunkai 1920: 563–68.

107. I discuss such risks associated with cocoon-firm and filature operation at length in Chapter 5.

108. This dispute was discussed widely in many Chinese commercial journals and newspapers of the time. I have pieced together this summary of its major turning points from many sources. I list here the most important, in chronological order: JSSGB 1021 (Oct. 19, 1916): 1–3; NSGB 3, no. 9 (Apr. 15, 1917, special reports section: 9–16; NSGB 3, no. 10 (May 15, 1917), special reports section: 27–37; JSSGB 1270 (June 25, 1917): 5–6; JSSGB 1280 (July 5, 1917), orders section: 7–9; NSGB 3, no. 12 (July 15, 1917), selections section: 2–3; JSSGB 1386 (Oct. 21, 1917), orders section: 3–4; NSGB 4, no. 7 (Feb. 15, 1918), selections section: 5–7; JSSYYZ 14 (May 1920): 16–19; JSSYYZ 15 (June 1920): 23–25; MGRB (Apr. 12, 1921), sec. 3: 10; MGRB (Apr. 23, 1921), sec. 3: 10; NSGB 7, no. 10 (May 15, 1921), political affairs section: 31; DELSDAG file 3234, miscellaneous reports from April through June 1929, on the history of cocoon-firm control and petitions for its reinstitution; GSBYK 2, no. 18 (Sept. 15, 1930), national economic affairs section: 3–4.

109. See sources listed in note 108.

110. Institute of Pacific Relations 1939: 237–38. Translated from Qian 1935: 73–74.

111. MGRB (June 5, 1917), sec. 3: 10.

112. NKGB 11 (May 1, 1929): 73–75; NKGB 19 (Jan. 1, 1930): 9–10;

NKGB 21 (Mar. 1, 1930): 28–29. See also Chapter 7 for discussion of the political ramifications of these events.

CHAPTER 4

1. For a fuller discussion of this literature, see Chapter 1.
2. L. M. Li 1981: 131–38; see also Zhang 1979, pt. 2: 53–54.
3. L. M. Li 1981: 134–35.
4. Wuxi ximenwai Jiangsu shengli yucan shiyansuo 1919–21: 40.
5. L. M. Li 1981: 135–36.
6. Yan 1923: ch. 10, p. 9; Gao and Yan 1980: 4.
7. For discussion of the phrase *quanke nongsang*, see Shu Xincheng et al. 1974: 1247.
8. The symbolic significance of the stone engravings erected over the door of Yan's residence was brought home to me in a visit to the site in 1980. I was accompanied on this visit by a professor from Nanjing University who is also a native of Wuxi. As a descendent of literati families of the area, and as a man who also had the surname Yan, an indication of possible ties of kinship with Yan Ziqing, the professor was personally elated by the opportunity to display the site and the remains of the stone engraving to me and to have me photograph and be photographed with them. Clearly, for him, the opportunity to reinforce the importance of the dissemination of knowledge of sericulture by a gentry member through the ritualistic display of the stone characters was an essential aspect of local elite heritage and was not to be taken lightly, even in the 1980's.
9. Zhang 1979, pt. 2: 53.
10. Yang 1955: 124–25.
11. Mann 1987: chs. 2–5.
12. One might even suggest that Pierre Bourdieu's arguments about "symbolic capital" are relevant here, as local elites used the term "wenshe" to evoke links to a wide repertoire of elite behavior designed to promote community well-being. On symbolic capital, see Bourdieu 1977: ch. 4, esp. 171–83.
13. The term "yang," or "foreign," also implies "modern" and "Western" and, from the point of view of the peasants who used it, referred to anything related to externally induced deviations from traditional activities or behavior in the local setting.
14. *Kaihua xiangzhi* 1916, 1: 52–54. In the twentieth century, the adjective "yang," or "foreign," continued to be used by the peasantry to describe individuals from the local elite involved in various aspects of silk-industry development. When sericulture extension-station workers, young female members of the local elite, went into the countryside in the 1920's and 1930's, peasants stood in their doorways gawking, calling these strangers who passed by "foreign teachers" (*yang xiansheng*). Fei Dasheng interview, May 18, 1981. See also Chapter 7, pp. 142–43, for further discussion on this point.

15. Kaihua was the one area of Wuxi that had some sericulture and production of handicraft silk prior to the Taiping Rebellion. For more on this, see the gazetteer passage in Chapter 3 at note 37.

16. *Kaihua xiangzhi* 1916, 1: 54–55.

17. Ibid.: 55–56.

18. Ibid.: 56–57.

19. Goodman 1990: 29–46. Goodman's discussion of terminology used for "fellow-provincial" organizations is far more highly nuanced than I have intimated here. I have referred only to the terms "huiguan" and "gongsuo" because they were the most commonly used; but in reality, there was a much fuller array of choices for naming such organizations, and the possibility of embedding sets of suborganization names within a larger, overarching "fellow-provincial" structure. Goodman's excellent study is dedicated to working out the complexities of such organizations' activities as they developed in Shanghai from the 1850's through the 1930's.

20. Peng 1965: 91.

21. Mann 1979b: 73–74.

22. Rowe 1984; Goodman 1995.

23. Jürgen Habermas's most salient arguments about the bourgeois public sphere are contained in two seminal works, one appearing in its original German version in 1962, translated by Thomas Burger with Frederick Lawrence as *The Structural Transformation of the Public Sphere: An Inquiry into a Category of Bourgeois Society* (Cambridge, Mass.: MIT Press, 1989); and the other, later work (original German published in 1981), *The Theory of Communicative Action*, vol. 2, *Lifeworld and System: A Critique of Functionalist Reason*, trans. Thomas McCarthy (Boston: Beacon Press, 1987). Rowe's portrayal of Hankow's merchant guilds makes no strong claims for China regarding Habermas's central concern with new forms of public communication within the bourgeois public sphere. Nonetheless, by evoking the image of the "public sphere," the clear implication is that Chinese merchant guilds were distinctively "modern" and "progressive," if not entirely identical with their European counterparts, and thus part of an "early modern" era in Chinese history. It is this implicit view of a parallel path to Western-style capitalism with which I disagree.

24. Gao Jingyue interview, May 24, 1980. Although I do not know what gods were enshrined in the Shijinshan temple, there were many forms of the god of wealth in the delta region, and local temples were sometimes dedicated to him by merchants interested in furthering their business careers (von Glahn 1993). The establishment of a gongsuo office at a local temple is a slightly different matter, but bears strong resemblance to traditional forms of merchant behavior through which divine sanctions for commercial activity were commonly sought.

25. Gao Jingyue interview, May 24, 1980. One of my meetings with Gao Jingyue, former director of the Wuxi Filature and Cocoon Trade Association during the 1940's, took place at a public park now located at Huishan. The arrangement of such a meeting at the original site of the formation of the

Wuxi Cocoon-Merchant Guild was important in a symbolic sense. Huishan is a gently rolling hilly area next to the city proper, and figures prominently in local lore about the county's founding. Legend holds that county founders (the founding "ancestors") chose the site for early settlement because of its natural beauty and its auspicious location. The close association of such a site with commercial activity shows that local elites in Wuxi, as in other delta locales, perceived strong ties between commerce, historical continuity, and community well-being, and that they used every opportunity to develop, strengthen, and demonstrate the connections.

26. Gao Jingyue interview, May 24, 1980.

27. Ibid.

28. See sources in Chapter 3, note 108.

29. *JSSYYZ* 15 (June 1920): 74–75.

30. DELSDAG, file no. 3242, subfile no. 32472.

31. *NSGB* 3, no. 12 (July 15, 1917), news section: 21.

32. Ibid.

33. *GSBYK* 1, no. 12 (June 15, 1929), domestic economic affairs section: 9–10.

34. This type of price fluctuation can be seen in daily newspaper reports on cocoon prices. See for example, *MGRB* (May 27, 1917), sec. 3: 10; *MGRB* (May 28, 1917), sec. 3: 11; *MGRB* (May 30, 1917), sec. 3: 10.

35. Wang 1973: 80; as cited in Mann 1987: 147–48.

36. Mann 1987: chs. 7 and 8.

37. Ibid.: ch. 8.

38. *JSSGB* 1277 (July 2, 1917), "Diaocha gexian shoukuan biao: Wuxi xian."

39. *JSSGB* 1650 (July 21, 1918): 24–25.

40. *JSSGB* (May 15, 1923): 7–8.

41. Mann 1987: ch. 8.

42. *NKGB* 4 (Nov. 1, 1928): 7; DELSDAG file no. 3234, "Fuzhu sijianye yu gailiang cansi canzhong shixiang, 1927–34."

43. Mann 1987: 164–70. Earlier works by Eastman (1974) and T'ien (1972) also demonstrate that working out suitable methods for funding expanding government at the central, provincial, and county levels was one of the central dynamics of Guomindang statemaking.

44. *NKGB* 3 (Oct. 1, 1928): 48ff.; *NKGB* 4 (Nov. 1, 1928): 48–54; *NKGB* 5 (Nov. 20, 1928): 10–16; *NKGB* 6 (Dec. 10, 1928): 53–58; *GSBYK* 1, no. 7 (Apr. 1, 1929), industry and commercial news section: 6.

45. On the institution of the bureau system to create new subunits of provincial administration at the county level, see Kuhn 1979: 122–24. Because Jiangsu was the Guomindang's new "capital province," many programs designed for implementation by the provincial government had the strong force of central government initiative behind them. Thus, as we shall see in more detail later, new programs for cocoon-firm control were pursued with great force and persistence by Jiangsu provincial agencies from 1928 onward, as they struggled to find new ways to promote programs for eco-

nomic development and more effective commercial taxation throughout the Yangzi delta, the core economic region controlled by the new national government.

46. *NKGB* 13 (July 1, 1929): 59.

CHAPTER 5

1. The two other major industries in Wuxi were cotton mills and flour-processing plants, many of which were owned by the Rong brothers, who went on from their efforts to found cocoon firms in Wuxi (see Chapter 3) to become two of China's most famous industrialists. A 1930 publication of the Wuxi County government entitled *Wuxi Yearbook* has the most comprehensive description of industrial development in Wuxi. See Wuxi xianzhengfu, Wuxi shizheng choubeichu 1930, section on industry. Other sources include Qian 1961; Mantetsu 1940; Chūshi kensetsu shiryō seibi jimusho 1941; and for the Rong brothers' activities, Shanghai shehui kexueyuan jingji yanjiusuo 1962.

2. L. M. Li (1981: ch. 6) and Eng (1986: ch. 3) provide the best overall discussions of the development of filatures in Shanghai and the Canton delta in English. So 1986 also discusses the development of filatures in the Canton delta. Tōa Kenkyūjo 1943: 132–33 and 142–46 also has general descriptions of the rapid flourishing of the filature industry in Shanghai, and especially in Wuxi, following World War I.

3. Chen 1957–61: 112; Wang 1979: 1272–76; L. M. Li 1981: 171; Eng 1986: 55–57, 79–84.

4. Eng 1986: 87–89.

5. Chapter 3 explores the problem of inadequate cocoon supplies for early Shanghai filatures. L. M. Li 1981: 167 discusses some of the reasons for locating filatures in Wuxi as opposed to Shanghai, including cheaper labor, savings on taxes, and proximity to cocoon supply. I return to the comparative advantages of building filatures in Wuxi later in this chapter.

6. Wuxi difangzhi bianji weiyuanhui 1959: 41–42, 57; Qian 1961: 123–27; Lü Huantai interview, May 24, 1980; Shen Yaoming interview, May 24, 1980; Gao and Yan 1987: 45–46; Wuxishi zhengxie wenshi ziliao yanjiu weiyuanhui 1981: 52–55.

7. Although sources vary, many cite approximately fifty filatures in Wuxi in the late 1920's. The reason for variation is that filatures once built were not always in operation; also, most filatures were in a constant state of flux in terms of their managerial personnel, rented out for contractual periods and often renamed in the process. I discuss this mode of filature operation at length below. Sources on the number of Wuxi filatures include Tōa kenkyūjo 1943: 132–33, 142–46; *Wuxi shizheng* 2 (1929): 107–13; Wuxi shizheng choubeichu 1929: 121–23; Wuxi xianzhengfu, Wuxi shizheng choubeichu 1930, industry section: 12–21; Mantetsu 1940: 79–80; Wuxi difangzhi bianji weiyuanhui 1959: 41–42; Lu 1921: 46–47; Zhu and Zhang 1923: 7–8; Jiangsu shengli disan shifan fushu xiaoxue diwuceng shangyeke 1923: 12; and DELSDAG file 3242, subfile 32472. I also include as Appendix

C a comprehensive listing of filatures in Wuxi compiled in Gao and Yan 1987: 51–52 and 55–59.

8. Wuxi difangzhi bianji weiyuanhui 1959: 41. See also Appendix C for a comprehensive listing of filature founders and their backgrounds.

9. The following account of the founding and development of the Gansheng filature comes from a reminiscence written in 1980 by Wang Huanan, nephew of the founder of the filature, Sun Heqing, and cousin of the filature's most prominent manager, Cheng Bingruo. Wang's father and grandfather also became filature investors beginning in 1917, and Wang himself went on to become manager of the Meixin filature in Wuxi. The reminiscence is found in Gao and Yan 1987: 38–40.

10. See Appendix C.

11. GSBYK 2, no. 1 (Jan. 1, 1930), investigation section: 2–5.

12. Ibid. For descriptions of early filature founders and investors, see Appendix C. See also Gao and Yan 1987: 31–50, for accounts of the founding of early filatures.

13. See Appendix C.

14. Gao and Yan 1987: 53–54.

15. Bergère 1983: 745–51.

16. I interviewed a group of former filature managers in Wuxi in 1980–81, several of whom had been to Japan as students. Gao Jingyue, the unofficial leader of this group, was the son of a comprador agent for the cocoon trade in Wuxi. He had studied in Japan, and when he returned to Wuxi, he entered filature management. A study of Wuxi students studying abroad in the period 1898 to 1920 reports that most of the 241 students who went abroad during this period went to Japan or the United States. See Wuxi difangzhi bianzuan weiyuanhui ban'gongshi, Wuxi xianzhi bianzuan weiyuanhui ban'gongshi 1986: 45–77.

17. Wuxishi zhengxie wenshi ziliao yanjiu weiyuanhui 1981: 54–55.

18. Zhuang Yaohe interview, May 27, 1980; Chūsi kensetsu shiryō seibi jimusho 1941: 42–43; Chen 1957–61: 113; NSGB 3, no. 9 (Apr. 15, 1917), special reports section: 14–15; Wuxi difangzhi bianji weiyuanhui 1959: 45–46; Mantetsu 1940: 85–86; Gao and Yan 1987: 66–70; Wuxishi fangzhi gongyeju saosi gongyeshi bianji xiaozu 1959: 26–27; Wuxishi zhengxie wenshi ziliao yanjiu weiyuanhui 1981: 54–55.

19. Qian 1988: 71; Wuxishi zhengxie wenshi ziliao yanjiu weiyuanhui 1981: 54–55.

20. Wuxi difangzhi bianji weiyuanhui 1959: 45–46.

21. NSGB 3, no. 9 (Apr. 15, 1917), special reports section: 14–15; GSBYK 2, no. 1 (Jan. 1, 1930), investigation section: 2–5; Chen 1957–61: 113; Zhuang Yaohe interview, May 27, 1980; Chūshi kensetsu shiryō seibi jimusho 1941: 39–43; Mantetsu 1940: 85–87; Wuxishi fangzhi gongyeju saosi gongyeshi bianji xiaozu 1959: 26–27; Wuxishi zhengxie wenshi ziliao yanjiu weiyuanhui 1981: 54–55.

22. Gao and Yan 1987: 49; L. M. Li 1981: 167.

23. *YHZB* 13, no. 34 (Sept. 3, 1929), weekly commerce section: 2–3; *YHZB* 13, no. 37 (Sept. 24, 1929), weekly commerce section: 4; *GSBYK* 2, no. 17 (Sept. 1, 1930), legislation section: 4–6; *SB* (Jan. 19, 1937), sec. 4: 14; L. M. Li 1981: 173; Lieu 1940: 92.

24. Gao and Yan 1987: 49; L. M. Li 1981: 167.

25. Gao and Yan 1987: 49; L. M. Li 1981: 167.

26. Wuxi xianzhengfu, Wuxi shizheng choubeichu 1930, industry section: 18.

27. Eng 1986: 87–94; L. M. Li 1981: 91–95.

28. Xu 1990: 152–61. This source reports that Japanese raw-silk sales first began to surpass the Chinese in the period from 1900 to 1906. Other reports stress the same phenomenon but disagree on exactly which year the switch in relative market shares first occurred. Many claim the shift occurred in 1909. See, for example, Shen 1934; and Yan n.d., "Chuncan daosi sibujin." This issue also was discussed at length in my interview with Zhou Kuangming, Nov. 8–13, 1980.

29. See, for example, reports about anxiety over weather, political disturbances, cocoon supply, and rising prices in *MGRB* (May 21, 1916), sec. 3: 10; (May 25, 1917), sec. 3: 10; (May 27, 1917), sec. 3: 10; (May 28, 1917), sec. 3: 11; (May 30, 1917), sec. 3: 10; (June 4, 1917), sec. 2: 7; (June 5, 1917), sec. 3: 10; (May 11, 1921), sec. 3: 11; (June 5, 1921), sec. 2: 8. A detailed petition requesting protection of silver shipments throughout the delta during cocoon-buying season can be found in *JSSGB* (May 16, 1923): 2–3. Generally speaking, it was the responsibility of cocoon merchants' guilds to start the process of petitioning for military protection for silver shipments. See Gao Jingyue interview, May 24, 1980, and *MGRB* (May 12, 1917), sec. 3: 10; (May 15, 1917), sec. 2: 7 and sec. 3, 10; (May 24, 1917), sec. 2: 7 and sec. 3: 10. Part of the rationale for the involvement of the military was that foreign buyers were involved in cocoon purchase, meaning that the Chinese government was obligated by the terms of international treaties to provide them with military protection. It is also clear from many of these newspaper reports that when interprovincial military activity was under way in Jiangsu and Zhejiang, there were negative effects on both cocoon production and marketing, causing a great deal of volatility in daily cocoon market prices. See, especially, *MGRB* (Apr. 18, 1916), sec. 2: 8; (Apr. 19, 1916), sec. 2: 8; (Apr. 27, 1916), sec. 3: 10; (Apr. 29, 1916), sec. 3: 10; (May 21, 1916), sec. 3: 10; (Apr. 6, 1916), sec. 3: 10.

30. *JSSYYZ* 15 (June 1920): 74–75; DELSDAG file 3242, subfile 32472.

31. The baohong system of cocoon-firm contracting, as described in Chapter 3, was still in wide use on the eve of Japanese takeover of the Wuxi silk industry in the late 1930's. See Zhang 1984: 79, and Gao 1983: 106.

32. On filature closings in Wuxi, see Mantetsu 1940: 94, where the claim is made that only the largest, most successful filatures operated year-round in Wuxi, with most remaining open only ten months of the year. See also *YHZB* 13, no. 34 (Sept. 3, 1929), weekly commerce section: 2–3; *YHZB*

13, no. 37 (Sept. 24, 1929), weekly commerce section: 4; *GSBYK* 2, no. 17 (Sept. 1, 1930), legislation section: 4–6; *SB* (Jan. 19, 1937), sec. 4: 14. These sources all report filature closings due to cocoon shortages.

33. Wuxi xianzhengfu, Wuxi shizheng choubeichu 1930, party affairs section: 21–26. Another source cites 36,350 as the total number of female filature workers, and an additional 5,417 child workers. See Gao and Yan 1987: 492; the original source for these numbers is a 1932 publication, *Zhongguo laodong nianjian.* It is likely that the number 19,000 is an understatement of the total number of female filature workers, therefore, that fails to count workers hired on a temporary basis and child labor. Also, the age range cited here for female filature workers is probably too high, failing to factor in child labor.

34. Gao and Yan 1987: 502.

35. The strike and the workers' wage demands were reported widely in the Wuxi press. See the press excerpts in Gao and Yan 1987: 512–29. Wang 1986 also reports that one of the major concessions granted to filature workers as a result of the strike was a raise in wages to fifty cents a day.

36. Honig 1986.

37. L. M. Li 1981: 183–84; Xu 1990: 287–88.

38. Xu 1990: 287–88.

39. Lillian M. Li (1981: 183–84) also discusses data on cocoon and raw-silk taxes. She reaches a different conclusion, though, saying that "it is difficult to see that the tax on cocoons posed a real obstacle to expansion or modernization." However, she does not take into account the problem of a price squeeze caused by relatively high cocoon prices for filatures relative to raw-silk prices, and the way in which cocoon-trade taxes exacerbated fear of losses by filature managers as a result.

40. Eng 1986: 87–94, and Lieu 1933: 115–22, have the best overall descriptions of the system of raw-silk purchase for export in Shanghai.

41. Lieu 1933: 118–22; Eng 1986: 89–90; *YHZB* 13, no. 36 (Sept. 17, 1929), reports section: 7.

42. *YHZB* 13, no. 38 (Oct. 1, 1929), miscellany section: 10–11.

43. *YHZB* 13, no. 39 (Oct. 8, 1929), miscellany section: 16–17.

44. *YHZB* 13, no. 37 (Sept. 24, 1929), weekly commerce section: 4; 13, no. 42 (Oct. 29, 1929), weekly commerce section: 3–4; 13, no. 44 (Nov. 12, 1929), weekly commerce section: 4–5; 13, no. 48 (Dec. 10, 1929), weekly commerce section: 5.

45. *YHZB* 13, no. 36 (Sept. 17, 1929), reports section: 5–7.

46. Eng (1986: 75 and 120–30) makes the argument for a "rentier mentality" pervading the filature industries of both Shanghai and the Canton delta. We should note here that Wuxi was not the only locale in which "split ownership/management" was used for development of the filature industry. The same system, with some variations, was found in filatures throughout Shanghai and the Canton delta as well. Thus, we should be alerted to the fact that traditions of commercial layering had far-reaching effects beyond the Yangzi delta, and also that the special risks associated

with raw-silk production and marketing tended to produce similar strategies for spreading risk.

47. Eng (ibid.: 70–79) summarizes the case most strongly, basing his argument on a wide array of sources from the period stressing the low rates of capital investment in the industry and the consequent "need" to borrow from native banks.

48. Wu 1993.

CHAPTER 6

1. See, for example, Brandt 1989 and Faure 1989.

2. When I used the remains of the SSRI survey, they were housed at the Institute of Economics of the Chinese Academy of Social Sciences in Beijing. Since that time, the materials have been difficult for others to access. A research team of American and Chinese scholars headed by David Zweig planned to use the materials in 1989, but the materials were withheld. I know of only one Chinese researcher, Professor Wu Baijun of the Chinese University of Science and Technology in Shanghai, who has produced a substantive study based on the materials (his Ph.D. dissertation, completed in 1993).

3. For further discussion of the value of Mantetsu survey materials, see Huang 1985, ch. 2. Elsewhere I have discussed the Mantetsu materials in the context of what constitutes peasant "rationality." For this analysis, inspired by the work of Russian theorist A. V. Chayanov in the 1920's, see Bell 1992.

4. For a complete list of other crops grown, see the data set OPS contained in Appendix B (Table B2).

5. A good general description of Wuxi's farming system appears in Mantetsu 1941, with the breakdown of land usage found in tables 5 and 10 following the main body of the text.

6. Mantetsu 1941: 9–11. For estimates of about one-third of the land in Wuxi being devoted to mulberry cultivation, see Lu 1921: 45; *GSBYK* 2, no. 15 (Aug. 1, 1930), investigation section: 3. Rong 1927: 109; Wuxi xianzhengfu, Wuxi shizheng choubeichu 1930, agriculture section: 5. Yu (1932: 171) states that in the vicinity of the market town of Lishe in the northwestern part of the county, mulberry fields were approximately one-fourth of total arable land.

7. Mantetsu 1941: tables 5 and 10.

8. As for most calculations of this type from the SSRI survey, I have relied on data available in the 128-household sample derived from the SSRI survey remains. See Appendix B for a full description of the sample and the variables developed from the survey.

9. Mantetsu 1941: 26.

10. *JNSWB* 9 (Apr. 21, 1900), commercial raw-materials section: 2; DELSDAG file no. 3504, subfile "Liangnianlai": 4; Sun 1931: 985; *MGRB* (May 21, 1916), sec. 3: 10; (May 11, 1921), sec. 3: 11; and (June 5, 1921), sec. 2: 8.

11. DELSDAG file no. 3242, subfile no. 32472; Qian 1935; *MGRB* (May 27, 1917), sec. 3: 10; (June 4, 1917), sec. 2: 7; and (June 5, 1917), sec. 3: 10.

12. Mantetsu 1941: 23 and table 5.

13. Ibid. A total of six rural surveys were conducted by Shanghai-based Mantetsu research teams during 1939 and 1940. In addition to the Wuxi survey, other surveys were conducted in Jiading, Taicang, Changshou, Songjiang, and Nantong counties. Philip Huang (1990) has made use of these surveys in his study of peasant family-based production in the Yangzi delta, and Kathy Walker (1993 and 1999) has made extensive use of the Nantong survey.

14. Mantetsu 1941: 28.

15. On topsoil and subsoil rights, see Chapter 2. By the time of land reform in Wuxi in the late 1940's and early 1950's, many rural investigators were preoccupied with the degree to which tenants' positions vis-à-vis landlords had declined since Qing times. Based on their firsthand investigations in several villages and townships, they claimed that landlords had the ability to confiscate land on which tenants held permanent tenure in the form of topsoil ownership rights if the tenant defaulted for three years. Land on which the tenant held no ownership rights could be bargained for yearly, so landlords could find new tenants willing to pay higher rents. See Sunan renmin xingzheng gongzhu tudi gaige weiyuanhui 1951: 1–10; Jiang 1951; Hui 1951; and Yu 1951.

16. In the Mantetsu-surveyed villages, less land was rented—about 25 percent of the total—and only ten households in the three villages worked rented land. These facts point to variation in class relations in different village settings, including the probability that many peasant families living in the Mantetsu-surveyed villages near the market town of Rongxiang had given up renting land from resident or absentee landlords, and that male family members instead were seeking other forms of work elsewhere (more on this below). It also helps to explain how many households in the three Mantetsu-surveyed villages, by avoiding rent, managed to get by with farms of such unusually small size—only 2.54 mu on average, as we have seen.

17. Perkins 1969: 14–15 and app. F. Perkins's main rationales for his definition of subsistence were that in 1957, no province of China had a per capita output as low as 400 jin; that in the 130-odd villages surveyed by Buck, fewer than ten fell below this level of grain output per capita; and that in over thirty countries at levels of development comparable to China in 1957–59, per capita grain supply was rarely below the level of 400 jin.

18. Estimates of per capita grain output, consumption, and household incomes in this chapter account for age and sex of family members using a standard formula, also used by Perkins, of 77 adult male equivalents per 100 members of the population (or, one adult male equivalent = men + 0.8 women + 0.5 children). Thus, in discussions concerning such issues, "per capita" more precisely means "per adult male equivalent."

19. The Mantetsu researchers also commented on the inability of Wuxi farming households to achieve self-sufficiency in grain production. They

found that families purchased, on average, about half the grain that they consumed, and that only 10 percent, or eight households of 80, had complete self-sufficiency in rice. Mantetsu 1941: 144–47.

20. Lu 1921: 45.

21. SSRI survey tables on sericulture. See also Bell 1994: 195–96.

22. SSRI survey tables on subsidiary occupations. See also Bell 1994: 196.

23. For patterns of work associated with sericulture in Wuxi, see Mantetsu 1941: 55–56 and table 11. For the problem of sleepless nights and peasant fatigue, see Rong 1927: 113, and Mao [1932] 1979.

24. On the question of the disposition of a women's earnings in Chinese households, see Salaff 1981.

25. In a previously published article (Bell 1994), I have considered in much greater detail and depth the interrelationships between silkworm raising and women's status. Previous studies by Topley (1975) and Stockard (1989) on women's work in filatures and silkworm raising in Guangdong have suggested possible positive outcomes for rural women's status because of new income-earning potential. But for a variety of reasons, from women's lack of direct control over their incomes to peasant beliefs about ritual pollution and silkworm death, I argue that we must be cautious before assuming any universal positive benefits accruing to peasant women through new forms of silk production.

26. SSRI survey tables on subsidiary occupations; see data set SUPINC in Appendix B for the way occupation categories were coded.

27. The village of Huangxiang to the immediate northwest of Wuxi City had a large number of women working in a silk filature that was relatively close to the village. Because of the poor quality of survey questionnaires from Huangxiang, I have not included any of these households in the 128-household sample currently under consideration. It is important to note, however, that many peasant women from Huangxiang worked in filatures because they could continue to reside at home. Thus, their additional non-waged economic contributions to family life, such as vegetable gardening, animal-tending, and child care, were not lost even as they went to work for some period each year in the filature. Also, the social stigma associated with sending women off to work outside the home was at least partially mitigated by this situation, as women continued to eat and sleep at home on a daily basis. Women in Huangxiang did not "migrate" in a formal sense—a subject to which I shall turn momentarily—and it was guaranteed that their factory earnings would return home to supplement family incomes overall.

28. Scattered evidence from the SSRI survey on mulberry markets provides insight into why this was so. Mulberries were bought and sold at the village level among farming families. There were no organized, larger-scale markets for mulberries, and prices fluctuated considerably from one locale to another and from one season to the next. There were no guarantees that additional mulberries would be available if a particular household needed

them, or what their prices would be. Thus, mulberry-market uncertainty worked against the possibility that small farming households would rely too heavily upon purchased mulberries to increase the size of their silkworm broods.

29. Mantetsu 1941: 104.

30. Ibid.: 103–4. Among ten households who were asked how much money came back home in 1940 from their family members who had migrated, two households said none; one said 6 yuan; one said 10 yuan; two said 40 yuan; one said 55 yuan; one said 100 yuan; one said 130 yuan; and one said 160 yuan.

31. Ibid.: 88–95 and tables 2 and 3.

32. The percentage of households with per capita incomes below 24 yuan is derived from a simple frequencies distribution of total per capita incomes for all 128 households in the SSRI-survey sample.

33. Although we should be cautious about generalizations based on survey data for only one year, there is nothing to indicate that the situation in 1929 in Wuxi was unusual in any respect. Prices reported by peasant households in the SSRI survey for cocoons, rice, and wheat correspond to trends in prices observed in the periodical literature for the period (for more on cocoon prices, see Chapter 5 above). Widely reported rural destitution in Wuxi during the early 1930's might thus be seen as resulting not only from the immediate, and relatively short-term, effects of the Great Depression on Wuxi's silk industry, but also from the difficulties many peasants were already having in making ends meet, even with the ability to sell their cocoons to local silk filatures fully intact. For more on rural destitution in Wuxi during the early 1930's, see Bell 1985.

CHAPTER 7

1. The literature on such individuals is much too voluminous to cite in its entirety here. Perhaps the best general introduction to research on China's increasingly complex intellectual currents in the early twentieth century is found in the chapters by Charlotte Furth and Benjamin Schwartz in *The Cambridge History of China*, vol. 12, pt. 1 (Cambridge: Cambridge University Press, 1983). Chapters by Andrew Nathan and Marie-Claire Bergère in the same volume, on the Peking government from 1916 to 1928 and on the activities of China's new bourgeoisie respectively, are also a very useful introduction to the political trajectories spawned by new intellectual currents. Wellington Chan's work on "merchants and mandarins," as he terms wealthy businessmen and high-ranking officials, is also a good overview of how such men began to take a new interest in industry and political forms to support it. Chan has a chapter in *The Cambridge History*, vol. 11, pt. 2 (Cambridge: Cambridge University Press, 1980), but his book (Chan 1977) provides an even better brief overview of late Qing intellectual shifts toward the importance of modern industry.

2. I use "modernity" here rather than "modernization" to indicate that my analysis involves more than a discussion of scientific technique and its

application to sericulture. In reaction to a previous generation of scholar-ship called "modernization theory," more recent writers choose the term "modernity" to indicate that complex, and highly varied, matrixes of ideas and social practices evolved in third-world countries as global capitalism impinged upon them in various ways in the early twentieth century. In this sense, "modernity" took different paths in different places as modern sci-ence and its related institutions were imported, adapted, and reconfigured. As this happened, the meanings and concrete implications of modernity also became hotly contested issues in varied local contexts.

3. The microorganism responsible for the French silkworm epidemic was identified and named "pebrine" by Louis Pasteur in the early 1860's. After Pasteur set to work on stemming the spread of the disease through cel-lular incubation of eggs, the epidemic was checked, but it was already too late for French sericulture to recover. On these developments, see Eng 1986: 26–27.

4. Hu Yuankai interview, May 23, 1980.

5. Native egg varieties typically produced 1 dan of dried cocoons for every 3 dan of fresh ones, and it took 6 dan of dried cocoons to spin 1 dan of raw silk. When improved silkworm eggs were used, it took only 2.5 to 2.6 dan of fresh cocoons to yield 1 dan of dried ones, and only 3.5 to 4 dan of dried cocoons to produce 1 dan of raw silk. For these estimates, see Yan n.d., "Chuncan daosi sibujin": 14–15. Obviously, filatures would have been will-ing to pay peasants more for cocoons produced with improved eggs because of these improving ratios. Also, as noted, the silk produced from improved eggs was of higher quality and thus received higher prices on the world market.

6. For more on changing product preferences in the international market for raw silk, see Chapter 3.

7. Eng 1986: 173–74.

8. Eng (1986) also attributes the Japanese success to rapid proliferation of traditional sericulture technique into new areas and to the expansion of mulberry acreage (pp. 174–75).

9. L. M. Li 1981: 87; Zhou Kuangming interview, Nov. 8–13, 1980; Yan n.d., "Chuncan daosi sibujin": 1.

10. Lillian Li and Robert Eng both provide accounts of early sericulture schools in the delta region. See Li 1981: 188–90; Eng 1986: 130–36.

11. Yin 1931: 13; Eng 1986: 132; L. M. Li 1981: 190.

12. Yin 1931: 13.

13. L. M. Li 1981: 190; Eng 1986: 132.

14. Yan n.d., "Chuncan daosi sibujin": 2; Zhang 1979, pt. 2: 54.

15. DELSDAG file no. 3504, "Ershinian zhounian gongzuo baogao": 4–5.

16. Yan n.d., "Chuncan daosi sibujin": 1.

17. Fei Dasheng interview, May 18, 1981.

18. Hu Yuankai interview, May 23, 1980.

19. Chen Yaorong interview, May 23, 1980.

20. Ibid.

21. Fei Dasheng interview, May 18, 1981; Hu Yuankai interview, May 23, 1980.

22. *JSJSYK* 2, no. 3 (Mar. 1, 1935), addenda section: 4–17.

23. Fei Dasheng interview, May 18, 1981; Hu Yuankai interview, May 23, 1980.

24. Wong 1979: 34.

25. Eng 1986: 134–35.

26. *JSSGB* 1030 (Oct. 19, 1916): 3–15.

27. Yin 1931: 13–14; *NSGB* 4, no. 2 (Sept. 1917), selections section: 15–16.

28. Liu Yuzhen 1919: 9–12; Yin 1931: 14.

29. Yin 1931: 14; *JSSGB* 1650 (Jul. 21, 1918): 24–25.

30. On cocoon-merchant resistance to sericulture reform surtaxes, see Chapter 4.

31. Complaints about the proliferation in the early 1920's of such surtaxes abound in commercial literature appearing after the establishment of the Guomindang government in Nanjing in 1927. To acknowledge such complaints seemed to be a way for the Guomindang leadership to absolve itself from blame for the "inherited" chaos in matters related to commercial surtaxes. See, for example, *NKGB* 4 (Nov. 1, 1928): 19.

32. Zhao 1935, vol. 1, ch. 4: 244–46.

33. *NKGB* 2 (Aug. 1, 1928): 9.

34. Liu Yuzhen 1919: 9–12.

35. *WXZZ* 4 (Oct. 1, 1923), industry section: 1; Liu Shudong 1919: 35–36; Gong 1921: 12.

36. *WXZZ* 4 (Oct. 1, 1923), industry section: 1; *WXZZ* 2 (Apr. 1, 1923), investigation section: 2.

37. *WXZZ* 4 (Oct. 1, 1923), industry section: 1; Liu Shudong 1919: 36; Gong 1921: 12; *WXZZ* 2 (Apr. 1, 1923), investigation section: 2; Chen Yaorong interview, May 23, 1980; Hu Yuankai interview, May 23, 1980.

38. Eastman 1974: 227–28.

39. The entire report is contained in *NKGB* 13 (Jul. 1, 1929): 113–23.

40. Ibid.: 119.

41. Funding levels for the new experiment stations were reported in ibid.: 120. The total provincial revenue for 1929–30 was 11,867,320 yuan, as reported in Zhao 1935, vol. 1, ch. 4: 246.

42. *NKGB* 10 (Apr. 1, 1929): 4–5; *NKGB* 13 (Jul. 1, 1929): 114–16.

43. Wuxi xianzhengfu, Wuxi shizheng choubeichu 1930, agriculture section: 2–3.

44. *YHZB* 13, no. 36 (Sept. 17, 1929), weekly commerce: 4.

45. *YHZB* 13, no. 34 (Sept. 3, 1929), weekly commerce: 2–3.

46. SSRI survey tables on sericulture. For details on the survey, see Chapter 1 and Appendix B.

47. Fei Dasheng interview, May 18, 1981.

48. *Nücan* 11 (Feb. 6, 1924): 1.

49. Ibid.: 3.

50. Zhang 1979, pt. 2: 54–55; *JNSWB* 9 (Apr. 21, 1900), commercial raw-materials section: 1.

51. *JNSWB* 12 (May 21, 1900), commercial affairs section: 6.

52. This impression has been formed by reading in the Hushuguan publication *Nücan* from the early 1920's through the mid-1930's. A particularly revealing article from 1924 reports on a conversation between the school's head, Zheng Qunqiang, and school graduates on the silkworm-egg breeding business. Zheng pointed out that improved silkworm-egg production could bring profit both to the peasants and to breedery owners (*Nücan* 10 [Jan. 20, 1924]: 4).

53. Hu Yuankai interview, May 23, 1980.

54. Ibid.

55. Chen Yaorong interview, May 23, 1980.

56. *NKGB* 18 (Dec. 1, 1929): 16–18, 65; *NKGB* 20 (Feb. 1, 1930): 18.

57. SSRI survey tables on sericulture.

58. Mantetsu 1941: 124. For more information about the Mantetsu survey, see Chapter 1 and Appendix B.

59. Ibid.: 144–47.

60. SSRI survey sample, tables on loans.

61. Mantetsu 1941: table 16.

62. *GSBYK* 1, no. 18 (Sept. 15, 1929), domestic economy section: 5–8.

63. *YHZB* 13, no. 34 (Sept. 3, 1929), weekly commerce section: 2–3.

64. *NKGB* 18 (Dec. 1, 1929): 4–6.

65. Kuhn 1975: 284.

66. *NKGB* 18 (Dec. 1, 1929): 4–6, 65.

67. *NKGB* 10 (Apr. 1, 1929): 4–6.

68. *Wuxi xianzheng gongbao*, no. 1 (May 1929), meeting minutes section: 4–5.

69. *NKGB* 12 (June 1, 1929): 16–17; 13 (Jul. 1, 1929): 20–21, 28.

70. *NKGB* 18 (Dec. 1, 1929): 13–14, 16–18.

71. Ibid.

72. *NKGB* 19 (Jan. 1, 1930): 9–10.

73. *NKGB* 11 (May 1, 1929): 73–75; 19 (Jan. 1, 1930): 9–10.

74. *NKGB* 5 (Nov. 20, 1928): 50–53.

75. *NKGB* 19 (Jan. 1, 1930): 9–10.

76. *NKGB* 8 (Feb. 1, 1929): 18; 11 (May 1, 1929): 24–25; 21 (Mar. 1, 1930): 66–72.

77. Sun 1948: 311.

78. *NKGB* 19 (Jan. 1, 1930): 9–10.

79. Ibid.

80. Ibid.; *NKGB* 21 (Mar. 1, 1930): 28–29.

81. *NKGB* 19 (Jan. 1, 1930): 9–10; 21 (Mar. 1, 1930): 28–29.

82. L. M. Li 1981: 188–96; Eng 1986: 130–36.

CHAPTER 8

1. Chandler 1977 is the classic statement on how new forms of management practice in nineteenth-century America resulted in the "vertical integration" of business, and an improved competitive potential for the most successful capitalist enterprises of the era. I say more on Chandler's arguments below.

2. The emphasis on business mergers rather than on "vertical integration" is suggested by the work of Naomi Lamoreaux (1985). I have more to say on this issue as part of my discussion of Wuxi silk-industry reorganization during the Great Depression.

3. Zhao and Yi 1982, 2: 52.

4. Wuxishi zhengxie wenshi ziliao yanjiu weiyuanhui 1981: 50; Gao and Yan 1987: 45.

5. Lü Huantai interview, May 24, 1980; Qian 1961: 126–27; Wuxi difangzhi bianji weiyuanhui 1959: 41.

6. Qian 1961: 127.

7. Lü Huantai interview, May 24, 1980; Qian 1961: 127; Wuxi difangzhi bianji weiyuanhui 1959: 42.

8. Lü Huantai interview, May 24, 1980; SB (May 6, 1934).

9. Qian 1961: 127.

10. Okumura 1978: 274.

11. Qian 1961: 127.

12. Wuxi difangzhi bianji weiyuanhui 1959: 43; Shen 1934: 34.

13. Lü Huantai interview, May 24, 1980; Wu Yaming interview, Nov. 7, 1980.

14. Wuxi difangzhi bianji weiyuanhui 1959: 43.

15. Hua 1931: 17; Wu Yaming interview, Nov. 7, 1980.

16. Lü Huantai interview, May 24, 1980. Lü Huantai was head of this New York office.

17. Coble 1980: 85.

18. Kong 1935: 72–73.

19. GSBYK 2, no. 3 (Feb. 1, 1930), commercial news section: 16.

20. GSBYK 4, no. 19 (Oct. 1, 1932), national economy section: 1–2; He 1933: 18.

21. Chūshi kensetsu shiryō seibi jimusho 1941: 40.

22. GSBYK 3, no. 2 (Jan. 15, 1931), commercial and industrial news section: 7–9.

23. Ibid.

24. This rate was raised in 1932 to 140 yuan per dan. See He 1933: 20; and Kong 1935: 72–73.

25. All export taxes on silk were suspended one year later, in May 1932. See He 1933: 20.

26. GSBYK 3, no. 10 (May 15, 1931), legislation section: 8–9.

27. Okumura 1978: 246.

28. DELSDAG file no. 1328, leaf 10.

29. Ibid., leaf 78.

30. Ibid., leaf 32; as discussed in Chapter 7, cocoons resulting from the use of improved silkworm eggs produced more silk per unit of their weight than did those which came from unimproved varieties.

31. One source reported that twenty-six filatures were operating full- or part-time in 1932, and that twenty-three filatures were completely closed. This estimate was based on a Ministry of Industry survey of industry in Wuxi conducted in 1932. Of the twenty-six open filatures, only seven or eight were operating full-time. See Chūshi kensetsu shiryō seibi jimusho 1941: 41–42. Another source stated that twenty-one filatures were operating in Wuxi in the fall of 1932, with 50 percent of these open only part-time. The method of part-time operation was to hire women to reel silk from cocoon stocks immediately on hand and then close the filature when the stocks were used up. See GSBYK 4, no. 19 (Oct. 1, 1932), national economy section: 1–2.

32. DELSDAG file no. 1328, leaf 13.

33. Ibid., leaves 106–7.

34. On the formation of the Commission for the National Economy in 1931, see GSBYK 3, no. 12 (June 15, 1931), legislation section: 4–5.

35. For the commission's role in the creation of various speciality subcommissions devoted to silk-industry development, see Zhang 1957, 3: 163–64.

36. Guan 1935: 1.

37. JSJSYK 2, no. 3 (Mar. 1935), report section: 57.

38. SB (May 17, 1934).

39. Shanghai shehui kexueyuan jingji yanjiusuo 1962, 1: 8; Qian 1961: 127.

40. Okumura 1978: 247.

41. SB (May 4, 1934); Okumura 1978: 250.

42. SB (June 2, 1934), sec. 4: 13.

43. SB (May 4, 1934); SB (May 17, 1934).

44. SB (May 4, 1934); SB (May 17, 1934).

45. SB (May 17, 1934).

46. Under new Guomindang organizational policy from 1930 onward, the name of all industry organizations changed to the form of tongye gonghui, literally, "association of those in the industry." Thus the cocoon-merchant organization in Wuxi was no longer known as a gongsuo, but rather as the Cocoon-Industry Association (jianye gonghui). This policy was reported upon widely in GSBYK throughout 1930. See, for example, GSBYK 2, no. 3 (Feb. 3, 1930), legislation section: 12–13; and 2, no. 7 (Apr. 1, 1930), industrial and commercial news section: 2–3.

47. SB (June 2, 1934), sec. 4: 13.   48. SB (May 26, 1934).

49. SB (May 27, 1934).   50. SB (June 2, 1934).

51. SB (June 3, 1934), sec. 3: 11.

52. Ibid.; SB (June 4, 1934), sec. 2: 8.

53. SB (June 3, 1934), sec. 3: 11.   54. SB (Jan. 20, 1935), sec. 3: 10.

55. Ibid.   56. SB (Feb. 10, 1935), sec. 3: 11.

57. *SB* (May 4, 1934).

58. *SB* (June 2, 1934), sec. 4: 13.

59. DELSDAG file no. 3242, cocoon firm tables: 42.

60. Guan 1935: 1.

61. Lü Huantai interviews, May 24, 1980 and May 28, 1981; Ku 1937b: 67–70.

62. DELSDAG file no. 3242, cocoon firm tables: 42; Lü Huantai interview, May 28, 1981.

63. Lü Huantai interviews, May 24, 1980, and May 28, 1981.

64. *SB* (May 17, 1934).

65. *SB* (Aug. 6, 1934), sec. 3: 10.

66. Ibid.

67. *SB* (Jan. 29, 1935), sec. 2: 8.

68. *SB* (Feb. 18, 1936), sec. 3: 9; (Mar. 12, 1936), sec. 3: 9.

69. Shen 1934: 34.

70. Ibid.

71. Ku 1937a: 104.

72. Ibid.: 106; also translated in Institute of Pacific Relations 1939: 187.

73. Chandler 1977.   74. Lamoreaux 1985.

75. Okumura 1978: 252.   76. *SB* (May 19, 1934).

77. "January Review," *Cansi tongji yuebao* (Jan. 1936); *SB* (Feb. 11, 1936), sec. 3: 9.

78. *SB* (Feb. 11, 1936), sec. 3: 9; Okumura 1978: 253.

79. *SB* (Feb. 2, 1936), sec. 3: 12.

80. As Naomi Lamoreaux (1985) points out, the American industries that experienced the most drastic mergers in the 1890's were precisely those that had just gone through rapid expansion in the immediate pre-depression years. Her argument is that in the absence of such rapid expansion, the conditions that might lead to price-cutting to gain market shares were not as likely to materialize. This seems to have held true in the case of the central China silk industry as well.

81. *SB* (May 18, 1934); *SB* (Jan. 28, 1935), sec. 3: 9.

82. *SB* (Feb. 5, 1936), sec. 3: 10.   83. Mantetsu 1940: 86.

84. Zhu 1936: 520.   85. Okumura 1978: 253.

86. Wuxi difangzhi bianji weiyuanhui 1959: 43–44; Qian 1961: 127.

87. Okumura 1978: 253–54; Zhu 1936: 520; Wuxi difangzhi bianji wei-yuanhui 1959: 43–44. This last source states that Xue was even beginning to establish cocoon firms as far away as the cocoon-producing areas of Anhui, Shandong, and Hubei.

88. Gao Jingyue interview, (May 28, 1981).

89. *SB* (Apr. 12, 1936), sec. 3: 10; *YHZB* 20, no. 18 (May 12, 1936), national news section: 8–9.

90. *SB* (June 2, 1936), sec. 3: 11.

91. Raw-silk prices are calculated from tables in L. M. Li 1981: 74–77. Cocoon prices had risen to highs of seventy yuan per dan in the late 1920's. See table on sericulture and cocoon production in the SSRI survey.

92. *SB* (June 1, 1936), sec. 4: 14.

93. *SB* (June 4, 1936), sec. 3: 10.

94. *SB* (June 7, 1936), sec. 3: 9.

95. For the critical writings of one such individual, see Ku Nong (a pseudonym meaning "the suffering peasant") 1937a and 1937b, and an abridged translation of the first of these articles in Institute of Pacific Relations 1939: 184–88.

96. This point of view came through strongly in a joint conversation-interview with several such men held in Wuxi on May 28, 1981. Participants in that discussion were Gao Jingyue, Lü Huantai, Gu Suruo, Zhang Enshen, and Xu Ruliang. For more on their backgrounds, see Chapter 9 and Appendix A.

97. Qian 1988: 80.

98. Relevant studies include Eastman 1974; T'ien 1972; and Bergère 1983 and 1989.

99. See, for example, Xu 1949.

100. Coble 1980; Kirby 1984.

101. Kirby 1984.

CHAPTER 9

1. Skinner's arguments about China's macroregions and urban development are laid out in two seminal articles, Skinner 1977b and 1977c.

2. See, for example, Schoppa 1982; Rankin 1986; and Esherick and Rankin 1990.

3. Pomeranz 1993.

4. Walker 1999. For the Rong brothers' political roles, see Shanghai shehui kexueyuan jingji yanjiusuo 1962: 204.

5. Gao Jingyue interview, Oct. 20, 1980.

6. Ibid.

7. Ibid.

8. Gu 1986: 67–72.

9. Lü Huantai interview, May 24, 1980.

10. Gu 1986: 71.   11. Zhang 1984.

12. Gu 1986: 71.   13. Gu 1986.

14. A dissertation by Kathrin Sears (1985) on Shanghai's cotton-textile capitalists and the nationalization of industry in the 1950's chronicles concerns with raw-material supply and pricing similar to those we have observed for Wuxi in the pre-1937 period. Sears describes a process of moving from "indirect controls," in which the state acted as regulator of cotton supply and prices, to "direct controls," in which the state assigned its own personnel to manage industry. Sears has a background chapter on Guomindang policy from 1945 to 1949 in which she demonstrates how "indirect controls" were already in operation before the Chinese Communist Party came to power. It is clear from Sears's work, in tandem with arguments I have made about Guomindang industrial policy during the early 1930's, that rich potential exists for research on economic policy during the 1940's,

a critical period in which further groundwork was laid in various ways by both Nationalists and Communists for the later contours of state-directed development. Although more difficult, another rich topic would be industrial development under Japanese occupation, since a wealth of material was collected and collated by Japanese researchers on industries in the Yangzi delta during the late 1930's and early 1940's. There is much material of this type on silk production in Wuxi under the Japanese.

15. For Mao's utopian vision and its influence on development policy, see Meisner 1986.

Bibliography

Titles of extensively cited Republican-period journals and newspapers appear in the Abbreviations, p. 223.

ARCHIVAL MATERIALS

Dierlishi dang'anguan (Number Two National History Archive, Nanjing). [Abbreviated DELSDAG.]

File no. 1328. Materials from the Ministry of Industry dated 1932.9.24. "Zhengli Jiang-Zhe chenchangsi chenjian weiyuanhui zhuyue huiyi an" (Monthly meeting reports of the committee to arrange for dealing with old stocks of filature silk and cocoons).

File no. 3234. Materials from the Executive Yuan. "Fuzhu sijianye yu gailiang cansi canzhong shixiang, 1927–1934" (Items related to assistance to the silk industry and sericulture and silkworm-egg improvement, 1927–34).

File no. 3242. Materials from the Ministry of Industry. Subfile no. 22741: "Ershier nianfen jiansi diaochabiao yi baodao gexian yilanbiao" (Tables by county for those already reporting on the investigation of cocoons and silk production in 1933); no. 32472: "Ershier nianfen jiansi chanliang deng diaocha biao xudao gexian yilanbiao" (Supplementary tables by county on the investigation of cocoon and silk production in 1933).

File No. 3243. Archival materials from the Ministry of Industry. Subfile no. 3, agriculture 3194: "Ershiernian chunqiu canye zhidao shishi gaikuang biao" (Tables on the implementation of spring and fall sericulture extension work in 1933).

File No. 3504. "Jiang-Zhe-Wan-Ni qudi canzhong qingxing" (The regulation of silkworm eggs in Jiangsu, Zhejiang, Anhui, and Shanghai). Subfiles: "Liangnianlai bensheng [Zhejiang] canzhong zhizao ji qudi jingguo gaikuang, Minguo ershinian-Minguo ershiernian" (The manufacture and regulation of silkworm eggs in Zhejiang for the past two years, 1931–33); "Ershinian zhounian gongzuo baogao" (Yearly work report for 1931); "Ershiyinian zhounian gongzuo baogao" (Yearly work report for 1932).

OTHER SOURCES

Balazs, Etienne. 1964. *Chinese Civilization and Bureaucracy: Variations on a Theme*. New Haven and London: Yale University Press.

Barclay, George W. 1958. *Techniques of Population Analysis*. New York: Wiley.

Barlow, Alfred. 1884. *The History and Principles of Weaving by Hand and Power*. London: Sampson Low, Marston, Searle, & Rivington.

Bell, Lynda S. 1985. "Explaining China's Rural Crisis: Observations from Wuxi County in the Early Twentieth Century." *Republican China* 11, no. 1 (Nov.): 15–31.

———. 1990. "From Comprador to County Magnate: Bourgeois Practice in the Wuxi County Silk Industry." In Esherick and Rankin 1990: 113–39.

———. 1992. "Farming, Sericulture, and Peasant Rationality in Wuxi County in the Early Twentieth Century." In Rawski and Li 1992: 207–42.

———. 1994. "For Better, For Worse: Women and the World Market in Rural China." *Modern China* 20, no. 2 (Apr.): 180–210.

Bergère, Marie-Claire. 1983. "The Chinese Bourgeoisie, 1911–1937." In John K. Fairbank, ed., *The Cambridge History of China*, vol. 12, pt. 1, *Republican China, 1912–1949*, pp. 722–827. Cambridge: Cambridge University Press.

———. 1989. *The Golden Age of the Chinese Bourgeoisie, 1911–1937*. Trans. Janet Lloyd. Cambridge: Cambridge University Press. Originally published as *L'Age d'Or de la Bourgeoisie Chinoise* (Paris: Editions Flammarion, 1986).

Bernhardt, Kathryn. 1992. *Rent, Taxes, and Peasant Resistance: The Lower Yangzi Region, 1840–1950*. Stanford, Calif.: Stanford University Press.

Boggs, Carl. 1976. *Gramsci's Marxism*. London: Pluto Press.

Boserup, Ester. 1965. *The Conditions of Agricultural Growth: The Economics of Agrarian Change Under Population Pressure*. Chicago: Aldine.

Bourdieu, Pierre. 1977. *An Outline of a Theory of Practice*. Trans. Richard Nice. Cambridge: Cambridge University Press.

Brandt, Loren. 1989. *Commercialization and Agricultural Development: Central and Eastern China, 1870–1937*. Cambridge: Cambridge University Press.

Brenner, Robert. 1976. "Agrarian Class Structure and Economic Development in Pre-Industrial Europe." *Past and Present* 70 (Feb.): 30–75.

———. 1977. "The Origins of Capitalist Development: A Critique of Neo-Smithian Marxism," *New Left Review* 104 (July/Aug.): 25–92.

Buck, John Lossing. 1937. *Land Utilization in China*. 2 vols. Shanghai: Commercial Press.

Chan, Wellington K. K. 1977. *Merchants, Mandarins, and Modern Enterprise in Late Ch'ing China*. Cambridge, Mass.: East Asian Research Center, Harvard University.

Chandler, Alfred D., Jr. 1977. *The Visible Hand: The Managerial Revolution in American Business*. Cambridge, Mass.: Belknap Press.

Chen Hansheng. 1988. *Sige shidai de wo* (My life through four eras). Beijing: Zhongguo wenshi chubanshe.

Chen Huayin. 1929. "Jiangsusheng renkou yu yiken tianmu zhi xilian" (Correlation between population and cultivated land in Jiangsu). *Tongji yuebao* 1, no. 3 (May): 44–48.

Ch'en Lu [Chen Lu], Yang Wan-chung [Yang Wanzhong], Chin Chia-hsiang [Jin Jiaxiang], and Wu Chien-fan [Wu Jianfan]. 1961. "Agricultural Regions of Su-chou [Suzhou] and Wu-hsi [Wuxi] in Kiangsu [Jiangsu] Province." Translated from the Chinese and published in English in JPRS (Joint Publications Research Service) publication no. 6990 (March 27, 1961), *Natural Regions of Communist China and Agricultural Regions in Kiangsu* [Jiangsu], pp. 1–37. Washington, D.C.: U.S. Government Printing Office. Originally published in *Dili xuebao* 25, no. 3 (June 1959): 180–200.

Chen Tingfang, trans. 1957–61. "Juyou fengjian de maiban xingzhide Zhongguo saosiye" (China's feudalistic, comprador-nature silk reeling industry). In Chen et al. 1957–61, 4: 111–13. Originally published as "Jindai Zhongguo zhi saosiye" (Modern China's silk reeling industry), translated from the Japanese, in *Chiye zhoukan* 1, nos. 46–47 (Nov.–Dec. 1943).

Chen Zhen, Yao Luohe, and Pang Xianzhi, eds. 1957–61. *Zhongguo jindai gongyeshi ziliao* (Materials on the history of China's modern industry). 4 vols. Beijing: Sanlian shudian.

Ch'eng, I-fan. 1988. "Development and Frustrations of Statecraft in Mid-Ming China: As Reflected in the Experiences of the Gu Family of Jiangnan During the Sixteenth Century." Ph.D. diss., University of California, Berkeley.

Chien, Helen Hsieh, trans. 1993. *The European Diary of Hsieh [sic] Fucheng: Envoy Extraordinary of Imperial China.* New York: St. Martin's.

Chūshi kensetsu shiryō seibi jimusho, ed. 1941. *Mushaku kōgyō jijō* (Wuxi industry). Shanghai: Chūshi kensetsu shiryō seibi jimusho.

Coble, Jr., Parks M. 1980. *The Shanghai Capitalists and the Nationalist Government, 1927–1937.* Cambridge, Mass.: Harvard University Press.

Cochran, Sherman. 1980. *Big Business in China: Sino-Foreign Rivalry in the Cigarette Industry, 1890–1930.* Cambridge, Mass.: Harvard University Press.

Dennerline, Jerry. 1981a. *The Chia-ting Loyalists: Confucian Leadership and Social Change in Seventeenth-Century China.* New Haven, Conn.: Yale University Press.

———. 1981b. "The New Hua Charitable Estate and Local-Level Leadership in Wuxi County at the End of the Qing." In Tang Tsou, ed., *Proceedings of the NEH Modern China Project, 1978–1980: Political Leadership and Social Change at the Local Level in China, from 1850 to the Present,* Select Papers from the Center for Far Eastern Studies, no. 4, pp. 19–70. Chicago: Center for Far Eastern Studies, University of Chicago.

———. 1988. *Qian Mu and the World of Seven Mansions.* New Haven, Conn.: Yale University Press.

Dongnan daxue nongke, ed. 1923–24. *Jiangsusheng nongye diaochalu* (Records of an investigation into agriculture in Jiangsu province). 3 vols. Changzhou (?): Jiangsusheng jiaoyu/shiye/xingzheng lianhehui.

Duara, Prasenjit. 1988. *Culture, Power and the State: Rural North China, 1900–1942.* Stanford, Calif.: Stanford University Press.

Eastman, Lloyd E. 1974. *The Abortive Revolution: China Under National-ist Rule, 1927–1937*. Cambridge, Mass.: Harvard University Press.

—. 1984. *Seeds of Destruction: Nationalist China in War and Revolu-tion, 1937–1949*. Stanford, Calif.: Stanford University Press.

Elman, Benjamin. 1984. *From Philosophy to Philology: Intellectual and So-cial Aspects of Change in Late Imperial China*. Cambridge, Mass.: Coun-cil on East Asian Studies, Harvard University

—. 1990. *Classicism, Politics, and Kinship: The Ch'ang-chou School of New Text Confucianism in Late Imperial China*. Berkeley: University of California Press.

Elvin, Mark. 1973. *The Pattern of the Chinese Past: A Social and Economic Interpretation*. Stanford, Calif.: Stanford University Press.

Eng, Robert Y. 1986. *Economic Imperialism in China: Silk Production and Exports, 1861–1932*. Berkeley: Institute of East Asian Studies, University of California.

Esherick, Joseph W. 1972. "Harvard on China: The Apologetics of Imperial-ism." *Bulletin of Concerned Asian Scholars* 4, no. 4 (Dec.): 9–16.

—. 1976. *Reform and Revolution in China: The 1911 Revolution in Hunan and Hubei*. Berkeley: University of California Press.

—. 1991. "Review of Loren Brandt's *Commercialization and Agricul-tural Development: Central and Eastern China, 1870–1937*." *Journal of Economic History* 51, no. 2 (June): 501–3.

Esherick, Joseph W., and Mary Backus Rankin, eds. 1990. *Chinese Local Elites and Patterns of Dominance*. Berkeley: University of California Press.

Faure, David. 1989. *The Rural Economy of Pre-Liberation China: Trade Ex-pansion and Peasant Livelihood in Jiangsu and Guangdong, 1870–1937*. Hong Kong: Oxford University Press.

Feng Hefa. 1935a. *Zhongguo nongcun jingji ziliao* (Materials on China's ru-ral economy). Shanghai: Liming shuju.

—. 1935b. *Zhongguo nongcun jingji ziliao xubian* (More materials on China's rural economy). Shanghai: Liming shuju.

Feuerwerker, Albert. 1992. "Presidential Address: Questions about China's Early Modern Economic History That I Wish I Could Answer." *Journal of Asian Studies* 51, no. 4 (Nov.): 757–69.

Fewsmith, Joseph. 1985. *Party, State, and Local Elites in Republican China: Merchant Organizations and Politics in Shanghai, 1890–1930*. Hono-lulu: University of Hawaii Press.

Fogel, Joshua. 1988. *Life Along the South Manchurian Railway: The Mem-oirs of Itō Takeo*. Armonk, N.Y.: M. E. Sharpe.

Food and Agriculture Organization of the United Nations. 1980. *China: Sericulture. Report on a FAO/UNDP Study Tour to the People's Repub-lic of China, 6 May to 4 June 1979*. Rome: Food and Agriculture Organi-zation of the United Nations.

Fox-Genovese, Elizabeth, and Eugene D. Genovese. 1983. *Fruits of Mer-*

chant Capital: Slavery and Bourgeois Property in the Rise and Expansion of Capitalism. New York: Oxford University Press.

Gao Jingyue. 1983. "Wuxi saosi gongye de fazhan he chiye guanli de yanbian, 1904–1956" (Development and evolution of industrial management in the Wuxi filature industry, 1904–1956). *Zhongguo shehui jingjishi yanjiu* 1: 102–10.

Gao Jingyue and Yan Xuexi. 1980. "Wuxi zuizao de sangyuan" (Wuxi's first mulberry tract). *Wuxi xianbao* (Aug. 20): 4.

———, eds. 1987. *Jindai Wuxi cansiye ziliao xuanji* (Collected materials on Wuxi's silk industry in the modern period). Huaiyin, Jiangsu: Jiangsu renmin chubanshe, Jiangsu guji chubanshe.

Goldstone, Jack A. 1991. *Revolution and Rebellion in the Early Modern World.* Berkeley: University of California Press.

Gong Zaiqing, ed. 1921. *Wuxi riyong youlan zhinan* (Wuxi daily travel guide). Wuxi: Su-Xi zhinan she.

Goodman, Bryna. 1995. *Native Place, City, and Nation: Regional Networks and Identities in Shanghai, 1853–1937.* Berkeley: University of California Press.

Gramsci, Antonio. [1929–35] 1971. *Selections from the Prison Notebooks of Antonio Gramsci.* Ed. and trans. Quintin Hoare and Geoffrey Nowell Smith. New York: International Publishers.

Gu Suruo. 1986. "Huiyi Wuxi saosi gongye de quanhangye gongsi heying" (Remembering consolidation of joint public-private management in the Wuxi silk-filature industry). *Wuxi wenshi ziliao,* no. 15 (Nov.): 59–72.

Guan Yida. 1935. "Jiangsusheng ershisannian canye tongzhi baogao" (Report on Jiangsu's sericulture control for 1934). *JSJSYK* 2, no. 3 (Mar.), report section: 1–6.

Guoli zhongyang yanjiuyuan shehui kexue yanjiusuo (Social Science Research Institute of the Academia Sinica). 1929. *Jiangsu Wuxi nongmindizhu jingji diaocha* (A survey of the peasant-landlord economy in Wuxi county, Jiangsu province). Wuxi.

Gutmann, Myron P. 1988. *Toward the Modern Economy: Early Industry in Europe, 1500–1800.* Philadelphia: Temple University Press.

Hauser, Ernest O. 1962. *Chumai de Shanghai tan.* Trans. Ji Ming. Beijing: Shangwu yin shudian. Originally published as *Shanghai: City for Sale* (New York: Harcourt, Brace, 1940).

He Bingxian. 1933. "Minguo ershiyinian Zhongguo gongshangye de huigu" (A review of Chinese commerce and industry in 1932). *GSBYK* 5, no. 1 (Jan. 1), articles section: 1–39.

Hinton, Harold C. 1956. *The Grain Tribute System of China, 1845–1911.* Chinese Economic and Political Studies. Cambridge, Mass.: Harvard University.

Ho, Ping-ti. 1959. *Studies on the Population of China, 1368–1953.* Cambridge, Mass.: Harvard University Press.

Honig, Emily. 1986. *Sisters and Strangers: Women in the Shanghai Cotton Mills, 1919–1949.* Stanford, Calif.: Stanford University Press.

Hua Yinchun. 1931(?). *Wuxi nongcun pinkun zhi yuanyin ji jiuzhi zhi fang-fa* (The reasons for rural impoverishment in Wuxi and methods for recovery). Wuxi: no publisher.

Huadong junzheng weiyuanhui tudi gaige weiyuanhui, ed. 1952. *Jiang-susheng nongcun diaocha* (Investigations in the Jiangsu countryside). Shanghai: Difang guoying Shanghaishi sanchang.

Huang, Philip C. C. 1985. *The Peasant Economy and Social Change in North China*. Stanford, Calif.: Stanford University Press.

———. 1990. *The Peasant Family and Rural Development in the Yangzi Delta, 1350–1988*. Stanford, Calif.: Stanford University Press.

Huang Yiping, ed. 1979. *Zhongguo jindai jingjishi lunwen xuanji* (Selected articles on China's modern economic history). 5 vols. Shanghai: Shanghai shifan daxue lishixi.

Hui Lin. 1951. "Wuxi Meicunqu sige xiang zutian zhaiwu jiben qingkuang diaocha" (An investigation of the basic circumstances relating to debt on rented land in four townships in Wuxi's Meicun ward). In Sunan renmin xingzheng gongzhu tudi gaige weiyuanhui 1951: 43–50.

Institute of Pacific Relations, ed. 1939. *Agrarian China. Selected Source Materials from Chinese Authors*. London: George Allen Unwin.

"January Review." 1936. *Cansi tongji yuebao* (Silk statistics monthly) (Jan.): English language summary at front.

Jiang Xingru. 1951. "Tan Wuxi nongcun qingkuang" (Discussing Wuxi's rural conditions). In Sunan renmin xingzheng gongzhu tudi gaige weiyuanhui 1951: 37–42.

Jiangsu shengli disan shifan fushu xiaoxue diwuceng shangyeke, ed. 1923. *Wuxi shiye xiankuang diaocha* (An investigation of current conditions of Wuxi industry). Wuxi: mimeo by the same agency.

Kaihua xiangzhi (A gazetteer of Kaihua township [Wuxi]). 3 vols. 1916.

Kirby, William C. 1984. *Germany and Republican China*. Stanford, Calif.: Stanford University Press.

Kōain kachū renrakubu, ed. 1941. *Chū-Shina jūyō kokubō shigen kiito chōsa hōkoku* (A report on an investigation of raw silk in central China, a raw material for national defense). Shanghai: Kōain kachū renrakubu.

Kong Fanlin. 1935. "Zhongguo nongcun wenti zhi jiantao" (A self-criticism of China's rural problems). *Nongcun jingji* 2, no. 12 (Oct. 1): 63–82.

Ku Nong (pseudonym). 1937a. "Yangcan hezuo yundong zai Wuxi" (The sericulture cooperative movement in Wuxi). *Zhongguo nongcun* 3, no. 6 (June 1): 103–6. Translated and abridged in Institute of Pacific Relations 1939: 184–88.

———. 1937b. "Sijian tongzhixia de Wuxi cansang" (Wuxi sericulture under [government policies of] cocoon control). In Zhongguo nongcun jingji yanjiuhui, ed., *Zhongguo nongcun dongtai* (Trends in rural China), pp. 62–70. Shanghai: Zhongguo nongcun jingji yanjiuhui.

Kuhn, Philip A. 1970. *Rebellion and Its Enemies in Late Imperial China:*

Militarization and Social Structure, 1796–1864. Cambridge, Mass.: Harvard University Press.

———. 1975. "Local Self-Government Under the Republic: Problems of Control, Autonomy, and Mobilization." In Wakeman and Grant 1975: 257–98.

———. 1979. "Local Taxation and Finance in Republican China." In [Mann] Jones 1979a: 100–136.

Lamoreaux, Naomi R. 1985. *The Great Merger Movement in American Business, 1895–1904.* Cambridge and New York: Cambridge University Press.

Lasek, Elizabeth. 1983. "Imperialism in China: A Methodological Critique." *Bulletin of Concerned Asian Scholars* 15, no. 1 (Jan.–Feb.): 50–64.

Li, Lillian M. 1981. *China's Silk Trade: Traditional Industry in the Modern World.* Cambridge, Mass.: Harvard University Press.

Li Wenzhi, ed. 1957. *Zhongguo jindai nongyeshi ziliao* (Materials concerning the agricultural history of modern China). Vol. 1, *1840–1911.* Beijing: Sanlian shudian.

———. 1981. "Lun Qingdai houqi Jiang-Zhe-Wan sansheng yuan Taiping Tianguo zhanlingqu tudi guanxi de bianhua" (On changes in land tenure in late Qing in areas of Jiangsu, Zhejiang, and Anhui formerly occupied by the Taipings). *Lishi yanjiu* 6 (Dec. 15): 81–96.

Li Wenzhi, Wei Jingyu, and Jing Junjian. 1983. *Ming/Qing shidai de nongye ziben zhuyi mengya wenti* (The agrarian sprouts of capitalism question during the Ming/Qing period). Vol. 1. Beijing: Zhongguo shehui kexue chubanshe.

Liang Fangzhong. 1980. *Zhongguo lidai hukou, tiandi, tianfu tongji* (China's dynastic statistics on household population, land, and land taxes). Shanghai: Shanghai renmin chubanshe.

Liao Kaisheng. 1930. "Shehui kexue yanjiusuo Wuxi nongcun diaocha jilüe" (A brief account of the Social Science Research Institute's rural survey in Wuxi). *Guoli zhongyang yanjiuyuan yuanwu yuebao* 1, no. 8 (Feb.): 9–15.

Lieu, D. K. 1933. *The Silk Reeling Industry in Shanghai.* Shanghai: Chinese Institute of Economic and Statistical Research.

———. 1936. *The Growth and Industrialization of Shanghai.* Shanghai: Chinese Institute of Pacific Relations.

———. 1940. *The Silk Industry of China.* Shanghai: Kelly and Walsh.

Lippit, Victor. 1974. *Land Reform and Economic Development in China.* White Plains, N.Y.: International Arts and Sciences Press.

———. 1978. "The Development of Underdevelopment in China." *Modern China* 4, no. 3 (July): 251–328.

Liu Shudong, chief ed. 1919. *Wuxi zhinan* (Guide to Wuxi). Wuxi: Xicheng yinshua gongsi.

Liu, Tessie P. 1994. *The Weaver's Knot: The Contradictions of Class Struggle and Family Solidarity in Western France, 1750–1914.* Ithaca, N.Y.: Cornell University Press.

Liu Yuzhen. 1919. "Canguan canye yanjiusuo cansang gailianghui ji" (Reports on visits to the Sericulture Experiment Bureau and the United Association for Sericulture Reform). In Wuxi Ximenwai Jiangsu shengli yucan shiyansuo 1919–21 (Jan. 1919, vol. 1), investigation section: 9–12.

Lu Guanying. 1921. "Jiangsu Wuxixian ershinianlai zhi siye guan" (An overview of the Wuxi silk industry during the last twenty years). NSGB 8, no. 1 (Aug. 15), articles and translations section: 45–47.

McElderry, Andrea Lee. 1976. Shanghai Old-Style Banks (Ch'ien-chuang), 1800–1935. Ann Arbor: University of Michigan Center for Chinese Studies.

MacKinnon, Stephen R. 1980. Power and Politics in Late Imperial China: Yuan Shi-kai in Beijing and Tianjin, 1901–1908. Berkeley: University of California Press.

———. 1990. "The Life and Times of Chen Han-sheng (1897–)." In Selected Papers in Asian Studies, Paper no. 35. [Tempe, Ariz.?]: Western Conference of the Association for Asian Studies.

[Mann] Jones, Susan, ed. 1979a. Select Papers from the Center for Far Eastern Studies. No. 3, 1978–79. Chicago: University of Chicago Press.

———. 1979b. "The Organization of Trade at the County Level: Brokerage and Tax Farming in the Republican Period." In [Mann] Jones, ed. 1979a: 70–99.

Mann, Susan. 1987. Local Merchants and the Chinese Bureaucracy, 1750–1950. Stanford, Calif.: Stanford University Press.

Mantetsu. 1940, 1941, 1942. See Minami Manshū tetsudō kabushiki kaisha, Shanhai jimusho chōsashitsu 1940, 1941, 1942.

Mao Jiaqi and Li Zufa, eds. 1988. Wuxi jindai jingji fazhan shilun (On the history of Wuxi's economic development in the modern period). Wuxi: Qiye guanli chubanshe.

Mao Tun [Mao Dun]. [1932] 1979. "Spring Silkworms." Translated and reprinted in Mao Tun, Spring Silkworms and Other Stories, pp. 1–26. Beijing: Foreign Languages Press.

Martin, Michael F. 1991. "Rural Living Conditions in Pre-Liberation China: A Survey of Three Recent Studies." Journal of Peasant Studies 19, no. 1 (Oct.): 122–37.

Medick, Hans. 1976. "The Proto-Industrial Family Economy: The Structural Function of Household and Family During the Transition from Peasant Society to Industrial Capitalism." Social History 1, no. 3 (Oct.): 291–315.

Meisner, Maurice. 1986. Mao's China and After: A History of the People's Republic. New York: Free Press.

Mendels, Franklin. 1972. "Proto-Industrialization: The First Phase of the Industrialization Process." Journal of Economic History 32, no. 1: 241–61.

Minami Manshū tetsudō kabushiki kaisha, Shanhai jimusho chōsashitsu (Shanghai Research Office of the South Manchurian Railway Company). 1940. Mushaku kōgyō jittai chōsa hōkokusho (A report of an investigation of industry in Wuxi). Shanghai: Minami Manshū tetsudō kabushiki kaisha, Shanhai jimusho chōsashitsu.

———. 1941. *Kōsoshō Mushakuken nōson jittai chōsa hōkokusho* (A report on an investigation of rural conditions in Wuxi County, Jiangsu Province). Shanghai: Minami Manshū tetsudō kabushiki kaisha, Shanhai jimusho chōsashitsu.

———. 1942. *Mushaku sōgō jittai chōsa hōkoku—kinyū no bu* (A comprehensive report on conditions in Wuxi—section on finance). Shanghai: Minami Manshū tetsudō kabushiki kaisha, Shanhai jimusho chōsashitsu.

Moulder, Frances V. 1977. *Japan, China and the Modern World Economy: Toward a Reinterpretation of East Asian Development ca. 1600 to ca. 1918.* Cambridge: Cambridge University Press.

Myers, Ramon H. 1970. *The Chinese Peasant Economy: Agricultural Development in Hopei and Shantung, 1890–1949.* Cambridge, Mass.: Harvard University Press.

———. 1991. "How Did the Modern Chinese Economy Develop?—A Review Article." *Journal of Asian Studies* 50, no. 3 (Aug.): 604–28.

Nathan, Andrew J. 1972. "Imperialism's Effects on China." *Bulletin of Concerned Asian Scholars* 4, no. 4 (Dec.): 3–8.

Nie Baozhang. 1979. *Zhongguo maiban zichanjieji de fasheng* (The rise of China's comprador bourgeoisie). Chongqing: Zhongguo shehuikexue chubanshe.

North, Douglass C. 1981. *Structure and Change in Economic History.* New York: Norton.

Nücan (Women's Sericulture). 1924. Hushuguan (Suzhou).

Okumura Satoshi. 1978. "Kyōkōka Kō-Setsu sanshigyō no saihen" (The reorganization of sericulture in Jiangsu and Zhejiang due to the depression). *Tōyōshi kenkyū* 37, no. 2 (Sept.): 242–78.

Peng Zeyi. 1963a. "Cong Mingdai guanying zhizao de jingying fanshi kan Jiangnan sizhiye shengchan de xingzhi" (A look at the nature of production in the Jiangnan silk-weaving industry from the management practices of the Imperial Silkworks in Ming times). *Lishi yanjiu* 2 (Feb.): 33–56.

———. 1963b. "Qingdai qianqi Jiangnan zhizao de yanjiu" (Research on the Jiangnan Imperial Silkworks in early Qing). *Lishi yanjiu* 4 (Apr.): 91–116.

———. 1963c. "Yapian zhanzheng qian Qingdai Suzhou sizhiye shengchan guanxi de xingshi yu xingzhi" (The structure and nature of the relations of production in the Suzhou silk-weaving industry in Qing times before the Opium War). *Jingji yanjiu* 10 (Oct.): 63–73.

———. 1965. "Shijiu shiji houqi Zhongguo chengshi shougongye shangye hanghui de chongjian he zuoyong" (The reestablishment and functions of Chinese urban handicraft and commercial guilds at the end of the nineteenth century). *Lishi yanjiu* 1 (Jan.): 71–102.

Perkins, Dwight H. 1969. *Agricultural Development in China, 1368–1968.* Chicago: Aldine.

Pomeranz, Kenneth. 1993. *The Making of a Hinterland: State, Society, and*

Economy in Inland North China, 1853–1937. Berkeley: University of California Press.

Priest, Quinton Gwynne. 1982. "Historiography and Statecraft in Eighteenth-Century China: The Life and Times of Chao I (1727–1814)." Ph.D. diss., University of California, Berkeley.

Qian Yaoxing. 1988. "Xueshi siye ziben jituan xingshuai" (The rise and fall of the Xue family silk-industry capital group). In Mao and Li 1988: 69–81.

Qian Zhaoxiong. 1935. "Shangye ziben caozongxia de Wuxi cansang" (Wuxi sericulture under the control of commercial capital). *Zhongguo nongcun* 1, no. 4 (Jan.): 71–74. Reprinted in Feng 1935b: 944–48; and in Institute of Pacific Relations 1939: 235–39 (an abridged English translation).

Qian Zhonghan. 1961. "Wuxi wuge zhuyao chanye ziben xitong de xingcheng yu fazhan" (The formation and development of five important industrial capital networks in Wuxi). In Zhongguo renmin zhengzhi xieshang huiyi quanguo weiyuanhui wenshi ziliao yanjiu weiyuanhui, ed., *Wenshi ziliao xuanji* 24, pp. 98–154. Beijing: Zhonghua shuju.

———. 1983. "Zhou Shunqing" (Zhou Shunqing). In Zhongguo renmin zhengzhi xieshang huiyi quanguo weiyuanhui wenshi ziliao yanjiu weiyuanhui, ed., *Gongshang jingji shiliao congkan* no. 4 [published in 1984], pp. 105–10. Beijing: Wenshi ziliao chubanshe.

Rankin, Mary Backus. 1986. *Elite Activism and Political Transformation in China: Zhejiang Province, 1865–1911*. Stanford, Calif.: Stanford University Press.

Rawski, Thomas G. 1989. *Economic Growth in Prewar China*. Berkeley: University of California Press.

Rawski, Thomas G., and Lillian M. Li, eds. 1992. *Chinese History in Economic Perspective*. Berkeley: University of California Press.

Rong An. 1927. "Gedi nongmin zhuangkuang diaocha: Wuxi" (Wide-ranging investigations of peasant conditions: Wuxi). *Dongfang zazhi* 24, no. 16 (Aug. 25): 109–13.

Rowe, William T. 1984. *Hankow: Commerce and Society in a Chinese City, 1796–1889*. Stanford, Calif.: Standford University Press.

———. 1989. *Hankow: Conflict and Community in a Chinese City, 1796–1895*. Stanford, Calif.: Stanford University Press.

———. 1990. "The Public Sphere in Modern China." *Modern China* 16, no. 3 (July): 309–29.

———. 1993. "The Problem of 'Civil Society' in Late Imperial China." *Modern China* 19, no. 2 (Apr.): 139–57.

Sable, Charles, and Jonathan Zeitlin. 1985. "Historical Alternatives to Mass Production: Politics, Markets and Technology in Nineteenth-Century Industrialization." *Past and Present* 108 (Aug.): 133–76.

Sahlins, Marshall. 1981. *Historical Metaphors and Mythical Realities: Structure in the Early History of the Sandwich Islands Kingdom*. Ann Arbor: University of Michigan Press.

———. 1985. *Islands of History*. Chicago: University of Chicago Press.

Salaff, Janet W. 1981. *Working Daughters of Hong Kong: Filial Piety or Power in the Family?* Cambridge: Cambridge University Press.

Schoppa, R. Keith. 1982. *Chinese Elites and Political Change: Zhejiang Province in the Early Twentieth Century.* Cambridge, Mass.: Harvard University Press.

Sears, Kathrin Elizabeth. 1985. "Shanghai's Textile Capitalists and the State: The Nationalization Process in China." Ph.D. diss., University of Michigan.

Shanghai shehui kexueyuan jingji yanjiusuo, ed. 1962. *Rongjia chiye shiliao* (Historical materials concerning the Rong family enterprises). Vol. 1, *1896–1937.* Shanghai: Renmin chubanshe.

Sheffield, Charles A. 1911. *Silk: Its Origin, Culture and Manufacture.* Florence, Mass.: The Corticelli Silk Mills.

Shehui jingji yanjiusuo. 1935. *Wuxi mishi diaocha* (An investigation of the Wuxi rice market). Shanghai: Shehui jingji yanjiusuo.

Shen Wenwei. 1934. "Fuxing Jiang-Zhe cansi shiye" (Revival of the silk industry in Jiangsu and Zhejiang). *Nongcun jingji* 1, no. 6 (Apr. 1): 32–35.

Shih Min-hsiung [Shi Minxiong]. 1976. *The Silk Industry in Ch'ing [Qing] China.* Ann Arbor: University of Michigan Center for Chinese Studies. English trans. by E-tu Zen Sun of *Qingdai sizhi gongye de fazhan* (Taibei: Zhongguo xueshu zhuzuo jiangzhu weiyuanhui, 1968).

Shu Xincheng et al., eds. 1974. *Cihai, hedingben* (Cihai dictionary, one-volume edition). Reprint of 1947 edition. Hong Kong: Zhonghua shuju, Xianggang fenju.

Skinner, G. William, ed. 1977a. *The City in Late Imperial China.* Stanford, Calif.: Stanford University Press.

———. 1977b. "Regional Urbanization in Nineteenth-Century China." In Skinner 1977a: 211–52.

———. 1977c. "Cities and the Hierarchy of Local Systems." In Skinner 1977a: 275–351.

So, Alvin Y. 1986. *The South China Silk District: Local Historical Transformation and World-System Theory.* Albany: State University of New York Press.

SSRI survey. 1929. See Guoli zhongyang yanjiuyuan shehui kexue yanjiusuo 1929.

Stockard, Janice E. 1989. *Daughters of the Canton Delta: Marriage Patterns and Economic Strategies in South China, 1860–1930.* Stanford, Calif.: Stanford University Press.

Stross, Randall E. 1986. *The Stubborn Earth: American Agriculturists on Chinese Soil, 1898–1937.* Berkeley: University of California Press.

Sun Bohe. 1948. "Minyuanlai woguo zhi cansiye" (The Chinese silk industry in the early years of the Republic). In Zhu 1948: 309–21.

Sun Ching-chih [Sun Jingzhi], chief ed. 1959. *Economic Geography of the East China Region (Shanghai, Kiangsu [Jiangsu], Anhwei [Anhui], Chejiang [Zhejiang]).* Translated from the Chinese and published with this title by JPRS (Joint Publications Research Service), pub. no. 11,438 (Dec. 7, 1961). Washington, D.C.: U.S. Government Printing Office. Translated from Sun Jingzhi, chief ed., *Huadong diqu jingji dili* (Beijing: Zhongguo kexueyuan dili yanjiusuo, Nov. 1959).

Sun, E-tu Zen. 1972. "Sericulture and Silk Textile Production in Ch'ing [Qing] China." In William Earl Willmott, ed., *Economic Organization in Chinese Society*, pp. 79–108. Stanford, Calif.: Stanford University Press.

Sun Guoqiao. 1931. "Wuxi zhidao yu yangcan shiye zhi yaodian" (The essentials of rice cultivation and sericulture in Wuxi). *Nongye zhoubao* 1, no. 25 (Oct. 16): 982–85.

Sunan renmin xingzheng gongzhu. 1950. "Sunan cansang qingkuang diaocha" (An investigation of conditions in sericulture in southern Jiangsu). In Huadong junzheng weiyuanhui tudi gaige weiyuanhui 1952: 375–79.

Sunan renmin xingzheng gongzhu tudi gaige weiyuanhui, ed. 1951. *Tudi gaige qian de Sunan nongcun* (The southern Jiangsu countryside before land reform). Shanghai: Shanghaishi jiaoqu, Sunanqu tudi gaige zhanlanhui.

Suzuki Chifu. 1981. "Shinmatsu Mushaku ni okeru santorihiki no hattatsu to gaikoku shihon" (The development of cocoon marketing and foreign capital in Wuxi during the late Qing). *Tōyō gakuhō* 63, nos. 1–2: 137–66.

T'ien, Hung-mao. 1972. *Government and Politics in Kuomintang [Guomindang] China, 1927–1937*. Stanford, Calif.: Stanford University Press.

Tōa dobunkai. 1920. *Shina shōbetsu zenshi* (A provincial gazetteer of China). Vol. 15, *Jiangsu*. Tokyo: Tōa dobunkai.

Tōa kenkyūjo, ed. 1943. *Shina sanshigyō kenkyū* (Research on China's silk industry). Tokyo: Osaka yagō shoten.

Topley, Marjorie. 1975. "Marriage Resistance in Rural Kwangtung [Guangdong]." In Margery Wolf and Roxane Witke, eds., *Women in Chinese Society*, pp. 67–88. Stanford, Calif.: Stanford University Press.

von Glahn, Richard. 1993. "Report on Recent Research." Report presented at the conference, "New Directions in the Sociocultural History of Late Imperial China," University of California, Los Angeles, Feb. 13.

Wakefield, David Ray. 1992. "Household Division in Qing and Republican China: Inheritance, Family Property, and Economic Development." Ph.D. diss., University of California, Los Angeles.

Wakeman, Frederic, Jr. 1975. "Introduction: The Evolution of Local Control in Late Imperial China." In Wakeman and Grant 1975: 1–25.

Wakeman, Frederic, Jr., and Carolyn Grant, eds. 1975. *Conflict and Control in Late Imperial China*. Berkeley: University of California Press.

Walker, Kathy Le Mons. 1993. "Economic Growth, Peasant Marginalization, and the Sexual Division of Labor in Early Twentieth-Century China: Women's Work in Nantong County." *Modern China* 19, no. 3 (July): 354–86.

———. 1999. *Chinese Modernity and the Peasant Path: Semicolonialism in the Northern Yangzi Delta*. Stanford, Calif.: Stanford University Press.

Wang Jingyu. 1979. "Guanyu Jichanglong saosichang de ruogan shiliao ji zhide yanjiu de jige wenti" (Some historical materials and several questions worthy of research concerning the Jichanglong silk filature). In Huang Yiping 1979: 1272–94. Originally published in *Xueshu yanjiu*, no. 6 (1962).

Wang Xiaotong. 1936. *Zhongguo shangye shi* (A history of Chinese commerce). Shanghai: Shangwu yinshuguan.

Wang, Yeh-chien. 1973. *Land Taxation in Imperial China, 1750–1911*. Cambridge, Mass.: Harvard University Press.

Wang Ying. 1986. "Wuxi saosi nügong diyici tongmeng zongbagong" (The first general strike by Wuxi's female filature workers). *Wuxi difang ziliao huibian* 8 (Dec.): 123–24.

Watson, Ernest. 1930. *The Principle Articles of Chinese Commerce*. Shanghai: Statistical Department of the Inspectorate General of Customs.

Wong, R. Bin. 1990. "The Development of China's Peasant Economy: A New Formulation of Old Problems." *Peasant Studies* 18, no. 1 (Fall): 5–26.

———. 1992. "Chinese Economic History and Development: A Note on the Myers-Huang Exchange." *Journal of Asian Studies* 51, no. 3 (Aug.): 600–611.

Wong, Siu-lun. 1979. *Sociology and Socialism in Contemporary China*. London: Routledge & Kegan Paul.

Wu Baijun. 1993. "Gongyehua chuqi quyu ziben de xingcheng" (Capital formation in [China's] earliest industrial areas). *Zhongguo jingjishi yanjiu* 2: 22–30.

Wuxi difangzhi bianzuan weiyuanhui ban'gongshi, Wuxi xianzhi bianzuan weiyuanhui ban'gongshi, eds. 1986. "Wuxi de zaoqi chuguo liuxuesheng" (Wuxi's earliest students to study abroad). *Wuxi difang ziliao huibian* 8 (Dec.): 33–77.

Wuxi difangzhi bianji weiyuanhui, ed. 1959. *Wuxi gushixuan* (Selected stories from Wuxi). Wuxi: Wuxi renmin chubanshe.

Wuxi-Jinkui xianzhi (A gazetteer of Wuxi and Jinkui counties). 40 vols. 1813.

Wuxi-Jinkui xianzhi (A gazetteer of Wuxi and Jinkui counties). 40 vols. 1881.

Wuxishi fangzhi gongyeju saosi gongyeshi bianji xiaozu, ed. 1959. *Wuxi saosi gongye shi* (A history of the Wuxi filature industry). Mimeographed manuscript held by the history office at the Wuxi Number One Silk Factory.

Wuxi shizheng (Wuxi city government). 1929.

Wuxi shizheng choubeichu, ed. 1929. "Wuxi saosichang yilanbiao" (A table of Wuxi's filatures). *Wuxi shizheng choubei shilu* 3 (Dec. 1): 121–23.

Wuxishi zhengxie wenshi ziliao yanjiu weiyuanhui, comp. 1981. "Wuxi Yongtai sichang shiliao pianduan" (Miscellaneous reflections on materials concerning the history of Wuxi's Yongtai silk filature). *Wuxi wenshi ziliao* 2: 48–70. Portions of this article, and an earlier unpublished version of it written in 1963, appear in Gao and Yan 1987: 37–38 and 43–49.

Wuxi xianzhengfu, ed. 1935. *Wuxi gailan* (Wuxi overview). Wuxi: Wuxi xianzhengfu.

Wuxi xianzhengfu, Wuxi shizheng choubeichu, eds. 1930. *Wuxi nianjian* (Wuxi yearbook), no. 1. Wuxi: Wuxi xianzhengfu, Wuxi shizheng choubeichu.

Wuxi xianzheng gongbao (Wuxi county government bulletin). 1929.

Wuxi Ximenwai Jiangsu shengli yucan shiyansuo, ed. 1919–21. *Jiangsu shengli yucan shiyansuo huikan* (Collected writings from the Jiangsu provincial sericulture experiment bureau). Wuxi: Wuxi Ximenwai Jiangsu shengli yucan shiyansuo.

Wuxi Yongtai sichang disi-wu ceng lianxiban lianhe biye jinian tekan chuban weiyuanhui. 1936. *Yongtai sichang disi-wu ceng lianxiban lianhe biye jinian tekan* (A joint commemorative graduation volume of the fourth and fifth training staffs of the Yongtai silk filature). Wuxi: Xiecheng yinwuju.

Wuxi zazhi (Wuxi magazine). 1923.

Xi-Jin shi xiaolu (A brief record of what is known about Wuxi and Jinkui counties). 1752.

Xi-Jin xiangtu dili (The rural geography of Wuxi and Jinkui counties). 1909. 2 vols.

Xu Dixin. 1949. *Guanliao ziben lun* (On comprador capital). Shanghai: Haiyan shudian.

Xu Dixin and Wu Chengming, eds. 1985. *Zhongguo ziben zhuyi de mengya* (The sprouts of Chinese capitalism). Beijing: Renmin chubanshe.

Xu Xinwu, ed. 1981. *Yapian zhanzheng qian Zhongguo mianfangzhi shougongye de shangpin shengchan yu ziben zhuyi mengya wenti* (Commercial production in the Chinese cotton handicraft industry before the Opium War and the sprouts of the capitalism question). Nanjing: Jiangsu renmin chubanshe.

————. 1990. *Zhongguo jindai saosi gongye shi* (A history of China's modern silk-filature industry). Shanghai: Shanghai renmin chubanshe.

Yan Jinqing, ed. 1923. *Yan Lianfang [Yan Ziqing] yigao* (The posthumous manuscripts of Yan Lianfang [Yan Ziqing]). Wuxi Municipal Library local history collection

Yan Xuexi. N.d. "Chuncan daosi sibujin: Ji jiechu de cansi jiaoyujia he gexinjia Zheng Qunqiang xiansheng" (A lifelong commitment to sericulture: A record of the prominent sericulture educator and innovator, Mr. Zheng Qunqiang). Manuscript. [Based on Zheng's own record of his life.]

Yang Renshan. 1955. *Wuxi Yang Renshan xiansheng yizhu, 1856–1932* (The posthumous work of Wuxi's Mr. Yang Renshan, 1856–1932). Hong Kong: Dongnan yinwu chubanshe.

Yin Liangying. 1931. *Zhongguo canye shi* (A history of Chinese sericulture). Nanjing: Guoli zhongyang daxue cansang xuehui.

Yin Weihe, ed. 1936. *Jiangsu liushiyi xianzhi* (A gazetteer of Jiangsu's sixty-one counties). 2 vols. Shanghai: Shangwu yinshuguan.

Young, Ernest P. 1977. *The Presidency of Yuan Shih-kai. Liberalism and*

Dictatorship in Early Republican China. Ann Arbor: University of Michigan Press.

Young, John. 1966. *The Research Activities of the South Manchurian Railway Company, 1907–1945: A History and Bibliography.* New York: East Asian Institute, Columbia University.

Yu Caiyou. 1951. "Wuxi Xinduxiang nongcun diaocha" (A rural investigation in Wuxi's Xindu township). In Sunan renmin xingzheng gongzhu tudi gaige weiyuanhui 1951: 51–56.

Yu Lin. 1932. "Jiangsu nongcun shuailuo de yige suoyin" (An index of rural Jiangsu's decline). *Xin chuangzao* 2, nos. 1 and 2: 169–81. Reprinted in Feng 1935a: 400–421.

Zelin, Madeleine. 1984. *The Magistrate's Tael: Rationalizing Fiscal Reform in Eighteenth-Century Ch'ing China.* Berkeley: University of California Press.

Zhang Enshen. 1984. "Jiefang qianhou wo jingying saosi gongye de huigu" (Reminiscences of my management experience in the silk-filature industry before and after Liberation). *Wuxi wenshi ziliao* 7 (May 10): 79–94.

Zhang Kai. 1979. "Mantan lishishang Jiangsu de canye" (An informal history of Jiansu sericulture). *Canye keji* no. 2 (July): 54–56 (pt. 1); no. 3 (Oct.): 53–56 (pt. 2).

Zhang Yongquan and Zhang Zhenhua. 1988. "Wuxi de tubuye" (Wuxi's cotton cloth trade). In Mao and Li 1988: 249–59.

Zhang Youyi, ed. 1957. *Zhongguo jindai nongyeshi ziliao* (Materials concerning the agricultural history of modern China). Vol. 2, *1911–27*, and vol. 3, *1927–37*. Beijing: Sanlian shudian.

Zhao Jing and Yi Menghong, eds. 1982. *Zhongguo jindai jingji sixiang ziliao xuanji* (Selected materials on China's modern economic thought). Beijing: Zhonghua shuju.

Zhao Ruheng, ed. 1935. *Jiangsu shengjian* (Jiangsu provincial yearbook). 2 vols. Shanghai: Xin Zhongguo jianshe xuehui.

Zhu Chuxin. 1936. "Zhongguo de sijianye" (China's raw-silk and cocoon industries). *Shenbao zhoukan* 1, no. 22 (June 7): 519–20.

Zhu Hebao. 1895. *Jiangsu quansheng yutu* (A comprehensive book of maps for Jiangsu Province). 3 vols. Nanjing(?): Jiangsu shuju.

Zhu Sihuang, ed. 1948. *Minguo jingjishi—Yinhang zhoubao sanshi zhoujinian kan* (An economic history of the Republic—A thirty-year anniversary volume issued by *Banker's Weekly*). Shanghai: Yinhang xuehui.

Zhu Zhengxin and Zhang Zhengxing. 1923. *Xiuzheng Wuxi xin xiangtu jiaokeshu* (A new textbook on local conditions in Wuxi). Rev. ed. Wuxi: Hangyu yanjiusuo.

Character List

For words or phrases that commonly appear in their English equivalent, I include translations in this list for the reader's convenience. I have not included characters for nontechnical words or phrases still in common usage. The exceptions to this rule are names of places and persons that, without characters provided, would be difficult to know. Well-known names such as Shanghai, Nanjing, and Chiang K'ai-shek do not appear in the list.

Anding canzhong zhizaochang (silkworm-egg breedery) 安定蠶種製造場
anmin tongshang 安民通商
Baishuidang 白水蕩
Baofeng sichang (silk filature) 寶丰絲廠
baohong 包烘
baojiao 包交
baolan ren 包攬人
baoshou 包手
Baotai sichang (silk filature) 寶泰絲廠
baozhengjin 保證金
baozhuang 包莊
Beimenwai 北門外
Cai Jingde 蔡經德
Cai Xiaofeng 蔡曉峰
Caizhengbu (Ministry of Finance) 財政部
Caizhengting (Department of Finance) 財政廳
Cansang gailiangqu (Sericulture Reform District) 蠶桑改良區
Cansang mofanqu (Model Sericulture District) 蠶桑模範區
canshibu (sericulture affairs office) 蠶事部

Cansi gailiang weiyuanhui (Commission for Sericulture Reform) 蠶絲改良委員會
Canye gaijin guanli weiyuanhui (Commission for the Administration of Sericulture Improvement) 蠶業改進管理委員會
Cao Yousheng 曹有聲
caoliang 漕糧
chandijuan 產地捐
changping cang 常平倉
changping sang 常平桑
changping sangyuan 常平桑園
Changshou xian (county) 常熟縣
Changzhou 常州
chaojiao 抄交
Chen Hansheng 陳翰笙
Chen Meifang 陳梅芳
Chen Qiyuan 陳啓沅
Chen Yaorong 陳堯榮
Chen Zhongxing 陳仲行
Chen Zhuoyun 陳倬云
Chen Zirong 陳子容
Cheng Bingruo 程炳若
chengpian sangyuan 成片桑園
Da Sheng 大生

Dafeng canzhong zhizaochang (silkworm-egg breedery) 大丰蠶種製造場

dan (a measure of volume) 石

dan (a measure of weight) 擔

Dangkou 蕩口

Dantu xian (county) 丹徒縣

Danyang xian (county) 丹陽縣

Dedayu sichang (silk filature) 德大裕絲廠

Deng Peilin 鄧培林

Dexing sichang (silk filature) 德興絲廠

dibao 地保

ding 丁

Ding Xingchu 丁杏初

Dingchang sichang (silk filature) 鼎昌絲廠

Dingsheng sichang (silk filature) 鼎盛絲廠

Dong Fureng 董福礽

Dongfang hezuoshe (cooperative) 東方合作社

Dongting 東亭

Dongwutang 東吳塘

Dongxian yanghang (foreign firm) 東線洋行

Dongze zhen (market town) 東澤鎮

duzi 獨資

Fangqian xiang (township) 坊前鄉

Fei Dasheng 費達生

Fei Xiaotong 費孝通

Feng Yibao 馮宜寶

Fucheng sichang (silk filature) 福成絲廠

Fuguan sichang (silk filature) 福綸絲廠

fuzheng gailiang jianshui or *jianjuan* 附正改良繭稅 or 繭捐

gailiang canzhong 改良蠶種

gailiangfei 改良費

Ganfeng sichang (silk filature) 乾丰絲廠

ganjian 乾繭

ganjian gongyi juan 乾繭公益捐

Ganshen erchang (Ganshen filature number two) 乾牲二廠

Ganshen sichang (silk filature) 乾牲絲廠

Gantai sichang (silk filature) 乾泰絲廠

Ganyuan sichang (silk filature)— founded 1913 乾元絲廠

Ganyuan sichang (silk filature)— founded 1922 乾源絲廠

Gao Jingyue 高景嶽

Gao Shufang 高叔方

gengdao 粳稻

Gengyu sichang (silk filature) 庚餘絲廠

gong (labor day) 工

Gong A' liu 龔阿六

Gong Canju 龔燦巨

Gongheyong sichang (silk filature) 公和永絲廠

gongshi 公事

gongsuo 公所

Gu Dasan 顧達三

Gu Mianfu 顧勉夫

Gu Suruo 顧酥若

Guan Yida 管義達

Guanchang sichang (silk filature) 綸昌絲廠

guandu shangban 官督商辦

Guangdong Sanshui lijinju (lijin bureau) 廣東三水釐金局

Guangsheng qianzhuang (native bank) 廣生錢莊

Guohuo yinhang (Native Goods Bank) 國貨銀行

Guoli zhongyang yanjiuyuan, shehui kexue yanjiusuo (Social Science Research Institute of the Academia Sinica) 國立中央研究院, 社會科學研究所

Hangzhou canxueguan (Hangzhou School for Sericulture) 杭州蠶學館

He Xizhang 何錫章

Hefeng sichang (silk filature) 禾丰絲廠

Henglin xiang (township) 橫林鄉
Hengyi sichang (silk filature) 恒益絲廠
Hezhong cansang gailiang hui (United Association for Sericulture Reform) 合衆蠶桑改良會
hezi 合資
Hongxu sichang (silk filature) 宏緒絲廠
Hongyu sichang (silk filature) 宏裕絲廠
Hu Guangyong 胡光鏞
Hu Yuankai 胡元凱
Hua Guanyi 華綸翼
Hua Shaochun 華少純
Hua Yizhi 華繹之
Hua Zhisan 華芝三
Huachang jianhang (cocoon firm) 華昌繭行
Huaishang shi (township) 懷上市
Huang Jinfan 黃錦帆
Huang Zhuoru 黃卓儒
Huang Zuoqing 黃佐卿
Huangbudun 黃埠墩
Huangtujingqiao 黃土涇橋
Huangxiang 黃巷
Huaxin sichang (silk filature) 華新絲廠
Huaxin zhisi yangchengsuo 華新製絲養成所
huiguan 會館
Huishan 惠山
Huiyuan sichang (silk filature) 匯源絲廠
huohao guigong 火耗歸公
huotian 活田
Hushuguan nüzi canye xuexiao (Hushuguan Sericulture School for Girls) 滸墅關女子蠶業學校
Ji Yunchu 季云初
Jiading xian (county) 嘉定縣
Jiang Shengjin 江生金
Jiangnan 江南
Jiangning xian (county) 江寧縣
Jiangsu shengli canzhong jianyansuo (Jiangsu Silkworm-Egg In-spection Bureau) 江蘇省立蠶種檢驗所
Jiangsu shengli Wuxi cansi shiyanchang (Jiangsu Provincial Sericulture Experiment Station in Wuxi) 江蘇省立無錫蠶絲試驗場
Jiangsu shengli yucan shiyansuo (Jiangsu Provincial Sericulture Experiment Bureau) 江蘇省立育蠶試驗所
Jiangsusheng canye xuexiao (Jiangsu Provincial Sericulture School) 江蘇省蠶業學校
Jiangsusheng canzhong gongsi (Jiangsu Provincial Silkworm-Egg Company) 江蘇省蠶種公司
Jiangsusheng nongye kexueyuan (Jiangsu Provincial Academy of Agricultural Science) 江蘇省農業科學院
Jiangsusheng nongye kexueyuan Zhenjiang canye yanjiusuo (Sericulture Research Institute of the Jiangsu Provincial Academy of Agricultural Science, in Zhenjiang) 江蘇省農業科學院鎮江蠶業研究所
Jiangsusheng sichou gongyeju (Jiangsu Provincial Silk-Industry Bureau) 江蘇省絲綢工業局
Jiangyin xian (county) 江陰縣
Jiang-Zhe sichou jizhi lianhehui (Jiangsu-Zhejiang United Silk Weavers' Association) 江浙絲綢機織聯合會
Jiang-Zhe-Wan sichang jianye zonggongsuo (Jiangsu-Zhejiang-Anhui Silk Producers' Guild) 江浙皖絲廠繭業總公所
jianhang (cocoon firm) 繭行
jianjuan (cocoon tax) 繭捐
jianshang (cocoon merchant) 繭商
jianshang gongsuo (cocoon-merchant guild) 繭商公所

jiansheju (bureaus of reconstruction) 建設局

Jiansheting (Department of Reconstruction) 建設廳

jianye gonghui 繭業公會

Jiaotong yinhang (Bank of Communications) 交通銀行

Jiatai sichang (silk filature) 嘉泰絲廠

Jiaxing xian (county) 嘉興縣

jihu 機戶

Jingcheng sichang (silk filature) 竟成絲廠

Jingjiang xian (county) 靖江縣

jingshi jimin 經世濟民

Jinji sichang (silk filature) 錦記絲廠

Jinkui xian (county) 金匱縣

Jintai sichang (silk filature) 錦泰絲廠

Jintan xian (county) 金壇縣

Jiuyu sichang (silk filature) 九餘絲廠

Kachū sanshi kabushiki kaisha (Central China Silk Company) 華中蠶絲株式會社

Kaihua wenshe (culture association) 開化文社

Kaihua xiang (township) 開化鄉

Kaiyuan xiang (township) 開原鄉

Kesanglu (Cottage for the Study of Mulberry Cultivation) 課桑廬

kexue yangcan 科學養蠶

Liangxi lu (road) 梁溪路

lijin 釐金

Lin Dichen 林迪臣

Lishe zhen (market town) 禮社鎮

Liu Yuqing 劉虞卿

Liyang xian (county) 溧陽縣

Longchang sichang (silk filature) 隆昌絲廠

Longting 龍亭

Lü Huantai 呂渙泰

Lu Peizhi 陸培之

Lu Youfeng 陸佑豐

luodishui 落地稅

Luoshe zhen (market town) 洛社鎮

Lüyuan renmin gongshe (Lüyuan People's Commune) 侶元人民公社

Ma Hanqing 馬漢卿

Maocun 毛村

Mei Guihe 糜桂和

Meicun 梅村

Meixin sichang (silk filature) 美新絲廠

Minami Manshū tetsudō kabushiki kaisha, Shanhai jimusho chōsashitsu (Mantetsu Shanghai Office) 南滿洲鐵道株式會社, 上海事務所調查室

Minfeng sichang (silk filature) 民豐絲廠

Mochou Hu (Mochou Lake) 莫愁湖

Nanchang sichang (silk filature) 南昌絲廠

Nanhai xian (county) 南海縣

Nantong xian (county) 南通縣

Ni Shaowen 倪紹雯

Ni Zicheng 倪子成

nonghui 農會

Nongkuangbu (Ministry of Agriculture and Mines) 農礦部

Nongkuangting (Department of Agriculture and Mines) 農礦廳

Nongmin yinhang (Peasant Bank) 農民銀行

Nongshangbu (Ministry of Agriculture and Commerce) 農商部

Nücan (Women's sericulture) 女蠶

nuodao 糯稻

Peng Zeyi 彭澤益

Qian Fenggao 錢鳳高

Qian Shilin 錢石麟

Qiang Zhuoren 強卓人

Qianliuxiang 前劉巷

qianzhuang (native bank) 錢莊

Qijun jianhang (cocoon firm) 其均繭行

Qingfeng sichang (silk filature) 慶
豐絲廠
Quanguo jingji weiyuanhui (Commission for the National Economy) 全國經機委員會
quanke nongsang 勸課農桑
quzhang 區長
Ren Ruduo 任汝鐸
Renchang jianhang (cocoon firm)
仁昌繭行
Rong Desheng 榮德生
Rong Zongjing 榮宗敬
Rongji sichang (silk filature) 榮記
絲廠
Rongxiang zhen (market town) 榮
鄉鎮
Ruichang sichang (silk filature) 瑞
昌絲廠
Ruifeng sichang (silk filature) 瑞
豐絲廠
Runde sichang (silk filature) 潤德
絲廠
Runkang sichang (silk filature) 潤
康絲廠
sangyuan 桑園
sanliandan 三連單
Sanwuguan canzhong zhizaochang (Sanwuguan Silkworm-egg Breedery) 三五館蠶種制
造場
saosichang (silk filature; see also
sichang) 繅絲廠
Shan Chongli 單崇禮
Shan Shaowen 單紹聞
Shan Youxian 單有先
shantang 善堂
Shaoxiang 邵巷
Shaoxing xian (county) 紹興縣
Shen Baixian 沈百先
Shen Bingcheng 沈秉成
Shen Gengyang 沈庚揚
Shen Jusun 沈菊蓀
Shen Yeyun 沈謁云
Shen Zhonghua 沈仲華
Shenchang sichang (silk filature)
慎昌絲廠

Shengchang tiehao (iron brokerage
firm) 升昌鐵號
shengsi (raw silk) 生絲
Shengsi jianyanju (Raw-Silk Inspection Bureau) 生絲檢驗局
Shengyu sichang (silk filature) 盛
裕絲廠
Shengze xian (county) 盛澤縣
shenshang 紳商
Shi Liangcai 史良才
shi/ying ye (split owner-ship/management) 實營業
Shijinshan miao (temple) 十金山
廟
Shitangwan zhen (market town)
石塘灣鎮
Shiyebu (Ministry of Industry) 實
業部
shiyechang 實業廠
Shiyeting (Department of Industry)
實業廳
shuitian (paddy land; rice/wheat
land) 水田
shuiwu gongsuo 稅務公所
Shunde xian (county) 順德縣
sichang (silk filature; see also
saosichang) 絲廠
Songjiang xian (county) 松江縣
Su Jiashan 蘇嘉善
Sun Bingru 孫炳如
Sun Boyu 孫伯瑜
Sun Heqing 孫鶴卿
Sun Xunchu 孫詢芻
Sun Zhongjun 孫中均
Suxiang 蘇巷
Suzhou Hushuguan canye xuexiao
(Suzhou School for Sericulture
in Hushuguan) 蘇州滸墅關蠶
業學校
Suzhou siye yanjiusuo (Suzhou
Silk-Industry Institute) 蘇州絲
業研究所
Tai Hu (Lake Tai) 太湖
Taicang xian (county) 太倉縣
Taifeng sichang (silk filature) 泰丰
絲廠

Taifu sichang (silk filature) 泰孚絲廠

tanding rudi 攤丁入地

tanding rumu 攤丁入畝

Tang Baoqian 唐保謙

Tangjiatang 唐家塘

tankuan 攤款

Tao Haiyong 陶海鏞

tiandi (subsoil) 田底

tianmian (topsoil) 田面

Tianxia shi (township) 天下市

tie 帖

Tongfeng sichang (silk filature) 同豐絲廠

tongguo lijin 通過釐金

tongye gonghui 同業公會

tuzhong (unimproved egg varieties) 土種

Wang Huanan 王化南

Wang Juancang 王卷藏

Wang Songlu 王頌魯

Wang Yisun 王貽蓀

Wang Yousun 王佑蓀

Wanyi sichang (silk filature) 萬益絲廠

Wanyuan sichang (silk filature) 萬源絲廠

wenshe 文社

wenshi ziliao 文史資料

Wu Dengyun 吳登澐

Wu Qifeng 吳起鳳

Wu Shirong 吳世榮

Wu Yaming 武亞明

Wufeng sichang (silk filature) 五豐絲廠

Wujiang xian (county) 吳江縣

Wujin xian (county) 武進縣

Wuxi gongsi heying saosi erchang (Wuxi Number Two Joint Public-Private Silk Factory) 無錫公司和營繅絲二廠

Wuxi gongsi heying saosi sanchang (Wuxi Number Three Joint Public-Private Silk Factory) 無錫公司和營繅絲三廠

Wuxi gongsi heying saosi yichang (Wuxi Number One Joint Public-Private Silk Factory) 無錫公司和營繅絲一廠

Wuxi jianhangye gongsuo (Wuxi Cocoon-Merchant Guild) 無錫繭行業公所

Wuxi saosi yichang (Wuxi Number One Silk Factory) 無錫繅絲一廠

Wuxi sichangye xiehui (Wuxi Silk-Filature Association) 無錫絲廠業協會

Wuxi sijianye tongye gonghui (Wuxi Silk-Industry Association) 無錫絲繭業同業公會

Wuxi xian (county) 無錫縣

Wuxian (Wu county) 吳縣

Wuxishi fangzhi gongyeju, saosi gongyeshi bianji xiaozu (Silk-Industry Editorial Group of the Wuxi Municipal Textile-Industry Bureau) 無錫市紡織工業局，繅絲工業史編輯小組

Wuxishi kexue puji xiehui cansi yanjiu shi (Sericulture-and-Silk Research Section of the Wuxi Municipal Association for the Dissemination of Science) 無錫市科學普及協會蠶絲研究室

Wuxishi renmin daibiao dahui (Wuxi Municipal People's Congress) 無錫市人民代表大會

Xiajiabian zhen (market town) 夏家邊鎮

xiandao 秈稻

xiangbao 鄉保

Xiaodingxiang 小丁巷

Xiaofangxiang 小房巷

Xiaoshatou 小沙頭

Xichang sichang (silk filature) 錫昌絲廠

Xidafang 西大房

Xiguan sichang (silk filature) 錫綸絲廠

Xihui gongyuan (Xihui Park) 錫惠公園

Xi-Jin 錫金 (無錫 and 金匱)

Xincheng yinhang (bank) 信誠銀行

Xingsheng sichang (silk filature) 興勝絲廠

Xinguan sichang (silk filature) 新綸絲廠

Xingye zhisi gufen youxian gongsi (Xingye Silk Company) 興業製絲股份有限公司

Xizhang canzhong zhizaochang (Xizhang Silkworm-egg Breedery) 西漳蠶種制造場

Xu Daosun 許稻蓀

Xu Jinrong 徐錦榮

Xu Ruliang 許汝良

Xu Yiru 徐怡如

Xue cangting (granary) 薛倉廳

Xue Fucheng 薛福成

Xue Nanming 薛南溟

Xue Runpei 薛潤培

Xue Shouxuan 薛壽萱

Xue Zukang 薛祖康

Xushe 許舍

Yan Shenyu 嚴慎予

Yan Xuexi 嚴學熙

Yan Ziqing 嚴紫卿

Yang Ganqing 楊干卿

Yang Hanxi 楊翰西

Yang Renshan 楊仁山

Yang Zhongzi 楊仲滋

yangchengsuo 養成所

Yangmuqiao 楊木橋

Yangzhou 楊州

Yichang sichang (silk filature) 怡昌絲廠

Yifeng sichang (silk filature) 義丰絲廠

yiji 義集

yingyechang 營業廠

Yixing xian (county) 宜興縣

yizhuang 義莊

Yongchang sichang (silk filature) 永昌絲廠

Yongfurun sichang (silk filature) 永孚潤絲廠

Yongji sichang (silk filature) 永吉絲廠

Yongsheng sichang (silk filature) 永盛絲廠

Yongtai sichang (silk filature) 永泰絲廠

Yongyu sichang (silk filature) 永裕絲廠

Youcheng sichang (silk filature) 有成絲廠

Yu Yiting 于義庭

Yuankang sichang (silk filature) 源康絲廠

Yuchang sichang (silk filature) 裕昌絲廠

Yuguan sichang (silk filature) 餘綸絲廠

yujian 餘繭

Yunda sichang (silk filature) 允大絲廠

Yuqi zhen (market town) 玉祁鎮

Yusheng sichang (silk filature) 裕生絲廠

Zeng Jikuan 曾濟寬

Zengxing sichang (silk filature) 增興絲廠

Zhaimen 寨門

Zhang Dingan 章定安

Zhang Enshen 張恩深

Zhang Gongquan 張公權

Zhang Jian 張謇

Zhang Kai 章楷

Zhang Shouyong 張壽鏞

Zhang Shuping 張叔平

Zhang Zhanhua 張湛華

Zhang Zizhen 張子振

zhangfang 脹房

Zhangtangxiang 張塘巷

Zhangxiangqiao 張巷橋

Zhejiang xingye yinhang (Zhejiang Xingye Bank) 浙江興業銀行

Zhenfeng sichang (silk filature) 振丰絲廠

Zheng Bingquan 鄭炳泉

Zheng Qunqiang 鄭群疆

Zheng Ziqing　鄭子卿
Zhenguan sichang (silk filature)
　鎮綸絲廠
Zhengxiang　鄭巷
Zhenjiang　鎮江
Zhenyi sichang (silk filature)　振藝
　絲廠
Zhenyi xinchang (new filature)　振
　藝新廠
Zhenyuan sichang (silk filature)
　振元絲廠
Zhenze zhen (market town)　震澤
　鎮
zhidaosuo　指導所
zhidaozu　指導組
Zhongguo minzhu jianguohui　中
　國民主建國會
Zhongguo renmin zhengzhi xie-
　shang huiyi Wuxishi wei-
　yuanhui (Wuxi Municipal Com-
　mittee of the Chinese People's
　Political Consultative Congress)
　中國人民政治協商會議無錫市
　委員會

Zhongguo yinhang (Bank of China)
　中國銀行
Zhongyang yinhang (Central Bank)
　中央銀行
Zhou Kuangming　周匡明
Zhou Shunqing　周舜卿
Zhou Yuanxun　周元勳
Zhou Yueshan　周月山
Zhou Zhaofu　周肇甫
Zhouxinzhen (market town)　周新
　鎮
Zhu Jing'an　朱靜庵
Zhu Lanfang　祝蘭舫
Zhuang Hao　莊濠
Zhuang Yaohe　莊幺鶴
ziben zhuyi mengya　資本主義
　萌芽
Zikang sichang (silk filature)　滋康
　絲廠
zikou banshui　子口半稅
zong　宗
zumi　租米
zutian　租田
zuzao　租灶

Index

In this index an "f" after a number indicates a separate reference on the next page, and an "ff" indicates separate references on the next two pages. A continuous discussion over two or more pages is indicated by a span of page numbers, e.g., "57–59." *Passim* is used for a cluster of references in close but not consecutive sequence.

Library of Congress Cataloging-in-Publication Data

Bell, Lynda Schaefer
  One industry, two Chinas : silk filatures and peasant-family
production in Wuxi County, 1865–1937 / Lynda S. Bell
    p.   cm.
  Includes bibliographical references and index.
  ISBN 0-8047-2998-0 (cloth : alk. paper)
   1. Silk industry—China—Wu-hsi hsien (Kiangsu Province)—History.
2. China—Economic Policy. 3. China—Commerce—History. I. Title.
HD9926.C63W82 1999
338.4'767739'0951222—dc21   99-10135
                                              CIP

This book is printed on acid-free, archival quality paper.

Original printing 1999
Last figure below indicates year of this printing:
08 07 06 05 04 03 02 01 00 99

Designed and typeset by John Feneron
Typeset in 9.5/12.5 Trump Mediaeval